OCT 9 1995

2013
2016

Sacred

AND

Legendary Art.

VOL. I.

The Assumption of the Magdalena.

𝕾𝖆𝖈𝖗𝖊𝖉

AND

𝕷𝖊𝖌𝖊𝖓𝖉𝖆𝖗𝖞 𝕬𝖗𝖙.

BY MRS. JAMESON.

VOLUME I.

CONTAINING

LEGENDS OF THE ANGELS AND ARCHANGELS, THE EVANGELISTS,

THE APOSTLES, THE DOCTORS OF THE CHURCH,

AND ST. MARY MAGDALENE,

AS REPRESENTED IN THE FINE ARTS.

NEW EDITION.

AMS PRESS
NEW YORK

Ref,
755
J31s
1970
V.1

Reprinted from the edition of 1896, New York
First AMS EDITION published 1970
Manufactured in the United States of America

International Standard Book Number:
Complete set: 0-404-03551-5
Volume 1: 0-404-03552-3

Library of Congress Card Catalog Number: 71-124594

AMS PRESS, INC.
NEW YORK, N.Y. 10003

PREFACE

THE THIRD EDITION.

———◦◦◦———

THE Author ventures to hope that, on comparing this Third Edition of 'Sacred and Legendary Art' with the two preceding, it will be found greatly improved, and rendered more worthy of the kind approbation and sympathy with which it has been received. The whole has been carefully revised; the references to the pictures and other works of Art corrected from the latest authorities, and many new examples have been added. All the Illustrations, which were formerly etched on copper, have been newly etched on steel; two have been omitted, and three others, as more interesting and appropriate, have been substituted; and twelve new woodcuts have been introduced. In a work so multifarious in its nature, and comprising so many hundred subjects and references, there may remain some errors and omissions, but they have not occurred from want of care; and I must not omit to express due thanks for the observations and corrections which have been forwarded to me from time to time, and which have been in this Edition carefully attended to.

January 1857.

A. J.

b

PREFACE

THE FIRST EDITION.

(1848.)

———•◦•———

THIS book was begun six years ago, in 1842. It has since been often laid aside, and again resumed. In this long interval, many useful and delightful works have been written on the same subject, but still the particular ground I had chosen remained unoccupied; and, amid many difficulties, and the consciousness of many deficiencies, I was encouraged to proceed, partly by the pleasure I took in a task so congenial—partly by the conviction that such a work has long been wanted by those who are not contented with a mere manual of reference, or a mere catalogue of names. This book is intended not only to be consulted, but to be read—if it be found worth reading. It has been written for those who are, like myself, unlearned; yet less, certainly, with the idea of instructing, than from a wish to share with others those pleasurable associations, those ever new and ever various aspects of character and sentiment, as exhibited in Art, which have been a source of such vivid enjoyment to myself.

This is the utmost limit of my ambition; and, knowing that I cannot escape criticism, I am at least anxious that there should be no mistake as to purpose and intention. I hope it will be clearly understood that I have taken throughout the æsthetic and not the religious view of those productions of Art which, in as far as they are informed with a true and earnest feeling, and steeped in that beauty which emanates from genius inspired by faith, may cease to be Religion, but cannot cease to be Poetry; and as poetry only I have considered them.

The difficulty of selection and compression has been the greatest of all my difficulties; there is not a chapter in this book which might not have been more easily extended to a volume than compressed into a few pages. Every reader, however, who is interested in the subject, may supply the omissions, follow out the suggestions, and enjoy the pleasure of discovering new exceptions, new analogies, for himself. With regard to the arrangement, I am afraid it will be found liable to objections ; but it is the best that, after long consideration and many changes, I could fix upon. It is not formal, nor technical, like that of a catalogue or a calendar, but intended to lead the fancy naturally from subject to subject as one opened upon another, with just sufficient order to keep the mind unperplexed and the attention unfatigued amid a great diversity of objects, scenes, stories, and characters.

The authorities for the legends have been the *Legenda Aurea* of Voragine, in the old French and English translations ; the *Flos Sanctorum* of Ribadeneira, in the old French translation ; the *Perfetto Legendario*, editions of Rome and Venice ; the *Legende delle Sante Vergini*, Florence and Venice ; the large work of Baillet, *Les Vies des Saints*, in thirty-two volumes, most useful for the historical authorities ; and Alban Butler's *Lives of the Saints.* All these have been consulted for such particulars of circumstance and character as might illustrate the various representations, and then compressed into a narrative as clear as I could render it. Where one authority only has been followed, it is usually placed in the margin.

The First Part contains the legends of the scriptural personages and the primitive fathers.

The Second Part contains those sainted personages who lived, or are supposed to have lived, in the first ages of Christianity, and whose real history, founded on fact or tradition, has been so disguised by poetical embroidery, that they have in some sort the air of ideal beings. As I could not undertake to go through the whole calendar, nor yet to make my book a catalogue of pictures and statues, I have confined myself to the saints most interesting and important, and (with very few exceptions) to those works of Art of which I could speak from my own knowledge.

The legends of the monastic orders, and the history of the Franciscans and Dominicans, considered merely in their connection with the revival and development of the Fine Arts in the thirteenth and fourteenth centuries, open so wide a range of speculation,—the characteristics of these religious enthusiasts of both sexes are so full of interest and beauty as artistic conceptions, and as psychological and philosophical studies so extraordinary, that I could not, in conscience, compress them into a few pages : they form a volume complete in itself, entitled 'Legends of the Monastic Orders.'

The little sketches and woodcuts are trifling as illustrations, and can only assist the memory and the fancy of the reader; but I regret this the less, inasmuch as those who take an interest in the subject can easily illustrate the book for themselves. To collect a portfolio of prints, including those works of Art which are cited under each head as examples, with a selection from the hundreds of others which are not cited, and arrange them in the same order—with reference, not to schools, or styles, or dates, but to subject merely—would be an amusing, and I think not a profitless, occupation. It could not be done in the right spirit without leading the mind far beyond the mere pleasure of comparison and criticism, to 'thoughts more elevate and reasonings high' of things celestial and terrestrial, as shadowed forth in form by the wit and the hand of man.

CONTENTS

OF

THE FIRST VOLUME.

———◆◦◆———

OF ANGELS AND ARCHANGELS.

THE FOUR EVANGELISTS.

THE TWELVE APOSTLES.

THE DOCTORS OF THE CHURCH.

VOL. I.   *c*

ST. MARY MAGDALENE, ST. MARTHA, ST. LAZARUS, ST. MAXIMIN, ST. MARCELLA, ST. MARY OF EGYPT, AND THE BEATIFIED PENITENTS.

Character of Mary Magdalene. Disputes concerning her Identity. The Popular
and Scriptural Legend. The old Provençal Legend. The Devotional Representations : as Patron Saint ; as Penitent. Sacred Subjects in which
she is introduced. Legendary Subjects. La Danse de la Madeleine. The

LIST OF ILLUSTRATIONS

IN

THE FIRST VOLUME.

———◆———

𝔚𝔬𝔬𝔡𝔠𝔲𝔱𝔰.

Etchings.

1   Laus Deo !

𝔈𝔫𝔱𝔯𝔬𝔡𝔲𝔠𝔱𝔦𝔬𝔫.

I. OF THE ORIGIN AND GENERAL SIGNIFICANCE OF THE LEGENDS REPRESENTED IN ART.

WE cannot look round a picture gallery—we cannot turn over a portfolio of prints after the old masters, nor even the modern engravings which pour upon us daily, from Paris, Munich, or Berlin —without perceiving how many of the most celebrated productions of Art, more particularly those which have descended to us from the early Italian and German schools, represent incidents and characters taken from the once popular legends of the Catholic Church. This form of ' *Hero-Worship* ' has become, since the Reformation, strange to us—as far removed from our sympathies and associations as if it were antecedent to the fall of Babylon and related to the religion of Zoroaster, instead of being left but two or three centuries behind us, and closely connected with the faith of our forefathers and the history of civilisation and Christianity. Of late years, with a growing passion for the works of Art of the Middle Ages, there has arisen among us a desire to comprehend the state of feeling

which produced them, and the legends and traditions on which they
are founded ;—a desire to understand, and to bring to some surer
critical test, representations which have become familiar without
being intelligible. To enable us to do this, we must pause for a
moment at the outset; and, before we plunge into the midst of things,
ascend to higher ground, and command a far wider range of illustration than has yet been attempted, in order to take cognizance of
principles and results which, if not new, must be contemplated in a
new relation to each other.

The Legendary Art of the Middle Ages sprang out of the legendary literature of the preceding ages. For three centuries at least,
this literature, the only literature which existed at the time, formed
the sole mental and moral nourishment of the *people* of Europe.
The romances of Chivalry, which long afterwards succeeded, were
confined to particular classes, and left no impress on Art, beyond
the miniature illuminations of a few manuscripts. This legendary
literature, on the contrary, which had worked itself into the life of
the people, became, like the antique mythology, as a living soul
diffused through the loveliest forms of Art, still vivid and vivifying,
even when the old faith in its mystical significance was lost or forgotten. And it is a mistake to suppose that these legends had their
sole origin in the brains of dreaming monks. The wildest of them
had some basis of truth to rest on, and the forms which they gradually assumed were but the necessary result of the age which produced them. They became the intense expression of that inner life,
which revolted against the desolation and emptiness of the outward
existence; of those crushed and outraged sympathies which cried
aloud for rest, and refuge, and solace, and could nowhere find them.
It will be said, ' In the purer doctrine of the GOSPEL.' But where
was that to be found ? The Gospel was not then the heritage of the
poor: Christ, as a comforter, walked not among men. His own
blessed teaching was inaccessible except to the learned : it was shut
up in rare manuscripts ; it was perverted and sophisticated by the
passions and the blindness of those few to whom it *was* accessible.
The bitter disputes in the early Church relative to the nature of the
Godhead, the subtle distinctions and incomprehensible arguments

of the theologians, the dread entertained by the predominant Church of any heterodox opinions concerning the divinity of the Redeemer, had all conspired to remove *Him*, in His personal character of Teacher and Saviour, far away from the hearts of the benighted and miserable people—far, far away into regions speculative, mysterious, spiritual, whither they could not, dared not follow Him.   In this state of things, as it has been remarked by a distinguished writer, ' Christ became the object of a remoter, a more awful adoration.   The mind began, therefore, to seek out, or eagerly to seize, some other more material beings in closer alliance with human sympathies.'   And the same author, after tracing in vivid and beautiful language the dangerous but natural consequences of this feeling, thus sums up the result: ' During the perilous and gloomy days of persecution, the reverence for those who endured martyrdom for the religion of Christ had grown up out of the best feelings of man's improved nature.   Reverence gradually grew into veneration, worship, adoration: and although the more rigid theology maintained a marked distinction between the honour shown to the martyrs, and that addressed to the Redeemer and the Supreme Being, the line was too fine and invisible not to be transgressed by excited popular feeling.' [1]

' We live,' says the poet, ' through admiration, hope, and love.' Out of these vital aspirations—not indeed always ' well or wisely placed,' but never, as in the heathen mythology, degraded to vicious and contemptible objects—arose and spread the universal passion for the traditional histories of the saints and martyrs,— personages endeared and sanctified in all hearts, partly as examples of the loftiest virtue, partly as benign intercessors between suffering humanity and that Deity who, in every other light than as a God of Vengeance, had been veiled from their eyes by the perversities of schoolmen and fanatics, till He had receded beyond their reach, almost beyond their comprehension.   Of the prevalence and of the incalculable influence of this legendary literature from the seventh to the tenth century, that is, just about the period when Modern Art was struggling into existence, we have a most striking picture in Guizot's ' Histoire de la Civilisation.'   ' As after the

[1] Milman, Hist. of Christianity, iii. 540.

siege of Troy (says this philosophical and eloquent writer) there
were found, in every city of Greece, men who collected the traditions and adventures of heroes, and sung them for the recreation
of the people, till these recitals became a national passion, a
national poetry; so, at the time of which we speak, the traditions
of what may be called the heroic ages of Christianity had the same
interest for the nations of Europe.   There were men who made it
their business to collect them, to transcribe them, to read or recite
them aloud, for the edification and delight of the people.   And this
was the only literature, properly so called, of that time.'

Now, if we go back to the *authentic* histories of the sufferings
and heroism of the early martyrs, we shall find enough there, both
of the wonderful and the affecting, to justify the credulity and
enthusiasm of the unlettered people, who saw no reason why they
should not believe in one miracle as well as in another.   In these
universally diffused legends, we may recognise the means, at least
one of the means, by which a merciful Providence, working through
its own immutable laws, had provided against the utter depravation,
almost extinction, of society.   Of the ' Dark Ages,' emphatically so
called, the period to which I allude was perhaps the darkest; it
was ' of Night's black arch the key-stone.'   At a time when men
were given over to the direst evils that can afflict humanity,—ignorance, idleness, wickedness, misery; at a time when the everyday
incidents of life were a violation of all the moral instincts of mankind; at a time when all things seemed abandoned to a blind
chance, or the brutal law of force; when there was no repose, no
refuge, no safety anywhere; when the powerful inflicted, and the
weak endured, whatever we can conceive of most revolting and
intolerable; when slavery was recognised by law throughout
Europe; when men fled to cloisters, to shut themselves from
oppression, and women to shield themselves from outrage; when
the manners were harsh, the language gross; when all the softer
social sentiments, as pity, reverence, tenderness, found no resting-
place in the actual relations of life; when for the higher ranks
there was only the fierce excitement of war, and on the humbler
classes lay the weary, dreary monotony of a stagnant existence,
poor in pleasures of every kind, without aim, without hope; *then*—

wondrous reaction of the ineffaceable instincts of good implanted within us!—arose a literature which reversed the outward order of things, which asserted and kept alive in the hearts of men those pure principles of Christianity which were outraged in their daily actions; a literature in which peace was represented as better than war, and sufferance more dignified than resistance; which exhibited poverty and toil as honourable, and charity as the first of virtues; which held up to imitation and emulation self-sacrifice in the cause of good, and contempt of death for conscience' sake; a literature in which the tenderness, the chastity, the heroism of woman, played a conspicuous part; which distinctly protested against slavery, against violence, against impurity in word and deed; which refreshed the fevered and darkened spirit with images of moral beauty and truth; revealed bright glimpses of a better land, where 'the wicked cease from troubling,' and brought down the angels of God with shining wings and bearing crowns of glory, to do battle with the demons of darkness, to catch the fleeting soul of the triumphant martyr, and carry it at once into a paradise of eternal blessedness and peace!

Now the Legendary Art of the three centuries which comprise the revival of learning, was, as I have said, the reflection of this literature, of this teaching. Considered in this point of view, can we easily overrate its interest and importance?

When, after the long period of darkness which followed upon the decline of the Roman Empire, the Fine Arts began to revive, the first, and for several ages the only, impress they received was that of the religious spirit of the time. Painting, Sculpture, Music, and Architecture, as they emerged one after another from the 'formless void,' were pressed into the service of the Church. But it is a mistake to suppose, that in adroitly adapting the reviving Arts to her purposes, in that magnificent spirit of calculation which at all times characterised her, the Church from the beginning selected the subjects, or dictated the use that was to be made of them. We find, on the contrary, edicts and councils *repressing* the popular extravagances in this respect, and denouncing those apocryphal versions of sacred events and traditions which had become the delight of the people. But vain were councils and edicts; the tide was too strong to be so checked. The Church found herself obliged to accept and mould to her own objects the exotic elements she could not eradicate. She *absorbed*, so to speak, the evils and errors she could not expel. There seems to have been at this time a sort of compromise between the popular legends, with all their wild mixture of northern and classical superstitions, and the Church legends properly so called. The first great object to which reviving Art was destined, was to render the Christian places of worship a theatre of instruction and improvement for the people, to attract and to interest them by representations of scenes, events, and personages, already so familiar as to require no explanation, appealing at once to their intelligence and their sympathies; embodying in beautiful shapes (beautiful at least in their eyes) associations and feelings and memories deep-rooted in their very hearts, and which had influenced, in no slight degree, the progress of civilisation, the development of mind. Upon these creations of ancient Art we cannot look as *those* did for whom they were created; we cannot annihilate the centuries which lie between us and them; we cannot, in simplicity of heart, forget the artist in the image he has placed before us, nor supply what may be deficient in his work, through a reverentially excited fancy. We are critical, not credulous. We no longer accept this polytheistic form of Christianity; and there is little danger, I suppose, of our falling again into the strange excesses of superstition to which it led. But if we have not much sympathy with modern imitations of Mediæval Art, still less should we sympathise with that narrow puritanical jealousy which holds the monuments of a real and earnest faith in contempt. All that God has permitted once to exist in the past should be considered as the possession of the present; sacred for example or warning, and held as the foundation on which to build up what is better and purer. It should seem an established fact, that all revolutions in religion, in government, and in art, which begin in the spirit of scorn, and in a sweeping destruction of the antecedent condition, only tend to a reaction. Our puritanical ancestors chopped off the heads of Madonnas and Saints, and paid vagabonds to smash the storied windows of our cathedrals; —*now*, are these rejected and outraged shapes of beauty coming back to us, or are we not rather going back to them? As a Protestant, I might fear lest in doing so we confound the eternal spirit of Christianity with the mutable forms in which it has deigned to speak to the hearts of men, forms which must of necessity vary with the degree of social civilisation, and bear the impress of the feelings and fashions of the age which produce them; but I must also feel that we ought to comprehend, and to hold in due reverence, that which has once been consecrated to holiest aims, which has shown us what a magnificent use has been made of Art, and how it may still be adapted to good and glorious purposes, if, while we respect these time-consecrated images and types, we do not allow them to fetter us, but trust in the progressive spirit of Christianity to furnish us with new impersonations of the good—new combinations of the beautiful. I hate the destructive as I revere the progressive spirit. We must laugh if any one were to try and persuade us that the sun was guided along his blazing path by ' a fair-haired god who touched a golden lyre; ' but shall we therefore cease to adore in the Apollo Belvedere the majestic symbol of light, the most divine impersonation of intellectual power and beauty? So of the corresponding Christian symbols :—may that time never come, when we shall look up to the effigy of the winged and radiant angel trampling down the brute-fiend, without a glow of faith in the perpetual supremacy and final triumph of good over evil!

It is about a hundred years since the passion, or the fashion, for collecting works of Art, began to be generally diffused among the rich and the noble of this land; and it is amusing to look back and to consider the perversions and affectations of the would-be connoisseurship during this period;—the very small stock of ideas on which people set up a pretension to taste—the false notions, the mixture of pedantry and ignorance, which everywhere prevailed. The publication of Richardson's book, and Sir Joshua Reynolds's Discourses, had this advantage,—that they, to a certain degree, diffused a more elevated idea of Art as *Art*, and that they placed connoisseurship on a better and truer basis. In those days we had Inquiries into the Principles of Taste, Treatises on the Sublime and Beautiful, Anecdotes of Painting; and we abounded in Antiquarian Essays on disputed Pictures and mutilated Statues; but then, and up to a late period, any inquiry into the true spirit and significance of works of Art, as connected with the history of Religion and Civilisation, would have appeared ridiculous—or perhaps dangerous:—we should have had another cry of 'No Popery,' and Acts of Parliament forbidding the importation of Saints and Madonnas. It was fortunate, perhaps, that connoisseurs meddled not with such high matters. They talked volubly and harmlessly of 'hands,' and 'masters,' and 'schools,'—of 'draperies,' of 'tints,' of 'handling,'—of 'fine heads,' 'fine compositions;' of the 'grace of Raphael,' and of the 'Correggiosity of Correggio.' The very manner in which the names of the painters were pedantically used instead of the name of the subject, is indicative of this factitious feeling; the only question at issue was, whether such a picture was a genuine 'Raphael?' such another a genuine 'Titian?' The spirit of the work—whether *that* was genuine; how far it was influenced by the faith and the condition of the age which produced it; whether the conception was properly characteristic, and of *what* it was characteristic—of the subject? or of the school? or of the time?—whether the treatment corresponded to the idea within our own souls, or was modified by the individuality of the artist, or by received conventionalisms of all kinds?—these were questions which had not then occurred to any one; and I am not sure that we are much wiser even now: yet, setting aside all higher considerations, how can we do common justice to the artist, unless we can bring his work to the test of truth? and how can we do this, unless we know what to look for, what was *intended* as to incident, expression, character? One result of our ignorance has been the admiration wasted on the flimsy mannerists of the later ages of Art; men who apparently had no definite *intention* in anything they did, except a dashing outline, or a delicate finish, or a striking and attractive management of colour.

It is curious, this general ignorance with regard to the subjects of Mediæval Art, more particularly now that it has become a reigning fashion among us. We find no such ignorance with regard to the subjects of Classical Art, because the associations connected with them form a part of every liberal education. Do we hear any one say, in looking at Annibal Caracci's pictures in the National Gallery,

' Which is Silenus, and which is Apollo?' Who ever confounds a Venus with a Minerva, or a Vestal with an Amazon; or would endure an undraped Juno, or a beardless Jupiter? Even the gardener in Zeluco knew Neptune by his 'fork,' and Vulcan by his 'lame leg.' We are indeed so accustomed, in visiting the churches and the galleries abroad, and the collections at home, to the predominance of sacred subjects, that it has become a mere matter of course, and excites no particular interest and attention. We have heard it all accounted for by the fact that the Church and Churchmen were the first, and for a long time the only, patrons of Art. In every sacred edifice, and in every public or private collection enriched from the plunder of sacred edifices, we look for the usual proportion of melancholy martyr-doms and fictitious miracles,—for the predominance of Madonnas and Magdalenes, St. Catherines and St. Jeromes; but why these should predominate, why certain events and characters from the Old and the New Testament should be continually repeated, and others comparatively neglected; whence the predilection for certain legend-ary personages, who seemed to be multiplied to infinity, and the rarity of others;—of this we know nothing.

We have learned, perhaps, after running through half the galleries and churches in Europe, to distinguish a few of the attributes and characteristic figures which meet us at every turn, yet without any clear idea of their meaning, derivation, or relative propriety. The palm of victory, we know, designates the martyr triumphant in death. We so far emulate the critical sagacity of the gardener in Zeluco that we have learned to distinguish St. Laurence by his gridiron, and St. Catherine by her wheel. We are not at a loss to recognise the Magdalene's 'loose hair and lifted eye,' even when without her skull and her vase of ointment. We learn to know St. Francis by his brown habit and shaven crown and wasted ardent features: but how do we distinguish him from St. Anthony or St. Dominick? As for St. George and the Dragon—from the St. George of the Louvre,— Raphael's,—who sits his horse with the elegant tranquillity of one assured of celestial aid, down to him ' who swings on a sign-post at mine hostess's door,'—he is our familiar acquaintance. But who is that lovely being in the first blush of youth, who, bearing aloft the symbolic cross, stands with one foot on the vanquished dragon?

'That is a copy after Raphael.' And who is that majestic creature
holding her palm branch, while the unicorn crouches at her feet?
'That is the famous Moretto at Vienna.' Are we satisfied?—not in
the least! but we try to look wiser, and pass on.

In the old times the painters of these legendary scenes and subjects
could always reckon securely on certain associations and certain sympathies in the minds of the spectators. We have outgrown these
associations, we repudiate these sympathies. We have taken these
works from their consecrated localities, in which they once held each
their dedicated place, and we have hung them in our drawing-rooms
and our dressing-rooms, over our pianos and our side-boards—and
now what do they say to us? That Magdalene, weeping amid her
hair, who once spoke comfort to the soul of the fallen sinner,—that
Sebastian, arrow-pierced, whose upward ardent glance spoke of
courage and hope to the tyrant-ridden serf,—that poor tortured slave,
to whose aid St. Mark comes sweeping down from above,—can they
speak to *us* of nothing save flowing lines and correct drawing and
gorgeous colour? Must we be told that one is a Titian, the other
a Guido, the third a Tintoret, before we dare to melt in compassion
or admiration?—or the moment we refer to their ancient religious
signification and influence, must it be with disdain or with pity?
This, as it appears to me, is to take not a rational, but rather a most
irrational as well as a most irreverent, view of the question; it is to
confine the pleasure and improvement to be derived from works of
Art within very narrow bounds; it is to seal up a fountain of the
richest poetry, and to shut out a thousand ennobling and inspiring
thoughts. Happily there is a growing appreciation of these larger
principles of criticism as applied to the study of Art. People look
at the pictures which hang round their walls, and have an awakening
suspicion that there is more in them than meets the eye—more than
mere connoisseurship can interpret; and that they have another,
a deeper significance than has been dreamed of by picture dealers
and picture collectors, or even picture critics.

II. Of the Distinction to be drawn between the Devotional and the Historical Subjects.

At first, when entering on a subject so boundless and so diversified, we are at a loss for some leading classification which shall be distinct and intelligible, without being mechanical. It appears to me that all sacred representations, in as far as they appeal to sentiment and imagination, resolve themselves into two great classes, which I shall call the DEVOTIONAL and the HISTORICAL.

Devotional pictures are those which portray the objects of our veneration with reference only to their sacred character, whether standing singly or in company with others. They place before us no action or event, real or supposed. They are neither portrait nor history. A group of sacred personages where no action is represented, is called in Italian a ' *sacra conversazione ;* '—the word *conversazione*, which signifies a society in which there is communion, being here, as it appears to me, used with peculiar propriety. All subjects, then, which exhibit to us sacred personages, alone or in groups, simply in the character of superior beings, must be considered as *devotionally* treated.

But a sacred subject, without losing wholly its religious import, becomes historical the moment it represents any story, incident, or action, real or imagined. All pictures which exhibit the events of Scripture story; all those which express the actions, miracles, and martyrdoms of saints, come under this class ; and to this distinction I must call the attention of the reader, requesting that it may be borne in mind throughout this work.

We must also recollect that a story, action, or fact, may be so represented as to become a symbol expressive of an abstract idea ; and some Scriptural and some legendary subjects may be devotional, or historical, according to the sentiment conveyed : for example, the Crucifixion and the Last Supper may be so represented as either to exhibit an event, or to express a symbol of our Redemption. The Raising of Lazarus exhibits in the Catacombs a mystical emblem of the general resurrection ; in the grand picture by Sebastian del Piombo, in our National Gallery, it is a scene from the life of

our Saviour. Among the legendary subjects, the Penance of the
Magdalene, and St. Martin Dividing his Cloak, may be merely
incidents, or they may be symbolical, the first of penitence, the
latter of charity, in the general sense. And, again, there are some
subjects which, though expressing a scene or an action, are *wholly*
mystical and devotional in their import; as the Vision of St.
Augustine, and the Marriage of St. Catherine.

Among the grandest of the devotional subjects, we may reckon
those compositions which represent the whole celestial hierarchy;
the divine personages of the Trinity, the angels and archangels,
and the beatified spirits of the just. Such is the subject called the
' Paradiso,' so often met with in pictures and ecclesiastical decoration, where Christ is enthroned in glory; such is also the Coronation of the Virgin, that ancient and popular symbol of the triumph
of Religion or the Church; the Adoration of the Lamb; and the
Last Judgment, from the Apocalypse. The order of precedence in
these sacred assemblages was early settled by ecclesiastical authority,
and was almost as absolute as that of a modern code of honour.
First after the Trinity, the Virgin Mary, as *Regina Angelorum*, and
St. John the Baptist; then, in order, the Evangelists; the Patriarchs,
the Prophets; the Apostles; the Fathers; the Bishops; the Martyrs;
the Hermits; the Virgins; the Monks, Nuns, and Confessors.

As examples, I may cite the Paradiso of Angelico, in the
Florence Academy; the Coronation of the Virgin by Hans Hemling,
in the Wallerstein collection, which contains not less than fifty-two
figures, all individualised with their proper attributes; and which,
if it were possible, should be considered in contrast with the Coronation by Angelico. The Flemish painter seems to have carried his
intense impression of earthly and individual life into the regions of
heaven; the Italian, through a purer inspiration, seems to have
brought all Paradise down before us upon earth. In the Adoration of
the Lamb by Van Eyck, there are not fewer than two hundred figures.
For the Last Judgment, the grand compositions of Orcagna in the
Campo Santo,—of Luca Signorelli and Angelico at Orvieto,—and the
fresco of Michael Angelo in the Sistine Chapel, may be consulted.

Where the usual order is varied, there is generally some reason

for it; for instance, in the exaltation of a favourite saint, as we
sometimes find St. Dominick and St. Francis by the side of St. Peter
and St. Paul; and among the miniatures of that extraordinary MS.,
—the Hortus Deliciarum, now at Strasbourg, painted for a virgin
abbess,—there is a ' Paradiso,' in which the painter, either by her
command or in compliment to her, has placed the virgins immediately after the angels.

The representation of the Virgin and Child with saints grouped
around them, is a devotional subject familiar to us from its constant
recurrence.   It also frequently happens that the tutelary saint of the
locality, or the patron saint of the votary, is represented as seated on
a raised throne in the centre; and other saints, though under every
other circumstance taking a superior rank, become here accessaries,
and are placed on each side or lower down in the picture: for example, where St. Augustine is enthroned, and St. Peter and St. Paul
stand on each side, as in a picture by B. Vivarini,[1] or where St.
Barbara is enthroned, and Mary Magdalene and St. Catherine stand
on each side, as in a picture by Matteo di Siena.[2]

In such pictures, the votary or donor is often introduced kneeling
at the feet of his patron, either alone or accompanied by his wife and
other members of his family: and to express the excess of his
humility, he is sometimes so diminutive in proportion to the colossal
object of his veneration, as to be almost lost to sight; we have
frequent examples of this *naïveté* of sentiment in the old mosaics and
votive altar-pieces; for instance, in a beautiful old fresco at Assisi,
where the Magdalene, a majestic figure about six feet high, holds out
her hand in benediction to a little Franciscan friar about a foot in
height: but it was abandoned as barbarous in the later schools of
Art, and the votary, when retained, appears of the natural size; as
in the *Madonna del Donatore* of Raphael,[3] where Sigismond Conti is
almost the finest and most striking part of that inestimable picture
and in the *Madonna* of the Meyer family by Holbein.[4]

When a bishop is introduced into a group of saints kneeling, while
all the others are standing, he may be supposed to be the *Donatore*

[1] Venice ; SS. Giovanni e Paolo.   [2] Siena ; San Dominico.
[3] Rome ; Vatican.   [4] Dresden Gal.

or *Divoto*, the person who presents the picture.   When he is standing, he is one of the bishop-patrons or bishop-martyrs, of whom there
are some hundreds, and who are more difficult to discriminate than
any other pictured saints.

And this leads me to the subject of the so-called *anachronisms* in
devotional subjects, where personages who lived at different and
distant periods of time are found grouped together.   It is curious to
find the critics of the last century treating with pity and ridicule, as
the result of ignorance or a barbarous unformed taste, the noblest
and most spiritual conceptions of poetic Art.   Even Sir Joshua
Reynolds had so little idea of the true object and feeling of such
representations, that he thinks it necessary to apologise for the error
of the painter, or the mistaken piety of his employer.   We must
remember that the personages here brought together in their sacred
character belong no more to our earth, but to heaven and eternity :
for them there is no longer time or place ; they are here assembled
together in the perpetual ' communion of saints,'—immortal contemporaries in that kingdom where the Angel of the Apocalypse
proclaimed ' that there should be time no longer.'
Such groups are sometimes arranged with an artless solemnity, all
the personages standing and looking straight out of the picture at
the worshipper.   Sometimes there is a touch of dramatic sentiment,
which, without interfering with the solemn devotional feeling, lights
up the whole with the charm of a purpose ; as in the Correggio at
Parma, where St. Jerome presents his translation of the Scriptures
to the infant Christ, while an angel turns the leaves, and Mary
Magdalene, symbol of redemption and reconciliation, bends to kiss
the feet of the Saviour.

Our ancestors of the Middle Ages were not particular in drawing
that strong line of demarcation between the classical, Jewish, and
Christian periods of history, that we do.   They saw only Christendom
everywhere ; they regarded the past only in relation to Christianity.
Hence we find in the early ecclesiastical monuments and edifices
such a strange assemblage of Pagan, Scriptural, and Christian
worthies ; as, Hector of Troy, Alexander the Great, King David,

Judas Maccabeus, King Arthur, St. George, Godfrey of Boulogne, Lucretia, Virginia, Judith, St. Elizabeth, St. Bridget (as in the Cross of Nuremburg). In the curious Manual of Greek Art, published by Didron, we find the Greek philosophers and poets entering into a scheme of ecclesiastical decoration, as in the carved stalls in the Cathedral of Ulm, where Solon, Apollonius, Plutarch, Plato, Sophocles, are represented, holding each a scroll, on which is inscribed a passage from their works, interpreted into an allusion to the coming of Christ: and I have seen a picture of the Nativity in which the sibyls are dancing hand-in-hand around the cradle of the new-born Saviour. This may appear profane to some, but the comprehension of the whole universe within the pale of Christianity strikes me as being in the most Catholic, as well as in the most poetical, spirit.

It is in devotional subjects that we commonly find those anthropomorphic representations of the Divinity which shock devout people; and which no excuse or argument can render endurable to those who see in them only ignorant irreverence or intentional profaneness. It might be pleaded that the profaneness is not intentional; that emblems and forms are, in the imitative arts, what figures of speech are in language; that only through a figure of speech can any attempt be made to place the idea of Almighty power before us. Familiar expressions, consecrated by Scripture usage, represent the Deity as reposing, waking, stretching forth His hand, sitting on a throne; as pleased, angry, vengeful, repentant; and the ancient painters, speaking the language proper to their art, appear to have turned these emblematical words into emblematical pictures. I forbear to say more on this point, because I have taken throughout the poetical and not the religious view of Art, and this is an objection which must be left, as a matter of feeling, to the amount of candour and knowledge in the critical reader.

In the sacred subjects, properly called HISTORICAL, we must be careful to distinguish between those which are *Scriptural*, representing scenes from the Old or New Testament, and those which are *Legendary*.

Of the first, for the present, I do not speak, as they will be fully treated hereafter.

The historical subjects from the lives of the saints consist principally of *Miracles* and *Martyrdoms.*

In the first, it is worth remarking that we have no pictured
miracle which is not imitated from the Old or the New Testament
(unless it be an obvious emblem, as where the saint carries his own
head). There is no act of supernatural power related of any saint
which is not recorded of some great Scriptural personage. The
object was to represent the favourite patron as a copy of the great
universal type of beneficence, CHRIST OUR REDEEMER. And they
were not satisfied that the resemblance should lie in character only;
but should emulate the power of Christ in His visible actions. We
must remember that the common people of the Middle Ages did not,
and could not, distinguish between miracles accredited by the testimony of Scripture and those which were fabrications, or at least exag-
gerations. All miracles related as divine interpositions were to them
equally possible, equally credible. If a more extended knowledge
of the natural laws renders us in these days less credulous, it also
shows us that many things were possible, under particular conditions,
which were long deemed supernatural.

We find in the legendary pictures, that the birth of several saints is
announced by an angel, or in a dream, as in the stories of St. Catherine,
St. Roch, &c. They exhibit precocious piety and wisdom, as in the
story of St. Nicholas, who also calms a tempest, and guides the
storm-tossed vessel safe to land. They walk on the water, as in the
stories of St. Raymond and St. Hyacinth ; or a river divides, to let
them pass, as in the story of St. Alban. Saints are fed and comforted miraculously, or delivered from prison by angels ; or resist
fire, like the 'Three Children.' The multiplication of bread, and the
transformation of water into wine, are standing miracles. But
those which most frequently occur in pictures, are the healing of
the sick, the lame, the blind; the casting out of demons, the restoration of the dead, or some other manifestation of compassionate
and beneficent power.

Some of the pictured legends are partly Scriptural, partly historical, as the story of St. Peter ; others are clearly religious apologues
founded on fact or tradition, as those of St. Mary of Egypt and St.
Christopher ; others are obviously and purely allegorical, as the Greek

story of St. Sophia (*i.e*, Heavenly Wisdom, *ΣΟΦΙΑ*) and her celestial progeny, St. Faith, St. Hope, and St. Charity, all martyred by the blind and cruel Pagans. The names sound as if borrowed from the ' Pilgrim's Progress ; ' and it is curious to find Bunyan's allegorical legend, the favourite picture-book of the people, appearing just at the time when the legends and pictures of the saints became objects of puritanical horror, and supplying their place in the popular imagination.

Martyrdoms are only too common : they present to us Christianity under its most mystical aspect—the deification of suffering ; but to render these representations effective, they should be pathetic without being terrible, they should speak to us

Of melancholy fear subdued by faith,
Of blessed consolations in distress ;

but not of the horrid cruelty of man towards man. It has been well remarked by my friend M. Rio (to whose charming and eloquent exposition of Christian Art I refer with ever-new delight), that the early painters of Western Christendom avoided these subjects, and that their prevalence in ecclesiastical decoration marked the decline of religious feeling, and the degeneracy of Art. But this remark does not apply to Byzantine Art ; for we find from the exact description of a picture of the martyrdom of St. Euphemia (both the picture and the description dating from the third century), that such representations were then common, and were appealed to in the same manner as now, to excite the feelings of the people.

The martyrdoms generally met with are those of St. Peter and St. Paul, St. Stephen Protomartyr, St. Laurence, St. Catherine, and St. Sebastian. These we find everywhere, in all countries and localities. Where the patron of the church or chapel is a martyr, his martyrdom holds a conspicuous place, often over the high altar. and accompanied by all the moving circumstances which can excite the pity, or horror, or enthusiasm of the pious votaries ; but in the best examples we find the saint preparing for his death, not suffering the torments actually inflicted ; so that the mind is elevated by the sentiment of his courage, not disturbed and disgusted by the spectacle of his agonies.

III. Of certain Patron Saints,

WHILE such assemblages of holy persons as are found grouped together in devotional pictures are to be considered as quite independent of chronology, we shall find that the selection has been neither capricious nor arbitrary, and, with a little consideration, we shall discover the leading idea in the mind of the artist—that, at least, which was intended to be conveyed to the mind of the spectator, and which was much more intelligible in former times than it is now.

Sometimes we find certain saints placed in companionship, because they are the joint patrons and protectors of the city or locality for which the picture was painted. Thus in the Bologna pictures we constantly find the bishop St. Petronius, St. Eloy, St. Dominick, and the warrior St. Proculus ; while in the Venetian pictures we have perpetual St. Marks, St. Georges, and St. Catherines.

Or, secondly, they are connected by kindred powers and attributes. Thus we find St. Sebastian, the patron against pestilence, in company with St. Roch, who ministered to the sick of the plague. Thus St. Catherine and St. Jerome, the two patrons of school theology, are often found in companionship. Where St. Catherine and St. Barbara are found together, the first figures as patroness of the ecclesiastical, and the second of the military, power—or they represent respectively the contemplative and the active life.

Or, thirdly, they are combined in the fancy by some inevitable association ; as St. Augustine and St. Stephen are often in the same picture, because St. Augustine dedicated some of his most eloquent works to the glory of the martyr.

Or they were friends on earth, for which reason St. Cyprian and St. Cornelius are placed together.

Or their relics repose in the same spot ; whence St. Stephen and St. Laurence have become almost inseparable. When St. Vincent and

St. Laurence are placed together (as in a lovely composition of Parmigiano, where they sit reading out of the same book), it is because of the similarity of their fate, and that the popular tradition supposed them to be brothers.

A point of more general importance, and capable of more definite explanation, is the predominance of certain sacred personages in particular schools of Art. St. Cosmo and St. Damian, for instance, are perpetually recurring in the Florentine pictures as the patron saints of the Medici family. In the Lombard pictures St. Ambrose is often found without his compeers—not as doctor of the Church, but as bishop of Milan. In the Siena pictures, we may look for the nun St. Catherine of Siena, and St. Ansano, the apostle of the Sienese, holding his banner and palm. And in the Augustine chapels and churches, St. Augustine figures, not as doctor of the Church, but as patriarch of the Order.

A bishop-martyr, holding his palm, and not otherwise designated either by name or attribute, would be—in one of Perugino's pictures, St. Ercolano or St. Costanzo; in a Florentine picture, St. Donato or St. Romulo; if the picture were painted in the march of Ancona, it would probably be St Apollinaris of Ravenna; at Naples it would be St. Januarius; at Paris, or in a picture painted for a French church, of which there are many in Italy, it would be St. Denis; and in German prints, St. Boniface or St. Lambert. I need not further multiply examples.

If the locality from which the picture came will sometimes deter mine the names of the personages, so the personages represented will often explain the purpose and intended situation of the picture. There is in Lord Ashburton's gallery a noble group representing together St. Peter, St. Leonard, St. Martha, and Mary Magdalene. Such a combination points it out at once as intended for a charitable institution, and, on inquiry, we find that it was painted for the chapel of a brotherhood associated to redeem prisoners, to ransom slaves, to work for the poor, and to convert the sinner to repentance. Many such interesting and instructive analogies will be pointed out in the course of the following pages, and the observer of works of Art will discover others for himself.

I add here, in alphabetical order, those countries and localities of which the patron saints are distinguished in works of Art.[1]

ANCONA : St. Cyriacus, *Bishop;* and his mother Anna, *Martyr.*

AREZZO : St. Donato, *Bishop.*

ASTI, NOVARA, and all through the cities of PIEDMONT and the north of Italy, we find the *Warrior,* St. Maurice, and his companions St. Secundus, St. Alexander, and the other Martyrs of the Theban Legion.

AUGSBURG : St. Ulrich, *Bishop;* St. Afra, *Martyr.*

AUSTRIA : St. Leopold, St. Stephen, St. Maximilian, St. Coloman.

BAMBERG : St. Henry and St. Cunegunda, *Emperor* and *Empress.*

BARCELONA : St. Eulalia, *Martyr.* (In Spanish pictures only.)

BAVARIA : St. George, *Martyr.*

BERGAMO : St. Alexander, *Warrior;* St. Grata, *Widow.*

BOHEMIA : St. John Nepomuck, *Priest;* St. Wenceslaus, *King;* St. Ludmilla, *Queen;* St. Vitus, *young Martyr;* St. Procopius, *Hermit.*

BOLOGNA : St. Petronius, *Bishop;* St. Dominick, *Friar;* St. Proculus, *Warrior Martyr;* St. Eloy (Eligio), *Bishop* and *Smith.*

BRESCIA : St. Faustinus and Jovita ; St. Julia, St. Afra, *Martyrs.*

BRUGES : St. John the Baptist.

BURGUNDY : St. Andrew, *Apostle.*

COLOGNE : The Three Kings ; St. Ursula, *Virgin Martyr;* St. Gereon, *Warrior Martyr.*

COMO : St. Abbondio, *Bishop.*

CORTONA : St. Margaret, *Nun* and *Penitent.*

CREMONA : St. Omobuono, *Secular Habit.*

FERRARA : St. Geminiano, *Bishop;* St. George, *Martyr;* St. Barbara, *Martyr.*

FIESOLE : St. Romolo, *Bishop.*

FLORENCE : St. John the Baptist ; St. Zenobio, St. Antonino, *Bishops;* St. Reparata, *Virgin Martyr;* St. Cosmo and Damian (the Apothecary Saints, especial patrons of the Medici family) ; St. Verdiana, *Nun;* St. Miniato, *Warrior.*

FRANCE : St. Michael, *Angel;* St. Dionysius (Denis), *Bishop;* St. Geneviève, *Virgin;* St. Martin, *Bishop.*

GENOA : St. George, St. Laurence, *Martyrs.*

GHENT : St. Bavon, *Prince* and *Hermit.*

GRENOBLE : St. Hugh the Carthusian.

IRELAND : St. Patrick, *Bishop;* St. Bridget, *Abbess.*

LUCCA : St. Martin, *Bishop;* St. Frediano, *Priest;* St. Zita, *Virgin.*

LIEGE : St. Hubert, *Bishop* and *Huntsman;* St. Lambert, *Bishop.*

MADRID : St. Isidore, *Labourer;* St. Dominick, *Friar* (Patron of the Escurial, St. Laurence).

---

[1] The Saints who do not appear in these volumes will be found in the 'Legends of the Monastic Orders.'

MANTUA : St. Andrew ; St. Barbara ; St. George and St. Longinus, *Warrior Saints.*

MARSEILLES and all PROVENCE : St. Lazarus ; St. Mary Magdalen ; St. Martha ; St. Marcella.

MESSINA : St. Agatha, *Martyr.*

MILAN : St. Ambrose, *Bishop* and *Doctor;* St. Gervasius and St. Protasius, *Martyrs;* St. Maurice, St. Victor, *Warriors.*

MODENA : St. Geminiano, *Bishop.*   (In pictures of the Correggio School.)

NAPLES : St. Januarius, *Martyr.*

NOVARA : St. Gaudenzio, *Bishop.*

NUREMBURG : St. Laurence, *Martyr;* St. Sebald, *Pilgrim* and *Hermit.*   (The latter an important person in pictures and prints of the Albert Dürer school.)

PADUA : St. Anthony of Padua, *Friar.*

PARIS : St. Geneviève, *Virgin;* St. Germain, *Bishop;* St. Hippolitus, *Martyr.*

PARMA : St. John, B. ; St. Thomas the Apostle ; St. Bernard, *Monk;* St. Hilary (Ilario), *Bishop.*

PERUGIA : St. Ercolano and St. Costanzo, *Bishops.*

PIACENZA : St. Justina, *Martyr;* St. Antoninus, *Warrior* (Theban Legion).

PIEDMONT and SAVOY : St. John, B. ; St. Maurice and St. George, *Warriors;* St. Amadeus, *King.*

PISA : St. Ranieri, *Hermit;* St. Torpé, *Warrior;* St. Ephesus and St. Potita, *Warriors.*   (These only in the ancient Pisan school.)

RAVENNA : St. Appolinaris, *Bishop.*

RIMINI : St. Julian, *Martyr.*   (A young saint, popular all through the north and down the east coast of Italy.)

SEVILLE : St. Leander, *Bishop;* St. Justina, St. Rufina, *Sisters* and *Martyrs.* (These are only found in Spanish pictures.)

SICILY : St. Vitus, *Martyr ;* St. Rosalia, *Recluse* (Palermo) ; St. Agatha (Messina), St. Lucia (Syracuse), *Martyrs.*

SIENNA : St. Ansano, *Martyr;* St. Catherine of Siena, *Nun;* St. Bernardino, *Friar.*

THURINGIA and all that part of SAXONY : St. Elizabeth of Hungary ; St. Boniface, *Bishop.*

TOLEDO : St. Ildefonso, *Bishop;* and St. Leocadia, *Martyr.*   (Only in Spanish pictures.)

TREVISO : St. Liberale, *Warrior.*

TURIN : St. John the Baptist ; St. Maurice, *Warrior.*

UMBRIA : All through this region and the eastern coast of Italy, very important in respect to Art, the favourite saints are—St. Nicholas, *Bishop;* St. Francis of Assisi, *Friar;* St. Clara, *Nun;* St. Julian, *Martyr;* and St. Catherine, *Virgin Martyr.*

VALENCIA : St. Vincent, *Martyr.*

VENICE : St. Mark, *Apostle;* St. George, St. Theodore, *Warriors;* St. Nicholas, *Bishop;* St. Catherine, St. Christina, *Virgin Martyrs.*

VERCELLI : St. Eusebius, *Bishop;* St. Thronestus, *Warrior* (Theban Legion).

VERONA : St. Zeno, *Bishop;* St. Fermo, *Martyr;* St. Euphemia, *Martyr.*

VOTIVE PICTURES are those which have been dedicated in certain religious edifices, in fulfilment of vows ; either as the expression of thanksgiving for blessings which have been vouchsafed, or propitiative against calamities to be averted. The far greater number of these pictures commemorate an escape from danger, sickness, death ; and more especially, some visitation of the plague, that terrible and frequent scourge of the Middle Ages. The significance of such pictures is generally indicated by the presence of St. Sebastian or St. Roch, the patrons against the plague ; or St. Cosmo and St. Damian, the healing and medical saints ; accompanied by the patron saints of the country or locality, if it be a public act of devotion ; or, if dedicated by private or individual piety, the donor kneels, presented by his own patron saint. In general, though not always, this expressive group is arranged in attendance on the enthroned Madonna and her divine Son, as the universal protectors from all evil. Such pictures are among the most interesting and remarkable of the works of sacred Art which remain to us, and have often a pathetic and poetical beauty, and an historical significance, which it is a chief purpose of these volumes to interpret and illustrate.

IV. OF CERTAIN EMBLEMS AND ATTRIBUTES.

To know something of the attributes and emblems of general application, as well as those proper to each saint, is absolutely necessary ; but it will also greatly assist the fancy and the memory to *understand* their origin and significance. For this reason I will add a few words of explanation.

The GLORY, NIMBUS, or AUREOLE—the Christian attribute of sanctity, and used generally to distinguish all holy personages—is of pagan origin. It expressed the luminous nebula (Homer, *Il.* xxiii. 205), supposed to emanate from, and surround, the Divine Essence, which stood, 'a shade in midst of its own brightness.' Images of the gods were decorated with a crown of rays, or with stars ; and when the Roman emperors assumed the honours due to

St. Domian.   St. Mark.   St. Roch.   A. J. fecit.
St. Cosmo.   St. Sebastian.

A Venetian votive picture against the plague.

divinity, they appeared in public crowned with golden radii. The colossal statue of Nero wore a circle of rays, imitating the glory of the sun. This ornament became customary; and not only the first Cæsars, but the Christian emperors, adopted the same divine insignia; and it became at length so common that we find it on some medals, round the heads of the consuls of the later empire. Considered in the East as *the attribute of power only*, whether good or evil, we find, wherever early Art has been developed under Byzantine influences, the nimbus thus applied. Satan, in many Greek, Saxon, and French miniatures, from the ninth to the thirteenth century, wears a glory. In a psalter of the twelfth century, the Beast of the Apocalypse with seven heads, has six heads surrounded by the nimbus; the seventh, wounded and drooping, is without the sign of power.

But in Western Art the associations with this attribute were not merely those of dignity, but of something divine and consecrated. It was for a long time avoided in the Christian representations as being appropriated by false gods or heathen pride; and when first adopted does not seem clear.[1] The earliest example cited is a gem of St. Martin of the early part of the sixth century, in which the glory round his head seems to represent his apotheosis; and in all instances it is evidently intended to represent divine glory and beatitude.

The glory round the head is properly the nimbus or aureole. The oblong glory surrounding the whole person, called in Latin the *vesica piscis*, and in Italian the *mandorla* (almond) from its form, is confined to figures of Christ and the Virgin, or saints who are in the act of ascending into heaven. When used to distinguish one of the three divine persons of the Trinity, the glory is often cruciform or triangular. The square nimbus designates a person living at the time the work was executed. In the frescoes of Giotto at Assisi, the allegorical personages are in some instances distinguished by the hexagonal nimbus. In other instances it is circular. From the fifth to the twelfth century the nimbus had the form

[1] 'Avant le 5me siècle le nimbe chrétien ne se voit pas sur les monuments *authentiques.* (Didron, Iconographie, p. 101.)

of a disc or plate over the head.[1] From the twelfth to the
fifteenth century, it was a broad golden band, round, or rather
behind the head, composed of circle within circle, often adorned
with precious stones, and sometimes having the name of the saint
inscribed within it. From the fifteenth century it was a bright
fillet over the head, and in the seventeenth century it disappeared
altogether, in pictures the glory is always golden, the colour of
light; in miniatures and stained glass I have seen glories of various
colours, red, blue, or green.[2]

The FISH was the earliest, the most universal, of the Christian
emblems, partly as the symbol of water and the rite of baptism,
and also because the five Greek letters which express the word Fish
form the anagram of the name of Jesus Christ. In this sense we
find the fish as a general symbol of the Christian faith upon the
sarcophagi of the early Christians; on the tombs of the martyrs in
the Catacombs; on rings, coins, lamps, and other utensils; and
as an ornament in early Christian architecture. It is usually a
dolphin, which among the pagans had also a sacred significance.
The passage in the Gospel, ' Follow me, and I will make ye
fishers of men,' is supposed to have originated the use of this
symbol; and I may observe here, that the fish placed in the hands
of St. Peter has probably a double or treble signification, alluding
to his former occupation as a fisherman, his conversion to Christianity, and his vocation as a Christian apostle, *i.e.*, a fisher of men,
in the sense used by Christ; and in the same sense, we find it
given as an attribute to bishops who were famous for converting
and baptizing, as St. Zeno of Verona, and Gregory of Tours.

---

[1] A metal circle, like a round plate, was fastened on the head of those statues placed in
the open air, to defend them from the rain or dust. Some of the ancient glories are very
like those plates, but I do not think they are derived from them.

[2] I believe these coloured glories to be symbolical, but am not sure of the application
of the colours. Among the miniatures of the *Hortus Deliciarum*, painted in 1180, is a
representation of the celestial paradise, in which the virgins, the apostles, the martyrs,
and confessors wear the golden nimbus; the prophets and the patriarchs, the white or silver
nimbus; the saints who strove with temptation, the red nimbus; those who were married
have the nimbus green, while the beatified penitents have theirs of a yellowish white, somewhat shaded. (Didron, Iconographie Chrétienne p. 168.)

The CROSS.—About the tenth century the Fish disappeared, and the Cross—symbol of our redemption, from the apostolic times— became the sole and universal emblem of the Christian faith. The cross placed in the hand of a saint is usually the Latin cross (1), the form ascribed to the cross on which our Saviour suffered. Other crosses are used as emblems or ornaments, but still having the same signification : as the Greek cross (2), in which the arms are all of the same length ; the transverse cross, on which St.

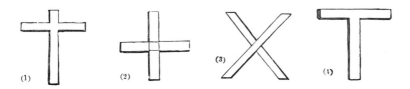

Andrew is supposed to have suffered, in this form (3) ; the Egyptian cross, sometimes placed in the hands of St. Philip the apostle, and it was also the form of the crutch of St. Anthony, and embroidered on his cope or robe, hence it is called St. Anthony's cross (4). There is also the Maltese cross, and various ornamental crosses. The double cross on the top of a staff, instead of the crosier, is borne by the Pope only ; the staff with a single cross by the Greek bishops.

At first, the Cross was a sign only. When formed of gold or silver, the five wounds of Christ were signified by a ruby or carbuncle at each extremity, and one in the centre. It was not till the sixth century that the Cross became a CRUCIFIX, no longer an emblem, but an *image*.

The LAMB, in Christian Art, is the peculiar symbol of the Redeemer, as the sacrifice without blemish ; in this sense it is given as an attribute to John the Baptist. The lamb is also the general emblem of innocence, meekness, modesty ; in this sense it is given to St. Agnes, of whom Massillon said so beautifully, ' Peu de pudeur, où il n'y a pas de religion ; peu de religion, où il n'y a pas de pudeur.'

The PELICAN, tearing open her breast to feed her young with her own blood, was an early symbol of our redemption through Christ.

One or both of these emblems are frequently found in ancient crosses and crucifixes; the lamb at the foot, the pelican at the top, of the cross.

The DRAGON is the emblem of sin in general, and of the sin of idolatry in particular; and the dragon slain and vanquished by the power of the Cross, is the perpetually recurring myth, which, varied in a thousand ways, we find running through all the old Christian legends; not subject to misapprehension in the earliest times; but as the cloud of ignorance darkened and deepened, the symbol was translated into a fact. It has been suggested that the dragon, which is to us a phantasm and an allegory, which, in the Middle Ages, was the visible shape of the demon adversary of all truth and goodness, might have been, as regards form, originally *a fact;* for wherever we have dragon legends, whether the scene be laid in Asia, Africa, or Europe, the imputed circumstances and the form are little varied. The dragons introduced into early painting and sculpture so invariably represent a gigantic winged crocodile, that it is presumed there must have been some common origin for the type chosen as if by common consent; and that this common type may have been some fossil remains of the Saurian species, or even some far-off dim tradition of one of these tremendous reptiles surviving in Heaven knows what vast desolate morass or inland lake, and spreading horror and devastation along its shores. At Aix, a huge fossilised head of one of the Sauri was for a long time preserved as the head of the identical dragon subdued by St. Martha; and St. Jerome relates that he had himself beheld at Tyre the bones of the sea monster to which Andromeda had been exposed—probably some fossil remains, which in the popular imagination were thus accounted for. Professor Owen told me, that the head of a dragon in one of the legendary pictures he had seen in Italy, closely resembled in form that of the *Deinotherium Giganteum.* These observations have reference only to the type adopted when the old Scripture allegory took form and shape. The dragon of Holy Writ is the same as the serpent, *i.e.*, personified sin, the spiritual enemy of mankind.

The Scriptural phrase of the 'jaws of hell' is literally rendered in the ancient works of Art by the huge jaws of a dragon, wide open and emitting flames, into which the souls of sinners are tumbled headlong. In pictures, sin is also typified by a serpent or snake; in this form it is placed under the feet of the Madonna, sometimes with an apple in its mouth; sometimes, but only in late pictures of the seventeenth century, winding its green scaly length round and round a globe, significant of the subjugation of the whole earth to the power of sin till delivered by the Redeemer. On this subject I shall have much more to say when treating of the pictures of the Fall of Man, and the subjects taken from the Apocalypse: for the present we need only bear in mind the various significations of the popular Dragon myth, which may shadow forth the conquest over sin, as in the legends of St. Michael and St. Margaret; or over paganism, as in the legends of St. Sylvester and St. George; or sometimes a destroying flood, as in the legend of St. Martha, where the inundation of the Rhone is figured by a dragon emerging from the waters and spreading around death and pestilence,—like the Python of the Grecian myth.

The LION, as an ancient Christian symbol, is of frequent recurrence, more particularly in architectural decoration. Antiquaries are not agreed as to the exact meaning attached to the mystical lions placed in the porches of so many old Lombard churches; sometimes with an animal, sometimes with a man, in their paws. But we find that the lion was an ancient symbol of the Redeemer, 'the Lion of the tribe of Judah:' also of the resurrection of the Redeemer; because, according to an oriental fable, the lion's cub was born dead, and in three days its sire licked it into life. In this sense it occurs in the windows of the cathedral at Bourges. In either sense it may probably have been adopted as a frequent ornament in the church utensils, and in ecclesiastical decoration, supporting the pillars in front, or the carved thrones, &c.—The lion also typifies solitude—the wilderness; and, in this sense, is placed near St. Jerome and other saints who did penance, or lived as hermits in the desert; as in the legends of St. Paul the hermit, St. Mary of Egypt, St. Onofrio. Further, the lion as an attribute denoted death in the amphitheatre, and with this signification is placed near certain martyrs, as St. Ignatius and St. Euphemia. The

lion, as the type of fortitude and resolution, was placed at the feet
of those martyrs who had suffered with singular courage, as St.
Adrian and St. Natalia.[1]

When other wild beasts, as wolves and bears, are placed at the feet
of a saint attired as abbot or bishop, it signifies that he cleared waste
land, cut down forests, and substituted Christian culture and civilisation for paganism and the lawless hunter's life: such is the significance
in pictures of St. Magnus, St. Florentius, and St. Germain of Auxerre.

The HART or HIND was also an emblem of double signification. It
was a type of solitude and of purity of life, and was also a type of
piety and religious aspiration, adopted from the forty-second Psalm,
' Like as the hart panteth after the water-brooks, so panteth my soul
for Thee, O God! '

When the original meaning of the lion, the hart, and other emblems,
was no longer present to the popular mind, legends were invented to
account for them ; and that which had been a symbol, became an incident, or an historical attribute,—as in the stories of the lion healed
by St. Jerome, or digging the grave of St. Paul ; the miraculous stag
which appeared to St. Eustace and St. Hubert ; the wounded doe in
the legend of St. Giles ; and the hind which spoke to St. Julian.

The PEACOCK, the bird of Juno, was an ancient pagan symbol,
signifying the apotheosis of an empress, as we find from many of
the old Roman coins and medals. The early Christians, accustomed
to this interpretation, adopted it as a general emblem of the mortal
exchanged for the immortal existence ; and, with this signification,
we find the peacock with outspread train on the walls and ceilings
of catacombs, the tombs of the martyrs, and many of the sarcophagi,
down to the fourth and fifth centuries. It is only in modern times
that the peacock has become the emblem of worldly pride.

The CROWN, as introduced in Christian Art, is either an emblem or
an attribute. It has been the emblem from all antiquity of victory,

---

[1] In the example of St. Jerome, a lion may have originally typified any hindrance in
the way of study or of duty ; in allusion to the text, ' The slothful man saith, There is a
lion by the way.' Prov. xxvi. 13.

and of recompense due to superior power or virtue. In this sense the word and the image are used in Scripture in many passages : for example, ' Henceforth there is laid up for me a crown of glory.' And in this sense, as the recompense of those who had fought the good fight to the end, and conquered, the crown became the especial symbol of the glory of martyrdom. In very ancient pictures, a hand is seen coming out of heaven holding a wreath or circlet; afterwards it is an angel who descends with a crown, which is sometimes a coronet of gold and jewels, sometimes a wreath of palm or myrtle. In general only the female martyrs wear the symbolical crown of glory; martyrs of the other sex hold the crown in their hands, or it is borne by an angel. Hence we may presume that the crown, which among the Jews was the especial ornament of a bride, signified the bride or spouse of Christ—one dedicated to virginity for his sake; and in this sense, down to the present time, the crown is placed on the head of a nun at the moment of consecration. Therefore in the old pictures of female martyrs we may interpret the crown in this double sense, as signifying at once the bride and the martyr.

But it is necessary also to distinguish between the *symbol* and the *attribute:* thus, where St. Cecilia and St. Barbara wear the crown, it is the symbol of their glorious martyrdom ; when St. Catherine and St. Ursula wear the crown, it is at once as the symbol of martyrdom and the attribute of their royal rank as princesses.

The crown is also the symbol of sovereignty. When it is placed on the head of the Virgin, it is as Queen of Heaven, and also as the ' Spouse ' of Scripture allegory.

But the crown is also an attribute, and frequently, when worn by a saint or placed at his feet, signifies that he was royal or of princely birth: as in the pictures of Louis of France, St. William, St. Elizabeth, St. Helena, and many others.

The crowns in the Italian pictures are generally a wreath, or a

simple circle of gold and jewels, or a coronet radiated with a few points. But in the old German pictures the crown is often of most magnificent workmanship, blazing with jewels.

I have seen a real silver crown placed on the figures of certain popular saints, but as a votive tribute, not an emblem.

The SWORD is also either a symbol or an attribute. As a symbol, it signifies generally a martyrdom by any violent death, and, in this sense, is given to many saints who did not die by the sword. As an attribute, it signifies the particular death suffered, and that the martyr in whose hand or at whose feet it is placed was beheaded: in this sense it is given to St. Paul, St. Catherine, and many others. It is given also to the warrior-martyrs, as the attribute of their military profession. Other symbols of martyrdom are the AXE, the LANCE, and the CLUB.

ARROWS, which are attributes, St. Ursula, St. Christina, and St. Sebastian.

The PONIARD, given to St. Lucia.

The CAULDRON, given to St. John the Evangelist and St. Cecilia.

The PINCERS and SHEARS, St. Apollonia and St. Agatha.

The WHEELS, St. Catherine.

FIRE and FLAMES are sometimes an emblem of martyrdom and punishment, and sometimes of religious fervour.

A BELL was supposed to have power to exorcise demons, and for this reason is given to the haunted St. Anthony.

The SHELL signifies pilgrimage.

The SKULL, penance.

The ANVIL, as an attribute of martyrdom, belongs to St. Adrian only.

The PALM, the ancient classical symbol of victory and triumph, was early assumed by the Christians as the universal symbol of martyrdom, and for this adaptation of a pagan ornament they found warrant in Scripture : Rev. vii. 9, 'And after this I beheld, and, lo, a great multitude stood before the throne clothed with white robes and with palms in their hands.' . . . 'And he said to me, These are they which came out of great tribulation.' Hence in pictures of martyrdoms an angel descends with the palm; hence it is figured on the tombs of early martyrs, and placed in the hands of those who suffered in the cause of truth, as expressing their final victory over the powers of sin and death.

> The sensual think with reverence of the palm
> Which the chaste votary wields.

The palm varies in form from a small leaf to the size of a palm branch, almost a tree. It is very small in the early Italian pictures, very large in the Spanish pictures. In the Siena pictures it has a

bunch of dates depending from it. It is only in late pictures that the palm, with a total disregard to the sacredness of its original signification, is placed on the ground, or under the feet of the saint.

The STANDARD, or banner, is also the symbol of victory, the spiritual victory over sin, death, and idolatry. It is borne by our Saviour after His resurrection, and is placed in the hands of St. George, St. Maurice, and other military saints ; in the hands of some victorious martyrs, as St. Julian, St. Ansano, and of those who preached the

Gospel among infidels; also in the hands of St. Ursula and St. Reparata, the only female saints, I believe, who bear this attribute.

The OLIVE, as the well-known emblem of peace and reconciliation, is figured on the tombs of the early martyrs; sometimes with, sometimes without, the dove. The olive is borne as the attribute of peace by the angel Gabriel, by St. Agnes, and by St. Pantaleon; sometimes also by the angels in a Nativity, who announce 'peace on earth.'

The DOVE in Christian Art is the emblem of the Holy Ghost; and, besides its introduction into various subjects from the New Testament, as the Annunciation, the Baptism, the Pentecost, it is placed near certain saints who are supposed to have been particularly inspired, as St. Gregory, St. Thomas Aquinas, St. Hilarius, and others.

The dove is also a symbol of simplicity and purity of heart, and, as such, it is introduced into pictures of female saints, and especially of the Madonna and Child.

It is also the emblem of the soul; in this sense it is seen issuing from the lips of dying martyrs, and is found in pictures of St. Eulalia of Merida, and St. Scholastica the sister of St. Benedict.

The LILY is another symbol of purity, of very general application. We find it in pictures of the Virgin, and particularly in pictures of the Annunciation. It is placed significantly in the hand of St. Joseph, the husband of the Virgin Mary, his staff, according to the legend, having put forth lilies; it is given, as an emblem merely, to St. Francis, St. Anthony of Padua, St. Dominick, and St. Catherine of Siena, to express the particular purity of their lives.

The UNICORN is another ancient symbol of purity, in allusion to the fable that it could never be captured except by a virgin stainless in mind and life; it has become in consequence the emblem peculiarly of *female* chastity, but in Christian Art is appropriate only to the Virgin Mary and St. Justina.

The FLAMING HEART expresses fervent piety and love: in early pictures it is given to St. Augustine, merely in allusion to a famous passage in his ' Confessions ; ' but in the later schools of Art it has become a general and rather vulgar emblem of spiritual love : in this sense it is given to St. Theresa ; St. Maria Maddalena de' Pazzi, a Florentine nun ; and some of the Jesuit saints.

The BOOK in the hands of the Evangelists and the Apostles is an attribute, and represents the Gospel. In the hand of St. Stephen it is the Old Testament ; in the hand of any other saint it may be the Gospel, but it may also be an emblem only, signifying that the saint was famous for his learning or his writings ; it has this sense in pictures of St. Catherine, the Doctors of the Church, St. Thomas Aquinas, and St. Bonaventura.

A CHURCH placed in the hands of a saint signifies that he was the founder of some particular church : in this sense St. Henry bears the cathedral of Bamberg ; or, that he was the protector and first bishop of the Church, as St. Petronius bears the cathedral of Bologna. I must except the single instance of St. Jerome ; the church in his hands signifies no particular edifice, but, in a general sense, the Catholic Church, of which he was the great support and one of the primitive fathers ; to render the symbol more expressive, rays of light are seen proceeding from the portal.

The SCOURGE in the hand of a saint, or at his feet, signifies the penances he inflicted upon himself ; but in the hand of St. Ambrose, it signifies the penance he inflicted upon others.

The CHALICE, or Sacramental Cup, with the Host, signifies Faith ; it is given to St. Barbara. The Cup, with the Serpent, is the attribute of St. John.

The SHIP.—The Ark of Noah, floating safe amid the Deluge, in which all things else were overwhelmed, was an obvious symbol of the Church of Christ. Subsequently the *Ark* became a ship. St. Ambrose likens the Church of God to a ship, and the Cross to the mast set in the midst of it. ' *Arbor quædam in navi est crux in ecclesia.*' The Bark of St. Peter tossed in the storm, and by the

Redeemer guided safe to land, was also considered as symbolical. These mingled associations combined to give to the emblem of the ship a sacred significance. Every one who has been at Rome will remember the famous mosaic of the ship tossed by the storms, and assailed by demons, called THE NAVICELLA, which was executed by Giotto for the old Basilica of St. Peter's, and is now under the Portico, opposite to the principal door. I believe that in the pictures of St. Nicholas and St. Ursula the ship had originally a sacred and symbolical significance, and that the legends were afterwards invented or modified to explain the emblem, as in so many other instances.

The ANCHOR is the Christian symbol of immovable firmness, hope, and patience; and in this sense we find it very frequently in the catacombs, and on the ancient Christian gems. It was given to several of the early saints as a symbol. Subsequently a legend was invented to account for the symbol, turning it into an attribute, as was the case with the lion and the stag. For example: to St. Clement the anchor was first given as the symbol of his constancy in Christian hope, and thence we find, subsequently invented, the story of his being thrown into the sea with the anchor round his neck. On the vane of the Church of St. Clement in the Strand, the anchor, the parish device, was anciently placed; and as in the English fancy no anchor can be well separated from a ship, they have lately placed a ship on the other side—the original signification of the anchor, as applied to St. Clement the martyr, being unknown or forgotten.

The LAMP, LANTERN, or TAPER, is the old emblem of piety: ' Let your light so shine before men : '—and it also signifies wisdom. In the first sense we find this attribute in the hand of St. Gudula, St. Geneviève of Paris, and St. Bridget; while the lamp in the hand of St. Lucia signifies celestial light or wisdom.

FLOWERS and FRUITS, often so beautifully introduced into ecclesiastical works of Art, may be merely ornamental; Crivelli, and some of the Venetian and Lombard painters, were fond of rich festoons of fruit, and backgrounds of foliage and roses. But in some instances they have a definite significance. Roses are symbolical in pictures of the Madonna, who is the ' *Rose of Sharon*.'[1] The wreath of roses on the brow of St. Cecilia, the roses and fruits borne by St. Dorothea, are explained by the legends.

The apple was the received emblem of the Fall of man and original sin. Placed in pictures of the Madonna and Child, either in the hand of the infant Christ, or presented by an angel, it signified Redemption from the consequences of the Fall. The pomegranate, bursting open, and the seeds visible, was an emblem of the future— of hope in immortality. When an apple, a pear, or a pomegranate is placed in the hand of St. Catherine as the mystical *Sposa* of Christ, which continually occurs, particularly in the German pictures, the allusion is to be taken in the Scriptural sense : ' The *fruit* of the Spirit is love, joy, peace.'

V. Of the Significance of Colours.

In very early Art we find colours used in a symbolical or mystic sense, and, until the ancient principles and traditions were wholly worn out of memory or set aside by the later painters, certain colours were appropriate to certain subjects and personages, and could not arbitrarily be applied or misapplied. In the old specimens of stained glass we find these significations scrupulously attended to. Thus :—

White, represented by the diamond or silver, was the emblem of light, religious purity, innocence, virginity, faith, joy, and life. Our Saviour wears white after His resurrection. In the judge it indicated integrity; in the rich man humility; in the woman chastity. It was the colour consecrated to the Virgin, who, however, never wears white except in pictures of the Assumption.

Red, the ruby, signified fire, divine love, the Holy Spirit, heat, or the creative power, and royalty. White and red roses expressed

[1] *Vide* ' Legends of the Madonna.'

love and innocence, or love and wisdom, as in the garland with which the angel crowns St. Cecilia. In a bad sense, red signified blood, war, hatred, and punishment. Red and black combined were the colours of purgatory and the Devil.

BLUE, or the sapphire, expressed heaven, the firmament, truth, constancy, fidelity. Christ and the Virgin wear the red tunic and the blue mantle, as signifying heavenly love and heavenly truth.[1] The same colours were given to St. John the evangelist, with this difference,—that he wore the blue tunic and the red mantle; in later pictures the colours are sometimes red and green.

YELLOW, or gold, was the symbol of the sun; of the goodness of God; initiation, or marriage; faith, or fruitfulness. St. Joseph, the husband of the Virgin, wears yellow. In pictures of the apostles, St. Peter wears a yellow mantle over a blue tunic. In a bad sense, yellow signifies inconstancy, jealousy, deceit; in this sense it is given to the traitor Judas, who is generally habited in dirty yellow.

GREEN, the emerald, is the colour of spring; of hope, particularly hope in immortality; and of victory, as the colour of the palm and the laurel.

VIOLET, the amethyst, signified love and truth: or passion and suffering. Hence it is the colour often worn by the martyrs. In some instances our Saviour, after His resurrection, is habited in a violet instead of a blue mantle. The Virgin also wears violet after the crucifixion. Mary Magdalene, who as patron saint wears the red robe, as penitent wears violet and blue, the colours of sorrow and of constancy. In the devotional representation of her by Timoteo della Vite,[2] she wears red and green, the colours of love and hope.

GREY, the colour of ashes, signified mourning, humility, and inno-

[1] In the Spanish schools the colour of our Saviour's mantle is generally a deep rich violet.   [2] Bologna Gal.

cence accused; hence adopted as the dress of the Franciscans (the Grey Friars); but it has since been changed for a dark rusty brown.

BLACK expressed the earth, darkness, mourning, wickedness, negation, death; and was appropriate to the Prince of Darkness. In some old illuminated MSS., Jesus, in the Temptation, wears a black robe. White and black together signified purity of life, and mourning or humiliation; hence adopted by the Dominicans and the Carmelites.

The mystical application of attributes and colours was more particularly attended to in that class of subjects I have distinguished as *devotional*. In the sacred historical pictures we find that the attributes are usually omitted as superfluous, and characteristic propriety of colour often sacrificed to the general effect.

These introductory observations and explanations will be found illustrated in a variety of forms as we proceed; and readers will be led to make comparisons and discover analogies and exceptions for themselves. I must stop here;—yet one word more.

All the productions of Art, from the time it has been directed and developed by Christian influences, may be regarded under three different aspects. 1. The purely religious aspect, which belongs to one mode of faith; 2. The poetical aspect, which belongs to all; 3. The artistic, which is the individual point of view, and has reference only to the action of the intellect on the means and material employed. There is pleasure, intense pleasure, merely in the consideration of Art as *Art;* in the faculties of comparison and nice discrimination, brought to bear on objects of beauty; in the exercise of a cultivated and refined taste on the productions of mind in any form whatever. But a three-fold, or rather a thousand-fold, pleasure is theirs who to a sense of the poetical unite a sympathy with the spiritual in Art, and who combine with delicacy of perception, and technical knowledge, more elevated sources of pleasure, more variety of association, habits of more excursive thought. Let none imagine, however, that, in placing before the uninitiated these unpretending volumes, I assume any such superiority as is here implied. Like a child that has sprung on a little way before its playmates, and caught a glimpse through an opening portal of some varied Eden within, all gay with flowers and musical with birds, and haunted by divine shapes which beckon onward; and, after one rapturous survey, runs back and catches its companions by the hand and hurries them forwards to share the new-found pleasure, the yet unexplored region of delight; even so it is with me:—I am on the outside, not the inside, of the door I open.

2   After Gaudenzio Ferrari, at Saronno.

PART I.

YE too must fly before a chasing hand,
Angels and saints in every hamlet mourned!
Ah! if the old idolatry be spurned,
Let not your radiant shapes desert the land!
Her adoration was not your demand,—
The fond heart proffered it,—the servile heart,
And therefore are ye summoned to depart ;
Michael, and thou St. George, whose flaming brand
The Dragon quelled ; and valiant Margaret,
Whose rival sword a like opponent slew ;
And rapt Cecilia, seraph-haunted queen
Of harmony ; and weeping Magdalene,
Who in the penitential desert met
Gales sweet as those that over Eden blew !   —WORDSWORTH.

'I can just remember,' says a theologian of the last century, 'when the women first taught me to say my prayers, I used to have an idea of a venerable old man, of a composed, benign countenance, with his own hair, clad in a morning gown of a grave-coloured flowered damask, sitting in an elbow chair.' And he proceeds to say that, in looking back to these beginnings, he is in no way disturbed at the grossness of his infant theology. The image thus shaped by the imagination of the child was, in truth, merely one example of the various forms and conceptions fitted to divers states and seasons, and orders and degrees, of the religious mind, whether infant or adult, which represent the several approximations such minds at such seasons can respectively make to the completeness of faith. These imperfect ideas should be held to be reconciled and comprehended in that completeness, not rejected by it ; and the nearest approximation which the greatest of human minds can accomplish is surely to be regarded as much nearer to the imperfection of an infantine notion than to the fulness of truth. The gown of flowered damask and the elbow-chair may disappear ; the anthropomorphism of childhood may give place to the divine incarnation of the Second Person in after years ; and we may come to conceive of the Deity as Milton did when his epithets were most abstract :—

'So spake the SOVRAN PRESENCE.

But after all, these are but different grades of imperfection in the forms of doctrinal faith ; and if there be a devouter love on the part of the child for what is pictured in his imagination as a venerable old man, than in the philosophic poet for the 'Sovran Presence,' the child's faith has more of the efficacy of religious truth in it than the poet's and philosopher's. —(*Vide* 'Notes on Life,' by HENRY TAYLOR, p. 136.)

Gloria in excelsis Deo !

Of Angels and Archangels.

I. THE ANGELS.

THERE is something so very attractive and poetical, as well as soothing
to our helpless finite nature, in all the superstitions connected with
the popular notion of Angels, that we cannot wonder at their prevalence in the early ages of the world.   Those nations who acknowledged
one Almighty Creator, and repudiated with horror the idea of a
plurality of Gods, were the most willing to accept, the most enthusiastic in accepting, these objects of an intermediate homage; and
gladly placed between their humanity and the awful supremacy of an
unseen God, the ministering spirits who were the agents of His will,
the witnesses of His glory, the partakers of His bliss, and who in
their preternatural attributes of love and knowledge filled up that
vast space in the created universe which intervened between mortal
man and the infinite, omnipotent LORD OF ALL.

The belief in these superior beings, dating from immemorial antiquity, interwoven as it should seem with our very nature, and authorised by a variety of passages in Scripture, has descended to our time. Although the bodily forms assigned to them are allowed to be impossible, and merely allegorical, although their supposed functions as rulers of the stars and elements have long been set aside by a knowledge of the natural laws, still the co-existence of many orders of beings superior in nature to ourselves, benignly interested in our welfare, and contending for us against the powers of evil, remains an article of faith. Perhaps the belief itself, and the feeling it excites in the tender and contemplative mind, were never more beautifully expressed than by our own Spenser :—

> And is there care in heaven ? And is there love
> In heavenly spirits to these creatures base,
> That may compassion of their evils move ?
> There is !—else much more wretched were the case
> Of men than beasts ! But oh, th' exceeding grace
> Of highest God that loves His creatures so,
> And all His works with mercy doth embrace,
> That blessed angels He sends to and fro
> To serve to wicked man, to serve His wicked foe.
>
> How oft do they their silver bowers leave,
> And come to succour us that succour want ?
> How oft do they with golden pinions cleave
> The flitting skies, like flying pursuivant,
> Against foul fiends, to aid us militant ?
> They for us fight, they watch, and duly ward,
> And their bright squadrons round about us plant,
> And all for love, and nothing for reward !
> Oh, why should heavenly God to men have such regard !

It is this feeling, expressed or unexpressed, lurking at the very core of all hearts, which renders the usual representations of angels, spite of all incongruities of form, so pleasing to the fancy : we overlook the anatomical solecisms, and become mindful only of that emblematical significance which through its humanity connects it with us, and through its supernatural appendages connects *us* with heaven.

But it is necessary to give a brief summary of the Scriptural and theological authorities, relative to the nature and functions of angels, before we can judge of the manner in which these ideas have been attended to and carried out in the artistic similitudes. Thus angels are represented in the Old Testament—

1. As beings of a higher nature than men, and gifted with superior intelligence and righteousness.[1]

2. As a host of attendants surrounding the throne of God, and as a kind of celestial court or council.[2]

3. As messengers of His will conveyed from heaven to earth : or as sent to guide, to correct, to instruct, to reprove, to console.

4. As protecting the pious.

5. As punishing by command of the Most High the wicked and disobedient.[3]

6. As having the form of men ; as eating and drinking.

7. As wielding a sword.

8. As having power to slay.[4]

I do not recollect any instance in which angels are represented in Scripture as instigated by human passions ; they are merely the agents of the mercy or the wrath of the Almighty.

After the period of the Captivity, the Jewish ideas concerning angels were considerably extended and modified by an admixture of the Chaldaic belief, and of the doctrines taught by Zoroaster.[5] It is then that we first hear of good and bad angels, and of a fallen angel or impersonation of evil, busy in working mischief on earth and counteracting good; also of archangels, who are alluded to by name ; and of guardian angels assigned to nations and individuals; and these foreign ideas concerning the spiritual world, accepted and promulgated by the Jewish doctors, pervade the whole of the New Testament, in which angels are far more familiar to us as agents, more frequently alluded to, and more distinctly brought before us, than in the Old Testament. For example : they are represented—

[1] 2 Sam. xiv. 17.

[2] Gen. xxxii. 1, 2; Ps. ciii. 21 ; 1 Kings xxii. 19; Job i. 6.

[3] Gen. xxii. 11 ; Exod. xiv. 19 ; Num. xx. 16 ; Gen. xxi. 17 ; Judg. xiii. 3 ; 2 Kings i. 3 ; Ps. xxxiv. 7 ; Judith xiii. 20.

[4] 2 Sam. xxiv. 16 ; 2 Kings xix. 35 ; Gen. xviii. 8 ; Num. xxii. 31 ; 1 Chron. xxi. 16 ; Gen. xix. 13.

[5] Calmet.

1. As countless.

2. As superior to all human wants and weaknesses.

3. As the deputed messengers of God.

4. They rejoice over the repentant sinner.   They take deep interest in the mission of Christ.

5. They are present with those who pray; they bear the souls of the just to heaven.

6. They minister to Christ on earth, and will be present at His second coming.[1]

In the Gospel of St. John, which is usually regarded as the fullest and most correct exposition of the doctrines of Christ, angels are only three times mentioned, and in none of these instances does the word angel fall from the lips of Christ.   On the other hand, the writings of St. Paul, who was deeply versed in all the learning and philosophy of the Jews, abound in allusions to angels, and according to the usual interpretation of certain passages, he shows them divided into several classes.[2]   St. Luke, who was the friend and disciple of St. Paul, some say his convert, is more direct and explicit on the subject of angels than any of the other Evangelists, and his allusions to them much more frequent.

The worship of angels, which the Jews brought from Chaldea, was early introduced into the Christian Church.   In the fourth century the council of Laodicea published a decree against places of worship dedicated to angels under names which the Church did not recognise. But neither warning nor council seems to have had power to modify the popular creed, countenanced as it was by high authority.   All the Fathers are unanimous as to the existence of angels good and evil. They hold that it is evermore the allotted task of good angels to defend us against evil angels, and to carry on a daily and hourly combat against our spiritual foes : they teach that the good angels are worthy of all reverence as the ministers of God and as the protectors of the human race; that their intercession is to be invoked, and their

[1] Matt. xxvi. 53; Heb. xii. 22; Matt. xxii. 30; Luke xx. 36; Matt. xix. 24; Luke i. 11; Acts v. 19, *et passim ;* Luke xv. 10 ; 1 Peter i. 12 ; Luke xvi. 22; Heb. i. 14; 1 Cor. xi. 10 ; Matt. i. 20, xvi. 27, xxv. 31.

[2] Rom. viii. 38 ; Col. i. 16 ; Ephes. i. 21.

perpetual, invisible presence to be regarded as an incitement to good and a preventive to evil.

This, however, was not enough. Taking for their foundation a few Scripture texts, and in particular thė classification of St. Paul, the imaginative theologians of the Middle Ages ran into all kinds of extravagant subtleties regarding the being, the nature, and the functions of the different orders of angels. Except as far as they have been taken as authorities in Art, I shall set aside these fanciful disquisitions, of which a mere abstract would fill volumes. For our present purpose it is sufficient to bear in mind that the great theologians divide the angelic host into three hierarchies, and these again into nine choirs, three in each hierarchy : according to Dionysius the Areopagite, in the following order : 1. Seraphim, Cherubim, Thrones. 2. Dominations, Virtues, Powers. 3. Princedoms, Archangels, Angels. The order of these denominations is not the same in all authorities : according to the Greek formula, St. Bernard, and the Legenda Aurea, the Cherubim precede the Seraphim, and in the hymn of St. Ambrose they have also the precedence— *To Thee, Cherubim and Seraphim continually do cry*, &c. ; but the authority of St. Dionysius seems to be admitted as paramount, for, according to the legend, he was the convert and intimate friend of St. Paul, and St. Paul, who had been transported to the seventh heaven, had made him acquainted with all he had there beheld.

> Desire
> In Dionysius so intensely wrought
> That he, as I have done, ranged them, and named
> Their orders, marshalled in his thought ;
> .   .   .   .   For he had learned
> Both this and much beside of these our orbs
> From an eye-witness to Heaven's mysteries.   —DANTE, *Par.* 28.

The first three choirs receive their glory immediately from God, and transmit it to the second ; the second illuminate the third ; the third are placed in relation to the created universe and man. The first Hierarchy are as councillors ; the second as governors ; the third as ministers. The Seraphim are absorbed in perpetual love and adoration immediately round the throne of God. The Cherubim know and worship.　The Thrones sustain the seat of the Most High.　The Dominations, Virtues, Powers, are the Regents of stars and elements.　The three last orders, Princedoms, Archangels, and Angels, are the protectors of the great Monarchies on earth, and the executors of the will of God throughout the universe.

The term angels is properly applied to all these celestial beings; but it belongs especially to the two last orders, who are brought into immediate communication with the human race.　The word angel, Greek in its origin, signifies a messenger, or more literally, a *bringer of tidings*.

In this sense the Greeks entitle Christ, ' The great Angel of the will of God ; ' and I have seen Greek representations of Christ with wings to His shoulders.　John the Baptist is also an angel in this sense ; likewise the Evangelists ; all of whom, as I shall show hereafter, bear, as celestial messengers, the angel-wings.

In ancient pictures and illuminations which exhibit the glorification of the Trinity, Christ, or the Virgin, the hierarchies of angels are represented in circles around them, orb within orb.　This is called a glory of angels.　In pictures it is seldom complete : instead of nine circles, the painters content themselves with one or two circles only.　The innermost circles, the Seraphim and the Cherubim, are in general represented as *heads* merely, with two or four or six wings, and of a bright red or blue colour ; sometimes with variegated wings, green, yellow, violet, &c. This emblem—intended to shadow forth to human comprehension a pure spirit glowing with love and intelligence, in which all that is bodily is put away, and only the head, the seat of soul, and wings, the attribute of spirit and swiftness, retained—is of Greek

4 Greek Seraph : wings of gold and crimson. (Ninth century.)

origin.　When first adopted I do not know, but I have met with it in Greek MSS. of the ninth century.　Down to the eleventh century the faces were human, but not childish; the infant head was afterwards adopted to express innocence in addition to love and intelligence.

5   Cherubim, Italian. (Fourteenth century.)

Such was the expressive and poetical symbol which degenerated
in the later periods of Art into
those little fat baby heads, with
curly hair and small wings under
the chin, which the more they resemble nature in colour, feature,
and detail, the more absurd they
become, the original meaning
being wholly lost or perverted.

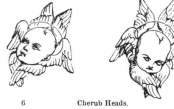

6   Cherub Heads.

In painting, where a glory of angels is placed round the Divine
Being or the glorified Virgin, those forming the innermost circles
are, or ought to be, of a glowing red, the colour of fire, that is, of
love; the next circle is painted blue, the colour of the firmament,
or light, that is, of knowledge.   Now as the word seraph is derived
from a Hebrew root signifying love, and the word cherub from a
Hebrew root signifying to know, should not this distinction fix
the proper place and name of the first two orders?   It is admitted
that the spirits which *love* are nearer to God than those which *know*,
since we cannot know that which we do not first love; that Love and
Knowledge, ' the two halves of a divided world,' constitute in their
union the perfection of the angelic nature; but the Seraphim, according to the derivation of their name, should *love* most; their whole
being is fused, as it were, in a glow of adoration; therefore they

should take the precedence, and their proper colour is red. The
Cherubim, 'the lords of those that know,' come next, and are to
be painted blue.

Thus it should seem that, in considering the religious pictures of
the early ages of Art, we have to get rid of certain associations as to
colour and form, derived from the phraseology of later poets and the
representations of later painters. ' Blue-eyed Seraphim,' and the
' blue depth of Seraph's eyes,' are not to be thought of any more
than ' smiling Cherubim.' The Seraphim, where distinguished by
colour, are red; the Cherubim blue: the proper character, where
character is attended to, is, in the Seraph, adoration; in the Cherub,
contemplation. So Milton—

> With thee bring
> Him who soars on golden wing,
> The Cherub, Contemplation.

I remember a little Triptyca, a genuine work of Fiesole, in which
one of the lateral compartments represents his favourite subject, the
souls of the blessed received into Paradise. They are moving from
the lower part of the picture towards the top, along an ascent paved
with flowers, all in white garments and crowned with roses. At one
side, low down, stands a blue Cherub robed in drapery spangled with
golden stars, who seems to encourage the blessed group. Above are
the gates of heaven. Christ welcomes to His kingdom the beatified
spirits, and on each side stands a Seraph, all of a glowing red, in
spangled drapery. The figures are not here merely heads and wings,
but full length, having all that soft peculiar grace which belongs to
the painter.[1]

In a Coronation of the Virgin,[2] a glory of Seraphim over-arches the
principal group. Here the angelic beings are wholly of a bright red
colour : they are human to the waist, with hands clasped in devotion :
the bodies and arms covered with plumage, but the forms terminating
in wings; all uniformly red. In the same collection is a small

---

[1] I know not whether it be necessary to observe here, that in early Art the souls of the
blessed are not represented as angels, nor regarded as belonging to this order of spiritual
beings, though I believe it is a very common notion that we are to rise from the dead with
the angelic attributes as well as the angelic nature. For this belief there is no warrant in
Scripture, unless Mark xii. 25 be so interpreted.

[2] Now in the Collection of Prince Wallerstein at Kensington Palace.

Greek picture of Christ receiving the soul of the Virgin; over His head hovers a large, fiery-red, six-winged Seraph; and on each side a Seraph with hair and face and limbs of glowing red, and with white draperies. Vasari mentions an Adoration of the Magi by Liberale of Verona, in which a group of angels, all of a red colour, stand as a celestial guard round the Virgin and her divine Infant.[1]

The distinction of hue in the red and blue angels we find wholly omitted towards the end of the fifteenth century. Cherubim with blue, red, green, and variegated wings, we find in the pictures of Perugino and other masters in the beginning of the sixteenth century, also in early pictures of Raphael. Liberale di Verona has given us, in a Madonna picture, Cherub heads without wings, and of a blue colour, emerging from golden clouds. And in Raphael's Madonna di San Sisto, the whole background is formed of Cherubim and Seraphim of a uni- form delicate bluish tinge, as if composed of air, and melting away into an abyss of golden glory, the principal figures standing relieved against this flood of living love and

7   Cherubim. (Liberale di Verona.)

light—beautiful! So are the Cherubim with many-coloured wings, which float in the firmament in Perugino's Coronation of the Virgin; but none of these can be regarded as so theologically correct, as the fiery-red and bright-blue Seraphim and Cherubim, of which are formed the hierarchies and glories which figure in the early pictures, the stained glass, the painted sculpture, and the illuminated MSS. from the tenth to the sixteenth century.

The next five choirs of angels, the Thrones, Dominations, Prince- doms, Virtues, Powers, though classed and described with great exactitude by the theologians, have not been very accurately discrimi- nated in Art. In some examples the Thrones have green wings, a fiery

[1] Vasari, p. 648. Fl. edit.

8   Part of a Glory of Angels surrounding the figure of Christ in a picture by Ambrogio Borgognone.

aureole, and bear a throne in their hands. The Dominations, Virtues,
and Powers, sometimes bear a globe and a long sceptre surmounted
by a cross. The Principalities, according to the Greek formula, should
bear a branch of lily. The Archangels are figured as warriors, and
carry a sword with the point upwards. The angels are robed as
deacons, and carry a wand. In one of the ancient frescoes in the
Cathedral at Orvieto, there is a complete hierarchy of angels, so
arranged as to symbolise the Trinity, each of the nine choirs being
composed of three angels, but the Seraphim only are distinguished by

their red colour and priority of place. In the south porch of the Cathedral of Chartres, each of the nine orders is represented by two angels; in other instances, one angel only represents the order to which he belongs, and nine angels represent the whole hierarchy.[1] Where, however, we meet with groups or rows of angels, as in the Greek mosaics and the earliest frescoes, all alike, all with the tiara, the long sceptre-like wands, and the orb of sovereignty, I believe these to represent the Powers and Princedoms of Heaven. The Archangels alone, as we shall see presently, have distinct individual names and attributes assigned to them.

The angels generally have the human form; are winged; and are endowed with immutable happiness and perpetual youth, because they are ever in the presence of Him with whom there is no change and no time. They are direct emanations of the beauty of the Eternal mind, therefore beautiful; created, therefore, not eternal, but created perfect, and immortal in their perfection. They are always supposed to be masculine; perhaps for the reason so beautifully assigned by Madame de Staël, 'because the union of power with purity (*la force avec la pureté*) constitutes all that we mortals can imagine of perfection.' There is no such thing as an o'd angel, and therefore there ought to be no such thing as an infant angel. The introduction of infant angels seems to have arisen from the custom of representing the regenerate souls of men as new-born infants, and perhaps also from the words of our Saviour when speaking of children, ' I say unto you, their angels do always behold the face of my Father which is in heaven.' Such representations, when religiously and poetically treated as spirits of love, intelligence, and innocence, are of exquisite beauty, and have a significance which charms and elevates the fancy; but from this, the true and religious conception, the Italian *putti* and *puttini*, and the rosy chubby babies of the Flemish school, are equally remote.

[1] I saw in the palace of the Bishop of Norwich an elegant little bas-relief in alabaster, exhibiting the nine choirs, each represented by a single angel. The first (the Seraphim) hold the sacramental cup; the Cherubim, a book; the Thrones, a throne; the Principalities, a bunch of lilies; the Archangels are armed. The other attributes are not clearly made out.

The figures have been ornamented with painting and gilding, now partially worn off; and the style is of the early part of the fifteenth century. It appeared to me to have formed one of the compartments of an altar-piece.

9   Egyptian winged genius. (Louvre.)

In early Art, the angels in the bloom of adolescence are always amply draped; at first, in the classical tunic and pallium; afterwards in long linen vestments with the alba and stole, as levites or deacons; or as princes, with embroidered robes and sandals, and jewelled crowns or fillets. Such figures are common in the Byzantine mosaics and pictures. The expression, in these early representations, is usually calm and impassive. Angels partially draped in loose, fluttering, meretricious attire, poised in attitudes upon clouds, or with features animated by human passion, or limbs strained by human effort, are the innovations of more modern Art. White is, or ought to be, the prevailing colour in angelic draperies, but red and blue of various shades are more frequent. Green often occurs; and in the Venetian pictures, yellow, or rather saffron-coloured robes are not unfrequent. In the best examples of Italian Art, the tints, though varied, are tender and delicate; all dark heavy colours and violent contrasts of

10   Winged figure from Nineveh.

colour are avoided. On the contrary, in the early German school, the angels have rich heavy voluminous draperies of the most intense and vivid colours, often jewelled and embroidered with gold. Flight, in such garments, seems as difficult as it would be to swim in coronation robes.

But, whatever be the treatment as to character, lineaments, or dress, wings are almost invariably the attribute of the angelic form. As emblematical appendages, these are not merely significant of the character of celestial messengers, for, from time immemorial, wings have been the Oriental and Egyptian symbol of power, as well as of swiftness; of the spiritual and aerial, in contradistinction to the human and the earthly. Thus, with the Egyptians, the winged globe signified power and eternity, that is, the Godhead; a bird, with a human head, signified the soul; and nondescript creatures, with wings, abound not only in the Egyptian paintings and hieroglyphics,

but also in the Chaldaic and Babylonian remains, in the Lycian and
Nineveh marbles, and on the gems and other relics of the Gnostics.
I have seen on the Gnostic gems figures with four wings, two springing from the shoulders and two from the loins.   This portentous
figure, from the ruins of Nineveh, is similarly constructed.   (10.)

   In Etruscan Art all their divinities are winged ; and where Venus
is represented with wings, as in many of the antique gems (and by
Correggio in imitation of them),[1] these brilliant wings are not, as
some have supposed, emblematical of the *transitoriness*, but of the
might, the majesty, and the essential divinity of beauty.   In Scripture, the first mention of Cherubim with wings is immediately after
the departure of the Israelites from Egypt (Exod. xxxi. 2).   Bezaleel,
the first artist whose name is recorded in the world's history, and
who appears to have been, like the greatest artists of modern times,
at once architect, sculptor, and painter, probably derived his figures
of Cherubim with outstretched wings, guarding the mercy-seat, from
those Egyptian works of Art with which the Israelites must have
been familiarised.   Clement of Alexandria is so aware of the relative
similitude, that he supposes the Egyptians to have borrowed from
the Israelites, which is obviously the reverse of the truth.   How far
the Cherubim, which figure in the Biblical pictures of the present day,
resemble the carved Cherubim of Bezaleel, we cannot tell, but probably the idea and the leading forms are the same : for the ark, we
know, was carried into Palestine ; these original Cherubim were the
pattern of those which adorned the temple of Solomon, and these,
again, were the prototype after which the imagery of the second
temple was fashioned.   Although in Scripture the shape under which
the celestial ministers appeared to man is nowhere described, except
in the visions of the prophets (Dan. x. 5), and there with a sort of
dreamy incoherent splendour, rendering it most perilous to clothe the
image placed before the fancy in definite forms, still the idea of
wings, as the angelic appendages, is conveyed in many places distinctly, and occasionally with a picturesque vividness which inspires
and assists the artist.   For instance, in Daniel, ch. vii., ' they had
wings like a fowl.'   In Ezekiel, ch. i., ' their wings were stretched
upward when they flew ; when they stood they let down their wings: '

[1] As in the picture in our National Gallery, No. 10.

'I heard the noise of their wings as the noise of great waters:' and in Zechariah, ch. v., 'I looked, and behold there came out two women, and the wind was in their wings, for they had wings like the wings of a stork.' And Isaiah, ch. vi., in the description of the Seraphim, 'Each one had six wings; with twain he covered his face, and with twain he covered his feet, and with twain he did fly.' By the early artists this description was followed out in a manner more conscientious and reverential than poetical.

They were content with a symbol. But mark how Milton, more daring, could paint from the same original:—

11   Seraph
(Greek mosaic, Cathedral of Monreale.)

> A seraph winged; six wings he wore to shade
> His lineaments divine : the pair that clad
> Each shoulder broad, came mantling o'er his breast
> With regal ornament ; the middle pair
> Girt like a starry zone his waist, and round
> Skirted his loins and thighs with downy gold
> And colours dipped in heaven ; the third his feet
> Shadowed from either heel with feathered mail,
> Sky-tinctured grain.

I have sometimes thought that Milton, in his descriptions of angels, was not indebted merely to the notions of the old theological writers, interpreted and embellished by his own fancy: may he not, in his wanderings through Italy, have beheld with kindling sympathy some of those glorious creations of Italian Art, which, when I saw them, made me break out into his own divine language as the only fit utterance to express those forms in words?—But, to return—Is it not a mistake to make the wings, the feathered appendages of the angelic form, as like as possible to real wings—the wings of storks, or the wings of swans, or herons, borrowed for the occasion? Some modern painters, anxious to make wings look 'natural,' have done this; Delaroche, for instance, in his St. Cecilia. Infinitely more beautiful and consistent are the nondescript wings which the early

painters gave their angels :—large—so large, that when the glorious
creature is represented as at rest, they droop from the shoulders to
the ground ; with long slender feathers, eyed sometimes like the
peacock's train, bedropped with gold like the pheasant's breast,
tinted with azure and violet and crimson, 'colours dipped in heaven,'
—they are really angel-wings, not bird-wings.

Orcagna's angels in the Campo Santo are, in this respect, peculiarly
poetical. Their extremities are wings instead of limbs ; and in a
few of the old Italian and German painters of the fifteenth century
we find angels whose extremities are formed of light waving folds of
pale rose-colour or azure drapery, or of a sort of vapoury cloud, or,

12   Angels. (Orcagna.)

in some instances, of flames. The cherubim and seraphim which
surround the similitude of Jehovah when He appears to Moses in the

burning bush,[1] are an example of the
sublime and poetical significance which
may be given to this kind of treatment.
They have heads and human features
marvellous for intelligence and beauty ;
their hair, their wings, their limbs, end
in lambent fires ; they are 'celestial
Ardours bright,' which seem to have
being without shape.

Dante's angels have less of dramatic
reality, less of the aggrandised and
idealised human presence, than Milton's.

13   Fiery Cherub. (Raphael.)

They are wondrous creatures. Some of them have the quaint fan-

[1] Vatican : Raphael's fresco.

tastic picturesqueness of old Italian Art and the Albert Dürer school;
for instance, those in the Purgatorio, with their wings of a bright
green, and their green draperies, 'verde come fogliette,' kept in a
perpetual state of undulation by the breeze created by the fanning
of their wings, with features too dazzling to be distinguished:

> Ben discerneva in lor la testa bionda,
> Ma nelle facce l' occhio si smarria
> Come virtù ch' a troppo si confonda.[1]

And the Shape, glowing red as in a furnace, with an air from the
fanning of its wings, ' fresh as the first breath of wind in a May morning, and fragrant as all its flowers.' That these and other passages
scattered through the Purgatorio and the Paradiso assisted the fancy
of the earlier painters, in portraying their angelic Glories and winged
Beatitudes, I have little doubt; but, on the other hand, the sublime
angel in the Inferno—he who comes speeding over the waters with
vast pinions like sails, sweeping the evil spirits in heaps before him,
' like frogs before a serpent,' and with a touch of his wand making
the gates of the city of Dis fly open ; then, with a countenance solemn
and majestic, and quite unmindful of his worshipper, as one occupied
by higher matters, turning and soaring away—this is quite in the sentiment of the grand old Greek and Italian mosaics, which preceded
Dante by some centuries.[2]

But besides being the winged messengers of God to man, the
deputed regents of the stars, the rulers of the elements, and the dis-
pensers of the fate of nations, angels have another function in which
we love to contemplate them. They are the choristers of heaven.
Theirs is the privilege to sound that hymn of praise which goes up
from this boundless and harmonious universe of suns and stars and
worlds and rejoicing creatures, towards the God who created them :
theirs is the music of the spheres—

> They sing, and singing in their glory move ;

they tune divine instruments, named after those of earth's harmonies—

---

[1] *v.* Purg. c. viii. ; Par. c. xxxi. ; Purg. c. xxiv.

[2] The Cherubim in the upper lights of the painted windows at St. Michael's, Coventry, and
at Cirencester, are represented each standing on a white wheel with eight spokes. They
have six wings, of peacocks' feathers, of a rich yellow colour. A white cross surmounts the
forehead, and both arms and legs are covered with short plumage. The extremities are
human and bare. At Cirencester the Cherubim hold a book ; at Coventry a scroll.

The harp, the solemn pipe
And dulcimer, all organs of sweet stop,
All sounds on fret by string or golden wire,
.   .   .   And with songs
And choral symphonies, day without night,
Circle his throne rejoicing.

There is nothing more beautiful, more attractive, in Art than the representations of angels in this character. Sometimes they form a chorus round the glorified Saviour, when, after His sorrow and sacrifice on earth, He takes His throne in heaven; or, when the crown is placed on the head of the Maternal Virgin in glory, pour forth their triumphant song, and sound their silver clarions on high: sometimes they stand or kneel before the Madonna and Child, or sit upon the steps of her throne, singing,—with such sweet earnest faces! or playing on their golden lutes, or piping celestial symphonies; or they bend in a choir from the opening heavens above, and welcome, with triumphant songs, the liberated soul of the saint or martyr; or join in St. Cecilia's hymn of praise: but whatever the scene, in these and similar representations, they appear in their natural place and vocation, and harmonise enchantingly with all our feelings and fancies relative to these angelic beings, made up of love and music.

14   Angel.   (Francia.)   15   Piping Angel.   (Gian Bellini.)

Most beautiful examples of this treatment occur both in early painting and sculpture; and no one who has wandered through churches and galleries, with feeling and observation awake, can fail to remember such.   It struck me as characteristic of the Venetian school, that the love of music seemed to combine with the sense of harmony in colour; nowhere have I seen musical angels so frequently and so beautifully introduced : and whereas the angelic choirs of Fiesole, Ghirlandajo, and Raphael seem to be playing as an act of homage for the delight of the Divine Personages, those of Vivarini and Bellini and Palma appear as if enchanted by their own music; and both together are united in the grand and beautiful angels of Melozzo da Forlì, particularly in one who is bending over a lute, and another who with a triumphant and ecstatic expression strikes the cymbals.[1]   Compare the cherubic host who are pouring forth their hymns of triumph, blowing their uplifted trumpets, and touching immortal harps and viols in Angelico's ' Coronation, ' [2] or in Signorelli's ' Paradiso,' [3] with those lovely Venetian choristers, the piping boys, myrtle-crowned, who are hymning Bellini's Madonna,[4] or those who are touching the lute to the praise and glory of St. Ambrose in Vivarini's most beautiful picture; you will feel immediately the distinction in point of sentiment.

The procession of chanting angels which once surmounted the organ in the Duomo of Florence is a perfect example of musical angels applied to the purpose of decoration.   Perhaps it was well to remove this exquisite work of art to a place of safety, where it can be admired and studied as a work of art; but the removal has taken from it the appropriate expression.   How they sing!—when the tones of the organ burst forth, we might have fancied we heard their divine voices through the stream of sound !   The exquisite little bronze choristers round the high altar of St. Antonio in Padua are another example; Florentine in elegance of form, Venetian in sentiment, intent upon their own sweet song.

There is a third function ascribed to these angelic natures, which brings them even nearer to our sympathies; they are the deputed guardians of the just and innocent.   St. Raphael, whose story I shall presently relate, is the prince of the guardian angels.   The Jews held that the angels deputed to Lot were his guardian angels.[5]   The fathers of the Christian Church taught that every human being, from the

---

[1] In the sacristy of the Vatican.   [2] In the Louvre.   [3] In the Cathedral at Orvieto
[4] In the *Frari* at Venice.   [5] Gen. xviii., xlviii. 16.

hour of his birth to that of his death, is accompanied by an angel appointed to watch over him. The Mahometans give to each of us a good and an evil angel; but the early Christians supposed us to be attended each by a good angel only, who undertakes that office, not merely from duty to God, and out of obedience and great humility, but as inspired by exceeding charity and love towards his human charge. It would require the tongues of angels themselves to recite all that we owe to these benign and vigilant guardians. They watch by the cradle of the new-born babe, and spread their celestial wings round the tottering steps of infancy. If the path of life be difficult and thorny, and evil spirits work us shame and woe, they sustain us; they bear the voice of our complaining, of our supplication, of our repentance, up to the foot of God's throne, and bring us back in return a pitying benediction, to strengthen and to cheer. When passion and temptation strive for the mastery, they encourage us to resist; when we conquer, they crown us; when we falter and fail, they compassionate and grieve over us; when we are obstinate in polluting our own souls, and perverted not only in act but in will, they leave us—and woe to them that are so left! But the good angel does not quit his charge until his protection is despised, rejected, and utterly repudiated. Wonderful the fervour of their love—wonderful their meekness and patience—who endure from day to day the spectacle of the unveiled human heart with all its miserable weaknesses and vanities, its inordinate desires and selfish purposes! Constant to us in death, they contend against the powers of darkness for the emancipated spirit; they even visit the suffering sinner in purgatory; they keep alive in the tormented spirit faith and hope, and remind him that the term of expiation will end at last. So Dante[1] represents the souls in purgatory as comforted in their misery; and (which has always seemed to me a touch of sublime truth and tenderness) as rejoicing over those who were on earth conspicuous for the very virtues wherein themselves were deficient. When at length the repentant soul is sufficiently purified, the guardian angel bears it to the bosom of the Saviour.

The earlier painters and sculptors did not, apparently, make the same use of guardian angels that we so often meet with in works of Modern Art. Poetical allegories of angels guiding the steps of child-

[1] Purg. c. viii.

hood, extending a shield over innocence, watching by a sick-bed, do not, I think, occur before the seventeenth century; at least I have not met with such. The ancient masters, who really believed in the personal agency of our angelic guardians, beheld them with awe and reverence, and reserved their presence for great and solemn occasions. The angel who presents the pious votary to Christ or the Virgin, who crowns St. Cecilia and St. Valerian after their conquest over human weakness; the angel who cleaves the air ' with flight precipitant ' to break the implements of torture, or to extend the palm to the dying martyr, victorious over pain ; the angels who assist and carry in their arms the souls of the just; are, in these and all similar examples, representations of guardian angels.

Such, then, are the three great functions of the angelic host : they are Messengers, Choristers, and Guardians. But angels, without reference to their individuality or their ministry—with regard only to their species and their form, as the most beautiful and the most elevated of created essences, as intermediate between heaven and earth—are introduced into all works of Art which have a sacred purpose or character, and must be considered not merely as decorative accessories, but as a kind of presence, as attendant witnesses; and, like the chorus in the Greek tragedies, looking on where they are not actors. In architectural decoration, the cherubim with which Solomon adorned his temple have been the authority and example.[1] ' Within the oracle he made two cherubims, each ten cubits high, and with wings five cubits in length ' (the angels in the old Christian churches on each side of the altar correspond with these cherubim), ' and he overlaid the cherubims with gold, and carved all the walls of the house with carved figures of cherubims, and he made doors of olive tree, and he carved on them figures of cherubims.' So, in Christian art and architecture, angels, with their beautiful cinctured heads and outstretched wings and flowing draperies, fill up every space. The instances are so numerous that they will occur to every one who has given a thought to the subject. I may mention the frieze of angels in Henry the Seventh's Chapel, merely as an example at hand, and which can be referred to at any moment; also the angels

[1] 1 Kings vi. 23.

round the choir of Lincoln Cathedral, of which there are fine casts
in the Crystal Palace at Sydenham; and in some of the old churches
in Saxony which clearly exhibit the influence of Byzantine Art—for
instance, at Freyberg, Merseburg, Naumburg—angels with outspread
wings fill up the spandrils of the arches along the nave.

But, in the best ages of Art, angels were not merely employed as
decorative accessories; they had their appropriate place and a solemn
significance as a part of that theological system which the edifice, as
a whole, represented.

As a celestial host surrounding the throne of the Trinity; or of
Christ, as redeemer or as judge; or of the Virgin in glory; or the
throned Madonna and Child; their place is immediately next to the
Divine Personages, and before the Evangelists.

In what is called a Liturgy of Angels, they figure in procession on

MH   ΓΕ μβ each side of the choir, so as to have the
appearance of approaching the altar: they
wear the stole and alba as deacons, and
bear the implements of the mass.   In the
Cathedral of Rheims there is a range of
colossal angels as a grand procession along
the vaults of the nave, who appear as
approaching the altar: these bear not only
the gospel, the missal, the sacramental
cup, the ewer, the taper, the cross, &c., but
also the attributes of sovereignty, celestial
and terrestrial: one carries the sun, another
the moon, a third the kingly sceptre, a
fourth the globe, a fifth the sword; and
all these, as they approach the sanctuary,
they seem about to place at the feet of
Christ, who stands there as priest and king
in glory.   Statues of angels in an attitude
of worship on each side of the altar, as if

16   Angel bearing the Moon.
(Greek, 12th century.)

adoring the sacrifice—or bearing in triumph the instruments of
Christ's passion, the cross, the nails, the spear, the crown of thorns
—or carrying tapers—are more common, and must be regarded not
merely as decoration, but as a *presence* in the high solemnity.

In the Cathedral of Auxerre may be seen angels attending on the triumphant coming of Christ; and, which is most singular, they, as well as Christ, are on horseback (17).

17

When, in subjects from Scripture history, angels figure not merely as attendants and spectators, but as personages necessary to the action, they are either ministers of the divine wrath or of the divine mercy; agents of destruction, or agents of help and good counsel. As all these instances belong to the historical scenes of the Old or the New Testament, they will be considered separately, and I shall confine myself here to a few remarks on the introduction and treatment of angels in some subjects of peculiar interest.

In relating "the expulsion of Adam and Eve from Paradise," it is not said that an angel was the immediate agent of the divine wrath, but it is so represented in works of Art. In the most ancient treatment I have met with,[1] a majestic armed angel drives forth the delinquents, and a cherub with six wings stands as guard before the gate. I found the same *motif* in the sculptures on the façade of the Duomo at Orvieto, by Niccolò Pisano. In another instance, an ancient

18   Adam and Eve expelled.   (N. Pisano.)

Saxon miniature, the angel is represented not as driving them forth, but closing the door against them. But these are exceptions to the

[1] MS. 10th century, Paris, Bibl. Nationale.

usual mode of treatment, which seldom varies; the angel is not
represented in wrath, but calm, and stretches forth a sword which
is often (literally rendering the text) a waving, lambent flame. I
remember an instance in which the preternatural sword, 'turning
every way,' has the form of a wheel of flames.

An angel is expressly introduced as a minister of wrath in the story
of Balaam, in which I have seen no deviation from the obvious prosaic
treatment, rendering the text literally, 'And the ass saw the angel
of the Lord standing in the way, and his sword drawn in his hand.'

'The destroying angel, leaning from heaven, presents to David three
arrows, from which to choose—war, pestilence, or famine.' I have
found this subject beautifully executed in several MSS., for instance,
in the 'Heures d'Anne de Bretagne;' also in pictures and in prints.

'The destroying angel sent to chastise the arrogance of David, is
beheld standing between heaven and earth with his sword stretched
over Jerusalem to destroy it.' Of this sublime vision I have never
seen any but the meanest representations; none of the great masters
have treated it; perhaps Rembrandt might have given us the
terrible and glorious angel standing like a shadow in the midst of
his own intense irradiation. David fallen on his face, and the sons
of Ornan hiding themselves by their rude threshing-floor, with that
wild mixture of the familiar and the unearthly in which he alone has
succeeded.

'The chastisement of Heliodorus' has given occasion to the
sublimest composition in which human genius ever attempted to
embody the conception of the supernatural—Raphael's fresco in the
Vatican. St. Michael, the protecting angel of the Hebrew nation, is
supposed to have been the minister of divine wrath on this occasion;
but Raphael, in omitting the wings, and all exaggeration or altera-
tion of the human figure, has shown how unnecessary it was for *him*
to have recourse to the prodigious and impossible in form, in order
to give the supernatural in sentiment. The unearthly warrior and
his unearthly steed—the weapon in his hand, which is not a sword to
pierce, nor a club to strike, but a sort of mace, of which, as it seems,
a touch would annihilate; the two attendant spirits, who come glid-
ing above the marble floor, with their hair streaming back with the
rapidity of their aërial motion—are in the very spirit of Dante, and,

as conceptions of superhuman power, superior to anything in pictured form which Art has bequeathed to us.

In calling to mind the various representations of the angels of the Apocalypse let loose for destruction, one is tempted to exclaim, ' Oh, for a warning voice ! ' When the Muse of Milton quailed, and fell ten thousand fathom deep into Bathos, what could be expected from human invention ? In general, where this subject is attempted in pictures, we find the angels animated, like those of Milton in the war of heaven, with ' fierce desire of battle,' breathing vengeance, wrath, and fury. So Albert Dürer, in those wonderful scenes of his ' Apocalypse,' has exhibited them ; but some of the early Italians show them merely impassive, conquering almost without effort. punishing without anger. The immediate instruments of the wrath of God in the day of judgment are not angels, but devils or demons, generally represented by the old painters with every possible exaggeration of hideousness, and as taking a horrible and grotesque delight in their task. The demons are fallen angels, their deformity a consequence of their fall. Thus, in some very ancient representations of the expulsion of Lucifer and his rebel host, the degradation of the form increases with their distance from heaven.[1] Those who are uppermost are still angels ; they bear the aureole, the wings, and the tunic ; they have not yet lost all their original brightness : those below them begin to assume the bestial form : the fingers become talons, the heads become horned ; and at last, as they touch the confines of the gulf of hell, the transformation is seen complete, from the luminous angel into the abominable and monstrous devil, with serpent tail, claws, bristles, and tusks. This gradual transformation, as they descend into the gulf of sin, has a striking allegorical significance which cannot escape the reader. In a Greek MS. of the ninth century,[2] bearing singular traces of antique classical Art in the conception and attributes of the figures, I found both angels and demons treated in a style quite peculiar and poetical. The angels are here gigantic, majestic, Jove-like figures, with great wings. The demons are also majestic, graceful winged figures, but painted of a dusky grey colour (it may originally have been black). In one scene, where Julian the Apostate goes to seek the heathen divinities, they are thus represented,

---

[1] MS. 13th century, Breviaire de St. Louis.   [2] Paris, Bibl. Nat., No. 510. G. MS.

that is, as *black angels;* showing that the painter had here assumed
the devils or demons to be the discrowned and fallen gods of the
antique world.

These are a few of the most striking instances of angels employed as
ministers of wrath.   Angels, as ministers of divine grace and mercy,

> Of all those acts which Deity supreme
> Doth ease its heart of love in,

occur much more frequently.

The ancient heresy that God made use of the agency of angels in
the creation of the world, and of mankind, I must notice here, because
it has found its way into Art; for example, in an old miniature which
represents an angel having before him a lump of clay, a kind of
ébauche of humanity, which he appears to be moulding with his hands,
while the Almighty stands by directing the work.[1] This idea,
absurd as it may appear, is not perhaps more absurd than the notion
of those who would represent the Great First Cause as always
busied in fashioning or altering the forms in His visible creation,
like a potter or any other mechanic.   But as we are occupied at
present with the Scriptural, not the legendary subjects, I return to
the Old Testament.   The first time that we read of an angel sent as
a messenger of mercy, it is for the comfort of poor Hagar; when he
found her weeping by the spring of water in the wilderness, because
her mistress had afflicted her: and again, when she was cast forth
and her boy fainted for thirst.   In the representation of these subjects, I do not know a single instance in which the usual angelic form
has not been adhered to.   In the sacrifice of Isaac, 'the angel of the
Lord calls to Abraham out of heaven.'   This subject, as the received
type of the sacrifice of the Son of God, was one of the earliest in
Christian Art.   We find it on the sarcophagi of the third and fourth
centuries; but in one of the latest only have I seen a personage
introduced as staying the hand of Abraham, and this personage is
without wings.   In painting, the angel is sometimes in the act of
taking the sword out of Abraham's hand, which expresses the nature of
his message; or he lays one hand on his arm, and with the other points
to the ram which was to replace the sacrifice, or brings the ram in his

---

[1] As in the legend of Prometheus. (Plato, Protag. p. 320.)

arms to the altar ; but, whatever the action, the form of the angelic messenger has never varied from the sixth century.

In the visit of the angels to Abraham, there has been a variety caused by the wording of the text. It is not said that three *angels* visited Abraham, yet in most of the ancient representations the three celestial guests are winged angels. I need hardly observe that these

19   The Angels who visit Abraham. (Raphael.)

three angels are assumed to be a figure of the Trinity, and in some old illuminations the interpretation is not left doubtful, the angels being characterised as the three persons of the Trinity, wearing each the cruciform nimbus : two of them, young and beardless, stand behind ; the third, representing the Father, has a beard, and, before *Him*, Abraham is prostrated. Beautiful for grace and simplicity is the winged group by Ghiberti, in which the three seem to step and move together as one. More modern artists have given us the celestial visitants merely as men. Pre-eminent in this style of conception are the pictures of Raphael and Murillo. Raphael here, as elsewhere, a true poet, has succeeded in conveying, with exquisite felicity, the sentiment of power, of a heavenly presence, and of a mysterious significance. The three youths, who stand linked together hand in hand before the Patriarch, with such an air of benign and superior grace, want no wings to show us that they belong to the courts of heaven, and have but just descended to earth—

> So lively shines
> In them divine resemblance, and such grace
> The hand that formed them on their shape hath poured.

Murillo, on the contrary, gives us merely three young men, travellers, and has set aside wholly both the angelic and the mystic character of the visitants. [1]

The angels who descend and ascend the ladder in Jacob's dream are in almost every instance represented in the usual form; sometimes a few [2]—sometimes in multitudes [3]—sometimes as one only, who turns to bless the sleeper before he ascends; [4] and the ladder is sometimes a flight, or a series of flights, of steps ascending from earth to the empyrean. But here it is Rembrandt who has shown himself the poet; the ladder is a slanting stream of light; the angels are mysterious bird-like luminous forms, which emerge one after another from a dazzling fount of glory, and go floating up and down, —so like a dream made visible!—In Middle-Age Art this vision of Jacob occurs very rarely. I shall have to return to it when treating of the subjects from the Old Testament.

In the New Testament angels are much more frequently alluded to than in the Old; more as a reality, less as a vision; in fact, there is no important event throughout the Gospels and Acts in which angels do not appear, either as immediate agents, or as visible and present; and in scenes where they are not distinctly said to be visibly present, they are assumed to be so invisibly, St. Paul having said expressly that 'their ministry is continual.' It is therefore with undeniable propriety that, in works of Art representing the incidents of the Gospels, angels should figure as a perpetual presence, made visible under such forms as custom and tradition have consecrated.

I pass over, for the present, the grandest, the most important

[1] Sutherland Gallery.   [2] As in Raphael's fresco in the Vatican.
[3] As in the picture by Allston, painted for Lord Egremont, and now at Petworth.
[4] As in a picture by F. Bol.

mission of an angel, the announcement brought by Gabriel to the blessed Virgin. I shall have to treat it fully hereafter.[1] The angel who appears to Joseph in a dream, and the angel who commands him to flee into Egypt, was in both cases probably the same angel who hailed Mary as blessed above all women; but we are not told so; and according to some commentators it was the guardian angel of Joseph who appeared to him. In these and other scenes of the New Testament, in which angels are described as direct agents, or merely as a chorus of ministering attendants, they have the usual form, enhanced by as much beauty, and benignity, and aërial grace as the fancy of the artist could bestow on them. In the Nativity they are seen hovering on high, pouring forth their song of triumph; they hold a scroll in their hands on which their song is written: in general there are three angels; the first sings, *Gloria in excelsis Deo!* the second, *Et in terra pax!* the third, *Hominibus bonæ voluntatis!* but in some pictures the three angels are replaced by a numerous choir, who raise the song of triumph in the skies, while others are seen kneeling round and adoring the Divine Infant.

The happiest, the most beautiful, instance I can remember of this particular treatment is the little chapel in the Riccardi Palace at Florence. This chapel is in the form of a Greek cross, and the frescoes are thus disposed:—

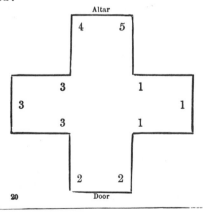

---

[1] See 'Legends of the Madonna,' p. 180.

The walls 1, 2, and 3, are painted with the journey of the Wise Men, who, with a long train of attendants mounted on horseback and gorgeously apparelled, are seen travelling over hill and dale led by the guiding star. Over the altar was the Nativity (now removed) ; on each side (4, 5) is seen a choir of angels, perhaps fifty in number, rejoicing over the birth of the Redeemer: some kneel in adoration, with arms folded over the bosom, others offer flowers ; some come dancing forward with flowers in their hands or in the lap of their robe ; others sing and make celestial music: they have glories round their heads, all inscribed alike, ' Gloria in excelsis Deo !' The naïve grace, the beautiful devout expression, the airy movements of these lovely beings, melt the soul to harmony and joy. The chapel having been long shut up, and its existence scarcely remembered, these paintings are in excellent preservation; and I saw nothing in Italy that more impressed me with admiration of the genuine feeling and piety of the old masters. The choral angels of Angelico da Fiesole already described are not more pure in sentiment, and are far less animated, than these.[1]

But how different from both is the ministry of the angels in some of the pictures of the sixteenth and seventeenth centuries, both German and Italian! The Virgin Mary is washing her Divine Infant; angels dry the clothes, or pour out water ; Joseph is planing a board, and angels assist the Infant Saviour in sweeping up the chips. In a beautiful little Madonna and Child, in Prince Wallerstein's collection, an angel is playing with the Divine Infant, is literally his *play-fellow ;* a very graceful idea, of which I have seen but this one instance.

In the Flight into Egypt, an angel often leads the ass. In the Riposo, a subject rare before the fifteenth century, angels offer fruit and flowers, or bend down the branches of the date-tree, that Joseph may gather the fruit ; or weave the choral dance, hand in hand, for the delight of the Infant Christ, while others make celestial music— as in Vandyck's beautiful picture in Lord Ashburton's collection. After the Temptation, they minister to the Saviour in the wilderness, and spread for Him a table of refreshment—

> . . . Celestial food divine,
> Ambrosial fruit, fetched from the tree of life,
> And from the fount of life ambrosial drink.

---

[1] For several curious and interesting particulars relative to these subjects. see the ' Legends cf the Madonna,' pp. 247, 256.

It is not said that angels were visibly present at the baptism of Christ; but it appears to me that they ought not therefore to be supposed absent, and that there is a propriety in making them attendants on this solemn occasion. They are not introduced in the very earliest examples, those in the catacombs and sarcophagi; nor yet in the mosaics of Ravenna; because angels were then rarely figured, and instead of the winged angel we have the sedge-crowned river god, representing the Jordan. In the Greek formula, they are required to be present 'in an attitude of respect:' no mention is made of their holding the garments of our Saviour; but it is certain that in Byzantine Art, and generally from the twelfth century, this has been the usual mode of representing them. According to the Fathers, our Saviour had no guardian angel; because He did not require one : notwithstanding the sense usually given to the text, 'He shall give His angels charge concerning thee, lest at any time thou dash thy foot against a stone,' the angels, they affirm, were not the guardians, but the servants, of Christ; and hence, I presume, the custom of representing them, not merely as present, but as ministering to Him during His baptism. The gates of San Paolo (tenth century) afford the most ancient example I have met with of an angel holding the raiment of the Saviour : there is only one angel. Giotto introduces two graceful angels kneeling on the bank of the river, and looking on with attention. The angel in Raphael's composition bows his head, as if awe-struck by the divine recognition of the majesty of the Redeemer ; and the reverent manner in which he holds the vestment is very beautiful. Other examples will here suggest themselves to the reader, and I shall resume the subject when treating of the life of our Saviour.

In one account of our Saviour's agony in the Garden of Gethsemane, it is expressly said that an angel 'appeared unto Him out of heaven, strengthening Him ; ' therefore, where this awful and pathetic subject has been attempted in Art, there is propriety in introducing a visible angel. Notwithstanding the latitude thus allowed to the imagination, or perhaps for that very reason, the greatest and the most intelligent painters have here fallen into strange errors, both in conception and in taste. For instance, is it not a manifest impropriety to take the Scripture phrase in a literal sense, and place a cup in the hand of the angel? Is not the word *cup* here, as elsewhere, used as a metaphor, signifying the destiny awarded by Divine will, as Christ had said before, ' Ye shall drink of my cup,' and as we say, ' His cup overfloweth with blessings?' The angel, therefore, who does not bend from heaven to announce to Him the decree He knew full well, nor to present the cup of bitterness, but to strengthen and comfort Him, should not bear the cup;—still less the cross, the scourge, the crown of thorns, as in many pictures.

Where our Saviour appears bowed to the earth, prostrate, half swooning with the anguish of that dread moment, and an angel is seen sustaining Him, there is a true feeling of the real meaning of Scripture; but even in such examples the effect is often spoiled by an attempt to render the scene at once more mystical and more palpable. Thus a painter equally remarkable for the purity of his taste and deep religious feeling, Niccolò Poussin, has represented Christ, in His agony, supported in the arms of an angel, while a crowd of child-angels, very much like Cupids, appear before Him with the instruments of the Passion; ten or twelve bear a huge cross; others hold the scourge, the crown of thorns, the nails, the sponge, the spear, and exhibit them before Him, as if these were the images, these the terrors, which could overwhelm with fear and anguish even the *human* nature of such a Being![1] It seems to me also a mistake, when the angel is introduced, to make him merely an accessory (as Raphael has done in one of his early pictures), a little figure in the air to help the meaning: since the occasion was worthy of angelic intervention, in a visible shape, bringing divine solace, divine sympathy, it should be represented under a form the most mighty and the most benign that Art could compass;—but has it been so? I can recollect no instance in which the failure has not been complete. If it be said that to render the angelic comforter so superior to the sorrowing and prostrate Redeemer would be to detract from *His* dignity as the principal personage of the scene, and thus violate one of the first rules of Art, I think differently—I think it could do so only in unskilful hands. Represented as it ought to be,

[1] The picture is, I suspect, not by Poussin, but by Stella. There is another, similar, by Guido; Louvre, 1057.

and might be, it would infinitely enhance the idea of that unimaginable anguish which, as we are told, was compounded of the iniquities and sorrows of all humanity laid upon *Him*. It was not the pang of the Mortal, but the Immortal, which required the presence of a ministering spirit sent down from heaven to sustain Him.

21   Lamenting Angel in a Crucifixion. (Campo Santo.)

In the Crucifixion, angels are seen lamenting, wringing their hands, averting or hiding their faces. In the old Greek crucifixions, one angel bears the sun, another the moon, on each side of the cross :—

> . . . Dim sadness did not spare,
> That time, celestial visages.

Michael Angelo gives us two unwinged colossal-looking angel heads, which peer out of heaven in the background of his Crucifixion in a manner truly supernatural, as if they sympathised in the consummation, but in awe rather than in grief.

Angels also receive in golden cups the blood which flows from the wounds of our Saviour. This is a representation which has the authority of some of the most distinguished and most spiritual among the old painters ; but it is, to my taste, particularly unpleasing and unpoetical. Raphael, in an early picture, the only Crucifixion he ever painted, thus introduces the angels ; and this form of the angelic ministry is a mystical version of the sacrifice of the Redeemer, not uncommon in Italian and German pictures of the sixteenth century.

As the Scriptural and legendary scenes, in which angels form the poetical machinery, will be discussed hereafter in detail as separate subjects, I shall conclude these general and preliminary remarks

with a few words on the characteristic style in which the principal
painters have set forth the angelic forms and attributes.

It appears that, previous to the end of the fourth century, there
were religious scruples which forbade the representation of angels,
arising, perhaps, from the scandal caused in the early Church by the
worship paid to these supernatural beings, and so strongly opposed
by the primitive teachers.   We do not find on any of the Christian
relics of the first three centuries, neither in the catacombs nor on the
vases or the sarcophagi, any figure which could be supposed to
represent what we call an angel.   On one of the latest sarcophagi we
find little winged figures, but evidently the classical winged genii,
used in the classical manner as ornament only.[1]   In the second Council of Nice, John of Thessalonica maintained that angels have the
human form, and may be so represented; and the Jewish doctors had
previously decided that God consulted His angels when He said,
' Let us make man after *our* image,' and that consequently we may
suppose the angels to be like men, or, in the words of the prophet,
' like unto the similitude of the sons of men.' [2]   (Dan x. 16.)

But it is evident that, in the first attempt at angelic effigy, it was
deemed necessary, in giving the human shape, to render it as superhuman, as imposing, as possible; colossal proportions, mighty over-
shadowing wings, kingly attributes,—these we find in the earliest
figures of angels which I believe exist—the mosaics in the Church of
Santa Agata at Ravenna (A.D. 400).   Christ is seated on a throne
(as in the early sarcophagi); He holds the Gospel in one hand, and
with the left gives the benediction.   An angel stands on each side;
they have large wings, and bear a silver wand, the long sceptre of
the Grecian kings; they are robed in classical drapery, but wear the
short pallium (the ' garb succinct for flight '); their feet are san-
daled, as prepared for a journey, and their hair bound by a fillet.
Except in the wings and short pallium, they resemble the figures of
Grecian kings and priests in the ancient bas-reliefs.

This was the truly majestic idea of an angelic presence (in contradistinction to the angelic *emblem*), which, well or ill executed, prevailed during the first ten centuries.   In the MS.[3] already referred

---

[1] Ciampini, p. 131, A.D. 394.   [2] Greek MS., A.D. 867.   [3] Paris, Bib. Nat., No. 510.

22   Angel.   (Greek MSS., ninth century.)

to, as containing such magnificent examples of this Godlike form
and bearing, I selected one group less ruined
than most of the others—Jacob wrestling with
the angel.   The drawing is wonderful for the
period, that of Charlemagne ; and see how the
mighty being grasps the puny mortal, who was
permitted for a while to resist him ! — ' He
touched the hollow of Jacob's thigh, and it was
out of joint ; '—the action is as significant as
possible.   In the original, the drapery of the
angel is white ; the fillet binding the hair,
the sandals, and the wings, of purple and
gold.

This lank, formal angel, is from the Greco-
Italian school of the eleventh century.   From
the eleventh to the thirteenth century, the
forms of the angels became, like all things in

23   A.D. 1000.

the then degraded state of Byzantine Art, merely conventional.
They are attired either in the imperial or the sacerdotal vestments,
as already described, and are richly ornamented, tasteless and stiff,
large without grandeur, and, in general, ill drawn; as in these
figures from Monreale (24).

24   Greek Angels. (Cathedral of Monreale. Eleventh century.)

On the revival of Art, we find the Byzantine idea of angels every-
where prevailing. The angels in Cimabue's famous ' Virgin and
Child Enthroned ' are grand creatures, rather stern; but this arose,
I think, from his inability to express beauty. The colossal angels at
Assisi (A.D. 1270), solemn sceptred kingly forms, all alike in action
and attitude, appeared to me magnificent (30).

In the angels of Giotto (A.D. 1310), we see the commencement of
a softer grace and a purer taste, further developed by some of his
scholars. Benozzo Gozzoli and Orcagna have left in the Campo
Santo examples of the most graceful and fanciful treatment. Of
Benozzo's angels in the Riccardi Palace I have spoken at length.
His master Angelico (worthy the name!) never reached the same
power of expressing the rapturous rejoicing of celestial beings, but
his conception of the angelic nature remains unapproached, unapproachable (A.D. 1430); it is only his, for it was the gentle, passion-

less, refined nature of the recluse, which stamped itself there. Angelico's angels are unearthly, not so much in form as in senti- ment; and superhuman, not in power but in purity. In other hands, any imitation of his soft ethereal grace would become feeble and insipid. With their long robes falling round their feet, and drooping many-coloured wings, they seem not to fly or to walk, but to float along, 'smooth sliding without step.' Blessed, blessed creatures! love us, only love us, for we dare not task your soft serene Beatitude by asking you to *help* us!

There is more sympathy with humanity in Francia's angels: they look as if they could weep, as well as love and sing.

Most beautiful are the groups of adoring angels by Francesco

25   Angels. (F. Granacci.)

Granacci,[1] so serenely tender, yet with a touch of grave earnestness which gives them a character apart: they have the air of guardian angels, who have discharged their trust, and to whom the Supreme utterance has voiced forth, ' Servant of God, well done!'

[1] In the Academy at Florence: they must have formed the side wings to an enthroned Madonna and Child.

The angels of Botticelli are often stiff, and those of Ghirlandajo
sometimes fantastic; but in both I have met with angelic countenances and forms which, for intense and happy expression, can
never be forgotten.   One has the feeling, however, that they used
human models—the *portrait* face looks through the *angel* face.   This
is still more apparent in Mantegna and Filippo Lippi.   As we might
have expected from the character of Fra Filippo his angels want
refinement: they have a boyish look, with their crisped curled hair,
and their bold beauty; yet some of them are magnificent for that
sort of angel-beings supposed to have a volition of their own.   Andrea
del Sarto's angels have the same fault in a less degree : they have,
if not a bold, yet a self-willed boyish expression.

Perugino's angels convey the idea of an unalterable sweetness :
those of his earlier time have much natural grace, those of his later
time are mannered.   In early Venetian Art the angels are charming;
they are happy affectionate beings, with a touch of that voluptuous
sentiment afterwards the characteristic of the Venetian school.

In the contemporary German school, angels are treated in a very
extraordinary and original style (26).   One cannot say that they are
earthly, or commonplace, still less are they beautiful or divine; but
they have great simplicity, earnestness, and energy of action.   They
appear to me conceived in the Old Testament spirit, with their grand
stiff massive draperies, their jewelled and golden glories, their wings
' eyed like the peacock, speckled like the pard,' their intense expression, and the sort of personal and passionate interest they throw into
their ministry.   This is the character of Albert Dürer's angels
especially; those of Martin Schoen and Lucus v. Leyden are of a
gentler spirit.

Leonardo da Vinci's angels do not quite please me, elegant, refined,
and lovely as they are :—' methinks they smile too much.'   By his
scholar Luini there are some angels in the gallery of the Brera,
swinging censers and playing on musical instruments, which, with the
peculiar character of the Milanese school, combine all the grace of a
purer, loftier nature.

Correggio's angels are grand and lovely, but they are like children
enlarged and sublimated, not like spirits taking the form of children :
where they smile it is truly, as Annibal Caracci expresses it, ' *con una*

26   Angel. German School. (Albert Dürer).

naturalezza e semplicità che innamora e sforza a ridere con loro;' but the smile in many of Correggio's angel heads has something sublime and spiritual, as well as *simple* and *natural.*

And Titian's angels impress me in a similar manner—I mean those in the glorious Assumption at Venice—with their childish forms and features, but with an expression caught from beholding the face of ' our Father that is in heaven : ' it is glorified infancy. I remember standing before this picture, contemplating those lovely spirits one after another, until a thrill came over me like that which I felt when Mendelssohn played the organ, and I became music while I listened.   The face of one of those angels is to the face of a child just what that of the Virgin in the same picture is compared with the fairest of the daughters of earth : it is not here superiority of beauty, but mind and music and love, *kneaded,* as it were, into form and colour.

I have thought it singular and somewhat unaccountable, that among the earliest examples of undraped boy-angels are those of Fra Bartolomeo—he who on one occasion, at the command of Savonarola, made a bonfire of all the undressed figures he could lay his hands on.

But Raphael, excelling in all things, is here excellent above all : his angels combine, in a higher degree than any other, the various faculties and attributes in which the fancy loves to clothe these pure immortal, beatified creatures.   The angels of Giotto, of Benozzo, of Fiesole, are, if not female, feminine; those of F. Lippi, and of A Mantegna, masculine; but you cannot say of those of Raphael that they are masculine or feminine.   The idea of sex is wholly lost in the blending of power, intelligence, and grace.   In his earlier pictures grace is the predominant characteristic, as in the dancing and singing angels in his Coronation of the Virgin.[1]   In his later pictures the sentiment in his ministering angels is more spiritual, more dignified. As a perfect example of grand and poetical feeling, I may cite the angels as ' Regents of the Planets,' in the Capella Chigiana.[2]   The cupola represents in a circle the creation of the solar system, according to the theological and astronomical (or rather *astrological*) notions which then prevailed—a hundred years before ' the starry Galileo and his woes.'   In the centre is the Creator; around, in eight compartments, we have, first, the angel of the celestial sphere, who seems to be listening to the divine mandate, ' Let there be lights in the firmament of heaven; ' then follow, in their order, the Sun, the Moon, Mercury, Venus, Mars, Jupiter, and Saturn.   The name of each planet is expressed by its mythological representative; the Sun by Apollo, the Moon by Diana: and over each presides a grand colossal winged spirit seated or reclining on a portion of the zodiac as on a throne.   I have selected two angels to give an idea of this peculiar and poetical treatment.   The union of the theological and the mythological attributes is in the classical taste of the time, and quite Miltonic.[3]   In Raphael's child-angels, the expression of power

---

[1] Gallery of the Vatican.   [2] S. Maria del Popolo, Rome.
[3] The mosaics in the dome of the Chigi chapel are so ill lighted that it is difficult to observe them in detail, but they have lately been rendered cheaply accessible in the fine set of engravings by Gruner, an artist who in our day has revived the pure and correct design and elegant execution of Marc Antonio.

Angels of the Planets from the Capella Crispi.

and intelligence, as well as innocence, is quite wonderful; for instance, look at the two angel-boys in the Dresden Madonna di San Sisto, and the angels, or celestial genii, who bear along the Almighty when He appears to Noah.[1] No one has expressed like Raphael the action of flight, except perhaps Rembrandt. The angel who descends to crown Santa Felicità cleaves the air with the action of a swallow;[2] and the angel in Rembrandt's Tobit soars like a lark with upward motion, spurning the earth.

Michael Angelo rarely gave wings to his angels; I scarcely recollect an instance, except the angel in the Annunciation: and his exaggerated human forms, his colossal creatures, in which the idea of power is conveyed through attitude and muscular action, are, to my taste, worse than unpleasing. My admiration for this wonderful man is so profound that I can afford to say this. His angels are superhuman, but hardly angelic: and while in Raphael's angels we do not feel the want of wings, we feel while looking at those of Michael Angelo that not even the 'sail-broad vans' with which Satan laboured through the surging abyss of chaos could suffice to lift those Titanic forms from earth, and sustain them in mid-air. The group of angels over the Last Judgment, flinging their mighty limbs about, and those that surround the descending figure of Christ in the Conversion of St. Paul, may be referred to here as characteristic examples. The angels, blowing their trumpets, puff and strain like so many troopers. Surely this is not angelic: there may be *power*, great imaginative and artistic power, exhibited in the conception of form, but in the beings themselves there is more of effort than of power: serenity, tranquillity, beatitude, ethereal purity, spiritual grace, are out of the question.

The later followers of his school, in their angelic as in their human forms, caricatured their great master, and became, to an offensive degree, forced, extravagant, and sensual.

When we come to the revival of a better taste under the influence of the Caracci, we find the angels of that school as far removed from the

[1] As in the fresco in the Vatican.

[2] See the engraving under this title by Marc Antonio; it is properly St. Cecilia, and not St. Félicité.

early Christian types as were their apostles and martyrs.   They have often great beauty, consummate elegance, but bear the same relation to the religious and ethereal types of the early painters that the angels of Tasso bear to those of Dante.   Turn, for instance, to the commencement of the *Gerusalemme Liberata*, where the angel is deputed to carry to Godfrey the behest of the Supreme Being.   The picture of the angel is distinctly and poetically brought before us; he takes to himself a form between boyhood and youth; his waving curls are crowned with beams of light; he puts on a pair of wings of silver tipped with gold, with which he cleaves the air, the clouds, the skies; he alights on Mount Lebanon, and poises himself on his balanced wings—

E si librò su l' adeguate penne.

This is exactly the angel which figures in the best pictures of the Caracci and Guido : he is supremely elegant, and nothing more.

I must not here venture on minute criticism, as regards distinctive character in the crowds of painters which sprung out of the eclectic school.   It would carry us too far; but one or two general remarks will lead the reader's fancy along the path I would wish him to pursue.   I would say, therefore, that the angels of Ludovico have more of sentiment, those of Annibal more of power, those of Guido more of grace; and of Guido it may be said that he excels them all in the expression of adoration and humility ; see, for instance, the adoring seraphs in Lord Ellesmere's ' Immaculate Conception.'   The angels of Domenichino, Guercino, and Albano, are to me less pleasing.   Domenichino's angels are merely human.   I never saw an angel in one of Guercino's pictures that had not, with the merely human character, a touch of vulgarity.   As for Albano, how are we to discriminate between his angels and his nymphs, Apollos, and Cupids?   But for the occasion and the appellation, it would be quite impossible to distinguish the Loves that sport round Venus and Adonis, from the Cherubim, so called, that hover above a Nativity or a Riposo ; and the little angels, in his Crucifixion, cry so like naughty little boys, that one longs to put them in a corner. This merely heathen grace and merely human sentiment is the general tendency of the whole school ; and no beauty of form or colour can, to the feeling and religious mind, redeem such gross violations of

27   Angels in a Nativity.   (Seventeenth century.)

propriety.   As for Poussin, of whom I think with due reverence, his
angels are often exquisitely beautiful and refined: they have a chastity

28   Angel : in a picture of Christ healing the Sick.   (N. Poussin)

and a moral grace which pleases at first view; but here again the
scriptural type is neglected and heathenised in obedience to the
fashion of the time.   If we compare the Cupids in his Rinaldo and

Armida, with the angels which minister to the Virgin and Child; or the Cherubim weeping in a Deposition, with the Amorini who are lamenting over Adonis; in what respect do they differ? They are evidently painted from the same models, the beautiful children of Titian and Fiamingo.

Rubens gives us strong well-built youths, with redundant yellow hair; and chubby naked babies, as like flesh and blood, and as natural, as the life: and those of Vandyck are more elegant, without being more angelic. Murillo's child-angels are divine, through absolute beauty; the expression of innocence and beatitude was never more perfectly given; but in grandeur and power they are inferior to Correggio, and, in all that should characterise a divine nature, immeasurably below Raphael.

Strange to say, the most poetical painter of angels in the seventeenth century is that inspired Dutchman, Rembrandt; not that his angels are scriptural; still less classical; and beautiful they are not, certainly—often the reverse; but if they have not the Miltonic dignity and grace, they are at least as unearthly and as poetical as any of the angelic phantasms in Dante,—unhuman, unembodied creatures, compounded of light and darkness, 'the somewhat between a *thought* and a *thing*,' haunting the memory like apparitions. For instance, look at his Jacob's Dream, at Dulwich; or his etching of the Angels appearing to the Shepherds,—breaking through the night, scattering the gloom, making our eyes ache with excess of glory,—the *Gloria in excelsis* ringing through the fancy while we gaze!

I have before observed that angels are supposed to be masculine, with the feminine attributes of beauty and purity; but in the seventeenth century the Florentine painter, Giovanni di S. Giovanni, scandalised his contemporaries by introducing into a glory round the Virgin, female angels (*angelesse*). Rubens has more than once committed the same fault against ecclesiastical canons and decorum; for instance, in his Madonna 'aux Anges' in the Louvre. Such aberrations of fancy are mere caprices of the painter, improprieties inadmissible in high Art.

Of the sprawling, fluttering, half-naked angels of the Pietro da Cortona and Bernini school, and the feeble mannerists of the seventeenth and eighteenth centuries, what shall be said? that they are worthy to illustrate Moore's Loves of the Angels? '*non ragioniam di lor ;*' no, nor even *look* at them! I have seen angels of the later Italian and Spanish painters more like opera dancers, with artificial wings and gauze draperies, dressed to figure in a ballet, than anything else I could compare them to.

The most original, and, in truth, the only new and original version of the Scripture idea of angels which I have met with, is that of William Blake, a poet painter, somewhat mad as we are told, if indeed his madness were not rather ' The telescope of truth,' a sort of poetical *clairvoyance*, bringing the unearthly nearer to him than to others. His adoring angels float rather than fly, and, with their half-liquid draperies, seem about to dissolve into light and love : and his rejoicing angels—behold them—sending up their voices with the morning stars, that ' singing, in their glory move ! '

29   ' All the sons of God shouted for joy ! '

As regards the treatment of angels in the more recent productions of Art, the painters and sculptors have generally adhered to received and known types in form and in sentiment. The angels of the old

Italians, Giotto and Frate Angelico, have been very well imitated by
Steinle and others of the German school: the Raffaelesque feeling
has been in general aimed at by the French and English painters.
Tenerani had the old mosaics in his mind when he conceived that
magnificent colossal Angel of the Resurrection seated on a tomb,
and waiting for the signal to sound his trumpet, which I saw in
his atelier, prepared, I believe, for the monument of the Duchess
Lanti.[1]

I pause here, for I have dwelt upon these celestial Hierarchies,
winged Splendours, Princedoms, Virtues, Powers, till my fancy is
becoming somewhat mazed and dazzled by the contemplation. I
must leave the reader to go into a picture-gallery, or look over a
portfolio of engravings, and so pursue the theme, whithersoever it
may lead him, and it *may* lead him, in Hamlet's words, ' to thoughts
beyond the reaches of his soul ! ' [2]

---

[1] It is now in the Lanti chapel in the church of the Lateran.

[2] Mr. Ruskin remarks very truly, that in early Christian Art there is ' a certain confidence,
in the way in which angels trust to their wings, very characteristic of a period of bold and
simple conception. Modern science has taught us that a wing cannot be anatomically joined
to a shoulder; and in proportion as painters approach more and more to the scientific as
distinguished from the contemplative state of mind, they put the wings of their angels on
more timidly, and dwell with greater emphasis on the human form with less upon the wings,
until these last become a species of decorative appendage, a mere *sign* of an angel. But in
Giotto's time an angel was a complete creature, as much believed in as a bird, and the way
in which it would or might cast itself into the air and lean hither and thither on its plumes,
was as naturally apprehended as the manner of flight of a chough or a starling. Hence
Dante's simple and most exquisite synonym for angel, '' Bird of God; '' and hence also a
variety and picturesqueness in the expression of the movements of the heavenly hierarchies
by the earlier painters, ill replaced by the powers of foreshortening and throwing naked limbs
into fantastic positions, which appear in the cherubic groups of later times.' The angels from
the Campo Santo at Pisa, numbered 12, 21, and 32, are instances of this bird-like form. They
are *Uccelli di Dio*. Those numbered 27, 28, and 37 are examples of the later treatment.

Archangels. (Cimabue. In San Francesco d'Assisi.)

II. The Archangels.

The Seven
Who in God's presence, nearest to His throne,
Stand ready at command.—MILTON.

HAVING treated of the celestial Hierarchy in general, we have now to
consider those angels who in artistic representations have assumed an
individual form and character. These belong to the order of Archangels, placed by Dionysius in the third Hierarchy : they take rank
between the Princedoms and the Angels, and partake of the nature
of both, being, like the Princedoms, Powers ; and, like the Angels,
Ministers and Messengers.

Frequent allusion is made in Scripture to the seven Angels who stand in the presence of God. (Rev. viii. 2, xv. 1, xvi. 1, &c.; Tobit xxii. 15.) This was in accordance with the popular creed of the Jews, who not only acknowledged the supremacy of the Seven Spirits, but assigned to them distinct vocations and distinct apellations, each terminating with the syllable *El*, which signifies God. Thus we have—

I. MICHAEL (*i.e.*, who is like unto God), captain-general of the host of heaven, and protector of the Hebrew nation.

II. GABRIEL (*i.e.*, God is my strength), guardian of the celestial treasury, and preceptor of the patriarch Joseph.

III. RAPHAEL (*i.e.*, the Medicine of God), the conductor of Tobit; thence the chief guardian angel.

IV. URIEL (*i.e.*, the Light of God), who taught Esdras. He was also regent of the sun.

V. CHAMUEL (*i.e.*, one who sees God?), who wrestled with Jacob, and who appeared to Christ at Gethsemane. (But, according to other authorities, this was the angel Gabriel.)

VI. JOPHIEL (*i.e.*, the Beauty of God), who was the preceptor of the sons of Noah, and is the protector of all those who, with an humble heart, seek after truth, and the enemy of those who pursue vain knowledge. Thus Jophiel was naturally considered as the guardian of the tree of knowledge, and the same who drove Adam and Eve from Paradise.

VII. ZADKIEL (*i.e.*, the Righteousness of God), who stayed the hand of Abraham when about to sacrifice his son. (But, according to other authorities, this was the archangel Michael.)

The Christian Church does not acknowledge these Seven Angels by name; neither in the East, where the worship of angels took deep root, nor yet in the West, where it has been tacitly accepted. Nor have I met with them as a series, *by name*, in any ecclesiastical work of Art, though I have seen a set of old anonymous prints in which they appear with distinct names and attributes: Michael bears the sword and scales; Gabriel, the lily; Raphael, the pilgrim's staff and gourd full of water, as a traveller. Uriel has a roll and a book : he is the interpreter of judgments and prophecies, and for this purpose was sent to Esdras :

31   The Archangels Michael and Raphael. (Campo Santo.)

—' The angel that was sent unto me, whose name was Uriel, gave me an answer.' (Esdras, ii. 4.) And in Milton—

> Uriel, for thou of those Seven Spirits that stand
> In sight of God's high throne, gloriously bright,
> The first art wont his great authentic will
> Interpreter through highest heaven to bring.

According to an early Christian tradition, it was this angel, and not Christ in person, who accompanied the two disciples to Emmaus.

Chamuel is represented with a cup and a staff; Jophiel with a flaming sword. Zadkiel bears the sacrificial knife which he took from the hand of Abraham.

But the Seven Angels, without being distinguished by name, are occasionally introduced into works of art. For example, over the arch of the choir in San Michele, at Ravenna (A.D. 545), on each side of the throned Saviour are the Seven Angels blowing trumpets like cow's horns :—' And I saw the Seven Angels which stand before God, and to them were given seven trumpets.' (Rev. viii. 2, 6.) In representations of the Crucifixion and in the Pietà, the Seven Angels are often seen in attendance, bearing the instruments of the Passion. Michael bears the cross, for he is ' the Bannerer of heaven ; ' but I do not feel certain of the particular avocations of the others.

In the Last Judgment of Orcagna, in the Campo Santo at Pisa (31), the Seven Angels are active and important personages. The angel who stands in the centre of the picture, below the throne of Christ, extends a scroll in each hand ; on that in the right hand is inscribed ' Come, ye blessed of my Father,' and on that in the left hand, ' Depart from me, ye accursed : ' him I suppose to be Michael, the angel of judgment. At his feet crouches an angel who seems to shrink from the tremendous spectacle, and hides his face : him I suppose to be Raphael, the guardian angel of humanity. The attitude has always been admired— cowering with horror, yet sublime. Beneath are other five angels, who are engaged in separating the just from the wicked, encouraging and sustaining the former, and driving the latter towards the demons who are ready to snatch them into flames. These Seven Angels have the garb of princes and warriors, with breastplates of gold, jewelled sword-belts and tiaras, rich mantles ; while the other angels who figure in the same scene are plumed, and bird-like, and hover above bearing the instruments of the Passion (32).

Again we may see the Seven Angels in quite another character, attending on St. Thomas Aquinas, in a picture by Taddeo Gaddi.[1] Here, instead of the instruments of the Passion, they bear the allegorical attributes of those virtues for which that famous saint and doctor is to be reverenced : one bears an olive-branch, *i.e.*, Peace ; the second, a book, *i.e.*, Knowledge ; the third, a crown and sceptre,

1 A.D. 1352. Florence, S. Maria Novella.

32

i.e., Power; the fourth, a church, *i.e.*, Religion; the fifth, a cross and shield, *i.e.*, Faith; the sixth, flames of fire in each hand, *i.e.*, Piety and Charity; the seventh, a lily, *i.e.*, Purity.

In general it may be presumed when seven angels figure together, or are distinguished from among a host of angels by dress, stature, or other attributes, that these represent 'the Seven Holy Angels who stand in the presence of God.' Four only of these Seven Angels are individualised by name, Michael, Gabriel, Raphael, and Uriel. According to the Jewish tradition, these four sustain the throne of the Almighty: they have the Greek epithet *arch*, or chief, assigned to them, from the two texts of Scripture in which that title is used (1 Thess. iv. 16; Jude 9); but only the three first, who in Scripture have a distinct personality, are reverenced in the Catholic Church as saints; and their gracious beauty, and their divine prowess, and their high behests to mortal man, have furnished some of the most important and most poetical subjects which appear in Christian Art.

The earliest instance I have met of the Archangels introduced by name into a work of art is in the old church of San Michele at Ravenna (A.D. 545). The mosaic in the apse exhibits Christ in the centre, bearing in one hand the cross as a trophy or sceptre, and in the other an open book on which are the words ' *Qui videt me videt et Patrem meum.*' On each side stand Michael and Gabriel, with vast wings and long sceptres; their names are inscribed above, but without the *Sanctus* and without the Glory. It appears, therefore, that at this time, the middle of the sixth century, the title of *Saint*, though in use, had not been given to the Archangels.

When, in the ancient churches, the figure of Christ or of the Lamb
appears in a circle of glory in the centre of the roof; and around, or
at the four corners, four angels who sustain the circle with outspread
arms, or stand as watchers, with sceptres or lances in their hands,
these I presume to be the four Archangels 'who sustain the throne
of God.' Examples may be seen in San Vitale at Ravenna; in the
chapel of San Zeno, in Santa Prassede at Rome; and on the roof of
the choir of San Francesco d'Assisi.

So the four Archangels, stately colossal figures, winged and armed
and sceptred, stand over the arch of the choir in the Cathedral of
Monreale, at Palermo.[1]

So the four angels stand at the four corners of the earth and hold
the winds, heads with puffed cheeks and dishevelled hair.[2] (Rev.
vii. 1.)

But I have never seen Uriel represented by name, or alone, in any
sacred edifice. In the picture of Uriel painted by Allston,[3] he is the
'Regent of the Sun,' as described by Milton; not a sacred or scriptural personage. On a shrine of carved ivory[4] I have seen the four
Archangels as keeping guard, two at each end; the three first are
named, as usual, St. Michael, St. Gabriel, St. Raphael; the fourth is
styled *St. Chérubin;* and I have seen the same name inscribed over
the head of the angel who expels Adam and Eve from Paradise.
There is no authority for such an appellation applied individually;
but I find, in a famous legend of the middle ages, 'La Pénitence
d'Adam,' that the angel who guards the gates of Paradise is thus
designated :—' Lorsque l'Ange Chérubin vit arriver Seth aux portes
de Paradis,' &c. The four Archangels, however, seldom occur together,
except in architectural decoration. On the other hand, devotional
pictures of the three Archangels named in the canonical Scriptures
are of frequent occurrence. They are often grouped together as patron
saints or protecting spirits; or they stand round the throne of Christ,
or below the glorified Virgin and Child, in an attitude of adoration.
According to the Greek formula, the three in combination represent
the triple power, military, civil, and religious, of the celestial hier-

[1] Greek mosaic, A.D. 1174.
[2] MS. of the Book of Revelation, fourteenth century. Trinity College, Dublin.
[3] Coll. of the Duke of Sutherland.   [4] Hôtel de Cluny, 399.

33   The Three Archangels (from an ancient Greek picture).

archy: St. Michael being habited as a warrior, Gabriel as a prince, and Raphael as a priest. In a Greek picture, of which I give an outline, the three Archangels sustain in a kind of throne the figure of the youthful Christ, here winged, as being Himself *the* supreme Angel (ἄγγελος), and with both hands blessing the universe. The Archangel Raphael has here the place of dignity as representing the Priesthood;

but in Western Art Michael takes precedence of the two others, and is usually placed in the centre as Prince or Chief: with him, then, as considered individually, we begin.

St. Michael.

Lat. Sanctus Michael Angelus.   *Ital.* San Michele, Sammichele.
Fr. Monseigneur Saint Michel.   (Sept. 29.)

'Michael, the Great Prince that standeth for the children of thy people.'—*Dan.* xii. 1.

It is difficult to clothe in adequate language the divine attributes with which painting and poetry have invested this illustrious arch-angel. Jews and Christians are agreed in giving him the pre-eminence over all created spirits. All the might, the majesty, the radiance, of Thrones, Dominations, Princedoms, Virtues, Powers, are centred in him. In him God put forth his strength when He exalted him chief over the celestial host, when angels warred with angels in heaven; and in him God showed forth his glory when He made him conqueror over the power of sin, and 'over the great dragon that deceived the world.'

To the origin of the worship paid to this great Archangel I dare not do more than allude, lest I stray wide from my subject, and lose myself, and my readers too, in labyrinths of Orientalism. But, in considering the artistic representations, it is interesting to call to mind that the glorification of St. Michael may be traced back to that primi-tive Eastern dogma, the perpetual antagonism between the Spirit of Good and the Spirit of Evil, mixed up with the Chaldaic belief in angels and their influence over the destinies of man. It was sub-sequent to the Captivity that the active Spirit of Good, under the name of Michael, came to be regarded as the especial protector of the Hebrew nation; the veneration paid to him by the Jews was adopted, or rather retained, by the Oriental Christians, and, though suppressed for a time, was revived and spread over the West, where we find it popular and almost universal from the eighth century.

The legends which have grown out of a few mystical texts of Scripture, amplified by the fanciful disquisitions of the theological writers, place St. Michael before us in three great characters:—
1. As captain of the heavenly hosts, and conqueror of the powers of hell. 2. As lord of souls, conductor and guardian of the spirits of the dead. 3. As patron saint and prince of the Church Militant.

When Lucifer, possessed by the spirit of pride and ingratitude, refused to fall down and worship the Son of man, Michael was deputed to punish his insolence, and to cast him out from heaven. Then Michael chained the revolted angels in middle air, where they are to remain till the day of judgment, being in the meantime perpetually tortured by hate, envy, and despair; for they behold man, whom they had disdained, exalted as their superior; above them they see the heaven they have forfeited; and beneath them the redeemed souls continually rising from earth, and ascending to the presence of God, whence they are shut out for ever.

'Now,' says the old Legend,[1] ' if it be asked wherefore the books of Moses, in revealing the disobedience and the fall of man, are silent as to the revolt and the fall of the angels, the reason is plain; and in this God acted according to his wisdom. For, let us suppose that a certain powerful lord had two vassals, both guilty of the crime of treason, and one of these is a nobleman of pure and lofty lineage, and the other a base-born churl:—what doth this lord? He hangs up the churl in the market-place as a warning and example to others;—but, for the nobleman, fearing the scandal that may arise among the people, and perhaps also some insult to the officers of the law, the judge causes him to be tried secretly, and shuts him up in a dungeon; and when judgment is pronounced against him, he sends to his prison, and puts him privily to death; and when one asketh after him, the answer is only " He is dead: "—and nothing more. Thus did God in respect to the rebel angels of old; and their fate was not revealed until the redemption of man was accomplished.'

This passage from the old Italian legend is so curiously charac-

[1] *v.* Il perfetto Legendario. 1659.

teristic of the feudal spirit of Christianity in the middle ages, that
I have ventured to insert it verbatim. If religion did, in some
degree, modify the institutions of chivalry, in a much greater degree
did the ruling prejudices of a barbarian age modify the popular
ideas of religion. Here, notwithstanding the primary doctrine of
Christ—the equality of all men before God, we have the distinction between noble and churl carried into the very councils of
Heaven.

But, to return to St. Michael: on whom, as the leader of his triumphant hosts, God bestowed many and great privileges. To him it
was given

> to bid sound th' archangel trumpet,

and exalt the banner of the Cross in the day of judgment; and to
him likewise was assigned the reception of the immortal spirits when
released by death. It was his task to weigh them in a balance (Dan.
v. 27; Ps. lxii. 9): those whose good works exceeded their demerits,
he presented before the throne of God; but those who were found
wanting he gave up to be tortured in purgatory, until their souls,
from being 'as crimson, should become as white as snow.' Therefore, in the hour of death, he is to be invoked by the faithful, saying, ' O Michael, militiæ cœlestis signifer, in adjutorium nostrum
veni, princeps et propugnator ! '

Lastly, when it pleased the Almighty to select from among the
nations of the earth one people to become peculiarly his own, He appointed St. Michael to be president and leader over that chosen people.[1]
'At that time shall Michael stand up, the great prince which standeth
for the children of thy people' (Dan. x. 13, xii. 1): and when the
power of the Synagogue was supposed to cease, and to be replaced by
the power of the Church, so that the Christians became the people
of God, then Michael, who had been the great prince of the Hebrew

---

[1] The Gnostics taught that the universe was created by the Seven Great Angels, who
ranked next to the *Eons*, or direct emanations from God : 'and when a distribution was
afterwards made of things, the chief of the creating angels had the people of the Jews particularly to his share ; a doctrine which in the main was received by many ancients.'—See
Lardner's ' History of the Early Heresies.' I have alluded to the angel pictured as the
agent in creation (p. 39), but the Seven creating Angels I have not met with in art. This
was one of the Gnostic fancies condemned by the early Church.

people, became the prince and leader of the Church militant in Christendom, and the guardian of redeemed souls, against his old adversary the Prince of Hell. (Rev. xii. 6, 7.)

The worship paid to St. Michael, and which originated in the far East, is supposed to have been adopted by the Oriental Christians in consequence of a famous apparition of the Archangel at Colossæ, in Phrygia, which caused him to be held in especial honour by the people of that city, and perhaps occasioned the particular warning of St. Paul addressed to the Colossians. But although the worship of angels was considered among the heresies of the early Church, we find Constantine no sooner master of the empire, and a baptized Christian, than he dedicates a church to the Archangel Michael (by his Greek name Michaëlion), and this church, one of the most magnificent in Constantinople, became renowned for its miracles, and the parent and model of hundreds more throughout the East.

In the West, the honours paid to St. Michael are of later date : that a church dedicated to him must have existed in Rome long before the year 500 seems clear, because at that time it is mentioned as having fallen into ruin. But the West had its angelic apparitions as well as the East, and St. Michael owes his wide-spread popularity in the middle ages to three famous visions which are thus recorded.

In the fifth century, in the city of Siponte, in Apulia (now Manfredonia), dwelt a man named Galgano or Garganus, very rich in cattle, sheep, and beasts ; and as they pastured on the sides of the mountain, it happened that a bull strayed and came not home ; then the rich man took a multitude of servants and sought the bull, and found him at the entrance of a cave on the very summit of the mountain, and, being wroth with the bull, the master ordered him to be slain ; but when the arrow was sent from the bow it returned to the bosom of him who sent it, and he fell dead on the ground : then the master and his servants were troubled, and they sent to inquire of the bishop what should be done. The bishop, having fasted and prayed three days, beheld in a vision the glorious Archangel Michael, who descended on the mountain, and told him that the servant had been slain because he had violated a spot peculiarly sacred to him, and he commanded that a church should be erected and sanctified there to his honour. And when they entered the cavern they found there three

altars already erected, one of them covered with a rich embroidered altar-
cloth of crimson and gold, and a stream of limpid water springing from
the rock which healed all diseases. So the church was built, and the
fame of the vision of Monte Galgano, though for some time confined
to the south of Italy, spread throughout Europe, and many pilgrimages were made to the spot on which the angelic footsteps had
alighted.

The second vision is much more imposing. When Rome was nearly
depopulated by a pestilence in the sixth century, St. Gregory, afterwards pope, advised that a procession should be made through the
streets of the city, singing the service since called the Great Litanies.
He placed himself at the head of the faithful, and during three days
they perambulated the city; and on the third day, when they had
arrived opposite to the mole of Hadrian, Gregory beheld the Archangel
Michael alight on the summit of that monument, and sheathe his
sword, bedropped with blood. Then Gregory knew that the plague
was stayed, and a church was there dedicated to the honour of the
Archangel : and the Tomb of Hadrian has since been called the
Castle of Sant' Angelo to this day.

This, of all the recorded apparitions of St. Michael, is the only one
which can be called poetical; it is evidently borrowed from the vision
of the destroying angel in Scripture. As early as the ninth century,
a church or chapel dedicated to St. Michael was erected on the summit
of the huge monument, which at that time must have preserved much
of its antique magnificence. The church was entitled *Ecclesia Sancti
Angeli usque ad Cœlos.* The bronze statue, which in memory of this
miracle now surmounts the Castle of St. Angelo, was placed there in
recent times by Benedict XIV., and is the work of a Flemish sculptor,
Verschaffelt. I suppose no one ever looked at this statue critically—
at least, for myself, I never could : nor can I remember now, whether,
as a work of art, it is above or below criticism ; perhaps both. With
its vast wings, poised in air, as seen against the deep blue skies of
Rome, or lighted up by the golden sunset, to me it was ever like what
it was intended to represent—like a vision.

A third apparition was that accorded to Aubert, bishop of Avranches
(A.D. 706). This holy man seems to have been desirous to attract to
his own diocese a portion of that sanctity (and perhaps other advan-

tages) which Monte Galgano derived from the worship of St. Michael. In the Gulf of Avranches, in Normandy, stands a lofty isolated rock inaccessible from the land at high water, and for ages past celebrated as one of the strongest fortresses and state prisons in France. In the reign of Childebert II., St. Aubert, bishop of Avranches, had a vision, in which the Archangel Michael commanded him to repair to this rock, then the terror of mariners, and erect a church to his honour on the highest point, where a bull would be found concealed, and it was to cover as much space as the bull had trampled with his hoofs; he also discovered to the bishop a well-spring of pure water, which had before been unknown. As the bishop treated this command as a dream, the Archangel appeared to him a second and a third time; and at length, to impress it on his waking memory, he touched his head with his thumb, and made a mark or hole in his skull, which he carried to the grave. This time the bishop obeyed, and a small church was built on the spot indicated; afterwards replaced by the magnificent Abbey Church, which was begun by Richard duke of Normandy, in 966, and finished by William the Conqueror. The poverty of invention shown in this legend, which is little more than a repetition of that of Monte Galgano, is very disappointing to the fancy, considering the celebrity of Mont-Saint-Michel as a place of pilgrimage, and as one of the most picturesque objects in European scenery, with its massive towers, which have braved the tempests of a thousand years, rising from the summit of the peak, and the sea weltering round its base. It failed not, however, in the effect anticipated. The worship of St. Michael became popular in France from the ninth century; the Archangel was selected as patron saint of France, and of the military order instituted in his honour by Louis XI. in 1469. The worship paid to St. Michael as patron saint of Normandy naturally extended itself to England after the Norman conquest, and churches dedicated to this archangel abound in all the towns and cities along the southern and eastern shores of our island; we also have a Mount St. Michael on the coast of Cornwall, in situation and in name resembling that on the coast of France. At this day there are few cities in Christendom which do not contain a church or churches dedicated to St. Michael, some of them of great antiquity.

I must not omit that St. Michael is considered as the angel of good

counsel :—that ' Le vrai office de Monseigneur Saint Michel est de
faire grandes revelations aux hommes en bas, en leur donnant moult
saints conseils,' and in particular, ' sur le bon nourissement que le
père et la mère donnent à leurs enfans.' [1] It is to be regretted that
' Monseigneur Saint Michel ' should be found rather remiss in this
part of his angelic functions.

We shall now see how far these various traditions and popular
notions concerning St. Michael have been carried out in Art.

In all representations of St. Michael, the leading idea, well or ill
expressed, is the same. He is young and beautiful, but ' severe in
youthful beauty,' as one who carries on a perpetual contest with the
powers of evil. In the earlier works of art he is robed in white, with
ample many-coloured wings, and bears merely the sceptre or the lance
surmounted by a cross, as one who conquered by spiritual might alone.
But in the later representations, those coloured by the spirit of
chivalry, he is the angelic Paladin, armed in a dazzling coat of mail,
with sword, and spear, and shield. He has a lofty open brow, long
fair hair floating on his shoulders, sometimes bound by a jewelled
tiara; sometimes, but not often, shaded by a helmet. From his
shoulders spring two resplendent wings. Thus we see him standing
by the throne of the Madonna, or worshipping at the feet of the
Divine Infant; an exquisite allegory of spiritual and intellectual
power protecting purity and adoring innocence.

There is a most beautiful little figure by Angelico, of St. Michael
standing in his character of archangel and patron of the Church
Militant, ' as the winged saint; ' no demon, no attribute except the
lance and shield. The attitude, so tranquilly elegant, may be seen
in this sketch (34). In the original the armour is of a dark crimson
and gold, the wings are of rainbow tints, vivid and delicate; a flame
of lambent fire rests on the brow.

But the single devotional figures of St. Michael usually represent
him as combining the two great characters of captain of the heavenly
host, and conqueror of the powers of hell. He stands armed, setting
his foot on Lucifer, either in the half-human or the dragon form, and
is about to transfix him with his lance, or to chain him down in the

[1] Le Livre des Angeles de Dieu, MS. Paris Bibl. Nat.

infernal abyss. Such, however varied in the attitude, expression, and accessories, is the most frequent and popular representation of St. Michael, when placed before us, as the universally received emblem of the final victory of good over evil.

In those churches of Christendom which have not been defaced by a blind destructive zeal, this image meets us at every turn : it salutes us in the porch as we enter, or it shines upon us in gorgeous colours from the window, or it is wreathed into the capitals of columns, or it stands in its holy heroic beauty over the altar. It is so common and so in harmony with our inmost being, that we rather feel its presence than observe it. It is the visible, palpable reflection of that great truth stamped into our very souls, and shadowed forth in every form of ancient belief,—the final triumph of the spiritual over the animal and earthly part of our nature. This is the secret of its perpetual repetition, and this the secret of the untired complacency with which we regard it; for even in the most inefficient attempts at expression, we have always the leading *motif* distinct and true, the winged virtue is always victorious above, and the bestial vice is always prostrate below : and if to this primal moral significance be added all the charm of poetry, grace, animated movement, which human genius has

34   St. Michael.   (Angelico, Fl. Acad.)

lavished on this ever blessed, ever welcome symbol, then, as we look up at it, we are ' not only touched, but wakened and inspired,' and the whole delighted imagination glows with faith and hope, and grateful triumphant sympathy,—so at least I have felt, and I must believe that others have felt it too.

In the earliest representations of this subject, we see the simplest form of the allegory, literally rendering the words of Scripture, ' The dragon shalt thou trample under foot ' (Ps. xci. 13). Here there is no risk of a divided interest or a misdirected sympathy. The demon, grovelling under the feet of the victorious spirit, is not the star-bright apostate who drew after him the third part of heaven; it is the bestial malignant reptile:—not the emblem of resistance, but the emblem of sin; not of the sin that aspires, which, in fact, is a contradiction in terms;—no sin aspires;—but of the sin which degrades and brutifies, as all sin does. In the later representations, where the demon takes the half-human shape, however hideous and deformed, the allegory may so be brought nearer to us, and rendered more terrible even by a horrid sympathy with that human face, grinning in despite and agony; but much of the beauty of the scriptural metaphor is lost.[1]

The representations of St. Michael and the dragon are so multifarious that I can only select a few among them as examples of the different styles of treatment.

The symbol, as such, is supposed to have originated with the Gnostics and Arians, and the earliest examples are to be found in the ancient churches on the western coast of Italy, and the old Lombard churches. I have never seen it in the old mosaics of the sixth century, but in the contemporary sculpture frequently. It would be difficult to point to the most ancient example, such is the confusion of dates as regards dedications, restorations, alterations; but I remember a carving in white marble on the porch of the Cathedral of Cortona (about the seventh century), which may be regarded as an

---

[1] Dr. Arnold has some characteristic remarks on the half-human effigies of Satan; he objects to the Miltonic representation :—' By giving a human likeness, and representing him as a bad man, you necessarily get some image of what is good, as well as of what is bad, for no man is entirely evil.'—' The hoofs, the horns, the tail, were all useful in this way, as giving you an image of something altogether disgusting; and so Mephistophiles, and the utterly contemptible and hateful character of the Little Master in Sintram, are far more true than the Paradise Lost.'—*Life*, vol. ii.

example of this primitive style of treatment: the illustration, from a slight sketch made on the spot, will be better than any description (35).

Another instance will be remembered by the traveller in Italy, the strange antique bas-relief on the façade of that extraordinary old church the San Michele at Pavia; not the figure in the porch, which is modern, but that which is above. In the Menologium Grecum is a St. Michael standing with a long sceptre, a majestic colossal figure, while kneeling angels adore him, and the demons crouch under his feet.[1]

By Martin Schoen: St. Michael, attired in a long loose robe and floating mantle, tramples on the demon; he has thrown down

35

the shield, and with his lance in both hands, but without effort, and even with a calm angelic dignity, prepares to transfix his adversary. The figure is singularly elegant. The demon has not here the usual form of a dragon, but is a horrible nondescript reptile, with multitudinous flexile claws, like those of a crab, stretched out to seize and entangle the unwary;—for an emblematical figure, very significant (36). In an old fresco by Guariente di Padova[2] the angel is draped as in Martin Schoen's figure, but the attitude is far less elegant.

Sometimes the dragon has a small head at the end of his tail, instead of the forked string. I recollect an instance of St. Michael transfixing the large head, while a smaller angel, also armed, transfixes the other head.[3] This is an attempt to render literally the description in the Apocalypse: ' For their power is in their mouth, and in their tails: for their tails were like unto serpents, and had heads, and with them they do hurt' (Rev. ix. 19). In a most elegant figure of St. Michael, from the choir of the San Giovanni, at Malta, I found the demon thus characterised, with a tail ending in the serpent head.

[1] Vatican MSS., No. 1613, A.D. 989.   [2] A.D. 1365.   Eremitani.   Padua.
[3] Greek Apocalypse MS.   Paris Bibl. Nat.

36   St Michael. (Martin Schoen.)

In an old Siena picture[1] St. Michael is seated on a throne: in one
hand a sword, in the other the orb of sovereignty ; under his feet lies
the dragon mangled and bleeding : a bad picture, but curious for the
singular treatment.

In the sixteenth century these figures of St. Michael become less
ideal and angelic, and more and more chivalrous and picturesque.   In
a beautiful altar-piece by Andrea del Sarto, now in the Florence
Academy, there is a fine martial figure of the Archangel, which, but
for the wings, might be mistaken for a St. George; and in the predella
underneath, on a small scale, he is conqueror of the demon.   The

[1] Siena Acad.

peculiarity here is, that the demon, though vanquished, makes a vain struggle, and has seized hold of the belt of the angel, who, with uplifted sword, and an action of infinite grace and dignity, looks superior down, as one assured of victory.

Raphael has given us three figures of St. Michael, all different, and one of them taking rank with his masterpieces.

The first is an early production, painted when he was a youth of nineteen or twenty, and now in the Louvre. St. Michael armed with a shield on which is a red cross, his sword raised to strike, stands with one foot on a monster; other horrible little monsters, like figures in a dream, are around him: in the background are seen the hypocrites and thieves as described by Dante; the first, in melancholy procession, weighed down with leaden cowls; the others, tormented by snakes: and, in the distance, the flaming dolorous city. St. Michael is here the vanquisher of the Vices. It is a curious and fantastic, rather than poetical, little picture.

The second picture, also in the Louvre, was painted by Raphael, in the maturity of his talent, for Francis I. : the king had left to him the choice of the subject, and he selected St. Michael, the military patron of France, and of that knightly Order of which the king was Grand Master.

St. Michael—not standing, but hovering on his poised wings, and grasping his lance in both hands—sets one foot lightly on the shoulder of the demon, who, prostrate, writhes up, as it were, and tries to lift his head and turn it on his conqueror with one last gaze of malignant rage and despair. The archangel looks down upon him with a brow calm and serious; in his beautiful face is neither vengeance nor disdain—in his attitude no effort; his form, a model of youthful grace and majesty, is clothed in a brilliant panoply of gold and silver; an azure scarf floats on his shoulders; his wide-spread wings are of purple, blue, and gold; his light hair is raised, and floats outward on each side of his head, as if from the swiftness of his downward motion. The earth emits flames, and seems opening to swallow up the adversary. The form of the demon is human, but vulgar in its proportions, and of a swarthy red, as if fire-scathed; he has the horns and the serpent-tail; but, from the attitude into which he is thrown, the monstrous form is so fore-shortened that it does not

37   The St. Michael painted by Raphael for Francis I.

disgust, and the majestic figure of the archangel fills up nearly the
whole space—fills the eye—fills the soul—with its victorious beauty.

That Milton had seen this picture, and that when his sight was
quenched the 'winged saint' revisited him in his darkness, who can
doubt ?—

> Over his lucid arms
> A military vest of purple flowed
> Livelier than Meliboœan, or the grain
> Of Sarra worn by kings and heroes old
> In time of truce.

By his side,
As in a glittering zodiac, hung the sword,
Satan's dire dread, and in his hand the spear.

A third St. Michael, designed by Raphael, exists only as an engraving.[1] The angel here wears a helmet, and is classically draped; he stands in an attitude of repose, his foot on the neck of the demon; one hand rests on the pummel of his sword, the other holds the lance.

It seems agreed that, as a work of art, there is only the St. Michael of Guido (in the Capuccini at Rome) which can be compared with that of Raphael; the moment chosen is the same; the treatment nearly the same; the sentiment quite different.

Here the angel, standing, yet scarcely touching the ground, poised on his outspread wings, sets his left foot on the head of his adversary; in one hand he brandishes a sword, in the other he holds the end of a chain, with which he is about to bind down the demon in the bottomless pit. The attitude has been criticised, and justly; the grace is somewhat mannered, verging on the theatrical; but Forsyth is too severe when he talks of the ' air of a dancing-master: ' one thing, however, is certain, we do not think about attitude when we look at Raphael's St. Michael; in Guido's, it is the first thing that strikes us; but when we look farther, the head redeems all; it is singularly beautiful, and in the blending of the masculine and feminine graces, in the serene purity of the brow, and the flow of the golden hair, there is something divine : a slight, very slight expression of scorn is in the air of the head. The fiend is the worst part of the picture; it is not a fiend, but a degraded prosaic human ruffian; we laugh with incredulous contempt at the idea of an angel called down from heaven to overcome such a wretch. In Raphael the fiend is human, but the head has the god-like ugliness and malignity of a satyr; Guido's fiend is only stupid and base. It appears to me that there is just the same difference—the same *kind* of difference— between the angel of Raphael and the angel of Guido, as between the description in Tasso and the description in Milton; let any one compare them. In Tasso we are struck by the picturesque elegance of the description as a piece of art, the melody of the verse, the

[1] By Marco di Ravenna. Bartsch, xiv. 106.

admirable choice of the expressions, as in Guido by the finished but
somewhat artificial and studied grace.   In Raphael and Milton we
see only the vision of a 'shape divine.'

One of the most beautiful figures of St. Michael I ever saw, occurs
in a coronation of the Virgin by Moretto, and is touched by his
peculiar sentiment of serious tenderness.[1]

In devotional pictures such figures of St. Michael are sometimes
grouped poetically with other personages, as in a most beautiful
picture by Innocenza da Imola,[2] where the archangel tramples on
the demon; St. Paul standing on one side, and St. Benedict on the
other, both of whom had striven with the fiend and had overcome
him: the Madonna and Child are seen in a glory above.

And again in a picture by Mabuse,[3] where St. Michael, as patron,
sets his foot on the black grinning fiend, and looks down on a kneeling votary, while the votary, with his head turned away, appears
to be worshipping, not the protecting angel, but the Madonna, to
whom St. Michael presents him (38).   Such votive pictures are not
uncommon, and have a peculiar grace and significance.   Here the
archangel bears the victorious banner of the cross;—he has conquered.   In some instances he holds in his hand the head of the
Dragon, and in *all* instances it is, or ought to be, the head of the
Dragon which is transfixed :—' Thou shalt bruise his head.'

Those representations in which St. Michael is not conqueror, but
combatant, in which the moment is one of transition, are less frequent;
it is then an *action*, not an *emblem*, and the composition is historical
rather than symbolical.   It is the strife with Lucifer ; ' when Michael
and his angels fought against the dragon, and the dragon fought
and his angels, and the great dragon was cast out.' (Rev. xii. 7.)   In
churches and chapels dedicated to St. Michael, or to 'the Holy Angels,'
this appropriate subject often occurs ; as in a famous fresco by Spinello
d'Arezzo, at Arezzo.[4]   In the middle of the composition, Michael,
armed with sword and shield, is seen combating the dragon with
seven heads, as described in the Apocalypse.   Above and around are
many angels also armed.   At the top of the picture is seen an empty

[1] Brescia. S. Maria delle Grazie.
[2] Milan, Brera.   [3] Boisserée Gallery.
[4] A.D. 1400. Engraved in Lusinio's 'Early Florentine Masters.'

38   St. Michael. (Mabuse, 1510.)

throne, the throne which Lucifer had 'set in the north;' below is seen
Lucifer, falling with his angels over the parapet of heaven. (Isaiah xiv.
13.)   The painter tasked his skill to render the transformation of the
spirits of light into spirits of darkness as fearful and as hideous as
possible; and, being a man of a nervous temperament, the continual
dwelling on these horrors began at length to trouble his brain.   He
fancied that Lucifer appeared to him in a dream, demanding by what
authority he had portrayed him under an aspect so revolting?—the

painter awoke in horror, was seized with delirious fever, and so died.

In his combat with the dragon, Michael is sometimes represented alone, and sometimes as assisted by the two other archangels, Gabriel and Raphael : as in the fresco by Signorelli, at Orvieto, where one of the angels, whom we may suppose to be Raphael, looks down on the falling demons, with an air of melancholy, almost of pity.

In a picture by Marco Oggione,[1] Michael has precipitated the demon into the gulf, and hovers above, while Raphael and Gabriel stand below on each side, looking on ; all are clothed in voluminous loose white draperies, more like priests than warriors ; but it is a fine picture.

In the large Rubens-room at Munich, there are two pictures of Michael subduing the revolted angels.   The large one, in which Michael is the principal figure, is not agreeable.   Rubens could not lift himself sufficiently above the earth to conceive and embody the spiritual, and heroic, and beautiful in one divine form; his St. Michael is vulgar. The smaller composition, where the fallen, or rather falling, angels fill the whole space, is a most wonderful effort of artistic invention.   At the summit of the picture stands St. Michael, the shield in one hand, in the other the forked lightnings of divine wrath; and from above the rebel host tumble headlong ' in hideous ruin and combustion hurled,' and with such affright and amazement in every face, such a downward movement in every limb, that we recoil in dizzy horror while we look upon it.   It is curious that Rubens should have introduced female reprobate spirits : if he intended his picture as an allegory, merely the conquest of the spiritual over the sensual, he is excusable ; but if he meant to figure the vision in the Apocalypse, it is a deviation from the proper scriptural treatment, which is inexcusable. This picture remains, however, as a whole, a perfect miracle of art : the fault is, that we feel inclined to applaud as we do at some astonishing *tour de force;* such at least was my own feeling, and this is not the feeling appropriate to the subject.   Though this famous picture is entitled the Fall of the Angels, I have some doubts as to whether this was the intention of the painter, whether he did not mean to express the fall of sinners, flung by the Angel of judgment into the abyss of wrath and perdition ?

[1] Milan.   Brera.

33   St. Michael as Angel of Judgment and Lord of Souls.   (Justice of Ghent.)

In those devotional pictures which exhibit St. Michael as Lord of souls, he is winged and unarmed, and holds the balance. In each scale sits a little naked figure, representing a human soul; one of these is usually represented with hands joined as in thankfulness— he is the *beato*, the elected; the other is in an attitude of horror—he is the rejected, the reprobate ; and often, but not necessarily, the idea is completed by the introduction of a demon, who is grasping at the descending scale, either with his talons, or with the long two-pronged hook, such as is given to Pluto in the antique sculpture.

Sometimes St. Michael is thus represented singly; sometimes very beautifully in Madonna pictures, as in a picture by Leonardo da Vinci (A.D. 1498), where St. Michael, a graceful angelic figure, with light flowing hair, kneels before the Madonna, and presents the balance to

40   St. Michael. (Signorelli, 1500. In the San Gregorio, Rome.)

the Infant, who seems to welcome the pious little soul who sits in
the uppermost scale.

I have seen this idea varied.   St Michael stands majestic with the
balance poised in his hands: instead of a human figure in either scale,
there are weights; on one side is seen a company of five or six little
naked shivering souls, as if waiting for their doom; on the other
several demons, one of whom with his hook is pulling down the
ascending scale.[1]   With or without the balance, St. Michael figures
as Lord of souls when introduced into pictures of the Assumption or
the Glorification of the Virgin.   To understand the whole beauty and
propriety of such representations, we must remember that, according
to one of the legends of the death of the Virgin, her spirit was con-

[1] Psalter of St. Louis.   Bib. de l'Arsenal, Paris.

signed to the care of St. Michael until it was permitted to reanimate
the spotless form, and with it ascend to heaven.

In one or two instances only, I have seen St. Michael without wings.
In general, an armed figure, unwinged and standing on a dragon, we
may presume to be a St. George; but where the balance is introduced,
it leaves no doubt of the personality—it is a St. Michael. Occasionally
the two characters—the protecting Angel of light and the Angel of
judgment—are united, and we see St. Michael, with the dragon under
his feet and the balance in his hand. This was a favourite and appropriate subject on tombs and chapels dedicated to the dead; such is
the beautiful bas-relief on the tomb of Henry VII. in Westminster
Abbey.

In some representations of the Last Judgment, St. Michael, instead
of the banner and cross, bears the scales; as in the very curious bas-
relief on the façade of the church of St. Trophime at Arles. St.
Michael here has a balance so large that it is almost as high as
himself; it is not a mere emblem, but a fact; a soul sits in each scale,
and a third is rising up; the angel holds out one hand to assist him.
In another part of the same bas-relief St. Michael is seen carrying a
human soul (represented as a little naked figure) and bringing it to
St. Peter and St. Paul. In a celebrated Last Judgment, attributed
by some authors to John Van Eyck, by others to Justus of Ghent,
St. Michael is grandly introduced.[1] High up, in the centre, sits
the Saviour, with the severe expression of the judge. Above Him
hover four angels with the instruments of the Passion, and below
Him three others sounding trumpets (*v.* p. 54).—I suppose the seven
pre-eminent angels: the Virgin and St. John the Baptist on
each side, and then the Apostles ranged in the usual manner.
' In the lower half of the picture stands St. Michael, clad in golden
armour, so bright as to reflect in the most complete manner all the
surrounding objects. His figure is slender and elegant, but colossal
as compared to the rest. He seems to be bending earnestly forward,
a splendid purple mantle falls from his shoulders to the ground, and
his large wings are composed of glittering peacock's feathers. He
holds the balance; the scale with the good rests on earth, but that
with the souls which are found wanting mounts into the air. A demon

[1] See ante, p. 111, for the figure of St. Michael.

stands ready to receive them, and towards this scale St. Michael points with the end of a black staff which he holds in his right hand.' This picture, which is a chef-d'œuvre of the early German school, is now in the church of St. Mary at Dantzig.

The historical subjects in which St. Michael is introduced exhibit him as prince of the Hebrew nation, and belong properly to the Old Testament.[1] 'After the confusion of tongues, and the scattering of the people, which occurred on the building of the Tower of Babel, every separate nation had an angel to direct it. To Michael was given in charge the people of the Lord. The Hebrews being carried away captive into the land of Assyria, Daniel prayed that they might be permitted to return when the seventy years of captivity were over; but the Angel of Persia opposed himself on this occasion to the angels Michael and Gabriel. He wished to retain the Jews in captivity, because he was glad to have, within the bounds of his jurisdiction, a people who served the true God, and because he hoped that in time the captive Jews would convert to the truth the Assyrians and Persians committed to his care.' This curious passage from one of the early Christian fathers, repre-senting the good angels as opposed to each other, and one of them as disputing the commands of God, is an instance of the confused ideas on the subject of angels which prevailed in the ancient Church, and which prevail, I imagine, in the minds of many even at this day.

In the story of Hagar in the wilderness, it is Michael who de-scends to her aid. In the sacrifice of Isaac, it is Michael who stays the arm of Abraham. It is Michael who brings the plagues on Egypt, and he it is who leads the Israelites through the wilderness. It was the belief of the Jews, and of some of the early Christian fathers, that through his angel (not in person) God spoke to Moses from the burning bush, and delivered to him the law on Mount Sinai; and that the angel so delegated was Michael.

It is Michael who combats with Lucifer for the body of Moses. (Jude ver. 9.) According to one interpretation of this curious passage

[1] St. Ephrem, Bib. Orient. tom. i. p. 78.   De Beausobre, vol. ii. p. 17.

of Scripture, the demon wished to enter and to possess the form of Moses, in order to deceive the Jews by personating their leader; but others say, that Michael contended for the body, that he might bury it in an unknown place, lest the Jews should fall into the sin of paying divine honours to their legislator. This is a fine picturesque subject; the rocky desert, the body of Moses dead on the earth, the contest of the good and evil angel confronting each other, —these are grand materials! It must have been rarely treated, for I remember but one instance—the fresco by L. Signorelli, in the Sistine Chapel in the Vatican.

It is Michael who intercepts Balaam[1] when on his way to curse the people of Israel, and puts blessings into his mouth instead of curses: a subject often treated, but as a fact rather than a vision.

It is Michael who stands before Joshua in the plain by Jericho:— ' And Joshua said unto him, Art thou for us, or for our adversaries? And he said, Nay; but as captain of the host of the Lord am I now come. And Joshua fell on his face to the earth, and did worship, and said unto him, What saith my Lord unto his servant? And the captain of the Lord's host said unto Joshua, Loose thy shoe from off thy foot; for the place whereon thou standest is holy.' (Joshua v. 13–15.) This subject is very uncommon. In the Greek MS. already alluded to, I met with a magnificent example—magnificent in point of sentiment, though half ruined and effaced; the God-like bearing of the armed angel, looking down on the prostrate Joshua, is here as fine as possible.

It is Michael who appears to Gideon.[2] It is Michael who chastises David.[3] It is Michael who exterminates the army of Sennacherib; a subject magnificently painted by Rubens. (Some suppose that on this occasion God made use of the ministry of an evil angel.[4])

It is Michael who descends to deliver the Three Children from the burning fiery furnace. The Three Children in the furnace is a subject which appears very early in the catacombs and on the sarcophagi as a symbol of the Redemption;—so early, that it is described by Tertullian;[5] but in almost all the examples given there are three figures

---

[1] Didron, Manuel grec., p. 101. [2] Judges vi. 11.
[3] 2 Sam. xxiv. 16. [4] Calmet.
[5] De Oratione, cap. xii.

only : where there is a fourth, it is, of course, the protecting angel, but he is without wings.[1]

Michael seizes the prophet Habakkuk by the hair of the head, and carries him to Babylon, to the den of lions, that he may feed Daniel.[2] This apocryphal subject occurs on several sarcophagi.[3] I have seen it also in illuminated MSS., but cannot at this moment refer to it. It occurs in a series of late Flemish prints after Hemskirk,—of which there are good impressions in the British Museum.

The Archangel Michael is not named in the Gospels; but in the legends of the Madonna, as we shall see hereafter, he plays a very important part, being deputed by Christ to announce to His mother her approaching end, and to receive her soul.   For the present I will only remark, that when, in accordance with this very ancient legend, an angel is represented kneeling before the Madonna, and holding in his hand a palm surmounted by stars, or a lighted taper, this angel is not Gabriel, announcing the conception of Christ, as is usually supposed, but Michael, as the angel of death.[4]

The legend of Monte Galgano I saw in a large fresco, in the Santa Croce at Florence, by a painter of the Giotto school; but in so bad a state, that I could only make out a bull on the top of a mountain, and a man shooting with a bow and arrow.   On the opposite wall is the combat of Michael with the dragon—very spirited, and in much better preservation.   To distinguish the apparition of St. Michael on Monte Galgano from the apparition on Mont St. Michel, in both of which a bull and a bishop are principal figures, it is necessary to observe, that, in the last-named subject, the sea is always introduced at the base of the picture, and that the former is most common in Italian, and the latter in French, works of art.   In the French stained glass of the thirteenth and fourteenth centuries, St. Michael is a very popular subject, either with the dragon, or the scales, or both.

Lately, in removing the whitewash from the east wall of the nave

---

[1] Bottari, Tab. xxii.   On the early Christian sarcophagi, as I have already observed, there are no winged angels.   In the oft-repeated subject of the 'Three Children in the burning fiery furnace,' the fourth figure, when introduced, may represent *a* son of God,—*i.e.*, ar angel ; or *the* Son of God, *i.e.*, Christ, as it has been interpreted in both senses.

[2] Bel and the Dragon, 26.   [3] Bottari, 15, 49, 84.   [4] See ' Legends of the Madonna.'

of Preston Church, near Brighton, was discovered the outline of a group of figures representing St. Michael, fully draped, and with large wings, bearing the balance ; in each scale a human soul. The scale containing the *beato* is assisted by a figure fully draped, but so ruined that it is not possible to say whether it represents the Virgin, or the guardian saint of the person who caused the fresco to be painted. I am told that in the old churches of Cornwall, and of the towns on the south coast, which had frequent intercourse with France, effigies of St. Michael occur frequently, both in painting and sculpture. On the old English coin, thence called an *angel*, we have the figure of St. Michael, who was one of the patron saints of our Norman kings.

I must now trust to the reader to contemplate the figures of St. Michael, so frequent and so varied in Art, with reference to these suggestions ; and leaving for the present this radiant Spirit, this bright similitude of a primal and universal faith, we turn to his angelic companions.

41   Egyptian hieroglyphic of the Genius of Good overcoming Evil (*v.* p. 108).

St. Gabriel.

Lat. Sanctus Gabriel.   *Ital.* San Gabriello, San Gabriele, L'Angelo Annunziatore.
Fr. St. Gabriel.

' I am GABRIEL, that stand in the presence of God.'—*Luke* i. 19.

IN those passages of Scripture where the Angel Gabriel is mentioned by name, he is brought before us in the character of a Messenger only, and always on important occasions.   In the Old Testament he is sent to Daniel to announce the return of the Jews from captivity and to explain the vision which prefigures the destinies of mighty empires.   His contest with the Angel of the kingdom of Persia, when St. Michael comes to his assistance, would be a splendid subject in fit hands ; I do not know that it has ever been painted.   In the New Testament the mission of Gabriel is yet more sublime : he first appears to the high priest Zacharias, and foretells the birth of John the Baptist,— a subject which belongs especially to the life of that saint.   Six months later, Gabriel is sent to announce the appearance of the Redeemer of mankind.[1]

In the Jewish tradition, Gabriel is the guardian of the celestial treasury.   Hence, I presume, Milton has made him chief guardian of Paradise :—

> Betwixt these rocky pillars Gabriel sat,
> Chief of the angelic guards, awaiting night.

As the Angel who announced the birth of Christ, he has been venerated as the Angel who presides over childbirth.   He foretells the birth of Samson, and, in the apocryphal legends, he foretells to Joachim the birth of the Virgin.   In the East, he is of great importance.   Mahomet selected him as his immediate teacher and inspirer, and he became the great protecting angel of Islamism : hence between Michael, the protector of the Jews and Christians,

---

[1] 'The stone on which stood the angel Gabriel when he announced to the most Blessed Virgin the great mystery of the Incarnation,' is among the relics enumerated as existing in the church of the Santa Croce at Rome.

and Gabriel, the protector of the Moslem, there is supposed to exist no friendly feeling—rather the reverse.

In the New Testament, Gabriel is a much more important personage than Michael; yet I have never met with any picture in which he figures singly as an object of worship. In devotional pictures he figures as the second of the three Archangels—' Secondo fra i primi,' as Tasso styles him; or in his peculiar character as the divine messenger of grace, ' *l'Angelo annunziatore.*' He then usually bears in one hand a lily or a sceptre; in the other a scroll on which is inscribed, ' AVE MARIA, GRATIA PLENA!' [1]

The subject called the ANNUNCIATION is one of the most frequent and most important, as it is one of the most beautiful, in the whole range of Christian Art. It belongs, however, to the history of the Virgin, where I shall have occasion to treat it at length; yet as the Angel Gabriel here assumes, by direct scriptural testimony, a distinct name and personality, and as the dignity and significance proper to a subject so often unworthily and perversely treated depend very much on the character and deportment given to the celestial messenger, I shall make a few observations in this place with respect to the treatment of the angel, only reserving the theme in its general bearing for future consideration.

In the early representations of the Annunciation it is treated as a religious mystery, and with a solemn simplicity and purity of feeling, which is very striking and graceful in itself, as well as in harmony with the peculiar manner of the divine revelation. The scene is generally a porch or portico of a temple-like building; the Virgin stands (she is very seldom seated, and then on a kind of raised throne); the angel stands before her, at some distance: very often, she is within the portico; he is without. Gabriel is a majestic being, generally robed in white, wearing the tunic and pallium *à l'antique*, his flowing hair bound by a jewelled tiara, with large many-coloured wings, and bearing the sceptre of sovereignty in the left hand, while the right is extended in the act of benediction as well as salutation : ' Hail! thou that art

---

[1] In Paradise he sings for ever the famous salutation :—

> Cantando *Ave Maria gratia plena*
> Dinanzi a lei le sue ali distese.
> DANTE, *Par.* 32.

highly favoured! Blessed art thou among women!' He is the
principal figure: the attitude of the Virgin, with her drapery drawn
over her head, her eyes drooping, and her hands folded on her bosom,
is always expressive of the utmost submission and humility. So
Dante introduces the image of the lowly Virgin receiving the angel
as an illustration of the virtue of Humility:—

> Ed avea in atto impressa esta favella
> ' Ecce ancilla Dei ! '—

and Flaxman has admirably embodied this idea, both in the lofty
angel with outspread arms, and the kneeling Virgin. Sometimes

42

the angel floats in, with his arms crossed over his bosom, but still
with the air of a superior being, as in this beautiful figure after
Lorenzo Monaco, from a picture in the Florence Gallery.

The two figures are not always in the same picture; it was a very general custom to place the Virgin and the Angel, the 'Annunziata' and the 'Angelo annunziatore,' one on each side of the altar, the place of the Virgin being usually to the right of the spectator; sometimes the figures are half-length: sometimes, when placed in the same picture, they are in two separate compartments, a pillar, or some other ornament, running up the picture between them; as in many old altar-pieces, where the two figures are placed above or on each side of the Nativity, or the Baptism, or the Marriage at Cana, or some other scene from the life and miracles of our Saviour. This subject does not appear on the sarcophagi; the earliest instance I have met with is in the mosaic series over the arch in front of the choir in the church of Santa Maria Maggiore, at Rome, executed in the fifth century. Here we have two successive moments represented together. In the first the angel is sent on his mission, and appears flying down from heaven; the earliest instance I have seen of an angel in the act of flight. In the second group the Virgin appears seated on a throne; two angels stand behind her, supposed to represent her guardian angels, and the angel Gabriel stands in front with one hand extended. The dresses are classical, and there is not a trace of the mediæval feeling, or style, in the whole composition.

In the Greek pictures, the Angel and the Virgin both stand; and in the Annunciation of Cimabue the Greek formula is strictly adhered to. I have seen pictures, of the fourteenth and fifteenth centuries, in which Gabriel enters as a princely ambassador, with three little angels bearing up his mantle behind: in a picture in the collection of Prince Wallerstein, one meek and beautiful angel bears up the rich robes of the majestic archangel, like a page in the train of a sovereign prince. But from the beginning of the fourteenth century we perceive a change of feeling, as well as a change of style. the veneration paid to the Virgin demanded another treatment. She becomes not merely the principal person, but the superior being; she is the 'Regina angelorum,' and the angel bows to her, or kneels before her as to a queen.[1] Thus in the famous altar-piece at Cologne,

[1] See the Ursuline Manual. 'When an angel anciently appeared to the patriarchs or prophets, he was received with due honour as being exalted above them, both by nature

43   The Angel Gabriel.   (Wilhelm of Cologne.   1440.)

the angel kneels; he bears a sceptre, and also a sealed roll, as if he
were a celestial ambassador delivering his credentials: about the same
period we sometimes see the angel merely with his hands folded over
his breast, and his head inclined, delivering his message as if to a
superior being.

    I cannot decide at what period the lily first replaced the sceptre in
the hand of the angel, not merely as the emblem of purity, but as the

and grace; but when an archangel visited Mary, he was struck with her superior dignity
and pre-eminence, and, approaching, saluted her with admiration and respect.   Though
accustomed to the lustre of the highest heavenly spirits, yet he was dazzled and amazed
at the dignity and spiritual glory of her whom he came to salute Mother of God, while
the attention of the whole heavenly court was with rapture fixed upon her.'

symbol of the Virgin from the verse in the Canticles usually applied to her: ' I am the rose of Sharon, and the lily of the valley.' A lily is often placed in a vase near the Virgin, or in the foreground of the picture : of all the attributes placed in the hand of the angel, the lily is the most usual and the most expressive.

The painters of Siena, who often displayed a new and original sentiment in the treatment of a subject, have represented the Angel Gabriel as the announcer of ' peace on earth ; ' he kneels before the Virgin, crowned with olive, and bearing a branch of olive in his hand, as in a picture by Taddeo Bartoli. There is also a beautiful St. Gabriel by Martin Schoen, standing, and crowned with olive. So Dante—

> L' angel che venne in terra col decreto
> Della molt' anni lagrimata pace.

Another passage in Dante which the painters seem to have had before them shows us the Madonna as queen, and the angel as adoring:—

> ' Qual è quel angel che con tanto giuoco
> Guarda negli occhi la nostra regina
> Innamorato sì che par di fuoco ?'
> Ed egli a me,—' Baldezza e leggiadria
> Quanta esser puote in angelo ed in alma
> Tutta è in lui, e si volem che sia ! '

It is in seeking this *baldezza e leggiadria* in a mistaken sense that the later painters have forgotten all the spiritual dignity of the Angel Messenger.

Where the angel bears a lighted taper, which the Virgin extends her hand to take from him ; or, kneeling, bears in his hand a palm-branch, surmounted by seven or twelve stars (44), the subject represented is not the announcement of the birth of the Saviour, but the death of the Virgin, a part of her legendary history which is rarely treated and easily mistaken ; then the announcing angel is not Gabriel, but Michael.[1]

In old German Art, the angel in the Annunciation is habited in

---

[1] The Annunciation and the Death of the Virgin, and the office and character of the announcing angel in both subjects, are fully treated and illustrated in the ' Legends of the Madonna,' pp. 179, 334.

44   Angel announcing the death of the Virgin. (F. Filippo Lippi.)

priestly garments richly embroidered (45).   The scene is often the bed-
room of the Virgin; and while the announcing angel enters and kneels
at the threshold of the door, the Holy Ghost enters at the window.   I
have seen examples in which Gabriel, entering at a door behind the
Virgin, unfolds his official 'Ave Maria.'   He has no lily, or sceptre,
and she is apparently conscious of his presence without seeing him.[1]

But in the representations of the sixteenth century we find neither
the solemnity of the early Italian nor the naïveté of the early German
school; and this divine subject becomes more and more materialised
and familiarised, until, losing its spiritual character, it strikes us as
shockingly prosaic.   One cannot say that the angel is invariably
deficient in dignity, or the Virgin in grace.   In the Venetian school
and the Bologna school we find occasionally very beautiful Annuncia-
tions; but in general the half-draped fluttering angels and the girlish-
looking Virgins are nothing less than offensive; and in the attempt

[1] As in a very curious print by 'Le Graveur de 1466;' and there are other instances.

45   The Archangel Gabriel.   (Van Eyck.)

to vary the sentiment the *naturalisti* have here run the risk of being much *too* natural.

In the Cathedral at Orvieto, the Annunciation is represented in front of the choir by two colossal statues by Francesco Mochi : to the right is the Angel Gabriel, poised on a marble cloud, in an attitude so fantastic that he looks as if he were going to dance ; on the other side stands the Virgin, conceived in a spirit how different !— yet not less mistaken ; she has started from her throne ; with one hand she grasps it, with the other she seems to guard her person against the intruder : majesty at once, and fear, a look of insulted dignity, are in the air and attitude,—'*par che minacci e tema nel tempo istesso*'—but I thought of Mrs Siddons while I looked, not of the Virgin Mary.

This fault of sentiment I saw reversed, but equally in the extreme,

in another example—a beautiful miniature.[1]   The Virgin, seated on
the side of her bed, sinks back alarmed, almost fainting; the angel
in a robe of crimson, with a white tunic, stands before her, half
turning away and grasping his sceptre in his hand, with a proud
commanding air, like a magnificent surly god—a Jupiter who had
received a repulse.

I pass over other instances conceived in a taste even more blameable
—Gabriels like smirking, winged lord chamberlains; and Virgins,
half prim, half voluptuous—the sanctity and high solemnity of the
event utterly lost.   Let this suffice for the present: I may now leave
the reader to his own feeling and discrimination.

St. Raphael.

Lat. Sanctus Raphael. *Ital.* San Raffaello. *Fr.* Saint Raphael. *Ger.* Der Heilige Rafael.

'I am RAPHAEL, one of the Seven Holy Angels which present the prayers of the Saints,
and which go in and out before the glory of the HOLY ONE.'—*Tobit* xii. 15.

I HAVE already alluded to the established belief, that every individual
man, nay, every created being, hath a guardian angel deputed to
watch over him:—Woe unto us, if, by our negligence or our self-will,
we offend him on whose vigilance we depend for help and salvation!
But the prince of guardian spirits, the guardian angel of all humanity,
is Raphael; and in this character, according to the early Christians,
he appeared to the shepherds by night ' with good tidings of great joy,
which shall be for all people.'   It is, however, from the beautiful
Hebrew romance of Tobit that his attributes are gathered: he is the
protector of the young and innocent, and he watches over the pilgrim
and the wayfarer.   The character imputed to him in the Jewish traditions has been retained and amplified by Milton; Raphael is the
angel sent by God to warn Adam:—

> . . . . .   The affable archangel
> Raphael; the sociable spirit that deigned
> To travel with Tobias, and secured
> His marriage with the seven times wedded maid.

---

[1] Chants Royaux.   Paris Bibl. Nat.   MS. No. 6989.

And the character of the angel is preserved throughout; his sympathy with the human race, his benignity, his eloquence, his mild and social converse. So when Adam blesses him :—

> . . . . Since to part,
> Go, heavenly guest, ethereal messenger,
> Sent from whose sovereign goodness I adore !
> Gentle to me and affable hath been
> Thy condescension, and shall be honoured ever
> With grateful memory. Thou to mankind
> Be good and friendly still, and oft return !

This character of benignity is stamped on all the best representations of Raphael, which, however, are not common : they occur principally in the chapels dedicated to the holy guardian angels; but there are also churches and chapels dedicated to him singly.

The devotional figures of Raphael exhibit him in the dress of a pilgrim or traveller, ' his habit fit for speed succinct,' sandals on his feet, his hair bound with a fillet or diadem, the staff in his hand, and sometimes a bottle of water or a wallet (*panetière*) slung to his belt. In this figure by Murillo (46), from one of the most beautiful pictures in the Leuchtenberg Gallery, Raphael is the guardian and guide of the votary who appears below—a bishop who probably bore the same name.[1]

Sometimes, as guardian spirit, he has a sword: the most beautiful example I could cite of this treatment is the figure in the Breviary of Anne of Bretagne (A.D. 1500); he wears a pale-green tunic bordered with gold, and wings of a deep rose-colour; he has a casket or wallet slung over his shoulder by a golden belt; in one hand he holds a sword, and the other is raised with a warning gesture; his countenance, beautiful and benign as possible, yet says, ' Take heed.' More commonly, however, he carries a small casket, box, or vase, supposed to contain the ' fishy charm ' against the evil spirits. (Tobit vi. 6, 7.)

Raphael, in his character of guardian angel, is generally represented as leading the youthful Tobias. When, in order to mark the difference between the celestial and the mortal being, Tobit is figured so small as to look like a child, and when the angel wears his spiritwings, and is not disguised, the whole subject becomes idealised : it

[1] Mr Stirling entitles this picture, ' An Angel appearing to a Bishop at his prayers.'

46   St. Raphael.   (Murillo.   Leuchtenberg Gallery)

is no longer an historical action, but a devotional allegory ; and
Tobias with his fish represents the Christian, the believer, guarded
and guided through his life-pilgrimage by the angelic monitor and
minister of divine mercy.

There is a small side chapel in the church of Saint Euphemia, at
Verona, dedicated to St. Raphael.   The walls are painted with frescoes from the story of Tobit ; and over the altar is that masterpiece
of Carotto, representing the three archangels as three graceful spirit-
like figures without wings.   The altar being dedicated to Raphael,
he is here the principal figure ; he alone has the glory encircling his

head, and takes precedence of the others; he stands in the centre leading Tobias, and looking down on him with an air of such saintly and benign protection, that one feels inclined to say or sing, in the words of the litany, 'Sancte Raphaël, adolescentium pudicitæ defensor, ora pro nobis!' Even more divine is the St. Michael who stands on the right, with one hand gathering up the folds of his crimson robe, the other leaning on his great two-handed sword; but such a head, such a countenance looking out upon us—so earnest, powerful, and serious!—we recognise the Lord of Souls, the Angel of Judgment. To the left of Raphael stands Gabriel, the Angel of Redemption; he holds the lily, and looks up to heaven adoring! this is the least expressive of the three heads, but still beautiful; and, on the whole, the picture left a stronger impression on my mind than any I had seen at Venice, the glorious Assumption excepted. The colouring in its glowing depth is like that of Giorgione. Vasari tells us, that this picture, painted when Carotto was young (about A.D. 1495), was criticised because the limbs of the angels were too slender; to which Carotto, famous for his repartees, replied, 'Then they will fly the better!' The drawing, however, it must be conceded, is not the best part of the picture.

The earliest picture of Titian which remains to us is a St. Raphael leading Tobias;[1] beautiful, but not equal, certainly, to that of Carotto. Raphael, as we might naturally suppose, painted his guardian angel and patron saint *con amore:*[2] we have by him two St. Raphaels; the first, a little figure, executed when he was a boy in the studio of his master Perugino, is now on one side of an altar-piece in the Certosa at Pavia. Later in life, and in one of his finest works, he has introduced his patron saint with infinite beauty of feeling: in the Madonna della Pesce,[3] the Virgin sits upon her throne, with the Infant Christ in her arms; the angel Raphael presents Tobias, who is not here a youth but a child; while the Infant Christ turns away from the wise bearded old doctor, who is intently studying his great book, to welcome the angel and his charge. The head of the angel, looking up in the face of the Madonna, is in truth sublime: it would be impossible to determine whether it belongs to a masculine or a feminine being; but none could

---

[1] In the church of S. Marziale, Venice. [2] Passavant's Rafael, vol. ii. pp. 6, 150.
[3] Madrid Gallery.

doubt that it is a *divine* being, filled with fervent, enthusiastic, adoring love.   The fish in the hand of Tobias has given its name to the picture; and I may as well observe that in the devotional pictures, where the fish is merely an attribute, expressing Christian baptism, it is usually very small; in the story it is a sort of monster, which sprang out of the river and would have devoured him.

All the subjects in which the Archangel Raphael is an actor belong to the history of Tobit.   The scenes of this beautiful scriptural *legend* —I must call it so—have been popular subjects of Art, particularly in the later schools, and have been admirably treated by some of the best Dutch and Flemish painters; the combination of the picturesque and poetical with the homely and domestic recommended it particularly to Rembrandt and his school.   Tobias dragging the fish ashore, while the angel stands by, is a fine picturesque landscape subject which has been often repeated.   The spirited little sketch by Salvator,[1] in which the figure of the guardian angel is admirable for power and animated grace; the twilight effect by Rembrandt;[2] another by Domenichino; three by Claude; may be cited as examples.

47   Archangel.   (Rembrandt.)

In such pictures, as it has been rightly observed, the angel ought

[1] Louvre, No. 358.   [2] In our National Gallery.

not to have wings : he is disguised as the friendly traveller. The dog, which ought to be omitted in the devotional pictures, is here a part of the story, and figures with great propriety.

Rembrandt painted the parting of Tobias and his parents four times; Tobias led by the angel, four times; Tobias healing his father, once ; the departure of the angel, twice. Of this last subject, the picture in the Louvre may be pronounced one of his finest ;—miraculous for true and spirited expression, and for the action of the soaring angel, who parts the clouds and strikes through the air like a strong swimmer through the waves of the sea (47).

The story of Tobit, as a series of subjects, has been very frequently represented, always in the *genre* and picturesque style of the later schools. I shall have to return to it hereafter ; here I have merely alluded to the devotional treatment, in order to direct attention to the proper character of the Archangel Raphael.

And thus we have shown

> . . . . how Holy Church
> Doth represent with human countenance
> Gabriel and Michaël, and him who made
> Tobias whole.—DANTE, *Par.* c. iv.

ADDITIONAL NOTES ON ANGELS.

1. In a picture by Gentile da Fabriano (*Berlin Gallery*, 1130), the Virgin and Child are enthroned, and on each side of the throne is a tree, on the branches of which are little red Seraphim winged and perched like birds, singing and making music. I remember also a little Dutch print of a Riposo (*v.* 'Legends of the Madonna,' p. 256), in which five little angels are perched on the trees above, singing and playing for the solace of the divine Infant. Thus we have Dante's idea of the *Uccelli di Dio*, reproduced in a more familiar form.

2. In the Convent of Sant-Angelo at Bologna, Camillo Procaccino painted the 'Acts of the Holy Angels' in the following order :—1. The Fall of the Dragon. 2. The Angels drive Adam and Eve from Paradise. 3. The three Angels visit Abraham. 4. The Angel stays the arm of Abraham. 5. The Angel wrestles with Jacob. 6. The Angels visit Jacob in a Dream. 7. The Angel delivers the three Children in the burning fiery Furnace. 8. The Angel slays the Host of Sennacherib. 9. The Angel protects Tobit. 10. The Punishment of Heliodorus. 11. The Annunciation to Mary. It will be remarked that all these subjects are strictly scriptural.

The Four Evangelists.

'Matthew wrote for the Hebrews ; Mark, for the Italians; Luke, for the Greeks ; for ALL, the great herald John.'—*Gregory Nazianzen.*

SINCE on the Four Evangelists, as the witnesses and interpreters of a revealed religion, the whole Christian Church may be said to rest as upon four majestic pillars, we cannot be surprised that representations of them should abound, and that their effigies should have been introduced into Christian places of worship from very early times.   Generally, we find them represented together, grouped, or in a series, sometimes in their collective character, as the *Four Witnesses ;* sometimes in their individual character, each as an inspired teacher, or beneficent patron.   As no authentic resemblances of these sacred personages have ever been known or even supposed to exist, such representations have always been either *symbolical* or *ideal.*   In the symbol, the aim was to embody, under some emblematical image, the spiritual mission ; in the ideal portrait, the artist, left to his own conception, borrowed from Scripture some leading trait (when Scripture afforded any authority for such), and adding, with what success his skill could attain, all that his imagination could conceive, as expressive of dignity and persuasive eloquence—the look ' commercing with the skies,' the commanding form, the reverend face, the ample draperies—he put the book or the pen into his hand, and thus the writer and the teacher of the truth was placed before us.

The earliest type under which the Four Evangelists are figured is an emblem of the simplest kind : four scrolls placed in the four angles of a Greek cross, or four books (the Gospels), represented allegorically those who wrote or promulgated them.   The second type chosen was more poetical—the four rivers which had their source in Paradise . representations of this kind, in which the Saviour, figured as a lamb holding the cross, or in His human form, with a lamb near Him, stands on an eminence, from which gush four rivers or fountains, are to be met with in the catacombs, on ancient sarcophagi preserved among the Christian relics in the Vatican, and in several old churches constructed between the second and the fifth century.

At what period the four mysterious creatures in the vision of Ezekiel (ch. i. 5) were first adopted as significant symbols of the Four Evangelists, does not seem clear. The Jewish doctors interpreted them as figuring the four Archangels,—Michael, Raphael, Gabriel, Uriel; and afterwards applied them as emblems of the Four Great Prophets,—Isaiah, Jeremiah, Ezekiel, and Daniel. By the early Oriental Christians, who typified the whole of the Old Testament, the transfer of the emblem to the Four Evangelists seems obvious and easy; we find it alluded to as early as the second century. The four 'Beasts' of corresponding form in the Revelation (chap. iv. 7), which stood round the throne of the Lamb, were likewise thus interpreted; but it was not till the fifth century that we find these symbols assuming a visible form, and introduced into works of Art. In the seventh century they had become almost universal, as distinctive attributes.

The general application of the Four Creatures to the Four Evangelists is of much earlier date than the separate and individual application of each symbol, which has varied at different times;

48   St. Matthew.   (Mosaic, fifth century.)

that propounded by St. Jerome, in his commentary on Ezekiel, has since his time prevailed universally. Thus, then, 1. To St. Matthew was given the CHERUB, or human semblance, because he begins his Gospel with the human generation of Christ; or, according to others, because in his Gospel the human nature of the Saviour is more insisted on than the divine. In the most ancient mosaics, the type is human, not angelic, for the head is that of a man with a beard. 2. St. Mark has the LION, because he has set forth the royal dignity of Christ; or, according to others, because he begins with the mission of the Baptist—'*the voice of one crying in the wilder-ness*'—which is figured by the lion; or, according to a third interpretation, the lion was allotted to St. Mark, because there was, in the Middle Ages, a popular belief that the young of the lion was born dead, and after three days was awakened to vitality by the breath of its sire; some authors, however, represent the lion as vivifying his young not by his breath, but by his roar. In either case the application is the same; the revival of the young lion was considered as symbolical of the resurrection, and Mark was commonly called the ' Historian of the Resurrection.' Another commentator observes that Mark begins his Gospel with ' roaring '—'the voice of one crying in the wilderness ; ' and ends it fearfully with a curse —' He that believeth not shall be damned; ' and that, therefore, his appropriate attribute is the most terrible of beasts, the lion.[1] 3. Luke has the Ox, because he has dwelt on the priesthood of Christ, the *ox* being the emblem of sacrifice. 4. John has the EAGLE, which is the symbol of the highest inspiration, because he soared upwards to the contemplation of the divine nature of the Saviour.

But the order in which, in theological Art, these symbols are placed, is not the same as the order of the Gospels according to the canon. Rupertus considers the Four Beasts as typical of the Incarnation, the Passion, the Resurrection, and the Ascension ; an idea previously dwelt upon by Durandus, who adds, that the man and the lion are placed on the right, because the incarnation and the resurrection are the joy of the whole earth; whilst the ox is on the left, because Christ's sacrifice was a trouble to the apostles ; and the eagle is above the ox, as suggestive of our Lord's upward flight into heaven : according to others, the proper order in the ascending scale is thus—at the lowest point on the left, the ox; to the right, the lion ; above the ox, the eagle; and above all, the angel.   So in Raphael's Vision of Ezekiel, the angel gazes into the face of the Holy One, the others form His throne.

I have dwelt on these fanciful interpretations and disquisitions, because the symbols of the Evangelists meet us at every turn ; in the mosaics of the old Italian churches, in the decorative sculpture of our old cathedrals, in the Gothic stained glass, in the ancient pictures

---

[1] Rupertus, Commentar. in Apocal. c. 4. Mark xvi. 16.

and miniatures, on the carved and chased covers of old books ; everywhere, in short, where enters the idea of their divine mission—and where is it not? The profound thought, as well as the vivid imagination, exercised in some of these early works of Art, is beginning to be appreciated ; and we should lose the half of what is poetical and significant and venerable in these apparently arbitrary and fanciful symbols, if we merely seized the general intention, and not the relative and appropriate meaning of each.

I will only add (for I have restricted myself to the consideration of the mysteries of faith only so far as they are carried into the forms of Art) that these symbols of the Four Evangelists were in their combination held to be symbolical of the Redeemer, in the fourfold character then universally assigned to Him, as man, as king, as high priest, and as God; according to this Latin verse :—

> Quatuor hæc Dominum signant animalia Christum :
> Est *Homo* nascendo, *vitulus*que sacer moriendo,
> Et *Leo* surgendo, cœlos *aquila*que petendo ;
> Nec minus hos scribas animalia et ipsa figurant.

This would again alter the received order of the symbols, and place the angelic or human semblance lower than the rest : but I have never seen them so placed, at least I can recollect no instance.

A Greek mosaic, existing in the Convent of Vatopedi, on Mount Athos, exhibits an attempt to reduce to form the wild and sublime imagery of the prophet Ezekiel : the Evangelists, or rather the Gospels, are represented as the tetramorph, or four-faced creature, with wings full of eyes, and borne on wheels of living flame (49.)

The Tetramorph, *i.e.*, the union of the four attributes of the Evangelists, in one figure, is in Greek Art always angelic or winged—a mysterious thing. The Tetramorph in Western Art has in some instances become monstrous, instead of mystic and poetical. In a miniature of the *Hortus Deliciarum*, we find the new Law, or Christianity, represented as a woman crowned and seated on an animal which, with the body of a horse, has the four heads of the mystic creatures ; and of the four feet, one is human ; one hoofed, for the ox; one clawed like an eagle's ; and one like a lion's : underneath is inscribed *Animal Ecclesiæ.* In some other examples, the Church, or

49   Tetramorph.

the new Law, is seated in a triumphal car, drawn by the eagle, the lion, and the ox, while the angel holds the reins and drives as charioteer.

The early images of the Evangelical symbol are uniformly represented with wings, for the same reason that wings were given to the angels,—they were angels, *i.e.*, bringers of good tidings: for instance, in the earliest example to which I can refer, a rude fragment of a bas-relief in terra-cotta, found in the cata-combs, which represents a lamb with a glory holding a cross; on the right, an angel in a sacerdotal garment (St. Mat-thew), on the left the winged ox (St. Luke), each holding a book.

In the most ancient Christian churches we find these symbols perpetually recur-ring, generally in or over the recess at the east end (the apsis, or tribune), where stands the altar. And as the image of Christ, as the Redeemer, either under the semblance of the lamb, or in His human likeness, as a grand, calm, solemn figure enthroned, and in the act of benediction, forms invariably the principal object; almost as

50   St. Luke. (Mosaic, A.D. 750.)

51   St Luke. (Mosaic, fifth century.)

invariably the Evangelists are either at the four corners, or ranged in a line above or below, or they are over the arch in front of the tribune. Sometimes they are the heads only of the mystic creatures on an azure

52 St. John. (Mosaic, eleventh century.)

ground, studded with stars, floating as in a firmament, thus (50); or the half figure ends in a leafy scroll, like the genii in an arabesque, as thus (51); or the creature is given at full length and entire, with four wings, holding the book, and looking much like a figure in heraldry (52, 53).

53 St Mark. (Mosaic.)

The next step was the combination of the emblem with the human form, i.e., the head of the lion, ox, or eagle, set upon the figure of a man. Here is a figure of St. John standing with the head of an eagle, holding the Gospel (54). There is another rudely engraved in Münter's work, with the eagle's head, wings upon the shoulders, and a scroll. I remember another of St. John seated, writing, with the head and clawed feet of an eagle, and the body and hands of a man. Such figures as a series I have seen in ornaments, and frequently in illuminated

VOL. I. S

MSS., but seldom in churches, and never of a large size. A very

ᴧ · N · N · E · S·

striking and comparatively modern example of this peculiar treatment occurs in a bas-relief on the door of the College of St. Stephen and St. Lawrence, at Castiglione, in which the Four Evangelists are represented as half-length human figures, amply draped and holding the Gospels, each with the emblematic head and large outspread wings (55). The bronze bas-reliefs of the Evangelists on each side of the choir of St. Antonio, at Padua, are similar in form, and very fine, both in conception and workmanship.

This series of full-length figures is from the first compartment of the Life of Christ by Angelico da Fiesole.[1] In the original the figures stand round a mystic circle, alternately with the prophets (56). We must remember, that however monstrous and grotesque such figures may appear to the eye, they are not more unnatural than the angelic representations with which we are so familiar that we see in

54   St John.

them beauty only—not considering that men with the wings of birds are as merely emblematical and impossible as men with animal heads. It is interesting, and leads the mind to many speculations, to remark

that the Babylonish captivity must have familiarised the Israelites with the combination of the human and animal attributes in the same figure. The gigantic bas-reliefs from Nineveh show us winged bulls with human heads, and the human form with the eagle's head and wings. This figure, for example (57), is not unlike some early figures of St. John, if we sub-

55   St. Mark.

stitute the book and the pen for the basket and the pine-cone.

In a few later examples the only symbolical attribute retained is a

[1] Fl. Acad.

56

pair of wings.   The next figure (58) is from a curious set of Evangelists, of a minute size, and exquisitely engraved by Hans Beham;

57

From Nineveh.

58

they are habited in the old German fashion; each has his book, his emblem, and in addition the expressive wings.

These animal symbols, whether alone or in combination with the human forms, were perfectly intelligible to the people, sanctified in their eyes by tradition, by custom, and by the most solemn associations. All direct imitation of nature was, by the best painters, carefully avoided. In this respect how fine is Raphael's Vision of Ezekiel! how sublime and how true in feeling and conception! where the Messiah comes floating along, upborne by the Four Creatures—mysterious, spiritual, wonderful beings, animals in form, but in all else unearthly, and the winged ox not less divine than the winged angel![1]   Whereas in the later times, when the artist piqued himself upon the imitation of nature, the mystic and venerable significance was wholly lost.   As a striking instance of this mistaken style of treatment, we may turn to the famous group of the Four Evangelists by Rubens,[2] grand, colossal, standing or rather moving figures, each with his emblem, if emblems they can be called which are almost as full of reality as nature itself: —the ox so like life, we expect him to bellow at us; the magnificent lion flourishing his tail, and looking at St. Mark as if about to roar at him!—and herein lies the mistake of the great painter, that, for the religious and mysterious emblem, he has substituted the creatures themselves: this being one of the instances, not unfrequent in Art, in which the literal truth becomes a manifest falsehood.

In ecclesiastical decoration the Four Evangelists are sometimes grouped significantly with the Four Greater Prophets; thus representing the connection between the new and the old Law.   I met with a curious instance in the Cathedral of Chartres.   The five great windows over the south door may be said to contain a succinct system of

[1] There is a small and beautiful picture by Giulio Romano in the Belvedere at Vienna, representing the emblems of the Four Evangelists grouped in a picturesque manner, which was probably suggested by Raphael's celebrated picture, which is in the Pitti palace at Florence.
[2] Grosvenor Gallery.

theology, according to the belief of the thirteenth century : here the Virgin, *i.e.*, the Church or Religion, occupies the central window; on one side is Jeremiah, carrying on his shoulders St. Luke, and Isaiah carrying St. Matthew; on the other side Ezekiel bears St. John, and Daniel St. Mark; thus representing the New Testament resting on the Old.

In ecclesiastical decoration, and particularly in the stained glass, they are often found in combination with the Four Doctors, the Evangelists being considered as witnesses, the Doctors as interpreters, of the truth ; or as a series with the Four Greater Prophets, the Four Sibyls, and the Four Doctors of the Church, the Evangelists taking the third place.

If, as late as the sixteenth century, we find the Evangelists still expressed by the mystic emblems (as in the fine bronzes in the choir of Sant' Antonio at Padua), as early as the sixth we have in the Greek MSS. and mosaics the Evangelists as venerable men, and promul-gators of a revelation ; as in San Vitale at Ravenna (A.D. 547) : on each side of the choir, nearest the altar, we find the prophets Isaiah and Jeremiah; then follow the Evangelists, two on each side, all alike, all classically draped in white tunics, each holding an open book, on which is inscribed 'Secundum Marcum,' 'Secundum Johannem,' &c.; and above each the animal symbol or attribute, large, full length, and grandly designed. In modern ecclesiastical decoration, the usual and appropriate situation of the Four Evangelists is imme-diately under the dome, nearest to the Saviour after the angels, or after the prophets, where either are introduced. I will mention here a few examples celebrated in the history of Art; premising that among the works of Leonardo, of Michael Angelo, and Raphael, we find no representations of the Four Evangelists; which is singular, considering that such figures entered necessarily into every scheme of theological decorative Art.

By Cimabue (A.D. 1270), larger than life, on the vault of the choir in San Francesco d'Assisi.

By Giotto (A.D. 1320), in the choir of Sant' Apollinare, at Ravenna; seated, and each accompanied by one of the doctors of the Church.

By Angelico (A.D. 1390), round the dome of the chapel of San Niccolò, in the Vatican; all seated, each with his emblem.

By Masaccio (A.D. 1420), round the dome of the chapel of the Passion in San Clemente, at Rome; admirable for simple grandeur.

By Perugino (A.D. 1490), on the dome of the chapel del Cambio, at Perugia; the heads admirable.

By Correggio (A.D. 1520), immediately under the cupola of San Giovanni, in four lunettes, magnificent figures: and again in the Cathedral of Parma, each seated in glory, with one of the doctors of the Church.

By Domenichino, two sets (A. D. 1620). Those in the Church of St. Andrea della Valle, at Rome, are considered his finest works, and celebrated in the history of Art: they are grand figures. The emblematical animals are here combined with the personages in a manner the most studied and picturesque; and the angels which sport around them, playing with the mane of St. Mark's lion, or the pallet and pencils of St. Luke, are like beautiful ' Amoretti,'—but we hardly think of angels. The series at Grotta-Ferrata is inferior.

The Four Evangelists by Valentin (A.D. 1632), in the Louvre, had once great celebrity, and have been often engraved; they appear to me signal examples of all that should be avoided in character and sentiment. St. Matthew, for example, is an old beggar; the model for the attendant angel is a little French *gamin*, ' à qui Valentin a commandé de sortir un bras de la manche de sa chemise, que de l'autre main il soutient gauchement.'

Le Sueur (A.D. 1655), has represented the Four Evangelists seated at a table writing; the Holy Ghost descends upon them in the form of a dove.

Towards the end of the seventeenth century, we find sets of the Evangelists in which the emblems are altogether omitted, and the personages distinguished by their situation, or by their names inscribed under or over them; but we miss those antique scriptural attributes which placed them before us as beings foreshadowed in the prophecies uttered of old; they have become mere men.

This must suffice for the Evangelists considered as a series and in their collective character; but it will be interesting to pause for a moment, and take a rapid retrospective view of the progress, from first to last, in the expression of an idea through form.

First, we have the mere *fact;* the four scrolls, or the four books.

Next, the *idea;* the four rivers of salvation flowing from on high, to fertilise the whole earth.

Thirdly, the *prophetic* Symbol; the winged cherub of fourfold aspect.

Next, the *Christian* Symbol; the four 'beasts' in the Apocalypse, with or without the angel-wings.

Then the combination of the *emblematical animal* with the *human* form.

Then the *human* personages, each of venerable or inspired aspect, as becomes the teacher and witness; and each attended by the scriptural emblem—no longer an emblem, but an attribute—marking his individual vocation and character.

And, lastly, the emblem and attribute both discarded, we have the human being only, holding his Gospel, *i.e., his* version of the doctrine of Christ.

St. Matthew.

Lat. S. Mattheus.   *Ital.* San Matteo.   *Fr.* Saint Matthieu.   *Ger.* St. Matthäus. (Sept. 21.)

St. Matthew among the Apostles takes the seventh or eighth place, but as an Evangelist he always stands first, because his Gospel was the earliest written.   Very little is certainly known concerning him, his name occurring but once in his own Gospel, and in the other Gospels only incidentally with reference to two events.

He was a Hebrew by birth; by profession a publican, or tax-gatherer, in the service of the Romans—an office very lucrative, but particularly odious in the sight of his countrymen.   His original name was Levi.   It is recorded in few words, that as he sat at the receipt of custom by the lake of Gennesareth, Jesus in passing by saw him, and said unto him, 'Follow me,' and he left all and followed Him; and further, that he made a feast in his house, at which many publicans and sinners sat down with the Lord and His disciples, to the great astonishment and scandal of the Jews.   So far the sacred record: the traditional and legendary history of St. Matthew is equally scanty. It is related in the *Perfetto Legendario* that, after the dispersion of the apostles, he travelled into Egypt and Ethiopia, preaching the Gospel; and having arrived in the capital of Ethiopia, he lodged in the house of the eunuch who had been baptized by Philip, and who entertained him with great honour. There were two terrible magicians at that time in Ethiopia, who by their diabolical spells and incantations kept all the people in subjection, afflicting them at the same time with strange and terrible diseases; but St. Matthew overcame them, and having baptized the people, they were delivered for ever from the malignant influence of these enchanters. And further, it is related that St. Matthew raised the son of the King of Egypt from the dead, and healed his daughter of the leprosy. The princess, whose name was Iphigenia, he placed at the head of a community of virgins dedicated to the service of God; and a certain wicked heathen king, having threatened to tear her from her asylum, was struck by leprosy, and his palace destroyed by fire. St. Matthew remained twenty-three years in Egypt and Ethiopia, and it is said that he perished in the ninetieth year of our era, under Domitian; but the manner of his death is uncertain; according to the Greek legend, he died in peace, but according to the tradition of the Western Church, he suffered martyrdom either by the sword or the spear.

ℓ♭   St. Matthew.

Few churches are dedicated to St. Matthew. I am not aware that he is the patron saint of any country, trade, or profession, unless it be that of tax-gatherer or exciseman; and this is perhaps the reason that, except where he figures as one of the series of evangelists or apostles, he is so seldom represented alone, or in devotional pictures. In a large altar-piece, the ' San Matteo ' of Annibal Caracci,[1] he is standing before the throne of the Madonna, as a pendant to John the Baptist, and gives his name to the picture: but such examples are uncommon. When he is portrayed as an evangelist, he holds a book or a pen; and the angel, his proper attribute and

[1] Dresden Gallery. No. 828.

attendant, stands by, pointing up to heaven, or dictating; or he holds the inkhorn, or he supports the book. In his character of apostle, St. Matthew frequently holds a purse or money-bag, as significant of his former vocation (56).

Neither are pictures from his life of frequent occurrence. The principal incident, entitled the 'Calling of Matthew,' has been occasionally, but not often, treated in painting. The *motif* is simple and not easily mistaken. St. Matthew is seated at a kind of desk with money before him; various personages bring tribute; on one side is seen Christ, with one or two of His disciples, generally Peter and Andrew; St. Matthew is either looking towards Him with an expression of awe-struck attention, or he is rising from his seat, as in the act to follow: the mere accessories and number of the personages vary with the period of the composition and the taste of the painter.

1. The earliest instance I can cite, probably the oldest which has come down to us, is in a Greek MS. of the ninth century.[1] St. Matthew sits with both hands on a heap of gold, lying on a table before him : he looks round at Christ, who is a little behind.

2. St. Matthew is about to rise to follow the Saviour; by Matteo di Ser Cambio of Perugia, who has represented his patron saint in a small composition.[2]

3. In the Queen's Gallery at Buckingham Palace, there is a very curious and interesting picture of this subject, by Mabuse, which once belonged to King Charles I., and is quaintly described in the old catalogue of his pictures as ' a very old, defaced, curious altar-piece, upon a thick board, where Christ is calling St. Matthew out of the custom-house; which picture was got in Queen Elizabeth's days, in the taking of Calus Malus (Cadiz), in Spain. Painted upon a board in a gilded arched frame, like an altar-piece; containing ten big figures, less than half so big as the life, and some twenty-two afar off less figures. Given to the King.' In the foreground there is a rich architectural porch, from which St. Matthew is issuing in haste, leaving his money-bags behind ; and in the background is seen the Lake of Gennesareth and shipping. This picture was among the booty taken in Essex's expedition against Cadiz in 1596, and probably stolen from some church.

[1] Paris, Bib. du Roi, No. 510.   [2] A.D. 1377. Eng. in Rossini, pl. 24.

4. In the Vienna Gallery I found three pictures of the same subject, all by Hemessen, very quaint and curious.

5. At Dresden the same subject in the Venetian style by Pordenone.

6. By Ludovico Caracci, a grand scenic picture, painted for the Mendicanti in Bologna.

7. In a chapel of the church of San Luigi de' Francesi, at Rome, there are three pictures by Caravaggio from the life of St. Matthew. Over the altar is the saint writing his Gospel, he looks up at the attendant angel, who is behind with outspread wings, and in the act of dictating. On the left is the calling of St. Matthew : the saint, who has been counting money, rises with one hand on his breast, and turns to follow the Saviour ; an old man, with spectacles on his nose, examines with curiosity the personage whose summons has had such a miraculous effect ; a boy is slyly appropriating the money which the apostle has thrown down. The third picture is the martyrdom of the saint, who, in the sacerdotal habit, lies extended on a block, while a half-naked executioner raises the sword, and several spectators shrink back with horror. There is nothing dignified or poetical in these representations ; and though painted with all that power of effect which characterised Caravaggio, then at the height of his reputation, they have also his coarseness of feeling and execution : the priests were (not without reason) dissatisfied ; and it required all the influence of his patron, Cardinal Giustiniani, to induce them to retain the pictures in the church where we now see them ;—here we sympathise with the priests, rather than with the artist and his patron.

The Feast which St. Matthew made for our Saviour and His disciples is the subject of one of Paul Veronese's gorgeous banquet scenes ; that which he painted for the refectory of the Convent of St. John and St. Paul at Venice. It is now in the Academy, filling up the end wall of one of the great rooms from side to side, and seeming to let in light and air through the lofty marble porticoes, which give us such a magnificent idea of the splendour which surrounded Levi before he left all to follow Jesus.

In all the representations of the death of St. Matthew, except those of the Greek or Byzantine school, he dies by the sword. The Greek artists uniformly exhibit him as dying in peace, while an angel swings the censer beside his bed: as on the ancient doors of San Paolo at Rome.

Pictures from the legendary life of St. Matthew are very rare. The most remarkable are the frescoes in the chapel of San Matteo at Ravenna, attributed to Giotto. They are so much ruined, that, of the eight subjects represented, only three—his vocation, his preaching and healing the sick in Ethiopia, and the baptism of the king and queen—can be made out. In the Bedford missal at Paris I found a miniature, representing St. Matthew ' healing the son and daughter of King Egyptus of the leprosy; ' but, as a subject of Art, he is not popular.

ST. MARK.

Lat. S. Marcus. *Ital.* San Marco Evangelista. *Fr.* St. Marc. *Ger.* Der Heilige Marcus. (April 25. A.D. 68.)

ST. MARK the Evangelist was not one of the twelve Apostles : his conversion apparently took place after the ascension. He was the companion and assistant of Paul and Barnabas, with whom he preached the Gospel among the Gentiles. According to the traditions received in the Roman Church, he was converted by St. Peter, and became his favourite disciple; attended him first to Aquileia, where they converted and baptized the people on the shores of the Adriatic, and thence to Rome. While there he wrote his Gospel for the use of the Roman converts,—some say from the dictation of the apostle. He afterwards, by command of St. Peter, went to preach the Gospel in Egypt; and after preaching in Lybia and Thebais for twelve years, he founded the church of Alexandria, subsequently one of the most celebrated of all the early Christian churches. The ire of the heathen being stirred up against him because of his miracles, they reviled him as a magician, and, during the feast of their god Serapis, seized him while in the act of worship, bound him, and dragged him along the streets and highways, and over stony and rocky places, till he perished miserably ; at the same time a dreadful tempest of hail and lightning fell upon his murderers, by which they were dispersed and destroyed. The Christians of Alexandria buried his mangled remains, and his sepulchre was regarded with great reverence for several centuries. About 815 A.D., some Venetian merchants trading to Alexandria carried off the relics (literally stole them,—'*convey* the wise it call!'), and they were deposited in the city of Venice, where the stately church of St. Mark was built over them.   Since that time, St. Mark has been honoured as the patron saint of Venice, and his legendary history has supplied the Venetian painters with many beautiful and picturesque subjects.

When St. Mark is represented as one of the Four Evangelists, either singly or grouped with the others, he is almost invariably accompanied by the lion, winged or unwinged, but generally winged, —which distinguishes him from St. Jerome, who is also accompanied by the lion, but unwinged, as we shall see hereafter.

In devotional representations, St. Mark often wears the habit of bishop, as first bishop of Alexandria.   He is thus represented in the colossal mosaic over the principal door of St. Mark's at Venice [1] in the pontificals of a Greek bishop, no mitre, short grey hair and beard; one hand raised in benediction, the other holding the Gospel.

Of the innumerable pictures in which St. Mark figures as patron of Venice, I can afford to give a few examples only.

1. A. Busati.   He is seated on a throne; an open book in one hand, bearing inscribed the Venetian motto ('*la Leggenda de' Veneti*') PAX TIBI, MARCE, EVANGELISTA MEUS; the other hand blessing: behind him a fig-tree, with leaves and no fruit; probably in allusion to the text, ch. xi. 13, which is peculiar to St. Mark.   On his right stands St. Andrew bearing a cross; on the left St. Bernardino of Siena; behind him the apple-tree which 'brought death into the world and all our woe.'   This votive picture, from its mystical accessories and the introduction of St. Bernardino, was probably painted for the Franciscans (*i Frari*) of Venice: it is now in the Academy there.

2. St. Mark on a lofty throne holds his Gospel in his hand; at his feet the four saints who are protectors against sickness and pestilence, St. Sebastian, St. Roch, St. Cosmo, and St. Damian: a splendid picture, in Titian's early manner.[2]   3. St. Mark plants the standard

---

[1] Designed by Titian, and executed by F. Zuccati.

[2] It is so like Giorgione in sentiment and colour that it has been attributed to him. For this expressive votive group, see the frontispiece to vol. ii., and the legends of the four patron saints above mentioned.

of Venice, by Bonifazio. And 4. ' San Marco che assista all' coscri-
zione maritima ; ' (*i.e.*, the enlisting of the mariners for the service of
the State) by G. del Moro, both curious instances of the manner in
which the Venetians mixed up their patron saint with all their
political and military transactions. 5. St. Mark presents the Doge
Leonardo Dona to the Virgin ; the most remarkable of a numerous
class of votive pictures common in the Venetian school, in which St.
Mark introduces either the Doge or some general or magnifico to the
Virgin.[1]

Among the devotional pictures of St. Mark, one of the most
famous is that of Fra Bartolomeo, in the Palazzo Pitti. He is
represented as a man in the prime of life, with bushy hair and a
short reddish beard, throned in a niche, and holding in one hand
the Gospel, in the other a pen ; the lion is omitted. The Frate
painted this picture for his own convent of San Marco at Florence.
It is much lauded and celebrated, but the attitude appeared to me
rather forced, and the features rather commonplace.

The legend which describes St. Mark as the disciple and amanuensis of St. Peter, has given occasion for those votive pictures in
which they are represented together. 1. In the treasury of St.
Mark's is preserved a golden reliquary of a square form, containing, it is said, a fragment of the original Gospel in the handwriting
of St. Mark : the chased cover represents St. Peter on a throne, and
before him kneels the evangelist, writing from his dictation.[2] 2. And
again, in an ancient Greek Evangelarium, St. Mark is seated,
writing; St. Peter stands before him with his hand raised as dictating. 3. In a beautiful picture by Angelico da Fiesole,[3] St. Peter is
in a pulpit preaching to the Romans ; and Mark, seated, is taking
down his words in a book. 4. St. Peter and St. Mark standing
together, the former holding a book, the latter a pen, with an inkhorn suspended from his girdle, by Bellini;[4] and 5, a similar one by
Bonvicino—very beautiful.[5] Such pictures are extremely interesting,

[1] Beneath the monument of Nicolò Orsini, in the SS. Giovanni-e-Paolo at Venice. A very
remarkable and beautiful picture of this class is in the Berlin Gallery (No. 316). St. Mark,
enthroned and holding his Gospel open on his knees, is instructing three of the *Procuradori
di San Marco*, who kneel before him in their rich crimson dresses, and listen reverently.

[2] Venice Ducal Palace.   [3] Fl. Gal.
[4] Venice Acad.   [5] Brera, Milan.

showing the opinion generally entertained of the origin of St. Mark's Gospel.

Historical pictures from the legendary life of St. Mark abound in the Venetian school, but are not often found out of Venice.

St. Mark preaching the Gospel at Alexandria, by Gentil Bellini,[1] a very large composition with numerous figures, is on many accounts extremely curious. The painter, who had been at Constantinople, transferred to Alexandria the Oriental scenery and costume with which he had become acquainted. The church of St. Euphemia at Alexandria, in the background, has the air of a Turkish mosque; a crowd of persons, men and women, in the costume of the Turks, surround the Saint, who is standing on a kind of pedestal or platform, ascended by a flight of steps, from which he addresses his audience with great fervour. Gentil Bellini painted this picture for the Scuola di San Marco, at Venice.

It is related that one day St. Mark, in his progress through the city of Alexandria, saw a poor cobbler, who had wounded his hand severely with his awl, so as to be incapacitated from gaining his bread: St. Mark healed the wound; and the cobbler, whose name was Anianus, being converted and properly instructed, became a zealous Christian, and succeeded St. Mark as Bishop of Alexandria. This miraculous cure of St. Anianus, and his subsequent baptism, are represented in two pictures by Mansueti.[2] In the Berlin Gallery is the cure of St. Anianus, by Cima da Conegliano; a large composition with many figures. The cure and baptism of St. Anianus, represented as a very aged man, form the subjects of two fine bas-reliefs on the façade of the School of St. Mark, by Tullio Lombardo, A.D. 1502.

In the Martyrdom of St. Mark, he is dragged through the streets by the enraged populace, who haul him along by a rope; a storm from above overwhelms the idolaters. The subject is thus represented by Angelico da Fiesole.[3]

A famous legend of St. Mark, which has been the subject of several pictures, can only be worthily given in the language of the old Venetian chronicle: there is something perfectly charming in the picturesque naïveté and matter-of-fact detail with which this

[1] Brera, Milan.   [2] A.D. 1500. Scuola di S. Marco, Venice.   [3] Fl. Gal.

wild and wonderful story is related; and if you, reader, have ever
stood on the steps of the Piazzetta and looked over to San Giorgio,
or San Niccolò, when the waves of the Lagune were foaming and
driving up to your feet, and storm-clouds stooping and lowering
seemed to touch the very domes and campanile around, then you
will have the whole scene as a reality before you.

  ' On the 25th of February 1340, there fell out a wonderful thing
in this land; for during three days the waters rose continually, and
in the night there was fearful rain and tempest, such as had never
been heard of. So great was the storm that the waters rose three
cubits higher than had ever been known in Venice; and an old
fisherman being in his little boat in the canal of St. Mark, reached
with difficulty the Riva di San Marco, and there he fastened his
boat, and waited the ceasing of the storm. And it is related that, at
the time this storm was at the highest, there came an unknown man,
and besought him that he would row him over to San Giorgio Maggiore, promising to pay him well; and the fisherman replied, " How
it is possible to go to San Giorgio? we shall sink by the way!"
But the man only besought him the more that he should set forth.
So, seeing that it was the will of God, he arose and rowed over to
San Giorgio Maggiore; and the man landed there, and desired the
boatman to wait. In a short while he returned with a young man;
and they said, " Now row towards San Niccolò di Lido." And the
fisherman said, " How can one possibly go so far with one oar?" And
they said, " Row boldly, for it shall be possible to thee, and thou shalt
be well paid." And he went; and it appeared to him as if the waters
were smooth. Being arrived at San Niccolò di Lido, the two men
landed, and returned with a third, and, having entered into the boat,
they commanded the fisherman that he should row beyond the two
castles. And the tempest raged continually. Being come to the
open sea, they beheld approaching, with such terrific speed that it
appeared to fly over the waters, an enormous galley full of demons
(as it is written in the Chronicles, and Marco Sabellino also makes
mention of this miracle): the said bark approached the castles to
overwhelm Venice, and to destroy it utterly; anon the sea, which
had hitherto been tumultuous, became calm; and these three men,
having made the sign of the cross, exorcised the demons, and com-

manded them to depart, and immediately the galley or the ship
vanished.   Then these three men commanded the fisherman to land
them, the one at San Niccolò di Lido, the other at San Giorgio
Maggiore, and the third at San Marco.   And when he had landed
the third, the fisherman, notwithstanding the miracle he had witnessed, desired that he would pay him; and he replied, " Thou art
right; go now to the Doge, and to the Procuratore of St. Mark, and
tell them what thou hast seen, for Venice would have been overwhelmed had it not been for us three.   I am St. Mark the Evangelist,
the protector of this city; the other is the brave knight St. George;
and he whom thou didst take up at the Lido is the holy bishop St.
Nicholas.   Say to the Doge and to the Procuratori[1] that they are to
pay you; and tell them likewise that this tempest arose because of a
certain schoolmaster dwelling at San Felice, who did sell his soul to
the devil, and afterwards hanged himself."   And the fisherman replied, " If I should tell them this, they will not believe me."   Then
St. Mark took off a ring which was on his finger, which ring was
worth five ducats; and he said, " Show them this, and tell them
when they look in the sanctuary they will not find it; " and thereupon he disappeared.   The next morning, the said fisherman presented himself before the Doge and related all he had seen the
night before, and showed him the ring for a sign.   And the Procuratori having sent for the ring, and sought in the usual place,
found it not; by reason of which miracle the fisherman was paid,
and a solemn procession was ordained, giving thanks to God, and
to the relics of the three holy saints, who rest in our land, and who
delivered us from this great danger.   The ring was given to Signor
Marco Loredano and to Signor Andrea Dandolo the Procuratori, who
placed it in the sanctuary; and, moreover, a perpetual provision
was made for the aged fisherman above mentioned.'[2]

This legend is the subject of two celebrated pictures :—The first,
attributed to Giorgione,[3] represents the storm.   A ship, manned
by demons, is seen towering over the waves : the demons appear to
be seized with consternation; some fling themselves headlong over
the side of their vessel, others are clinging to the rigging, others

[1] The *Procuradori* had the charge of the church and the treasury of St. Mark.
[2] Sanuto, Vite de' Duci Veneti.   [3] Acad. Venice.

sit on the masts which flame with fire, and the glare is seen over the murky sky and sea. More in front are two barks, one rowed by four satyr-like demons, splendid figures admirably painted, literally glowing as if they were red-hot, and full of fierce animation. In the other bark are seen the three saints, St. Mark, St. Nicholas, and St. George, rowed by the fisherman; sea-monsters are sporting amid the waves, demons bestride them; the city of Venice is just visible in the far-off distance. The whole picture is full of vigour and poetic feeling; the fiery glow of colour and the romantic style of Giorgione suited the subject; and it has been admirably restored.

The second picture is by Paris Bordone,[1] and represents the fisherman presenting the miraculous ring of St. Mark to the Doge Gradenigo. It is like a grand piece of scenic decoration; we have before us a magnificent marble hall, with columns and buildings in perspective; to the right, on the summit of a flight of steps, sits the Doge in council; the poor fisherman, ascending the steps, holds forth the ring. The numerous figures, the vivid colour, the luxuriant architecture, remind us of Paul Veronese, with, however, more delicacy, both in colour and execution.

A Christian slave, in the service of a certain nobleman of Provence, disobeyed the commands of his lord, and persisted in paying his devotions at the shrine of St. Mark, which was at some distance. On his return home, he was condemned to the torture. As it was about to be inflicted, the saint himself descended from heaven to aid his votary; the instruments of torture were broken or blunted, the oppressor and his executioners confounded. This legend is the subject of a celebrated picture by Tintoretto,[2] of which Mr Rogers had the original sketch. The slave lies on the ground amid a crowd of spectators, who look on, animated by all the various emotions of sympathy, rage, terror; a woman in front, with a child in her arms, has always been admired for the life-like vivacity of her attitude and expression. The executioner holds up the broken implements; St. Mark, with a headlong movement, seems to rush down from heaven in haste to save his worshipper; the dramatic grouping in this picture

[1] Acad. Venice. [2] Ibid.

is wonderful; the colouring, in its gorgeous depth and harmony, is in Mr Roger's sketch finer than in the picture.

In St. Mark's, at Venice, we find the whole history of St. Mark on the vault of the Cappella Zen (opening from the Baptistery), in a series of very curious mosaics of the twelfth century. The translation of the body of St. Mark; the carrying off the relics from Alexandria; their arrival in Venice; the grand religious ceremonies which took place on their arrival; are also represented in the mosaics over the portico of St. Mark's, executed chiefly between 1650 and 1680. We have the same legend in two compositions of Tintoretto:[1] in the first, the remains of St. Mark are taken forcibly from the tomb by the Venetian mariners; in the other, they are borne away to sea in a nightstorm, while in the air is seen hovering a bright transparent form,—the soul of the saint flitting with his body to Venice.

ST. LUKE.

Lat. Sanctus Luca. *Ital.* San Luca. *Fr.* Saint Luc. (Oct. 18.)

OF the real history of St. Luke we know very little. He was not an apostle; and, like St. Mark, appears to have been converted after the ascension. He was a beloved disciple of St. Paul, whom he accompanied to Rome, and remained with his master and teacher till the last. It is related, that, after the martyrdom of St. Peter and St. Paul, he preached the Gospel in Greece and Egypt; but whether he died a natural death, or suffered martyrdom, does not seem clear. The Greek traditions represent him as dying in peace, and his death was thus figured on the ancient doors of San Paolo at Rome. Others affirm that he was crucified at Patras with St. Andrew.

There is some ground for the supposition that Luke was a physician. (Col. iv. 14.) But the pretty legend which makes him a painter, and represents him as painting the portrait of the Virgin Mary, is unsupported by any of the earlier traditions. It is of Greek origin, still universally received by the Greek Church, which considers painting a religious art, and numbers in its calender of saints a long list of painters, as well as poets, musicians, and physicians. 'Les Grecs,' says Didron,

[1] Venice, Ducal Palace.

'semblent avoir canonisé des chrétiens uniquement parce qu'ils s'occupaient de soulager le corps ou de charmer l'esprit.' In the west of Europe, the legend which represents St. Luke as a painter can be traced no higher than the tenth century; the Greek painters introduced it; and a rude drawing of the Virgin discovered in the Catacombs, with an inscription purporting that it was 'one of seven painted by Luca,' confirmed the popular belief that St. Luke the Evangelist was meant. Thus originated the fame of innumerable Virgins of peculiar sanctity, all attributed to his hand, and regarded with extreme veneration. Such ancient pictures are generally of Greek workmanship, and of a black complexion.[1] In the legend of St. Luke we are assured that he carried with him everywhere two portraits, painted by himself; one of our Saviour, and one of the Virgin; and that by means of these he converted many of the heathen, for not only did they perform great miracles, but all who looked on these bright and benign faces, which bore a striking resemblance to each other, were moved to admiration and devotion. It is also said, that St. Luke painted many portraits of the Virgin, delighting himself by repeating this gracious image; and in the church of Santa Maria in Via Lata, at Rome, they still show a little chapel in which, 'as it hath been handed down from the first ages, St. Luke the Evangelist wrote, and painted the effigy of the Virgin-Mother of God.'

On the strength of this tradition, St. Luke has been chosen as the patron saint of painters. Academies of art are placed under his particular protection; their chapels are dedicated to him, and over the altar we see him in his charming and pious avocation, that of painting portraits of the Blessed Virgin for the consolation of the faithful.

[1] The little black virgin of the Monte della Guardia, near Bologna, I saw carried in grand procession through the streets of that city, in May 1847. The following inscription is engraved on a tablet in the church of San Domenico and San Sisto at Rome : 'Here at the high altar is preserved that image of the most blessed Mary, which, being delineated by St. Luke the Evangelist, received its colours and form divinely. This is that image with which St. Gregory the Great (according to St. Antonine), as a suppliant, purified Rome; and the pestilence being dispelled, the angel messenger of peace, from the summit of the castle of Adrian, commanding the Queen of Heaven to rejoice, restored health to the city.' A Virgin in the Ara Cœli pretends to the same honour : both these are black and ugly, while that in the S. Maria in Cosmedino is of uncommon dignity and beauty.—See 'Legends of the Madonna,' Introduction, p. xli.

The devotional figures of St Luke, in his character of evangelist, represent him in general with his Gospel and his attendant ox, winged or unwinged, as already described : but in Greek Art, and in those schools of Art which have been particularly under the Byzantine influence (as the early Venetian), we see St. Luke as evangelist young and beardless, holding the portrait of the Virgin as his attribute in one hand and his Gospel in the other. A beautiful figure of St. Luke as evangelist and painter is in the famous ' Heures d'Anne de Bretagne.' [1]

In an engraving by Lucas v. Leyden, executed as it should seem in honour of his patron saint, St. Luke is seated on the back of his ox writing the Gospel; he wears a hood like an old professor, rests his book against the horns of the animal, and his inkstand is suspended on the bough of a tree. But separate devotional figures of him as patron are as rare as those of St. Matthew.

St. Luke painting the Virgin has been a frequent and favourite subject. The most famous of all is a picture in the Academy of St. Luke, at Rome, ascribed to Raphael. Here St. Luke, kneeling on a footstool before an easel, is busied painting the Virgin with the Child in her arms, who appears to him out of heaven sustained by clouds : behind St. Luke stands Raphael himself, looking on. Another of the same subject, a very small and beautiful picture, also ascribed to Raphael, is in the Grosvenor Gallery. In neither of these pictures is the treatment quite worthy of that great painter, wanting his delicacy both of sentiment and execution. There is a most curious and quaint example in the Munich Gallery, attributed to Van Eyck; here the Virgin, seated under a rich Gothic canopy, holds on her lap the Infant Christ, in a most stiff attitude; St Luke, kneeling on one knee, is taking her likeness. There is another, similar in style, by Aldegraef, in the Vienna Gallery. Carlo Maratti represents St. Luke as presenting to the Virgin the picture he has painted of her. St. Luke painting the Madonna and Child, while an angel is grinding his colours, I remember in the Aguado Gallery; a late Spanish picture. [2]

---

[1] MS. A.D. 1500. Paris, Bib. Imp.   [2] F. Rizi. A.D. 1660.

St. Luke painting the Virgin.

St. Mark attended by St. Gregory.

St. John.

Lat. Sanctus Johannes. *Gr.* St. John Theologos, or the Divine. *Ital.* San Giovanni Evangelista. *Fr.* Saint Jean; Messire Saint Jehan. *Ger.* Der Heilige Johann. (Dec. 27, A.D. 99.)

Of St. Matthew, St. Mark, and St. Luke, so little is certainly known, that we have no data on which to found an individual portrait; therefore any representation of them as venerable and inspired teachers suffices to the fancy : but it is quite otherwise with St. John, the most distinguished of the evangelists, and the most beloved of the disciples of our Lord. Of him sufficient is known to convey a distinct impression of his personal character, and an idea of what his personal appearance may have been, supposing this outward semblance to have harmonised with the inward being.

He was the son of the fisherman Zebedee, and, with his brother James, among the first followers of the Saviour. He is emphatically called 'the disciple whom Jesus loved;' a preference which he merited, not only from the extreme purity of his life and character, but from his devoted and affectionate nature. He appears to have been at all times the constant companion of his divine Lord; and his life, while the Saviour was on earth, inseparable from His. In all the memorable circumstances recorded in the Gospel he was a party, or at least present. He witnessed the glory of the transfiguration; he leaned on the bosom of Jesus at the Last Supper; he stood by the cross in the hour of agony; he laid the body of his crucified Master in the sepulchre. After the death of the Virgin Mother, who had been confided to his care, he went about Judæa, preaching the Gospel with St. Peter. He then travelled into Asia Minor, where he founded the Seven Churches, and resided principally at Ephesus. During the persecution of the Christians under Domitian, St. John was sent in fetters to Rome; and, according to a tradition generally received in the Roman Church, he was cast into a caldron of boiling oil, but was miraculously preserved, and ' came out of it as out of a refreshing bath.' He was then accused of magic, and exiled to the island of Patmos, in the Ægean Sea, where he is said to have written his Revelation. After the death of the Emperor Domitian he was released, and returned to his church at Ephesus ; and for the use of the Christians there he is said to have written his Gospel, at the age of ninety. A few years afterwards he died in that city, being nearly a century old. All the incidents here touched upon occur frequently as subjects of Art, but most of them belong properly to the life of Christ.

The personal character of St. John, at once attractive and picturesque, has rendered him popular as a patron saint, and devotional pictures of him are far more numerous than of any of the other evangelists.

He is represented in one of his three characters : 1, as evangelist ; 2, as apostle; 3, as prophet; or the three are combined in one figure.

1. Of the early eagle symbol, I have spoken at length.

In Greek Art, whether as apostle or evangelist, St. John is always an aged man with white hair, and a venerable beard descending to his breast; and by the earlier Latin painters, where he figures as evangelist only, not as apostle, this type has been adhered to ; but the later painters set it aside, and St. John the Evangelist, nearly a century old, has all the attributes of the youthful apostle. He is beardless, with light curling hair, and eyes gazing upwards in a rapture of inspiration : he is sometimes seated with his pen and his book, sometimes standing; the attendant eagle always near him, and frequently holding the pen or inkhorn in his beak.

In some of the old prints and pictures, which represent St. John as writing the Gospel, his eyes are turned on the Virgin with the Infant Christ in her arms, who appear as a vision in the skies above; underneath, or on his book, is inscribed,—' The word was made flesh,' or some other text of the same import. The eagle at his side has sometimes the nimbus or a crown of stars,[1] and is then perhaps intended to figure the Holy Ghost.

I remember an instance in which the devil, intent on intercepting the message of reconcilement and ' goodwill towards men,' which was destined to destroy his empire on earth, appears behind St. John, and

[1] As in the Missal of Henry VIII. Bodleian, Oxford.

is oversetting the ink upon the pages ; another, in which he is stealing away the inkhorn.

2. As one of the series of apostles, St. John is always, in Western Art, young, or in the prime of life ; with little or no beard ; flowing or curling hair, generally of a pale brown or golden hue, to express the delicacy of his nature ; and in his countenance an expression of benignity and candour.   His drapery is, or ought to be, red, with a blue or green tunic. He bears in his hand the sacramental cup, from which a serpent is seen to issue.   St. Isidore relates that, at Rome, an attempt was made to poison St. John in the cup of the sacrament; he drank of the same, and administered it to the communicants without injury, the poison having by a miracle issued from the cup in the form of a serpent, while the hired assassin fell down dead at his feet.   According to another version of this story, the poisoned cup was administered by order of the Emperor Domitian.   According to a third version, Aristodemus, the high priest of Diana, at Ephesus, defied him to drink of the poisoned chalice, as a test of the truth of his mission ; St. John drank unharmed,—the priest fell dead.   Others say, and this seems the more probable interpretation, that the cup in the hand of St. John alludes to the reply given by our Saviour, when the mother

60   St. John.   (Hans Hemling.)

of James and John requested for her sons the place of honour in heaven,—' Ye shall drink indeed of my cup.'   As in other instances, the legend was invented to explain the symbol.   When the cup has the consecrated wafer instead of the serpent, it signifies the institution of the Eucharist.

Some of the old German representations of St. John are of singular beauty : for example, one by *Hans Hemling*, one by *Isaac von Melem*,[1] standing figures ; simple, graceful, majestic ; in the prime of youth,

[1] Both among the fine lithographs of the Boisserée Gallery. (*v*. Nos. 5, 15, 25.)

with a charming expression of devotion in the heads: both hold the sacramental cup with the serpent; no eagle; therefore St. John is here to be considered as the apostle only; when, with the cup, the eagle is placed by his side, he is represented in the double character of apostle and evangelist (61).

In the early Siena school, and in some old illuminations, I have seen St. John carrying in his hand a radiant circle, inscribed ' *In primo est verbum*,' and within the circle an eagle with outspread wings: but this is uncommon.

3. St. John as the prophet, the writer of the Revelation, is usually an aged man, with a white flowing beard, seated in a rocky desert; the sea in the distance, or flowing round him, to represent the island of Patmos; the eagle at his side. In the old frescoes, and the illuminated MSS. of the Apocalypse, this is the usual representation.

61   St. John. (Raphael.)

Some examples of the ideal and devotional figures of St. John, as evangelist and prophet, will give an idea of the variety of treatment in this favourite subject:—

1. Ancient Greek. St. John, with the head of an eagle and large wings, the figure fully draped, is soaring upwards. In such representations the inscription is usually ' *Quasi aquila ascendet et avolabit* ' (' Behold, he shall come up and fly as the eagle.' Jer. xlix. 22).

2. Perugino. St. John as an aged man, with long grey beard and flowing hair, attended by a black eagle, looking up at the Madonna in glory.[1]

3. Raphael (?). St. John, young and beautiful, mounted on the back of an eagle, and soaring heavenwards; in one hand he holds a

[1] Acad. Bologna.

tablet, in the other a pen ; sea and land below. This treatment, which recalls the antique Jupiter bestriding his eagle, appears to me at once too theatrical and too commonplace for Raphael.[1]

62   St John.

4. Correggio. St. John seated writing his Gospel; the eagle at his feet is pluming his wing; inscribed '*Altius cæteris Dei patefecit arcana*.' One of the series of Evangelists in the Duomo of Parma—wonderfully beautiful.

5. Domenichino. St. John, fulllength, life size; young and beautiful, in an ecstacy of inspiration, and sustained by two angels; the eagle at his feet: formerly in the Giustiniani Gallery;[2]—finer, I think, than the St. John in Sant' Andrea. Another, half length, a scroll in his hand, looking upwards as one to whom the glory of the heavens had been opened;—you see it reflected in his eyes,—while love, wonder, devotion, beam from his beautiful face and parted lips; behind him hovers the attendant eagle, holding the pen in his beak; near him is the chalice, with the serpent; so that here he is in his double character of apostle and evangelist.[3] Domenichino excelled in St. Johns, as Guido in Magdalenes; perhaps the most beautiful of all is that in the Brera, at Milan, where St. John bends on one knee at the foot of the throne of the Madonna and Child, his pen in one hand, the other pressed to his bosom, and looking up to them with an air of ecstatic inspiration. Two little angels, or rather *amoretti*, are in attendance : one has his arms round the neck of the eagle, sporting with it; the other holds up the cup and the serpent. Every detail is composed and painted to admiration ; but this is the artistic and picturesque, not the religious, version of the subject.

St. John is frequently represented with St. Peter, because, after the ascension, they taught and acted in concert. In such pictures, the

---

[1] Musée, Marseilles.   [2] Leigh Court, Gal. of Mr Miles.
[3] Petersburg, Gal. of Prince Narishken. Eng. by Müller.

contrast between the fiery resolve and sturdy, rugged grandeur which
is given to St. Peter, and the refinement, mildness, and personal grace
of St. John, produces a fine effect: as in Albert Dürer's picture,[1]
where John is holding open the Gospel, and Peter apparently reading
it ; two grand and simple figures, filling the mind as we gaze upon
them.   As this picture was painted *after* Albert Dürer became a Protestant, I have thought it possible that he might have had some
particular meaning in thus making Peter study the Gospel of John.
At all events, Albert Dürer was quite capable of such an intention ;
and, whether intended or not, the picture may be, and has been, thus
interpreted.   The prophets and the poets often say more than they
intended, for their light was for others more than for themselves : so
also the great painters—the Raphaels and Albert Dürers—prophets
and poets in their way.   When I have heard certain critics ridiculed
because they found more in the productions of a Shakespeare or a
Raphael than the poet or painter himself ever perceived or ' intended,'
such ridicule has appeared to me in the highest degree presumptuous
and absurd.   The true artist ' feels that he is greater than he knows.'
In giving form or utterance to the soul within him, does he account
to himself for all the world of thoughts his work will excite in the
minds of others?   Is its significance to be circumscribed either by
the intention and the knowledge of the poet, or the comprehension
of the age in which he lived?   That is the characteristic of the
second-rate, self-conscious poets or painters, whom we read or study
because they reflect to us a particular meaning—a particular period,
—but not of the Homers and Shakespeares, the Raphaels and Albert
Dürers; *they* speak to all times, to *all* men, with a suggestive
significance, widening, deepening with every successive generation ;
and to measure their depth of meaning by their own *intention*, or by
the comprehension of their own or any one generation, what is it
but to measure the star of heaven by its apparent magnitude ?—an
inch rule will do that !

But to return from this digression.   In devotional pictures we
often see St. John the Evangelist and St. John the Baptist standing
together ; or on each side of Christ, or of the Madonna and Child.

[1] Munich Gal.

There is a peculiar propriety and significance in this companionship : both are, then, to be considered as prophets; they were, besides, kinsmen, and bore the same name ; and St. John the Evangelist was the disciple of John the Baptist before he was called by Christ. Here, again, the contrast between the dark, emaciated, hairy prophet of the wilderness, and the graceful dignity of the youthful apostle, has a striking effect. An example at hand is the bronze bas-relief on the tomb of Henry VII.[1] Madonna pictures, in which the two St. Johns stand before her throne, occur frequently. I remember, also, a marble group of the Virgin and Child, in which the two St. Johns, as infants, are playing at her feet, one with his eagle, the other with his reed cross.[2]

As one who bore the most direct testimony to the Incarnation, St. John is often introduced into Madonna pictures and pictures of the Nativity ; but in the later schools only. In these instances he points significantly to the Child, and the sacramental cup and wafer is either in his hand or at his feet, or borne by an angel.

The historical and dramatic subjects in which St. John figures as a principal personage are very numerous. As the scriptural scenes belong properly to the life of Christ, I shall confine myself here to some observations on the manner in which St. John is introduced and treated in such pictures. In general he is to be distinguished from the other apostles by his youth and beauty and flowing hair, and by being placed nearest to Christ as the most beloved of His disciples.

'The mother of James and John imploring from our Saviour the highest place in heaven for her two sons.' (Matt. xx. 21): a picture by Bonifazio, in the Borghese Gallery, beautiful both in sentiment and colour. There is another example by Paul Veronese; and another, by Tintoretto, was in the Coesvelt Gallery. I must observe that, except in Venetian pictures, I have not met with this incident as a separate subject.

In the Last Supper, Peter is generally on the right of Christ, and St. John on the left : he leans his head down on the bosom of Christ

[1] Westmin. Abbey.   [2] Rome, S. Maria-sopra-Minerva.

(this is always the attitude in the oldest pictures); or he leans towards Christ, who places His hand upon his shoulder, drawing him towards Him with an expression of tenderness: this is the action in the fresco by Raphael lately discovered at Florence. But I must reserve the full consideration of this subject for another place.

Where, instead of the Last Supper, our Saviour is represented as administering the Eucharist, St. John is seen on His right hand, bearing the cup.

In the Crucifixion, when treated as a religious rather than an historical subject, St. John stands on the left of the Cross, and the Virgin on the right; both in attitudes of the profoundest grief and adoration mingled. In general the *motif* of this sacred subject does not vary; but I remember examples, in which St. John is seen trampling a Jew under his feet; on the other side the Virgin tramples on a veiled woman, signifying the old law, the synagogue, as opposed to the Christian Church, of which the Virgin was the received symbol.

When the Crucifixion is a *scene* or action, not a *mystery*, then St. John is beheld afar off, with the women who followed their divine Master to Calvary.

St. John and the Virgin Mary returning from the Crucifixion: he appears to be sustaining her slow and fainting steps. I have only once met with this beautiful subject, in a picture by Zurbaran, in the Munich Gallery.

In the Descent from the Cross, St. John is a chief actor; he generally sustains the head of the Saviour, and is distinguished by an expression of extreme sorrow and tenderness. In the Entombment he is sometimes one of the bearers, sometimes he follows lamenting. In a print of the Entombment after Andrea Mantegna, he is not only weeping and wringing his hands as usual, but absolutely crying aloud with the most exaggerated expression of anguish. In pictures of the Descent of the Holy Ghost, St. John is usually a conspicuous figure, and in the foreground. In the Assumption of the Virgin, he is also conspicuous, generally in front, as the pendant to St. Peter, and gazing upwards with ecstatic faith and devotion.

Of course there is great variety in these representations: the later painters thought less of individual character and significant propriety of arrangement than of artistic grouping; therefore the above re-marks have reference to the early painters only.

In the scenes taken from the Acts, St. John is always in com-panionship with St. Peter, and becomes the secondary figure.

St. John writing his Revelation in the island of Patmos is a subject which frequently occurs in MSS. of the Apocalypse, and in the chapels dedicated to St. John. The *motif* is generally the same in all; we have a desert island, with the sea in the distance, or flowing round it; St. John, seated on a rock or under a tree, is in the act of writing; or he is looking up to heaven, where the 'Woman crowned with stars,' or 'the Woman fleeing from the dra-gon,' appears as in his vision.[1] (Rev. xii.) Or he beholds St. Michael, armed, cast down the dragon in human form; he has the eagle and book, and looks up at the Virgin as in a picture by Ambrogio Figino.[2] The eagle is always in attendance as the symbol of inspiration in a general sense; when represented

63   St. John.   (Lucas v Leyden.)

with a diadem, or glory, as in some very early examples, it is a symbol of the Holy Ghost, which, among the Jews, was figured by the eagle.

The subjects from the legendary life of St. John are exceedingly interesting, but they are not easily recognised, and require particular attention; some are of frequent occurrence, others rarely met with.

1. Israel v. Meckenen. St. John Instructing his Disciples at Ephesus. (Acts iv. 37.) The scene is the interior of a Gothic church, the windows painted with heraldic emblazonments; St. John is seated expounding the Scriptures, and five disciples sit opposite to him with coarse ugly faces, but most intent, expressive countenances; in the background, a large chest full of money.

[1] *v.* 'Legends of the Madonna.'   [2] Brera, Milan.

2. Vatican, Chr. Mus. St. John drinking from the poisoned chalice; a man falls down dead at his feet, several figures look on with awe and astonishment: this is a frequent subject in the elder schools of Art, and in the illuminated MSS. of the Gospel and Apocalypse: but I have never met with a representation later than the beginning of the fourteenth century.[1]

3. It is related by Clement of Alexandria, that when St. John was at Ephesus, and before he was exiled to Patmos, he had taken to his care a young man of promising qualities of person and mind. During his absence he left him under the spiritual guidance of a certain bishop; but, after a while, the youth took to evil courses, and, proceeding from one excess to another, he at length became the leader of a band of robbers and assassins who struck terror into the whole country. When St. John returned to Ephesus, he went to the bishop and demanded ' the precious deposit he had left in his hands.' At first the priest did not understand him; but when St. John explained the allusion to his adopted son, he cast down his eyes with sorrow and shame, and told of what had befallen. Then St. John rent his garments, and wept with a loud voice, and cried out, ' Alas! alas! to what a guardian have I trusted our brother!' And he called for a horse and rode towards the forest in which the robbers sojourned; and when the captain of the robbers beheld his old master and instructor, he turned and would have fled from his presence; but St. John, by the most fervent entreaties, prevailed on him to stop and listen to his words. After some conference, the robber, utterly subdued, burst into tears of penitence, imploring forgiveness; and while he spoke, he hid beneath his robe his right hand, which had been sullied with so many crimes; but St. John, falling on his knees before him, seized that blood-polluted hand, and kissed it, and bathed it with his tears; and he remained with his re-converted brother till he had, by prayers and encouraging words and affectionate exhortations, reconciled him with Heaven and with himself.

This beautiful legend is the subject of some old engravings, in which

---

[1] We find among the relics exhibited on great occasions in the church of the S. Croce at Rome 'the cup in which St. John, the apostle and evangelist, by command of Domitian the emperor, drank poison without receiving any injury; which afterwards being tasted by his attendants, on the instant they fell dead.'

St. John is represented embracing the robber, who is weeping on his neck, having flung away his weapons. It has been, however, too rarely treated; I have never met with a picture of the subject; and yet it abounds in picturesque capabilities: the forest background—the contrast of youth and age—bright armour, flowing drapery, and the most striking and affecting moral, are here all combined.

4. Another very pretty apologue relating to St. John is sometimes included in a series of subjects from his life. Two young men, who had sold all their possessions to follow him, afterwards repented. He, perceiving their thoughts, sent them to gather pebbles and faggots, and, on their return, changed these into money and ingots of gold, saying to them, 'Take back your riches and enjoy them on earth, as you regret having exchanged them for heaven!' This story is represented on one of the windows of the Cathedral at Bourges. The two young men stand before St. John, with a heap of gold on one side, and a heap of stones and faggots on the other.

5. When St. John had sojourned in the island of Patmos a year and a day, he returned to his church at Ephesus; and as he approached the city, being received with great joy by the inhabitants, lo! a funeral procession came forth from the gates; and of those who followed weeping he inquired 'who was dead?' They said, 'Drusiana.' Now when he heard that name he was sad, for Drusiana had excelled in all good works, and he had formerly dwelt in her house; and he ordered them to set down the bier, and having prayed earnestly, God was pleased to restore Drusiana to life; she arose up, and the apostle went home with her and dwelt in her house.

This incident is the subject of a fine fresco, painted by Filippo Lippi, on the left hand wall of the Strozzi Chapel at Florence. It has the forcible expression and dramatic spirit of the painter, with that characteristic want of elevated feeling in the countenances and in the general treatment which is apparent in all his works: the group in one corner, of a child starting from a dog, is admired for its truth; but, by disturbing the solemnity of the marvellous scene, it repels like a falsehood.

6. There is another beautiful and picturesque legend relating to St. John, of which I have never seen any representation; but it may possibly have occasioned the frequent introduction of a partridge

into the pictures of sacred subjects, particularly in the Venetian
School. St. John had a tame partridge, which he cherished much;
and he amused himself with feeding and tending it. 'A certain
huntsman, passing by with his bow and arrows, was astonished
to see the great apostle, so venerable for his age and sanctity,
engaged in such an amusement. The apostle asked him if he always
kept his bow bent? He answered, that would be the way to render
it useless. "If," replied St. John, "you unbend your bow to prevent its being useless, so do I thus unbend my mind for the same
reason."'

7. The subject entitled the Martyrdom of St. John represents his
immersion in a caldron of boiling oil, by order of the Emperor
Domitian. According to the received tradition, this event took place
outside the Latin gate at Rome; and on the spot stands the chapel of
San Giovanni *in Olio*, commemorating his miraculous deliverance,
which is painted in fresco on the walls. The subject forms, of course,
one of a series of the life of St. John, and is occasionally met with in
old prints and pictures; but it is uncommon. The treatment affords
little variety; in Albert Dürer's famous woodcut, St. John is sitting
in a pot of boiling oil; one executioner is blowing the fire, another
is pouring oil from a ladle on the saint's head; a judge, probably
intended for Domitian, is seated on a throne to the left, and there
are numerous spectators. Padovanino painted this subject for the
San Pietro at Venice; Rubens, with horrible truth of detail, for the
altar-piece of St. John at Malines.

It is the martyrdom in the boiling oil which gives St. John the
right to bear the palm, with which he is occasionally seen.

8. St. John, habited in priest's garments, descends the steps of an
altar into an open grave, in which he lays himself down, not in death,
but in sleep, until the coming of Christ: 'being reserved alive with
Enoch and Elijah (who also knew not death), to preach against the
Antichrist in the last days.' This fanciful legend is founded on the
following text: 'Peter, seeing the disciple whom Jesus loved following, saith unto Jesus, Lord, and what shall this man do? Jesus
saith unto him, If I will that he tarry till I come, what is that to
thee? Then went this saying abroad among the brethren that that
disciple should not die' (John xxi. 21, 22.)

The legend which supposes St. John reserved alive has not been generally received in the Church, and as a subject of painting it is very uncommon. It occurs in the Menologium Græcum,[1] where the grave into which St. John descends is, according to the legend, '*fossa in crucis figuram*' (in the form of a cross). In a series of the deaths of the Apostles,[2] St. John is ascending from the grave; for, according to the Greek legend, St. John died without pain or change, and immediately rose again in bodily form, and ascended into heaven to rejoin Christ and the Virgin.

In a small and very curious picture which I saw at Rome,[3] forming part of a Predella, there is a tomb something like the Xanthian tombs in form; one end is open; St. John, with a long grey beard, is seen issuing from it, and, as he ascends, he is met by Christ, the Virgin, St. Peter, and St. Paul, who are descending from above; while figures below look up with astonishment. On the ancient doors of San Paolo he is lying in an open grave or sarcophagus.

Of the miracles performed by John after his death, two are singularly interesting in the history of Art; both have been treated in sculpture.

9. When the Empress Galla Placidia was returning from Constantinople to Ravenna with her two children (A.D. 425), she encountered a terrible storm. In her fear and anguish she vowed a vow to St. John the Evangelist, and, being landed in safety, she dedicated to his honour a magnificent church. When the edifice was finished, she was extremely desirous of procuring some relics of the Evangelist, wherewith to consecrate his sanctuary; but as it was not the manner of those days to exhume, and buy and sell, still less to steal, the bodies of holy men and martyrs, the desire of the pious empress remained unsatisfied. However, as it is related, St. John himself took pity upon her; for one night, as she prayed earnestly, he appeared to her in a vision; and when she threw herself at his feet to embrace and kiss them, he disappeared, leaving one of his slippers or sandals in her hand, which sandal was long preserved.

The antique church of Galla Placidia still exists at Ravenna, to

---

[1] Vatican MSS., tenth century.   [2] MSS., ninth century.   Paris Nat. Library.
[3] Vatican, Christian Museum.

keep alive, after the lapse of fourteen centuries, the memory of her
dream, and of the condescension of the blessed apostle. Not much
of the original building is left; the superb mosaics have all disappeared, except a few fragments, in which may be traced the storm
at sea, and Galla Placidia making her vow. Over the principal
porch, which is of white marble, in the Lombard style, and richly
and elegantly ornamented, the miracle of the slipper is represented
in two bas-reliefs, one above the other. The lower compartment,
or lunette, represents a tabernacle, and within it an altar; St. John
the Evangelist is seen offering incense; on the other side is Barbation, the confessor of the empress; she, prostrate at the feet of the
apostle, seems to take off his sandal : on each side are six hovering
angels bearing the implements of the mass. In the upper compartment, Galla Placidia is seen kneeling at the feet of Christ, and
offering to him the sacred sandal, while the Evangelist stands on
one side, and Barbation on the other. These bas-reliefs are not
older than the twelfth century, and are in excellent preservation :
I should suppose, from the style of the grouping, that they were
copied, or imitated, from the older mosaics, once in the interior of
the church.

10. The other miracle has the rare interest of being English in its
origin and in its representation. 'King Edward the Confessor had,
after Christ and the Virgin Mary, a special veneration for St. John
the Evangelist. One day, returning from his church at Westminster, where he had been hearing mass in honour of the evangelist,
he was accosted by a pilgrim, who asked of him an alms for the love
of God and St. John. The king, who was ever merciful to the poor,
immediately drew from his finger a ring, and, unknown to any one,
delivered it to the beggar. When the king had reigned twenty-four
years, it came to pass that two Englishmen, pilgrims, returning from
the Holy Land to their own country, were met by one in the habit
of a pilgrim, who asked of them concerning their country; and being
told they were of England, he said to them, " When ye shall have
arrived in your own country, go to King Edward, and salute him in
my name : say to him, that I thank him for the alms which he
bestowed on me in a certain street in Westminster; for there, on a
certain day, as I begged of him an alms, he bestowed on me this

ring, which till now I have preserved, and ye shall carry it back to him, saying that in six months from this time he shall quit the world, and come and remain with me for ever." And the pilgrims, being astounded, said, " Who art thou, and where is thy dwelling-place ? " And he answered, saying, " I am John the Evangelist. Edward, your king, is my friend, and for the sanctity of his life I hold him dear. Go now, therefore, deliver to him this message and this ring, and I will pray to God that ye may arrive safely in your own country." When St. John had spoken thus he delivered to them the ring, and vanished out of their sight. The pilgrims, praising and thanking the Lord for this glorious vision, went on their journey; and being arrived in England, they repaired to King Edward, and saluted him, and delivered the ring and the message, relating all truly. And the king received the news joyfully, and feasted the messengers royally. Then he set himself to prepare for his departure from this world. On the eve of the Nativity, in the year of our Lord 1066, he fell sick, and on the eve of the Epiphany following he died. The ring he gave to the Abbot of Westminster, to be for ever preserved among the relics there.'[1]

According to one account,[2] the pilgrims met the king near his palace at Waltham, at a place since called *Havering*. The writer adds,—' In allusion to this story, King Edward II. offered at his coronation a pound of gold made in the figure of a king holding a ring, and a mark of gold (8 oz.) made like to a pilgrim putting forth his hand to receive the ring.' These must have been two little statuettes of gold.

The legend of King Edward and St. John the Evangelist is represented, with other legends of the same monarch, along the top of the screen of Edward the Confessor's chapel. It is in three compartments. The first represents King Edward bestowing the ring on St. John in the disguise of a pilgrim; Westminster Abbey is seen behind. The second shows us the meeting of the pilgrims and St. John in Palestine; he holds what seems a palm. In the third the pilgrims deliver the ring to King Edward, who is seated at table. The sculpture is very rude; the figures disproportioned and ungraceful. They are supposed to be of the time of Henry VI.

[1] Johannis Brompton Cronicon, 955.   [2] Dart's Hist. of Westminster.

The same legend was painted on one of the windows of Romford church, in Essex, but whether it still exists there I know not.[1]

Before I quit the subject of the Evangelists, it is worth while to observe that, in Greek Art, not only the Four Evangelists, but the six writers of the Acts and Epistles, are considered as a sacred series. In an ancient and beautiful MS. of the *Epistole Canoniche*, presented by the Queen of Cyprus to Pope Innocent VIII., they are thus represented, two and two together :—

St. Luke, with a very thoughtful, earnest countenance, holds a scroll, on which is written in Greek the commencement of the Acts, ' The former treatise have I made, O Theophilus,' &c.; and St. James, with a long, very earnest, and refined face, holds a single roll.

St. Peter, with a broad, coarse, powerful physiognomy, strongly characterised, holds two rolls ; and St. John, with a long, and very refined face, grey hair and beard, holds three rolls.

St. Jude, with a long white beard and very aquiline nose, holds one roll. St. Paul, bald in front, with long brown hair and beard, and a refined face, bears many rolls tied up together.

All the figures are on a gold ground, about six inches in height, very finely conceived, though, as is usual in Byzantine Art, formal and mechanical in execution. They look like small copies of very grand originals. The draperies are all classical ; a pale violet or brown tunic and a white mantle, as in the old mosaics ; the rolls in their hands corresponding with the number of their writings.

[1] *v.* Legend of St. Edward the Confessor in the 'Legends of the Monastic Orders,' p. 99.

The Twelve Apostles.

NEXT to those who recorded the Word of God, were those called by Christ to the task of diffusing His doctrine, and sent to preach the kingdom of heaven 'through all nations.'

The earliest representations of the Twelve Apostles appear to have been, like those of the Four Evangelists, purely emblematical: they were figured as twelve sheep, with Christ in the midst, as the Good Shepherd, bearing a lamb in His arms; or, much more frequently, Christ is Himself the Lamb of God, raised on an eminence and crowned with a cruciform nimbus, and the apostles were ranged on each side as sheep. Instances are to be met with in the old Christian bas-reliefs. In the old Roman churches[1] we find this representation but little varied, and the situation is always the same. In

64

the centre is the lamb standing on an eminence, from which flow the four rivers of Paradise; on one side six sheep issuing from the city of Jerusalem, on the other six sheep issuing from the city of Bethlehem, the whole disposed in a line forming a sort of frieze, just below the decoration of the vault of the apsis. The church of S. M. Maggiore exhibits the only exception I have met with; there we find a group of sheep, entering, not issuing from, the gates of Jerusalem and Bethlehem: in this case, however, the sheep may represent believers, or disciples in general, not the Twelve Apostles. Upon the great crucifix in the apsis of San Clemente, at Rome, are twelve doves, which appear to signify the Twelve Apostles.

The next step was to represent the Apostles as twelve men all alike, each with a sheep, and Christ in the middle, also with a sheep,

1 Rome. S. M. in Trastevere. S. Prassede. S. Clemente. S. Cecilia.

sometimes larger than the others. We find this on some of the sarcophagi.[1] Again, a little later, we have them represented as twelve venerable men, bearing tablets or scrolls in their hands, no emblems to distinguish one from another, but their names inscribed over or beside each. They are thus represented in relief on several ancient sarcophagi now in the Christian Museum in the Vatican, and in several of the most ancient churches at Rome and Ravenna, ranged on each side of the Saviour in the vault of the apsis, or standing in a line beneath.

But while in the ancient Greek types, and the old mosaics, the attributes are omitted, they adhere almost invariably to a certain characteristic individual representation, which in the later ages of painting was wholly lost, or at least neglected. In these eldest types, St. Peter has a broad face, white hair, and short white beard : St. Paul, a long face, high bold forehead, dark hair and beard : St. Andrew is aged, with flowing white hair and beard : St. John, St. Thomas, St. Philip, young and beardless : St. James Major and St. James Minor, in the prime of life, short brown hair and beard ; both should bear a resemblance more or less to the Saviour, but St. James Minor particularly : St. Matthew, St. Jude, St. Simon, St. Matthias, aged, with white hair. The tablets or scrolls which they carry in their hands bear, or are supposed to bear, the articles of the Creed. It is a tradition, that, before the apostles dispersed to preach the Gospel in all lands, they assembled to compose the declaration of faith since called the Apostles' Creed, and that each of them furnished one of the twelve propositions contained in it, in the following order:—St. Peter : *Credo in Deum Patrem omnipotentem, creatorem cœli et terræ.* St. Andrew : *Et in Jesum Christum Filium ejus unicum, Dominum nostrum.* St. James Major : *Qui conceptus est de Spiritu Sancto, natus ex Maria Virgine.* St. John : *Passus sub Pontio Pilato, crucifixus, mortuus et sepultus.* St. Philip : *Descendit ad inferos, tertia die resurrexit à mortuis.* St. James Minor : *Ascendit ad cœlos, sedet ad dexteram Dei Patris omnipotentis.* St. Thomas : *Inde venturus est judicare vivos et mortuos.* St. Bartholomew : *Credo in Spiritum Sanctum.* St. Matthew : *Sanctam Ecclesiam Catholicam ; sanctorum communionem.*

[1] Bottari, Tab. xxviii.

St. Simon : *Remissionem peccatorum.*   St. Matthias : *Carnis resur-rectionem.*   St. Thaddeus : *Et vitam æternam.*

The statues of the apostles on the shrine of the Virgin in the San Michele at Florence exhibit a fine example of this arrangement.   I give the figure of St. Philip, holding his appropriate sentence of the Creed on a scroll (65).

In later times, the Apostles, instead of being disposed in a line, are grouped round the Saviour in glory, or they form a circle of heads in medallions : as statues, they ornament the screen in front of the altar, or they are placed in a line on each side of the nave, standing against the pillars which support it.   From the sixth century it became usual to distinguish each of them by a particular emblem or attribute borrowed from some circumstance of his life or death.   Thus, taking them in order, according to the canon of the mass—

St. Peter bears the keys or a fish.

St. Paul, the sword : sometimes two swords.

St. Andrew, the transverse cross.

St. James Major, the pilgrim's staff.

St. John, the chalice with the serpent; sometimes the eagle also ; but the eagle, as I have observed, belongs to him properly only in his character of Evangelist.

65   Orcagna

St. Thomas, a builder's rule : also, but more seldom, a spear.

St. James Minor, a club.

St. Philip, the staff or crosier, surmounted by a cross ; or a small cross in his hand.

St. Bartholomew, a large knife.

St. Matthew, a purse.

St. Simon, a saw.

St. Thaddeus (or Jude), a halberd or lance.

St. Matthias, a lance.

The origin and meaning of these attributes will be explained presently : meantime it must be borne in mind, that although in sacred Art the Apostles are always twelve in number, they are not always the same personages. St. Jude is frequently omitted to make room for St. Paul. Sometimes, in the most ancient churches (as in the Cathedral of Palermo), St. Simon and St. Matthias are omitted, and the evangelists St. Mark and St. Luke figure in their places. The Byzantine manual published by Didron omits James Minor, Jude, and Matthias ; and inserts Paul, Luke, and Mark. This was the arrangement on the bronze doors of San Paolo-fuori-le-Mura at Rome, executed by Byzantine artists in the tenth century, and now destroyed.

On an ancient pulpit, of beautiful workmanship, in the Cathedral of Troyes, the arrangement is according to the Greek formula.[1] Thus—

S. John B.	S. Matthew.	S. Philip.	S. Mark.	S. Paul.	J. Christ.	S. Peter.	S. Luke.	S. Andrew.	S. Thomas.	The Virgin.	S. Simon.	S. Bartholomew.	S. James.	S. John.	An Angel.

Here, John the Baptist figures in his character of angel or messenger; and St. Paul, St. Mark, and St. Luke take the place of St. James Minor, St. Jude, and St. Matthias.

The earliest instance of the Apostles entering into a scheme of ecclesiastical decoration, as the consecrated and delegated teachers of a revealed religion, occurs in the church of San Giovanni in Fonte at Ravenna.[2] In the centre of the dome is the Baptism of Christ, represented quite in the classical style ; the figure of the Saviour being entirely undraped, and the Jordan, signified by an antique river god, sedge-crowned, and bearing a linen napkin as though he were an attendant at a bath. Around, in a circle, in the manner of radii, are the Twelve Apostles. The order is,—Peter, Andrew, James, John, Philip, Bartholomew, Simon, Jude, James Minor, Matthew, Thomas, Paul; so that Peter and Paul stand face to face at one extremity of

[1] The churches in the eastern provinces of France, particularly in Champagne, exhibit marked traces of the influence of Greek Art in the eleventh and twelfth centuries.

[2] A.D 451.   Ciampini, Vet. Mon. p. 1, c. iv.

the circle, and Simon and Bartholomew back to back at the other. All wear pointed caps, and carry the oblation in their hands. Peter has a yellow vest and white mantle; Paul, a white vest and a yellow mantle, and so all around alternately. The name of each is inscribed over his head, and without the title *Sanctus*, which, though admitted into the Calendar in 449, was not adopted in works of Art till some years later, about 472.

In the next instance, the attributes had not yet been admitted, except in the figures of St. Peter and St. Paul.

MOSAIC (A.D. 816). Christ, in the centre, stands on an eminence; in one hand He holds an open book, on which is inscribed *Pax vobis*. St. Peter, with the keys and a cross, stands on the right; and Christ, with His right hand, points to the cross. St. Paul is on the left, with his sword; beyond, there are five Apostles on one side, and four on the other: in all, eleven (Judas being properly omitted). Each holds a book, and all are robed in white; underneath the whole is inscribed, in Latin, the words of our Saviour, ' Go ye, and teach all nations.' On the arch to the right, Christ is seated on a throne, and presents the keys to St. Peter, who kneels on one side, and the standard to Constantine, who kneels on the other (alluding, of course, to the famous standard). On the arch to the left, St. Peter is throned, and presents the stole to Pope Leo III., and the standard to Charlemagne. This singular monument, a kind of *résumé* of the power of the Church, is a restoration of the old mosaic, executed by order of Leo III. in the Triclinium of the old palace of the Lateran, and now on one side of the Scala Santa, the side facing the Porta San Giovanni.

MOSAIC, in the old basilica of St. Paul (A.D. 1206). In the centre an altar veiled, on which are the Gospels (or perhaps, rather, the *Book of Life*, the seven-sealed book in the Revelations), and the instruments of the Passion. Behind it rises a large Greek cross, adorned with gold and jewels. Underneath, at the foot of the altar, five small figures standing and bearing palms, representing those who suffered for the cause of Christ; and on each side, kneeling, the monk Aginulph, and Giovanni Gaetano Orsini, afterwards Nicholas III. On each side of the altar, a majestic angel: one bears a scroll, inscribed GLORIA IN EXCELSIS DEO; the other, ET IN TERRA PAX

HOMINIBUS BONÆ VOLUNTATIS. Beyond these the Apostles, six on each
side, bearing scrolls with the articles of the Creed. They are much
alike, all in white robes, and alternately with each stands a palm-
tree, the symbol of victory and resurrection. This composition, of a
colossal size, formed a kind of frieze (taking the place of the emblematical lamb and twelve sheep) round the apsis of the Basilica.

In sculpture, the Apostles, as a series, entered into all decorative
ecclesiastical architecture : sometimes on the exterior of the edifice,
always in the interior. In our English cathedrals they are seldom
found unmutilated, except when out of the reach of the spoiler; such
was the indiscriminate rage which confounded the venerable effigies
of these delegated teachers of the truth with the images which were
supposed to belong exclusively to the repudiated religion !
Where the scheme of decoration is purely theological, the proper
place of the Apostles is after the Angels, Prophets, and Evangelists ;
but when the *motif,* or leading idea, implies a special signification,
such as the Last Judgment, Paradise, the Coronation of the Madonna,
or the apotheosis of a saint, then the order is changed, and the
Apostles appear immediately after the Divine Personages and before
the angels, as forming a part of the council or court of heaven ;
—' When the Son of man shall come in His glory, ye also shall sit
on twelve thrones, judging the twelve tribes of Israel.' [1] Such is the
arrangement in the Campo Santo, in Angelico's ' Paradiso ' in the
Florence Gallery, in Raphael's ' Disputa,' and many other instances:
and I may add the architectural treatment on the façade of Wells
Cathedral, where, immediately under the Saviour sitting in judgment,
stand the Twelve Apostles, and beneath them the hierarchy of angels,
each of the nine choirs being here expressed by a single angel. [2]
Therefore to determine the proper place of the Apostles, it is necessary to observe well and to understand what has been the design
of the artist, and the leading idea of the whole composition, whether
strictly *theological* or partly *scenic.* In all monuments which have
a solemn or a sacred purpose,—altars, pulpits, tombs,—the Apostles

[1] Matt. xix. 28; and Luke xxii. 30.
[2] I must refer the reader to Mr Cockerell's illustrations and restorations of the rich and
multifarious and significant sculpture of Wells Cathedral.

find an appropriate place, either in connection with other sacred personages, or as a company apart,—the band of teachers. The range of statues along the top of the screen in front of the choir of St. Mark's at Venice will be remembered by all who have seen them : in the centre stand the Virgin and St. Mark, and then the Apostles, six on each side, grand solemn figures, standing there as if to guard the sanctuary. These are by Jacobelli, in the simple religious style of the fifteenth century, but quite Italian. In contrast with them, as the finest example of German sculptural treatment, we have the Twelve Apostles on the tomb of St. Sebald, in his church at Nuremburg, cast in bronze by Peter Vischer (about 1500). These have become well known by the casts which have lately been brought to England ; they are about two feet high, all remarkable for the characteristic expression of the heads, and the grand simplicity of the attitudes and draperies.

There are instances of the Apostles introduced into a scheme of ecclesiastical decoration as devotional figures, but assuming, from the style of treatment and from being placed in relation with other personages, a touch of the dramatic and picturesque. Such are Correggio's Apostles in the cupola of the duomo at Parma (1532), which may be considered as the most striking instance that could be produced of studied contrast to the solemnity and simplicity of the ancient treatment : here the *motif* is essentially *dramatic*. They stand round the dome as spectators would stand in a gallery or balcony, all in picturesque attitudes, studiously varied (some, it must be confessed, rather extravagant), and all looking up with amazement, or hope, or joy, or adoration, to the figure of the glorified Virgin ascending into heaven.

Another series of Apostles in the San Giovanni at Parma, which Correggio had painted earlier (1522), are conceived, I think, in a finer spirit as to character, but, perhaps, not more appropriate to the scene Here the Twelve Apostles are seated on clouds round the glorified Saviour, as they are supposed to be in heaven : they are but partially draped. In the heads but little attention has been paid to the ancient types, except in those of St. Peter and St. Paul ; but they are sublime as well as picturesque in the conception of character and expression.

The Apostles in Michael Angelo's Last Judgment (A.D. 1540) exhibit a still further deviation from the antique style of treatment. They stand on each side of the Saviour, who is not here Saviour and Redeemer, but inexorable Judge. They are grandly and artificially grouped, all without any drapery whatever, and with forms and attitudes which recall an assemblage of Titans holding a council of war, rather than the glorified companions of Christ. In early pictures of Christ in glory, the Apostles, His companions in heaven as on earth, form, with the Patriarchs and Prophets, the celestial court or council : they sit upon thrones to the right and to the left.[1] Raphael's ' Disputa' in the Vatican is a grand example of this arrangement.

Sets of the Apostles, in devotional pictures and prints, are so common, that I shall particularise only a few among the most interesting and celebrated. Engravings of these can easily be referred to.

1. A set by Raphael, engraved by Marc Antonio : grand, graceful figures, and each with his appropriate attribute. Though admirably distinguished in form and bearing, very little attention has been paid to the ancient types, except perhaps in St. Peter and St. John. Here St. James Minor is omitted to make room for St. Paul.

2. A set by Lucas van Leyden, smaller than Raphael's, but magnificent in feeling : here also the ancient types are for the most part neglected. These two sets should be compared as perfect examples of the best Italian and the most characteristic German manner. Some of the German sets are very curious and grotesque.

3. By H. S. Beham, a most curious set, in what may be called the ultra German style : they stand two and two together, like a procession of old beggars ; the workmanship exquisite. Another set by Beham, in which the figures stand singly, and which includes the Four Evangelists, dressed like old burgomasters, with the emblematical wings, has been already mentioned.

4. A set by Parmigiano, graceful and mannered, as is usual with him.

5. By Agostino Caracci. This set, famous as works of Art, must, when compared with those of Raphael and Lucas van Leyden, be pronounced absolutely vulgar. Here St. John is drinking out of his cup,—an idea which might strike some people as picturesque ; but

[1] Luke xxii. 30.

it is in vile taste. Thaddeus has a saw as well as Simon; Peter has the papal tiara at his feet; St. James Minor, instead of Thomas, carries the builder's rule; and St. Bartholomew has his skin thrown over his shoulders. This set is an example of the confusion which prevailed with respect to the old religious types and attributes, after the first half of the sixteenth century.

6. 'The Five Disciples,' by Albert Dürer, seem intended to form part of a complete set. We have St. Paul, St. Bartholomew, St. Thomas, St. Philip, and St. Simon. The two last are the finest, and are most grandly conceived.

These are examples of the simplest devotional treatment.

When the Apostles are grouped together in various historical scenes, —some scriptural, some legendary—they are more interesting as individual personages; and the treatment should be more characteristic. Some of these subjects belong properly to the life of Christ; as the Delivery of the Keys to Peter; the Transfiguration; the Entry into Jerusalem; the Last Supper; the Ascension. Others, as the Death and Assumption of the Virgin, will be considered in the Legends of the Madonna. But there are others, again, which refer more particularly to the personal history of the Apostles, as related in the Acts and in the Legends.

The Descent of the Holy Ghost was the first and most important event after the Ascension of Christ. It is thus described: " When the day of Pentecost was fully come, they were all with one accord in one place. And suddenly there came a sound from heaven, as of a rushing mighty wind, and it filled all the house where they were sitting. And there appeared unto them cloven tongues, like as of fire, and sat upon each of them, and they were all filled with the Holy Ghost, and began to speak with other tongues, as the Spirit gave them utterance. And there were dwelling at Jerusalem Jews, devout men, out of every nation under heaven. Now when this was noised abroad the multitude came together, and were confounded, because that every man heard them speak in his own language. . . . But this is that which was spoken by the prophet Joel.' (Acts ii. 1– 12, 16.)

According to the usual interpretation, the word *they*, in the first verse, does not signify the Apostles merely, but, with them, ' the women, and Mary the mother of Jesus, and His brethren : ' hence in so many representations of this subject the Virgin is not only present, but a principal person : Mary Magdalene and others are also frequently introduced.

1. The most striking example I have yet met with is the grand mosaic in the principal dome of St. Mark's at Venice.   In the apex of the dome is seen the Celestial Dove in a glory of light; rays proceed from the centre on every side, and fall on the heads of the Virgin and the Twelve Apostles, seated in a circle.   Lower down is a series of twelve figures standing all round the dome ; ' Parthians, Medes, and Elamites, the dwellers in Mesopotamia, Judea, Cappadocia, Pontus, Asia, Phrygia, Pamphylia, Cretes, and Arabians,'—each nation represented by one person, and all in strange dresses, and looking up with amazement.

2. The Twelve Apostles and the Virgin are seen above seated in an enclosure ; tongues of fire descend from heaven ; beneath is a closed door, at which several persons in strange foreign dresses, with turbans, &c., are listening with amazement.   One of these is in the Chinese costume,—a curious circumstance, considering the age of the picture, and which could have occurred at that date nowhere but at Venice.[1]

3. In the interior of a temple, sustained by slender pillars, the Twelve Apostles are seated in a circle, and in the midst the Virgin, tongues of fire on each head.   Here the Virgin is the principal person.[2]

4. An interior, the Twelve Apostles seated in a circle ; above them, the Celestial Dove in a glory, and from his beak proceed twelve tongues of flame : underneath, in a small arch, is the prophet Joel, as an old man crowned with a kingly crown and holding twelve rolls or scrolls, indicating the Gospel in so many different languages.   The allusion is to the words of Joel, ii. 28 : ' And I will pour out my Spirit upon all flesh.'[3]   This is the Greek formula, and it is curious that it should have been closely followed by Pinturicchio ;—thus :

5. In a rich landscape, with cypresses, palm-trees, and birds, the Virgin is seen kneeling ; St. Peter on the right, and James Minor on the left, also kneeling ; five other Apostles on each side.   The

---

[1] Venice Acad., fourteenth century.   [2] Rosini, vol. iii. p. 75.
[3] Convent of Chilandari, Mount Athos.

Celestial Dove, with outspread wings, descends in a glory surrounded by fifteen cherubim : there are no tongues of fire. The prophet Joel is seen above, with the inscription, ' *Effundam de Spiritu meo super omnem carnem.*'[1]

6. The Virgin and the Apostles seated; flames of fire stand on their heads; the Holy Ghost appears above in a glory of light, from which rays are poured on every side. Mary Magdalene, and another Mary, are present behind; astonishment is the prevailing expression in every face, except in the Virgin and St. Peter. The composition is attributed to Raphael.[2]

The next event of importance is the separation of the Twelve Apostles when they disperse to preach the Gospel in all lands. According to the ancient traditions, the Apostles determined by lot to what countries they should go: Peter went to Antioch; James the Great remained in Jerusalem and the neighbourhood; Philip went to Phrygia; John to Ephesus; Thomas to Parthia and Judea; Andrew to Scythia; Bartholomew to India and Judea. The Parting of the Apostles is a beautiful subject, of which I have met with but few examples; one is a woodcut after Titian. The Mission of the Apostles I remember to have seen by Bissoni over an altar in the Santa Giustina at Padua; they are preparing to depart; one reads from a book; another looses his shoes from his feet, in allusion to the text, ' Take neither purse, nor scrip, nor shoes;' several are bidding adieu to the Virgin. This picture struck me as dramatic; its merits otherwise I do not remember.

We have next ' The Twelve Baptisms.'[3] In the upper compartment Christ is standing in a majestic attitude, and on each side are six Apostles, all alike, and in white garments. The inscription above is in Greek : ' Go ye, and preach the Gospel to all nations.' Below in twelve smaller compartments, each of the Apostles is seen baptizing a convert: an attendant, in white garments, stands by each font, holding a napkin. One of the converts and his attendant are black, denoting

---

[1] Vatican, Sala del Pozzo.   [2] Vatican.
[3] Greek MS., ninth century. Paris, Bibl. du Roi, No. 510.

clearly the chamberlain of the Queen of Ethiopia. This is a very uncommon subject.

And, lastly, we have 'The Twelve Martyrdoms.' This is a more frequent series, in pictures and in prints, and occurs in a set of large fresco compositions in the church of San Nereo e Sant' Achilleo at Rome. In such representations the usual treatment is as follows :— 1. St. Peter is crucified with his head downwards. 2. St. Andrew, bound on a transverse cross. 3. St. James Major, beheaded with a sword. 4. St. John, in a caldron of boiling oil. 5. St. Philip, bound on a cross in the form of a T. 6. St. Bartholomew, flayed. 7. St. Thomas, pierced with a spear. 8. St. Matthew, killed with a sword. 9. St. James Minor, struck down with a club. 10. St. Simon and St. Jude together : one is killed with a sword, the other with a club. 11. St. Matthias has his head cloven by a halbert. 12. St. Paul is beheaded.[1]

The authority for many of these martyrdoms is wholly apocryphal,[2] and they sometimes vary ; but this is the usual mode of representation in Western Art. In early Greek Art a series of the Deaths of the Apostles often occurs, but they do not all suffer martyrdom ; and the subject of St. John in the caldron of boiling oil, so famous in the Latin Church, is, I believe, unknown, or, at least, so rare, that I have not found it in genuine Byzantine Art.

The most ancient series I have met with (in a Greek MS. of the ninth century) shows us five Apostles crucified : St. Peter and St. Philip with the head downwards ; St. Andrew on the transverse cross, as usual ; St. Simon and St. Bartholomew, in the same manner as our Saviour. St. Thomas is pierced by a lance ; and St. John is buried, and then raised by angels, according to the legend. The same series, similarly treated, ornamented the doors of the old Basilica of St. Paul, executed by Greek artists of the tenth century.[3]

Wherever the Apostles appear as a series, we expect, of course, some

---

[1] A set of martyrdoms is in the Frankfort Museum ; another is mentioned in Bartsch, viii. 22.

[2] Eusebius says that *all* the Apostles suffered martyrdom ; but this is not borne out by any ancient testimony.—*Lardner's Cred. of Gospel Hist.* vol. viii. p. 81.

[3] They were fortunately engraved for D'Agincourt's *Histoire de l'Art*, before they were destroyed by fire.

degree of discriminating propriety of character in each face and figure. We seek it when they merely form a part of the general scheme of significant decoration in the architectural arrangement of a place of worship ; we seek it with more reason when they stand before us as a series of devotional representations ; and still more when, as actors in some particular scene, they are supposed to be animated by sentiments called forth by the occasion, and modified by the individual character. By what test shall we try the truth and propriety of such representations ? We ought to know both what to require from the artist, and on what grounds to require it, before we can rest satisfied.

In the Gospel histories the Apostles are consistently and beautifully distinguished in temper and bearing. Their characters, whether exhibited at full length, or merely touched upon, are sustained with dramatic truth. The mediæval legends, however wild, are, as far as character goes, in harmony with these scriptural portraits, and fill up the outline given. It becomes therefore a really interesting speculation to observe, how far this variety of characteristic expression has been carried out in the early types, how far attended to, or neglected, by the great painters, since the revival of Art.

St. Peter and St. Paul.

Lat. SS. Petrus et Paulus. *Ital.* San Pietro or Piero, San Paolo. *Fr.* S. Pierre, S. Paul. *Spa.* San Pedro, San Pablo. (June 29 and 30.)

I HAVE already observed, that, as apostles and preachers of the Word, St. Peter and St. Paul take the first place. Even during their lives, a superiority was accorded to them ; and this superiority, as the acknowledged heads and founders of the Christian Church, under Christ, has been allowed down to the present time. The precedence is by common consent given to St. Peter; but they are held to be equal in faith, in merit, and in sanctity.

The early Christian Church was always considered under two great divisions : the church of the converted Jews, and the church of the Gentiles. The first was represented by St. Peter, the second by St.

VOL. I. A A

66   St. Paul.   St. Peter.   (Crivelli.)

Paul.   Standing together in this mutual relation, they represent the
universal Church of Christ; hence in works of Art they are seldom
separated, and are indispensable in all ecclesiastical decoration.   Their
proper place is on each side of the Saviour, or of the Virgin throned;
or on each side of the altar; or on each side of the arch over the choir.
In any case, where they stand together, not merely as Apostles, but
Founders, their place is next after the Evangelists and the Prophets.

    Thus seen almost everywhere in companionship, it becomes neces-
sary to distinguish them from each other; for St. Peter does not

always bear his keys, nor St. Paul his sword. In the earliest examples, these attributes are wholly omitted; yet I scarcely know any instance in which a distinct type of head has not been more or less attended to.

ΠΈΤΟϹ·ΟΚΟΡΥΦΔΙΟϹ
ῶΝ ΜΟϛΉ῾ϪΝ

67   St. Peter.
(Greek type, eleventh century.)

The ancient Greek type of the head of St. Peter, 'the Pilot of the Galilean Lake,' is so strongly characterised as to have the air of a portrait. It is either taken from the description of Nicephorus, so often quoted, or his description is taken from some very ancient representation: it certainly harmonises with all our preconceived notions of St. Peter's temperament and character. He is a robust old man, with a broad forehead, and rather coarse features, an open undaunted countenance, short grey hair, and short thick beard, curled, and of a silvery white: according to the descriptive portrait of Nicephorus, he had red weak eyes,—a peculiarity which it has not been thought necessary to preserve in his effigies. In some early pictures he is bald on the top of the head, and the hair grows thick around in a circle, somewhat like the priestly tonsure; and in some examples this tonsure has the form of a triple row of curls close to the head, a kind of tiara. A curious exception to this predominant, almost universal, type is to be found in Anglo-Saxon Art,[1] where St. Peter is always beardless, and wears the tonsure; so that but for the keys, suspended to a ring on his finger, one might take him for an elderly monk. It is a tradition that the Gentiles shaved the head of St. Peter in order to make

[1] St. Guthlac's Book. Ethelwold's Benedictional.

him an object of derision, and that this is the origin of the priestly tonsure.

The dress of St. Peter in the mosaics and Greek pictures is a blue tunic, with white drapery thrown over it, but in general the proper colours are a blue or green tunic with yellow drapery. On the early sarcophagi, and in the most ancient church mosaics, he bears merely

a scroll or book, and, except in the character of the head, he is exactly like St. Paul; a little later we find him with the cross in one hand, and the Gospel in the other. The keys in his hand appear as his peculiar attribute about the eighth century. I have seen him with one great key, but in general he carries two keys, one of gold and one of silver, to absolve and to bind; or, according to another interpretation, one is of gold, and one of iron, opening the gates of heaven and hell : occasionally, but rarely, he has a third key, expressing the dominion over heaven, and earth, and hell.[1]

68   St Peter with one Key.
(Taddeo Gaddi.)

St. Paul presents a striking contrast to St. Peter, in features as in character. There must have existed effigies of him in very early times, for St. Augustine says that a certain Marcellina, living in the second century, preserved in her Lararium, among her household gods, 'the images of Homer, Pythagoras, Jesus Christ, and Paul the apostle.' Chrysostom alludes to a portrait of Paul which hung in his chamber, but unfortunately he does not describe it. The earliest allusion to the personal appearance of St. Paul occurs in Lucian, where he is styled, in a tone of mocking disparagement, ' the bald-headed Galilean with a hook-nose.' The description given by Nicephorus, founded, we may presume, on tradition and on the existing portraits, has been the authority followed in the early representations. According to the ancient tradition, Paul was a man of small and meagre stature, with an aquiline nose, a high forehead, and sparkling

----

[1] As in the mosaic on the tomb of Otho II. (Lateran Mus.)

eyes. In the Greek type the face is long and oval, the nose aquiline, the forehead high and bald, the hair brown, the beard long, flowing, and pointed, and of a dark brown (in the Greek formula it is said that his beard should be greyish—I recollect no instance of St. Paul with a grey beard); his dress is like St. Peter's, a blue tunic and white mantle; he has a book or scroll in one hand, sometimes twelve rolls, which designate his epistles. He bears the sword, his attribute in a double sense; it signifies the manner of his martyrdom, and it is emblematical of the good fight fought by the faithful Christian, armed with ' the sword of the Spirit, which is the word of God' (Ephes. vi. 17). The life of St. Paul, after his conversion, was, as we know, one long spiritual combat :—' perplexed, but not in despair ; cast down, but not destroyed.'

69   St. Paul.
(Greek type, eleventh century.)

These traditional characteristic types of the features and persons of the two greatest apostles were long adhered to. We find them most strictly followed in the old Greek mosaics, in the early Christian sculpture, and the early pictures ; in all which the sturdy dignity and broad rustic features of St. Peter, and the elegant contemplative head of St. Paul, who looks like a Greek philosopher, form a most interesting and suggestive contrast. But, in later times, the old types, particularly in the head of St. Paul, were neglected and degraded. The best painters took care not to deviate wholly from the square head and short grey beard of St. Peter ; but, from the time of Sixtus IV., we find substituted for the head of St. Paul an arbitrary representation, which varied according to the model chosen by the artist— which was sometimes a Roman porter or a German boor ; sometimes the antique Jupiter or the bust of a Greek rhetorician.

I shall now give some examples, in chronological order, of the two great Apostles represented together, as Founders of the Church.

On the early sarcophagi (from A.D. 321 to 400), St. Peter and St. Paul stand on each side of the Saviour.   The former bears a cross, and is generally on the left hand of Christ.   The cross given to Peter, and often set with jewels, is supposed to refer to the passage in St. John, xxi. 19, ' Signifying by what death he should die: ' but it may surely bear another interpretation, *i.e.*, the spirit of Christianity transmitted to all nations by the first and greatest of the Apostles.   St. Paul carries a roll of writing; he has a very high bald forehead: in other respects the two Apostles are not particularly discriminated; they wear the classical costume.[1]   Similar figures of Peter and Paul occur on the ancient glass drinking-vessels and lamps preserved in the Vatican; but the workmanship is so rude, that they are merely curiosities, and cannot be cited as authorities.

Mosaic (Rome, A.D. 443) in Santa Maria Maggiore, over the arch which separates the sanctuary from the nave.   We have in the centre a throne, on which lies the roll, sealed with seven seals; above the throne rises a cross set with precious stones; on each side of the throne, St. Peter and St. Paul; they have no attributes, are habited in classical draperies, and the whole representation is strictly antique in style, without a trace of any of the characteristics of Mediæval Art.   This is the oldest representation I have met with next to those on the sarcophagi.

Mosaic (Rome, 6th century) in the church of Santa Sabina on the interior of the arch over the door.   We find on one side St. Peter, on the other St. Paul.   Under St. Peter stands a graceful female figure, veiled, and inscribed *Ecclesia ex circumcisione;* under St. Paul, a female figure, crowned, and inscribed *Ecclesia ex gentibus.*

Mosaic (Rome, A.D. 526) in St. Cosmo and St. Damian, on the vault of the apsis.   Christ stands in the centre, sustained by clouds; His right hand is raised in the attitude of one who exhorts (not blessing, as is the usual manner); the left hand holds the book of life; at His feet flows the river Jordan, the symbol of Baptism.   On each side, but lower down and much smaller in size, stand St. Peter and St. Paul; they seem to present St. Cosmo and St. Damian to

[1] Bottari, Tab. xxv.

the Saviour. Beyond these again, on either side, stand St. Theodore and the pope (Felix I.) who dedicated the church. Palm-trees, and a Phœnix crowned with a starry glory, emblems of Victory and Immortality, close this majestic and significant composition on each side. Here St. Peter and St. Paul are dignified figures, in which the Greek type is strongly characterised ; they wear long white mantles, and have no attributes.

MOSAIC (Milan, 9th century), in Sant' Ambrogio. Christ enthroned presents the Gospel to St. Paul, and the two keys to St. Peter.

MOSAIC (A.D. 936) on the tomb of Otho II. St. Peter and St. Paul together, rather more than half length, and above life size. St. Peter has three keys, suspended on a ring ; St. Paul, the book and sword. The original mosaic is preserved in the Vatican, and a copy is in the Lateran. This relic is, as a document, invaluable.

MOSAIC (A.D. 1216–1227), in the apsis of the old basilica of St. Paul. Christ is seated on a throne, with the cruciform glory and His name $\widehat{I C}$. $\widehat{X C}$. : the right hand gives the benediction in the Greek form ; He holds in His left an open book, inscribed VENITE BENEDICTI PATRIS MEI PERCIPITE REGNUM. (Matt. xxv. 34.) On the left, St. Peter with his right hand raised to Christ, and an open scroll in his left hand, inscribed TU ES CHRISTUS FILIUS DEI VIVI. On the other side of Christ, St. Paul ; his right hand on his breast, and in his left a scroll with these words, IN NOMINE JESU OMNE GENU FLECTATUR CŒLESTIUM TERRESTRIUM ET INFERNORUM. (Phil. xi. 10.) Beyond St. Peter stands his brother St. Andrew; and beyond St. Paul his favourite disciple Luke. At the foot of the throne kneels a diminutive figure of the Pope, Honorius III., by whom the mosaic was dedicated. Palm-trees close the composition on each side ; underneath runs the frieze of the Twelve Apostles, described at p. 173.

MOSAIC (12th century) in the Cathedral of Monreale at Palermo. St. Peter and St. Paul are seated on splendid thrones on each side of the tribune ; St. Peter holds in his left hand a book, and the right, which gives the benediction, holds also the two keys: over his head is inscribed, SANCTUS PETRUS PRINCEPS APOSTOLORUM CUI TRADITÆ SUNT CLAVES REGNI CŒLORUM.   St. Paul holds the sword with the point upwards like a sceptre, and the book as usual: the intellectual Greek character of the head is strongly discriminated.   The inscription is, SANCTUS PAULUS PRÆDICATOR VERITATIS ET DOCTOR GENTIUM GENTI.

Among the rich and curious bas-reliefs in front of the church of St. Trophime at Arles, we have St. Peter and St. Paul seated together receiving the souls of the just.   Each has two souls in his lap, and the Archangel Michael is bringing another.

In pictures, their proper place, as I have observed, is on each side of the throne of the Redeemer, or on each side of the Virgin and Child : sometimes they are standing together, or reading in the same book.

This must suffice for the devotional treatment of St. Peter and St. Paul, when represented as joint founders and patrons of the universal Christian Church.   Before I notice those historical subjects in which they appear together, I have to say a few words of the manner in which they are treated separately and distinctly.   And first of St. Peter.

The various events of the life of St. Peter are recorded in the Gospels and the Acts so minutely, that they may be presumed to be familiar to all readers.   From these we may deduce his character, remarkable for fervour and energy rather than sustained power.   His traditional and legendary history is full of incidents, miracles, and wonderful and picturesque passages.   His importance and popularity, considered as Prince of the Apostles and Founder of the Church of Rome, have extended with the influence of that powerful Church of which he is the head and representative, and multiplied, almost to infinitude, pictures and effigies of him in his individual character, as well as historical representations of his life and actions, wherever his paramount dignity is admitted.

It struck me, when wandering over the grand old churches of Ravenna, where the ecclesiastical mosaics are the most ancient that exist, and still in wonderful preservation, that St. Peter and St. Paul do not often appear, at least are in no respect distinguished from the other apostles.   Ravenna, in the fifth century, did not look to Rome for her saints.   On the other hand, among the earliest of the Roman mosaics, St. Peter is sometimes found sustaining the throne of Christ, without his companion St. Paul ; as in S. Maria-in-Trastevere, S. Maria Nuova, and others.   At Rome, St. Peter is *the* Saint, the *Santissimo*.   The secession of the Protestant Church dimmed his glory as Prince of the Apostles and universal Saint ; he fell into a kind of disrepute as identified with the See of Rome, which exposed his effigies, in England and Scotland particularly, to a sweeping destruction.   Those were disputatious days ; and Peter, the affectionate, enthusiastic, devoted, but somewhat rash apostle, veiled his head to the intellectual, intrepid, subtle philosopher Paul.

Let us now see how Art has placed before us the sturdy Prince of the Apostles.

I have already mentioned the characteristic type which belongs to him, and his prevalent attributes—the key, the cross, the book. When he figures among the disciples in the Gospel stories, he sometimes holds the fish as the symbol of his original vocation: if the fish be given to him in single devotional figures, it signifies also Christianity, or the rite of Baptism.

The figures of St. Peter standing, as Apostle and Patron Saint, with book and keys, are of such perpetual occurrence as to defy all attempts to particularise them, and so familiar as to need no further illustration.[1]

Representations of him in his peculiar character of Head and Founder of the Roman Church, and first universal bishop, are less common.   He is seated on a throne ; one hand is raised in the act of benediction; in the other he holds the keys, and sometimes a book or scroll, inscribed with the text, in Latin, ' Thou art Peter, and on this rock have I built my Church.'   This subject of the throned St. Peter

---

[1] One of the finest I have ever seen is the 'Saint Pierre au Donateur,' by Gaudenzio Ferrari ; holding his keys (both of gold), he presents a kneeling votary, a man of middle age, who probably bore his name.   The head of St. Peter is very characteristic, and has an energetic pleading expression, almost *demanding* what he requires for his votary.   The whole picture is extremely fine.   (*Turin Gallery*, No. 19.)

is very frequent in the older schools.   The well-known picture by Giotto, painted for Cardinal Stefaneschi, now in the sacristy of the Vatican, is very fine, simple, and solemn.   In a picture by Cima da Conegliano,[1] St. Peter is not only throned, but wears the triple tiara as Pope; the countenance is particularly earnest, fervent, almost fiery in expression: the keys lie at his feet; on one side stands St. John the Baptist, on the other St. Paul.

As a deviation from the usual form of this subject, I must mention an old bas-relief, full of character, and significantly appropriate to its locality— the church of San Pietro-in-Vincoli, at Rome. St. Peter, enthroned, holds in one hand the keys and the Gospel; with the other he presents his chains to a kneeling angel; this unusual treatment is very poetical and suggestive.

There are standing figures of St. Peter wearing the papal tiara, and brandishing his keys,—as in a picture by Cola dell' Amatrice (70). And I should think Milton had some such picture in his remembrance when he painted *his* St. Peter:—

> Last came and last did go
> The pilot of the Galilean Lake ;
> Two massy keys he bore of metals twain,
> (The golden opes, the iron shuts amain),
> He shook his *mitred* locks, and stern bespake.

When, in devotional pictures, St. Peter is accompanied by another apostle with no distinctive attributes, we may suppose it to be St. Mark, who was his interpreter, companion, and amanuensis at Rome. According to an early tradition, the Gospel of St. Mark was written down from the dictation of St.

[1] Milan, Brera (No. 189).

Peter.[1] In a miniature frontispiece to St. Mark's Gospel, the evangelist is seated writing, and St. Peter stands opposite, as if dictating. In a picture by Angelico,[2] Peter is preaching from a pulpit to a crowd of people : Mark, seated on one side, is diligently taking down his words. In a very fine picture by Bonvicino[3] they stand together; St. Peter is reading from a book; St. Mark holds a scroll and inkhorn; he is submitting to St. Peter the Gospel he has just penned, and which was afterwards confirmed by the apostle.

Lastly, a magnificent Venetian picture[4] represents St. Peter throned as bishop, with an earnest and rather stern countenance; he holds a book in his hand; two angels with musical instruments are seated on the steps of his throne: on his right hand stand John the Baptist, and St. Jerome as cardinal; on his left St. Ambrose; while St. Mark bends over a book, as if reading to this majestic auditory.

Those scenes and incidents related in the Gospels in which St. Peter is a principal or conspicuous figure, I shall enlarge upon when treating of the life of Christ, and will only indicate a few of them here, as illustrating the manner in which St. Peter is introduced and treated in such subjects.

We have, first, the Calling of Peter and Andrew in a picture by Basaiti,[5] where the two brothers are kneeling at the feet of the Saviour; the fishing boats and the Lake of Gennesareth in the background: and in the beautiful fresco by Ghirlandajo in the Sistine Chapel, where a number of contemporary personages are introduced as spectators. St. Andrew presenting St. Peter to our Saviour (as in a picture by Cavalucci, in the Vatican), is another version of the same subject; or St. Andrew is seen at the feet of Christ, while St. Peter is sitting on the edge of the boat, or descending from it in haste.

[1] 'What St. Clement says is to this purpose: that St. Peter's hearers at Rome were desirous of having his sermons writ down for their use ; that they made their request to Mark to leave them a written memorial of the doctrine they had received by word of mouth ; that they did not desist from their entreaties till they had prevailed upon him; and St. Peter confirmed that writing by his authority, that it might be read in the churches.'—LARDNER, *Cred.*, vol. i. p. 250.

[2] Fl. Gal. [3] Brera, Milan. [4] Gian Bellini: Venice. S. M. de' Frari. [5] Vienna Gal.

'Christ Walking on the Sea' is a familiar and picturesque subject, not to be mistaken. The most ancient and most celebrated representation is Giotto's mosaic (A.D. 1298), now placed in the portico of St. Peter's, over the arch opposite to the principal door. The sentiment in the composition of this subject is, generally, 'Lord, help me; or I perish:' St. Peter is sinking, and Christ is stretching out His hand to save him. It is considered as a type of the Church in danger, assailed by enemies, and saved by the miraculous interposition of the Redeemer; and in this sense must the frequent representations in churches be understood.

In the 'Miraculous Draught of Fishes,' St. Peter is usually on his knees looking up with awe and gratitude:—'Depart from me, O Lord! for I am a sinful man.' The composition of Raphael (the cartoon at Hampton Court) is just what we should seek for in Raphael, a masterpiece of dramatic expression,—the significant, the poetical, the miraculous predominating. The composition of Rubens, at Malines, which deserves the next place, should be looked at in contrast, as an instance of the picturesque and vigorous treatment equally characteristic of the painter;—all life and reality, even to the glittering fish which tumble in the net. 'St. Peter finding the tribute money' is a subject I have seldom met with; the *motif* is simple, and not to be mistaken.

In all the scenes of the life of our Saviour in which the Apostles are assembled,—in the Transfiguration, in the Last Supper, in the 'Washing the Feet of the Disciples,' in the scene of the agony and the betrayal of Christ,—St. Peter is introduced as a more or less prominent figure, but always to be distinguished from the other Apostles. In the third of these subjects, the washing of the feet, St. Peter generally looks up at Christ with an expression of humble expostulation, his hands on his head: the sentiment is—'Not my feet only, but my hands and my head.'

In the scene of the betrayal of Christ, St. Peter cutting off the ear of Malchus is sometimes a *too* prominent group; and I remember an old German print in which St. Peter, having cut off the ear, our Lord bends down to replace it.[1]

'St. Peter Denying the Saviour' is always one of the subjects in

---

[1] Bartsch. vi. 92.

the series of the Passion of Christ. It occurs frequently on the ancient sarcophagi as the symbol of repentance, and is treated with classical and sculptural simplicity, the cock being always introduced, as in the illustration (71): it is here to be understood as a general emblem of human weakness and repentance. As an action separately, or as one of the series of the life and actions of Peter, it has not been often painted; it seems to have been avoided in general by the early Italian painters as derogatory to the character and dignity of the Apostle. 'The only examples I can recollect are in the later Italian

71   Repentance of Peter. (Sarcophagus, third century.)

and Flemish schools. Teniers has adopted it as a vehicle for a guard-room scene; soldiers playing at cards, bright armour, &c. Rembrandt has taken it as a vehicle for a fine artificial light; and, for the same reason, the Caravaggio school delighted in it. The maiden, whose name in the old traditions is Balilla, is always introduced with a look and gesture of reproach, and the cock is often perched in the background.

'Christ turned and looked upon Peter:' of this beautiful subject, worthy of Raphael himself, I can remember no instance.

The 'Repentance of Peter' is a subject seldom treated in the earlier schools of Italy, but frequently by the later painters, and particularly by the Bologna school; in some instances most beautifully. It was a subject peculiarly suited to the genius of Guercino, who excelled in the expression of profound rather than elevated feeling.

There is a manner of representing the repentance of Peter which seems peculiar to Spanish Art, and is more ideal than is usual with that school. Christ is bound to a column and crowned with thorns; St. Peter kneels before Him in an attitude of the deepest anguish and humiliation, and appears to be supplicating forgiveness. Except in the Spanish school, I have never met with this treatment. The little picture by Murillo[1] is an exquisite example; and in the Spanish Gallery are two others, by Pedro de Cordova and Juan Juanes :—in the former, St. Peter holds a pocket-handkerchief with which he has been wiping his eyes, and the cock is perched on the column to which our Saviour is bound.

Another ideal treatment we find in a picture by Guercino; St. Peter is weeping bitterly, and opposite to him the Virgin is seated in motionless grief.

Half-length figures of St. Peter looking up with an expression of repentant sorrow, and wringing his hands, are of frequent occurrence, more especially in the later followers of the Bologna and Neapolitan schools of the seventeenth century: Ribera, Lanfranco, Caravaggio, and Valentin. In most of these instances, the total absence of ideal or elevated sentiment is striking;—any old bearded beggar out of the streets, who could cast up his eyes and look pathetic, served as a model.

I recollect no picture of the Crucifixion in which St. Peter is present.

'The Delivery of the Keys to Peter' and 'The Charge to Peter' (Feed my sheep), either in separate pictures or combined into one subject, have been, of course, favourite themes in a Church which founds its authority on these particular circumstances. The bas-relief over the principal door of St. Peter's at Rome represents the two themes in one: Christ delivers the keys to Peter, and the sheep are standing by. In the panels of the bronze doors beneath (A.D

[1] 'Le Christ à la Colonne.' *Louvre*, No. 550.

1431), we have the chain of thought and incident continued ; Peter delivers the emblematical keys to Pope Eugenius IV.

It is curious that, while the repentance of Peter is a frequent subject on the sarcophagi of the fourth century, the delivery of the keys to Peter occurs but once. Christ, as a beardless youth, presents to Peter two keys laid crosswise one over the other. Peter, in whose head the traditional type is most distinctly marked, has thrown his pallium over his outstretched hands, for, according to the antique ceremonial, of which the early sculpture and mosaics afford us so many examples, things consecrated could only be touched with covered hands. This singular example is engraved in Bottari.[1] An example of beautiful and solemn treatment in painting is Perugino's fresco in the Sistine Chapel. It contains twenty-one figures ; the conception is quite ideal, the composition regular even to formality, yet striking and dramatic. In the centre, Peter, kneeling on one knee, receives the keys from the hand of the Saviour ; the apostles and disciples are arranged on each side behind Christ and St. Peter ; in the background is the rebuilding of the Temple ;—a double allegory: ' Destroy this temple, I will build it up in three days : ' and also, perhaps, alluding to the building of the chapel by Sixtus IV.

In Raphael's cartoon[2] the scene is an open plain : Christ stands on the right ; in front, St. Peter kneels, with the keys in his hand ; Christ extends one hand to Peter, and with the other points to a flock of sheep in the background. The introduction of the sheep into this subject has been criticised as at once too literal and too allegorical,—a too literal transcript of the words, a too allegorical version of the meaning ; but I do not see how the words of our Saviour could have been otherwise rendered in painting, which must speak to us through sensible objects. The other apostles standing behind Peter show in each countenance the different manner in which they are affected by the words of the Saviour.

By Gian Bellini: a beautiful picture :[3] St. Peter kneeling, half-length, receives the keys from Jesus Christ, seated on a throne. Behind St. Peter stand the three Christian Graces, Faith, Hope, and Charity. Poussin has taken this subject in his series of the Seven Sacraments,[4] to represent the sacrament of Ordination. In this

---

[1] Tab. xxi.   [2] Hampton Court.   [3] Madrid Gal., No. 114.   [4] Bridgewater Gal.

instance again, the two themes are united; and we must also remember, that the allegorical representation of the disciples and
followers of Christ as sheep looking up to be fed is consecrated by
the practice of the earliest schools of Christian Art. Rubens has
rendered the subject very simply, in a picture containing only the
two figures, Christ and St. Peter;[1] and again with five figures, less
good.[2] Numerous other examples might be given; but the subject is
one that, however treated, cannot be easily mistaken.

A very ideal version of this subject is where St. Peter kneels at the
feet of the Madonna, and the Infant Christ, bending from her lap,
presents the keys to him; as in a singularly fine and large composition
by Crivelli,[3] and in another by Andrea Salaino. Another, very beautiful and curious, is in the possession of Mr Bromley of Wootten.[4]

After the ascension of our Saviour, the personal history of St. Peter
is mingled first with that of St. John, and afterwards with that of
St. Paul.

' Peter and John healing the lame man at the gate called Beautiful,'
is the subject of one of the finest of the cartoons at Hampton Court.
Perin del Vaga, Niccolò Poussin, and others less renowned, have also
treated it; it is susceptible of much contrast and dramatic effect.

' The sick are brought out and placed in the shadow of Peter and
John that they may be healed,' by Masaccio.[5]

' Peter preaching to the Early Converts:' the two most beautiful
compositions I have seen, are the simple group of Masaccio; and
another by Le Sueur, full of variety and sentiment.

' Peter and John communicate the Holy Ghost by laying their hands
on the Disciples,' by Vasari.[6] I do not well remember this picture.

The Vision of Peter: three angels sustain the curtain or sheet
which contains the various forbidden animals, as pigs, rabbits, &c.
(as in a print after Guercino).

' Peter baptizes the Centurion ' (very appropriately placed in the

---

[1] Cathedral at Malines.   [2] Gal. of the Hague.
[3] This picture, formerly in the Brera, is now in England, in the gallery of Lord Ward.
It is the finest and most characteristic specimen of the master I have ever seen.
[4] It is signed MĚDULA, and attributed to Giulio della Mendula; a painter (except
through this picture) unknown to me.
[5] Brancacci Chapel, Florence.   [6] Berlin Gal., No. 313.

baptistery of the Vatican). St. Peter meets the Centurion; he blesses the family of the Centurion. All commonplace versions of very interesting and picturesque subjects.

'The Death of Ananias.' Raphael's cartoon of this awful scene is a masterpiece of dramatic and scenic power; never was a story more admirably and completely told in painting. Those who had to deal with the same subject, as if to avoid a too close comparison with his unapproachable excellence, have chosen the death of Sapphira as the *motif*: as, for example, Niccolò Poussin.[1]

'Dorcas or Tabitha Restored to Life.' One of the finest and most effective of Guercino's pictures, now in the Palazzo Pitti: the simple dignity of the apostle, and the look of sick amazement in the face of the woman restored to consciousness, show how strong Guercino could be when he had to deal with natural emotions of no elevated kind. The same subject, by Costanzi, is among the great mosaics in St. Peter's. 'The Death of Dorcas,' by Le Sueur, is a beautiful composition. She lies extended on a couch; St. Peter and two other apostles approach the foot of it: the poor widows, weeping, show to St. Peter the garments which Dorcas had made for them (Acts ix. 39).

The imprisonment of Peter, and his deliverance by the Angel, were incidents so important, and offer such obvious points of dramatic effect, that they have been treated in every possible variety of style and sentiment, from the simple formality of the early mosaics, where the two figures—Peter sitting on a stool, leaning his head on his hand, and the Angel at his side—express the story like a vision,[2] down to the scenic and architectural compositions of Steenwick, where, amid a vast perspective of gloomy vaults and pillars, a diminutive St. Peter, with an Angel or a sentinel placed somewhere in the foreground, just serves to give the picture a name.[3]

Some examples of this subject are of great celebrity.

Masaccio, in the frescoes of the Brancacci Chapel, has represented Peter in prison looking through his grated window, and Paul outside communing with him. (The noble figure of St. Paul in this fresco

[1] Louvre, No. 685.

[2] As in the Greek mosaics in the Cathedral of Monreale, near Palermo.

[3] Several such pictures are in the royal collections at Windsor and Hampton Court.

was imitated by Raphael in the ' St. Paul preaching at Athens.') In
the next compartment of the series, Masaccio has given us the Angel
leading forth Peter, while the guard sleeps at the door : he sleeps as
one oppressed with an unnatural sleep. Raphael's fresco in the
Vatican is not one of his best, but he has seized on the obvious point
of effect, both as to light and grouping; and we have three separate
moments of the same incident, which yet combine most happily into
one grand scene. Thus in the centre, over the window, we see through
a grating the interior of the prison, where St. Peter is sleeping between
two guards, who, leaning on their weapons, are sunk in a deep charmed
slumber; [1] an angel, whose celestial radiance fills the dungeon with a
flood of light, is in the act of waking the apostle : on the right of the
spectator, the angel leads the apostle out of the prison ; two guards
are sleeping on the steps : on the left, the soldiers are roused from
sleep, and one with a lighted torch appears to be giving the alarm ;
the crescent moon faintly illumines the background.

The deliverance of St. Peter has always been considered as figurative
of the deliverance of the Church ; and the two other frescoes of this
room, the Heliodorus and the Attila, bear the same interpretation.
It is worth while to compare this dramatic composition of Raphael
with others wherein the story is merely a vehicle for àrtificial effects
of light, as in a picture by Gerard Honthorst; or treated like a supernatural vision, as by that poet, Rembrandt.

Those historical subjects in which St. Peter and St. Paul figure
together will be noticed in the life of St. Paul.

I come now to the legendary stories connected with St. Peter ;—an
inexhaustible source of popular and pictorial interest.

Peter was at Jerusalem as late as A.D. 52; then at Antioch; also
in Babylon: according to the most ancient testimonies he was at
Rome about A.D. 63 ; but the tradition, that he resided as bishop in
the city of Rome for twenty-five years, first related by Jerome, seems

---

[1] Moore makes a characteristic remark on this fresco ; he is *amazed* at the self-denial of
the painter who could cross this fine group with the black iron bars which represent the
prison.

questionable.[1] Among the legendary incidents which marked his sojourn in Rome, the first and the most important is the story of Simon Magus.

Simon, a famous magician among the Jews, had astonished the whole city of Jerusalem by his wonderful feats; but his inventions and sorceries were overcome by the real miracles of Peter, as the Egyptian magi had been conquered by Aaron. He offered the apostles money to buy the secret of their power, which Peter rejected with indignation. St. Augustine tells us, as a characteristic trait of the fiery-spirited apostle, that 'if he had fallen on the traitor Simon, he would certainly have torn him to pieces with his teeth.' The magician, vanquished by a superior power, flung his books into the Dead Sea, broke his wand, and fled to Rome, where he became a great favourite of the Emperor Claudius, and afterwards of Nero. Peter, bent on counteracting the wicked sorceries of Simon, followed him to Rome. About two years after his arrival, he was joined there by the Apostle Paul. Simon Magus having asserted that he was himself a god, and could raise the dead, Peter and Paul rebuked his impiety, and challenged him to a trial of skill in presence of the emperor. The arts of the magician failed; Peter and Paul restored the youth to life: and on many other occasions Simon was vanquished and put to shame by the miraculous power of the apostles. At length he undertook to fly up to heaven in sight of the emperor and the people; and, crowned with laurel, and supported by demons, he flung himself from a tower, and appeared for a while to float thus in the air: but St. Peter falling on his knees, commanded the demons to let go their hold, and Simon, precipitated to the ground, was dashed to pieces.

This romantic legend, so popular in the Middle Ages, is founded on some antique traditions not wholly unsupported by historical testimony.

There can be no doubt that there existed in the first century a

[1] Some Protestant writers have set aside St. Peter's ministry at Rome, as altogether apocryphal; but Gieseler, an author by no means credulous, considers that the historical evidence is in favour of the tradition (v. Text-book of Eccles. Hist. p. 53). This is the more satisfactory, because, even to Protestants, it is not agreeable to be at Rome and to be obliged to reject certain associations which add to the poetical, as well as to the religious, interest of the place.

superb landscape, in which are seen a lion and a lioness prowling in
the wilderness, while the saint is doing penance in the foreground.
By Agostino Caracci there is a famous engraving of ' St. Jerome
doing penance in a cave,' called from its size the *great* St. Jerome.
But to particularise further would be endless : I know scarcely any
Italian painter since the fifteenth century who has not treated this
subject at least once.

The Spanish painters have rendered it with a gloomy power, and
revelled in its mystic significance. In the Spanish gallery of the
Louvre I counted at least twenty St. Jeromes : the old German
painters and engravers also delighted in it, on account of its picturesque capabilities.

Albert Dürer represents St. Jerome kneeling before a crucifix,
which he has suspended against the trunk of a massy tree ; an open
book is near it ; he holds in his right hand a flint-stone, with
which he is about to strike his breast, all wounded and bleeding
from the blows already inflicted ; the lion crouches behind him, and
in the distance is a stag.

The penitent St. Jerome is not a good subject for sculpture ; the
undraped, meagre form, and the abasement of suffering, are disagreeable in this treatment : yet such representations are constantly
met with in churches. The famous colossal statue by Torrigiano,
now in the Museum at Seville, represents St. Jerome kneeling on a
rock, a stone in one hand, a crucifix in the other. At Venice, in
the Frari, there is a statue of St. Jerome, standing, with the stone
in his hand and the lion at his feet ; too majestic for the Penitent.
There are several other statues of St. Jerome at Venice, from the
Liberi and Lombardi schools, all fine as statues ; but the penitent
saint is idealised into the patron-saint of penitents.

When figures of St. Jerome as penitent are introduced in Madonna
pictures, or in the Passion of Christ, then such figures are devotional,
and symbolical, in a general sense, of Christian repentance.

There is an early picture of the Crucifixion, by Raphael,[1] in which
he has placed St. Jerome at the foot of the cross, beating his breast
with a stone (86).

The pictures from the life of St. Jerome comprise a variety of

[1] Collection of Lord Ward.

a few bones are near him—a naïve method of expressing his return
from death to life. The variety of expression in the countenances of
the assembled spectators is very fine. According to the custom of the
Florentine school at that time, many are portraits of distinguished
persons; and, considering that the fresco was painted at a period most
interesting in the Florentine history (A.D. 1440), we have much reason
to regret that these can no longer be discriminated.

4. 'The Fall of Simon Magus' is a favourite and picturesque
subject, often repeated. A most ancient and most curious version is
that on the walls of the Cathedral at Assisi, older than the time of
Giotto, and attributed to Giunta Pisano. (A.D. 1232.) On one side
is a pyramidical tower formed of wooden bars; Peter and Paul are
kneeling in front; the figure of the magician is seen floating in the
air and sustained by hideous demons;—very dreamy, poetical, and
fanciful. In Mr Ottley's collection I saw a small ancient picture of
the same subject, very curious, attributed to Benozzo Gozzoli.
Raphael's composition in the Vatican has the simplicity of a classical
bas-relief—a style which does not appear suited to this romantic
legend. The picture by L. Caracci at Naples I have not seen. Over
one of the altars of St. Peter, we now see the great mosaic, after
Vanni's picture of this subject; a clever commonplace treatment:
the scene is an amphitheatre, the emperor above in his balcony;
Peter and Paul in front, invoking the name of Christ, and Simon
Magus tumbling headlong, forsaken by his demons; in the background sit the vestals. Battoni's great picture in the S. Maria
degli Angeli at Rome is considered his best production; it is full
of well-studied academic drawing, but scenic and mannered.

The next subject in the order of events is styled the 'DOMINE, QUO
VADIS?' After the burning of Rome, Nero threw upon the Christians
the accusation of having fired the city. This was the origin of the
first persecution, in which many perished by terrible and hitherto
unheard-of deaths. The Christian converts besought Peter not to
expose his life, which was dear and necessary to the well-being of all;
and at length he consented to depart from Rome. But as he fled
along the Appian Way, about two miles from the gates, he was met
by a vision of our Saviour travelling towards the city. Struck with

amazement, he exclaimed, ' Lord! whither goest thou?' to which the
Saviour, looking upon him with a mild sadness, replied, 'I go to Rome
to be crucified a second time,' and vanished.   Peter, taking this for
a sign that he was to submit himself to the sufferings prepared for
him, immediately turned back and re-entered the city.   Michael
Angelo's famous statue, now in the church of S. Maria-sopra-Minerva
at Rome, is supposed to represent Christ as He appeared to Peter on
this occasion; and a cast or copy of it is in the little church of
' Domine, quo vadis?' erected on the spot sanctified by this mysterious meeting.

It is surprising that this most beautiful, picturesque, and, to my
fancy, sublime legend, has been so seldom treated; and never, as it
appears to me, in a manner worthy of its capabilities and its high significance.   It is seldom that a whole story can be told by two figures,
and these two figures placed in such grand and dramatic contrast;—
Christ in His serene majesty and radiant with all the glory of beatitude, yet with an expression of gentle reproach; the apostle at His
feet, arrested in his flight, amazed, and yet filled with a trembling
joy; and for the background the wide Campagna or the towering walls
of imperial Rome;—these are grand materials; but the pictures I
have met with are all ineffective in conception.   The best fall short
of the sublime ideal; most of them are theatrical and commonplace.

Raphael has interpreted it in a style rather too classical for the
spirit of the legend; with great simplicity and dignity, but as a *fact*,
rather than a vision conjured up by the stricken conscience and
tenderness of the affectionate apostle.   The small picture by Annibal
Caracci in our National Gallery is a carefully-finished academical study
and nothing more, but may be referred to as a fair example of the
usual mode of treatment.

Peter returned to Rome, persisted in his appointed work, preaching
and baptizing; was seized with St. Paul and thrown into the Mamer-
tine dungeons under the Capitol.   The two centurions who guarded
them, Processus and Martinian, and many of the criminals confined in
the same prison, were converted by the preaching of the apostle; and
there being no water to baptize them, at the prayer of St. Peter a
fountain sprang up from the stone floor; which may be seen at this
day.

'The Baptism of St. Processus and St. Martinian in the Dungeon,' by Trevisani, is in the baptistery of St. Peter's at Rome; they afterwards suffered for the faith, and were canonised. In the same church is the scene of their martyrdom by Valentino; they are seen bound and stretched on a hurdle, the head of one to the feet of the other, and thus beaten to death. The former picture—the Baptism—is commonplace; the latter, terrible for dark and effective expression; it is just one of those subjects in which the Caravaggio school delighted.

A few days after their incarceration, St. Peter and St. Paul were condemned to death. According to one tradition, St. Peter suffered martyrdom in the Circus of Caligula at the foot of the Vatican, and was crucified between two metæ, *i.e.*, the goals or terminæ in the Circus, round which the chariots turned in the race; but, according to another tradition, he was put to death in the court-yard of a barrack or military station on the summit of Mons Janicula, where the church of San Pietro in Montorio now stands; that is, on an eminence above the site of the Circus of Caligula. At his own request, and that his death might be even more painful and ignominious than that of his Divine Master, he was crucified with his head downwards.

In the earliest representations I have met with,[1] St. Peter is raised on the cross with his head downwards, and wears a long shirt which is fastened round his ankles. In the picture of Giotto,[2] the local circumstances, according to the first tradition, are carefully attended to : we have the cross erected between the two metæ, and about twenty soldiers and attendants; among them a woman who embraces the foot of the cross, as the Magdalene embraces the cross of the Saviour. Above are seen angels, who bear the soul of the martyred saint in a glory to heaven. Masaccio's composition[3] is very simple; the scene is the court-yard of a military station (according to the second tradition). Peter is already nailed upon a cross; three executioners are in the act of raising it with cords and a pulley to suspend it against a great beam of wood ; there are several soldiers, but no women, present.

---

[1] MS., Vatican, No. 5409. 10th century.   [2] In the sacristy of the Vatican.
[3] In the Brancacci Chapel at Florence.

72   Crucifixion of St. Peter.   (Giotto.)

In Guido's composition [1] there are only three figures, the apostle and
two executioners; it is celebrated as a work of Art, but it appeared
to me most ineffective.   On the other hand, Rubens has gone into
the opposite extreme; there are only three persons, the principal
figure filling nearly the whole of the canvas : it is full of vigour, truth,
and nature; but the brutality of the two executioners, and the agony
of the aged saint, too coarsely and painfully literal.   These simple
representations of the mere act or fact should be compared with the
fresco of Michael Angelo,[2] in which the event is evolved into a grand
drama.   Here the scene is evidently the summit of the Mons
Janiculum : in the midst of a crowd of soldiers and spectators, St.
Peter lies nailed to the cross, which a number of men are exerting
their utmost strength to raise from the ground.

The legend which makes St. Peter the keeper of the gate of

[1] In the Gallery of the Vatican.   [2] Vatican.   Cappella Paolina.

Paradise, with power to grant or refuse admission, is founded on the delivery of the keys to Peter. In most of the pictures which represent

73   From the fresco of Simone Memmi, Florence. (S. Maria Novella.)

the entrance of the blessed into Paradise or the New Jerusalem, Peter stands with his keys near the gate. There is a beautiful example in the great fresco of Simone Memmi in the chapel *de' Spagnuoli* at Florence: St. Peter stands at the open portal with his great key, and two angels crown with garlands the souls of the just as they enter joyously hand in hand.

The legend of St. Petronilla, the daughter of St. Peter (in French, Sainte Pernelle), has never been popular as a subject of Art, and I can remember no series of incidents from the life of St. Peter in which she is introduced, except those in the Carmine at Florence. It is apparently a Roman legend, and either unknown to the earliest artists, or neglected by them.   It is thus related :—

'The apostle Peter had a daughter born in lawful wedlock, who accompanied him in his journey from the East.   Being at Rome with him, she fell sick of a grievous infirmity which deprived her of the use of her limbs.   And it happened that as the disciples were at meat with him in his house, one said to him, "Master, how is it that thou, who healest the infirmities of others, dost not heal thy daughter Petronilla?" and St. Peter answered, "It is good for her to remain sick:" but, that they might see the power that was in the word of God, he commanded her to get up and serve them at table, which she did; and having done so, she lay down again helpless as before; but many years afterwards, being perfected by her long suffering, and praying fervently, she was healed.   Petronilla was wonderfully fair; and Valerius Flaccus, a young and noble Roman, who was a heathen, became enamoured of her beauty, and sought her for his wife, and he being very powerful, she feared to refuse him; she therefore desired him to return in three days, and promised that he should then carry her home.   But she prayed earnestly to be delivered from this peril; and when Flaccus returned in three days with great pomp to celebrate the marriage, he found her dead.   The company of nobles who attended him carried her to the grave, in which they laid her, crowned with roses; and Flaccus lamented greatly.'[1]

The legend places her death in the year 98, that is, 34 years after the death of St. Peter; but it would be in vain to attempt to reconcile the dates and improbabilities of this story.

St. Peter raising Petronilla from her sick-bed is one of the subjects by Masaccio in the Brancacci Chapel.   The scene of her entombment is the subject of a once celebrated and colossal picture by Guercino: the copy in mosaic is over the altar dedicated to her in St. Peter's: in front, and in the lower part of the picture, she is just seen as they are letting her down into the grave, crowned with roses; behind stands Flaccus with a handkerchief in his hand, and a crowd of

[1] v. Il perfetto Legendario.

spectators : in the upper part of the picture Petronilla is already in Paradise, kneeling, in a rich dress, before the feet of Christ, having exchanged an earthly for a heavenly bridegroom. This great picture exhibits, in a surpassing degree, the merits and defects of Guercino: it is effective, dramatic, deeply and forcibly coloured, and arrests attention : on the other hand, it is coarse, crowded, vulgar in sentiment, and repugnant to our better taste. There is a standing figure of Petronilla in the Duomo at Lucca, by Daniel di Volterra, very fine.[1]

The life of St. Peter, when represented as a series, generally comprises the following subjects, commencing with the first important incident after the Ascension of Christ.

1. Peter and John heal the lame man at the Beautiful Gate. 2. Peter heals the paralytic Eneas. 3. Peter raises Tabitha. 4. The angel takes off the chains of Peter. 5. He follows the angel out of the prison. 6. St. Peter and St. Paul meet at Rome. 7. Peter and Paul before Nero are accused by Simon Magus. 8. The fall of Simon Magus. 9. The crucifixion of St. Peter. This example is taken from the series of mosaics in the Cathedral of Monreale, at Palermo.

The fine series of frescoes in the Brancacci Chapel at Florence is differently arranged; thus :—1. The tribute money found in the fish

[1] There was an oratory in the church of the Franciscans at Varallo, in which they celebrated a yearly festival in honour of St. Petronilla. While Gaudenzio Ferrari was painting there the series of frescoes in the chapel of the crucifixion on the Sacro Monte, he promised to paint for the festival an effigy of the saint. The eve of the day arrived, and still it was not begun : the people murmured, and reproached him, which he affected to treat jestingly; but he arose in the night, and with no other light than the beams of the full moon, executed a charming figure of St. Petronilla, which still exists. She stands holding a book, a white veil over her head, and a yellow mantle falling in rich folds : she has no distinctive emblem. 'Gaudenzio, che in una bella notte d' estate dipinse fra ruvide muraglie una Santa tutta grazia e pudore mentre un pallido raggio di luna sbucato dalla frondosa chioma d' albero dolcemente gl' irradia la fronte calva e la barba rossiccia, presenta un non so che di ideale e di romanzesco che veramente rapisce.'—Opere di Gaudenzio Ferrari, No. 21. (Maggi, Turin. It is to be regretted that in this valuable work neither the pages nor the plates are numbered.)

by St. Peter. 2. Peter preaching to the converts. 3. Peter baptizes
the converts. In this fresco, the youth, who has thrown off his
garments and is preparing for baptism, is famous as the first really
graceful and well-drawn undraped figure which had been produced
since the revival of Art. 4. Peter and John heal the cripple at the
Beautiful Gate, and Petronilla is raised from her bed. 5. Peter in
his prison is visited by Paul. 6. Peter delivered by the angel. 7.
The resuscitation of the dead youth.   8. The sick are laid in the way
of Peter and John, ' that at the least the shadow of Peter passing
by might overshadow some of them.' 9. Peter and John distribute
alms ; a dead figure lies at the feet of the apostles, perhaps Ananias.
The situation of the fresco is very dark, so that it is difficult to distinguish the action and expression of the figures.   10. Peter and Paul
accused before Nero. 11. The crucifixion of Peter.

In St. Peter's at Rome, we have of course every scene from the
life of the apostle which could well be expressed by Art ; but none
of these are of great merit or interest : most of them are from the
schools of the seventeenth century.

ST. PAUL, though called to the apostleship after the ascension of
the Saviour, takes rank next to St. Peter as one of the chief witnesses
of the Christian faith.   Of all the apostles he is the most interesting ;
the one of whose personal character and history we know most, and
through the most direct and irrefragable testimony.   The events of
his life, as conveyed in the Acts and the Epistles, are so well known
that I need not here particularise them.   The legends connected with
him are very few.

The earliest single figure of St. Paul to which I can refer was found
painted on the walls of the cemetery of Priscilla, near Rome.[1]   He
stands, with outstretched arms, in the act of prayer (in the early ages
of Christianity the act of supplication was expressed in the classical
manner, that is, not with folded hands, but with the arms extended);
he has the nimbus ; his dress is that of a traveller, the tunic and
pallium being short, and his feet sandalled, perhaps to indicate his

---

[1] Second or third century. Bosio, p. 519.

many and celebrated travels; perhaps, also, it represents Paul praying for his flock before he departed from Macedon to return to Jerusalem (Acts xx.) : over this ancient figure, which, though ill drawn,
is quite classical in sentiment and costume, is inscribed PAULUS.
PASTOR . APOSTOLOS ; on his right hand stands the Good Shepherd,
in reference to the title of PASTOR, inscribed over his effigy. Another
figure of St. Paul, which appears to be of later date, but anterior to
the fifth century, was found in the catacombs at Naples : in this
effigy he wears the dress of a Greek philosopher ; the style in which
the drapery is worn recalls the time of Hadrian : he has no nimbus,
nor is the head bald ; he has sandals on his feet : over his head is
inscribed his name, PAULUS ; near him is a smaller figure similarly
draped, who offers him fruit and flowers in a vase ; probably the
personage who was entombed on the spot.

At what period the sword was given to St. Paul as his distinctive attribute, is with antiquaries a disputed point; certainly, much
later than the keys were given to Peter.[1] If we could be sure
that the mosaic on the tomb of Otho II., and another mosaic
already described, had not been altered in successive restorations,
these would be evidence that the sword was given to St. Paul as his
attribute as early as the 6th century ; but there are no monuments
which can be absolutely trusted as regards the introduction of
the sword before the end of the 11th century ; since the end of the
14th century, it has been so generally adopted, that in the devotional effigies I can remember no instance in which it is omitted.
When St. Paul is leaning on the sword, it expresses his martyrdom ; when he holds it aloft, it expresses also his warfare in the
cause of Christ : when two swords are given to him, one is the
attribute, the other the emblem ; but this double allusion does not
occur in any of the older representations. In Italy I never met
with St. Paul bearing two swords, and the only instance I can call
to mind is the bronze statue by Peter Vischer, on the shrine of St.
Sebald, at Nuremberg.

Although devotional representations of St. Paul separate from St.
Peter and the other apostles occur very rarely, pictures from his life

[1] v. Münter's Sinnbilder, p. 35.

and actions are commonly met with; the principal events are so
familiar, that they are easily recognised and discriminated even by
the most unlearned in biblical illustration; considered and treated
as a series, they form a most interesting and dramatic succession of
scenes, often introduced into the old churches; but the incidents
chosen are not always the same.

Paul, before his conversion, was present at the stoning of Stephen,
and he is generally introduced holding on his knees the garments
of the executioners. In some ancient pictures, he has, even while
looking on and 'consenting to the death' of the victim, the glory
round his head, as one who, while 'breathing out threatenings and
slaughter against the disciples of the Lord,' was already a 'chosen
vessel to bear His name before the Gentiles.' But in a set of pictures which relate expressly to St. Paul, the Martyrdom of Stephen
is, with proper feeling, omitted, and the series generally begins with
the CONVERSION OF PAUL,—in his character of apostle, the first
great event in his life. An incident so important, so celebrated,
and in all its accessories so picturesque and dramatic, has of course
been a frequent subject of artistic treatment, even as a separate
composition. In some of the old mosaics, the story is very simply,
and at the same time vividly, rendered. In the earliest examples,
St. Paul has the nimbus or glory while yet unconverted; he is
prostrate on the ground, grovelling on his hands and knees; rays
of light fall upon him out of heaven, where the figure of Christ,
half-length, is seen emerging from glory; sometimes it is a hand
only, which is the emblem of the Almighty Power; two or four
attendants at most are flying in terror. It is not said in Scripture
that St. Paul journeyed on horseback from Jerusalem to Damascus;
but the tradition is at least as old as the time of Pope Dalmasius
(A.D. 384), as it is then referred to. St. Augustine says he journeyed
on foot, because the Pharisees made a point of religion to go on foot,
and it is so represented in the old Greek mosaics. The expression,
'It is hard for thee to kick against the pricks,' has been oddly
enough assigned as a reason for placing Paul on horseback;[1] at all
events, as he bore a military command, it has been thought proper
in later times so to represent him, and also as surrounded by a

[1] v. Zani. Enc. della Belle Arti.

numerous cortége of attendants. This treatment admits, of course, of endless variety, in the disposition and number of the figures, in the attitudes and expression; but the moment chosen is generally the same.

1. The oldest example I can cite, next to the Greek mosaics, is an old Italian print mentioned by Zani. Paul, habited as a Roman warrior, kneels with his arms crossed on his breast, and holding a scroll, on which is inscribed in Latin, 'Lord, what shall I do?" Christ stands opposite to him, also holding a scroll, on which is written, 'Saul, Saul, why persecutest thou me?' There are no attendants. Zani does not give the date of this quaint and simple version of the story.

2. Raphael. Paul, habited as a Roman soldier, is lying on the ground as thrown from his horse; he looks upward to Christ, who appears in the clouds, attended by three child-angels : his attendants on foot and on horseback are represented as rushing to his assistance, unconscious of the vision, but panicstruck by its effect on *him :* one attendant in the background seizes by the bridle the terrified horse. The original cartoon of this fine composition (one of the tapestries in the Vatican) is lost.

3. Michael Angelo. Paul, a noble figure, though prostrate, appears to be struck motionless and senseless : Christ seems to be *rushing* down from heaven surrounded by a host of angels; those of the attendants who are near to Paul are flying in all directions, while a long train of soldiers is seen ascending from the background. This grand dramatic composition forms the pendant to the Crucifixion of Peter in the Cappella Paolina. It is so darkened by age and the smoke of tapers, and so ill lighted, that it is not easily made out; but there is a fine engraving, which may be consulted.

4. Another very celebrated composition of this subject is that of Rubens.[1] Paul, lying in the foreground, expresses in his attitude the most helpless and grovelling prostration. The attendants appear very literally frightened out of their senses; and the grey horse snorting and rearing behind is the finest part of the picture : as is usual with Rubens, the effects of physical fear and amazement are given with the utmost spirit and truth; but the scriptural dignity,

[1] In the Gallery of Mr Miles, at Leigh Court.

the supernatural terrors, of the subject are ill expressed, and the apostle himself is degraded. To go a step lower, Cuyp has given us a Conversion of St. Paul apparently for the sole purpose of introducing horses in different attitudes; the favourite dapple grey charger is seen bounding off in terror; no one looks at St. Paul, still less to Christ above—but the *horses* are admirable.

5. In Albert Dürer's print, a shower of *stones* is falling from heaven on St. Paul and his company.

6. There is a very curious and unusual version of this subject in a rare print by Lucas van Leyden. It is a composition of numerous figures. St. Paul is seen, blind and bewildered, led between two men; another man leads his frightened charger; several warriors and horsemen follow, and the whole procession seems to be proceeding slowly to the right. In the far distance is represented the previous moment—Paul struck down and blinded by the celestial vision.

' Paul, after his Conversion, restored to sight by Ananias,' as a separate subject, seldom occurs; but it has been treated in the later schools by Vasari, by Cavallucci, and by P. Cortona.

' The Jews flagellate Paul and Silas.' I know but one picture of this subject, that of Niccolò Poussin: the angry Jews are seen driving them forth with scourges; the Elders, who have condemned them, are seated in council behind : as we might expect from the character of Poussin, the dignity of the apostles is maintained,— but it is not one of his best pictures.

' Paul, after his Conversion, escapes from Damascus; ' he is let down in a basket (Acts ix. 25): the incident forms, of course, one of the scenes in his life when exhibited in a series, but I remember no separate picture of this subject, and the situation is so ludicrous and so derogatory that we can understand how it came to be avoided.

' The ecstatic vision of St. Paul, in which he was caught up to the third heaven ' (2 Cor. xii. 2.) Paul, who so frequently and familiarly speaks of angels, in describing this event, makes no mention of

them, but in pictures he is represented as borne upwards by angels.
I find no early composition of this subject. The small picture of
Domenichino is coldly conceived. Poussin has painted the ' Ravis-
sement de St. Paul' twice; in the first, the apostle is borne upon
the arms of four angels, and in the second he is sustained by three
angels. In rendering this ecstatic vision, the angels, always
allowable as machinery, have here a particular propriety; Paul is
elevated only a few feet above the roof of his house, where lie his
sword and book. Here the sword serves to distinguish the personage; and the roof of the house shows us that it is a vision, and not
an apotheosis. Both pictures are in the Louvre.

' Paul Preaching to the Converts at Ephesus.' In a beautiful
Raffaelesque composition by Le Sueur, the incident of the magicians
bringing their books of sorcery and burning them at the feet of the
apostle is well introduced. It was long the custom to exhibit this
picture solemnly in Notre Dame every year on the 1st of May. It
is now in the Louvre.

' Paul before Felix,' and ' Paul before Agrippa.' Neither of these
subjects has ever been adequately treated. It is to me inconceivable
that the old masters so completely overlooked the opportunity for
grand characteristic delineation afforded by both these scenes, the
latter especially. Perhaps in estimating its capabilities, we are
misled by the effect produced on the imagination by the splendid
eloquence of the apostle; yet, were another Raphael to arise, I would
suggest the subject as a pendant to the St. Paul at Athens.

' Paul performs miracles before the Emperor Nero ; ' a blind man,
a sick child, and a possessed woman are brought to him to be healed.
This, though a legendary rather than a scriptural subject, has been
treated by Le Sueur with scriptural dignity and simplicity.

' The Martyrdom of St. Paul' is sometimes a separate subject,
but generally it is the pendant to the martyrdom of St. Peter. According to the received tradition, the two apostles suffered at the
same time, but in different places; for St. Paul, being by birth a
Roman citizen, escaped the ignominy of the public exposure in the
Circus, as well as the prolonged torture of the cross. He was

beheaded by the sword outside the Ostian gate, about two miles from
Rome, at a place called the Aqua Salvias, now the 'Tre Fontane.'
The legend of the death of St. Paul relates that a certain Roman
matron, named Plautilla, one of the converts of St. Peter, placed herself on the road by which St. Paul passed to his martyrdom, in order
to behold him for the last time; and when she saw him, she wept
greatly, and besought his blessing.   The apostle then, seeing her
faith, turned to her and begged that she would give him her veil to
bind his eyes when he should be beheaded, promising to return it to
her after his death.   The attendants mocked at such a promise, but
Plautilla, with a woman's faith and charity, taking off her veil,
presented it to him.   After his martyrdom, St. Paul appeared to
her, and restored the veil stained with his blood.   It is also related,
that when he was decapitated the severed head made three bounds
upon the earth, and wherever it touched the ground a fountain sprang
forth.

In the most ancient representations of the martyrdom of St. Paul,
the legend of Plautilla is seldom omitted.   In the picture of Giotto
preserved in the sacristy of St. Peter's, Plautilla is seen on an
eminence in the background, receiving the veil from the hand of
Paul, who appears in the clouds above; the same representation, but
little varied, is executed in bas-relief on the bronze doors of St.
Peter's.   The three fountains gushing up beneath the severed head
are also frequently represented as a literal fact, though a manifest
and beautiful allegory, figurative of the fountains of Christian faith
which should spring forth from his martyrdom.

In all the melancholy vicinity of Rome, there is not a more melancholy spot than the 'Tre Fontane.'   A splendid monastery, rich with
the offerings of all Christendom, once existed there: the ravages of
that mysterious scourge of the Campagna, the malaria, have rendered
it a desert; three ancient churches and some ruins still exist, and a
few pale monks wander about the swampy dismal confines of the
hollow in which they stand.   In winter you approach them through
a quagmire; in summer, you dare not breathe in their pestilential
vicinity; and yet there is a sort of dead beauty about the place,
something hallowed as well as sad, which seizes on the fancy.   In
the church properly called 'San Paolo delle Tre Fontane,' and which

is so old that the date of the foundation is unknown, are three chapels with altars raised over as many wells or fountains; the altars are modern, and have each the head of St. Paul carved in relief. The water, which appeared to me exactly the same in all the three fountains, has a soft insipid taste, neither refreshing nor agreeable. The ancient frescoes have perished, and the modern ones are perishing. It is a melancholy spot.

To return, however, to that event which has rendered it for ages consecrated and memorable. Among the many representations of the decollation of St. Paul which exist in sculpture and in painting, I have not met with one which could take a high place as a work of Art, or which has done justice to the tragic capabilities of the subject.

After his martyrdom, the body of St. Paul was interred on a spot between the Ostian gate and the Aqua Salvias, and there arose the magnificent church known as San Paolo-*fuori-le-mura*. I saw this church a few months before it was consumed by fire in 1823; I saw it again in 1847, when the restoration was far advanced. Its cold magnificence, compared with the impressions left by the former structure, rich with inestimable remains of ancient Art, and venerable from a thousand associations, saddened and chilled me.

The mosaics in the old church, which represented the life and actions of St. Paul, were executed by the Greek mosaic masters of the eleventh century. They appear to have comprised the same subjects which still exist as a series in the church of Monreale near Palermo, and which I shall now describe.

1. Saul is sent by the high priest to Damascus. Two priests are seated on a raised throne in front of the Temple; Saul stands before them.

2. The Conversion of Saul, as already described (p. 214.)

3. Saul, being blind, is led by his attendants to the gate of Damascus.

4. Saul seated. Ananias enters and addresses him.

5. Paul is baptized: he is standing, or rather sitting, in a font, which is a large vase, and not much larger in proportion than a punch-bowl.

6. St. Paul disputes with the Jews. His attitude is vehement

and expressive; three Jewish doctors stand before him as if confounded and put to silence by his eloquent reasoning.

7. St. Paul escapes from Damascus; the basket, in which he is lowered down from a parapet, is about the size of a hand-basket.

8. St. Paul delivers a scroll to Timothy and Silas; he consigns to their direction the deacons that were ordained by the apostles and elders. (Acts xvi. 4.)

9. St. Paul and St. Peter meet at Rome, and embrace with brotherly affection. I believe this subject to represent the reconciliation of the two apostles after the dispute at Antioch. The inscription is, *Hic Paulus venit Romam et pacem fecit cum Petro.* (In the Christian Museum in the Vatican there is a most beautiful small Greek picture in which Peter and Paul are embracing; it may represent the reconciliation or the parting: the heads, though minute, are extremely characteristic.)

10. The Decollation of St. Paul at the Aqua Salvias; one fountain only is introduced.

This is the earliest instance I can quote of the dramatic treatment of the life and actions of St. Paul in a series of subjects. The Greek type of the head of St. Paul is retained throughout, strongly individualised, and he appears as a man of about thirty-five or forty. In the later schools of Art, which afford some celebrated examples of the life of St. Paul treated as a series, the Greek type has been abandoned.

The series, by Raphael, executed for the tapestries of the Sistine Chapel in the Vatican, consists of five large and seven small compositions.

1. The Conversion of Saul, already described: the cartoon is lost. 2. Elymas the sorcerer struck blind: wonderful for dramatic power. 3. St. Paul and Barnabas at Lystra. 4. Paul preaches at Athens. Of these three magnificent compositions we have the cartoons at Hampton Court. 5. St. Paul in prison at Philippi. The earthquake through which he was liberated is here represented allegorically as a Titan in the lower corner of the picture, with shoulders and arms heaving up the earth. This, which strikes us as rather pagan in conception, has, however, a parallel in the earliest Christian Art, where, in the baptism of Christ, the Jordan is sometimes represented by a classical river-god, sedge-crowned, and leaning on his urn.

The seven small subjects, which in the set of tapestries run under-neath as borders to the large compositions, are thus arranged :—

1. ' As for Saul, he made havoc of the church, entering into every house, and haling men and women committed them to prison' (Acts viii. 3). At one end of a long narrow composition Saul is seated in the dress of a Roman warrior, and attended by a lictor ; they bring before him a Christian youth ; farther on are seen soldiers 'haling men and women ' by the hair ; others flee in terror. This was erroneously supposed to represent the massacre at Prato, in 1512, by the adhe-rents of the Medici, and is so inscribed in the set of engravings by Bartoli and Landon.

2. John and Mark taking leave of the brethren at Perga in Pam-phylia. (Acts xiii. 3.)

3. Paul, teaching in the synagogue at Antioch, confounds the Jews. (Acts xviii. 3.)

4. Paul at Corinth engaged in tent-making with his host. This is an uncommon subject, but I remember another instance in a curious old German print, where, in the lower part of the composition, the apostle is teaching or preaching; and above there is a kind of gallery or balcony, in which he is seen working at a loom : ' You yourselves know that these hands have ministered to my necessities, labouring night and day, because we would not be chargeable unto you' (Acts xviii. 6).

5. Being at Corinth, he is mocked by the Jews. (Acts viii. 12.)

6. He lays his hand on the Christian converts.

7. He is brought before the judgment-seat of Gallio.[1]

' Paul, in the island of Melita, shaking the viper from his hand,' is not a common subject, and yet it is capable of the finest picturesque and dramatic effects : the storm and shipwreck in the background, the angry heavens above, the red firelight, the group of astonished mariners, and, pre-eminent among them, the calm intellectual figure of the apostle shaking the venomous beast from his hand,—these are surely beautiful and available materials for a scenic picture. Even if treated

---

[1] Those who consult the engravings by Santi Bartoli and Landon must bear in mind that almost all the references are erroneous. See Passavant's ' Rafael,' ii. 245.

as an allegory in a devotional sense, a single majestic figure, throwing the evil thing innocuous from him, which I have not yet seen, it would be an excellent and a significant subject.   The little picture by Elzheimer is the best example I can cite of the picturesque treatment. That of Le Sueur has much dignity ; those of Perino del Vaga, Thornhill, West, are all commonplace.

Thornhill, as everybody knows, painted the eight principal scenes of the life of the apostle in the cupola of St. Paul's.[1]   Few people, I should think, have strained their necks to examine them ; the eight original studies, small sketches *en grisaille*, are preserved in the vestry, and display that heartless, mindless, mannered mediocrity, which makes all criticism foolishness ; I shall, however, give a list of the subjects.

1. Paul and Barnabas at Lystra.   2. Paul preaching at Athens. 3. Elymas struck blind.   4. The converts burn their magical books. 5. Paul before Festus.   6. A woman seated at his feet ; I presume the Conversion of Lydia of Thyatira.   7. Paul let down in a basket. 8. He shakes the viper from his hand.

At the time that Thornhill was covering the cupola at 'the rate of £2 the square yard,' Hogarth, his son-in-law, would also try his hand.   He painted ' St. Paul pleading before Felix ' for Lincoln's Inn Hall ; where the subject, at least, is appropriate.   The picture itself is curiously characteristic, not of the scene or of the chief personage, but of the painter.   St. Paul loaded with chains, and his accuser Tertullus, stand in front ; and Felix, with his wife Drusilla, are seated on a raised tribunal in the background ; near Felix is the high priest Ananias.   The composition is good.   The heads are full of vivid expression—wrath, terror, doubt, fixed attention ; but the conception of character most ignoble and commonplace.   Hogarth was more at home when he took the same subject as a vehicle for a witty caricature of the Dutch manner of treating sacred subjects—their ludicrous anachronisms and mean incidents.   St. Paul, in allusion to his low stature, is mounted on a stool ; an angel is sawing through one leg of it ; Tertullus is a barrister, in wig, band, and gown ; the

---

[1] The clergy who permitted Sir James Thornhill to paint the cupola of St. Paul's with Scripture scenes, refused to admit any other paintings into the church.   Perhaps they were justified ; but not by the plea of Bishop Terrick—the fear of dolatry.

judge is like an old doting justice of peace, and his attendants like old beggars.

In the Florentine Gallery there is a very curious series of the lives of St. Peter and St. Paul in eight pictures, in the genuine old German style; fanciful, a... ated, full of natural and dramatic expression, and exquisitely finished,—but dry, hard, grotesque, and abounding in anachronisms.[1]

Among the few separate historical subjects in which St. Peter and St. Paul are represented together, the most important is the dispute at Antioch,—a subject avoided by the earliest painters. St. Paul says, 'When Peter was come to Antioch, I withstood him to the face, because he was to be blamed.' Guido's picture in the *Brera* at *Milan* is celebrated: Peter is seated, looking thoughtful, with downcast eyes, an open book on his knees; Paul, in an attitude of rebuke, stands over against him. There is another example by Rosso: here both are standing; Peter is looking down; Paul, with long hair and beard floating back, and a keen reproving expression, 'rebukes him to his face.' I presume the same subject to be represented by Lucas van Leyden in a rare and beautiful little print, in which St. Peter and St. Paul are seated together in earnest conversation. St. Peter holds a *key* in his right hand, and points with the other to a book which lies on his knees. St. Paul is about to turn the leaf, and his right hand appears to rebuke St. Peter; his left foot is on the *sword* which lies at his feet.

'The Parting of St. Peter and St. Paul, before they are led to death.' The scene is without the gates of Rome; and as the soldiers drag Peter away, he turns back to Paul with a pathetic expression. This picture, now in the Louvre, is one of Lanfranco's best compositions.[2]

When the crucifixion of St. Peter and the decollation of St. Paul

---

[1] This series, the most important work of the painter, Hans Schaufelein, is not mentioned in Kugler's Handbook. It is engraved in outline in the 'New Florence Gallery,' published in 1837.

[2] 'St. Paul prevents his jailor from killing himself' (Acts xvi.) has been lately painted by Claude Hallé, and is now in the Louvre. (École française, No. 283.)

are represented together in the same picture, such a picture must be considered as religious and devotional, not historical; it does not express the action as it really occurred, but, like many pictures of the crucifixion of our Saviour, it is placed before us as an excitement to piety, self-sacrifice, and repentance.   We have this kind of treatment in a picture by Niccolò dell' Abate:[1] St. Paul kneels before a block, and the headsman stands with sword uplifted in act to strike; in the background, two other executioners grasp St. Peter, who is kneeling on his cross and praying fervently: above, in a glory, is seen the Virgin; in her arms the Infant Christ, who delivers to two angels palm-branches for the martyred saints.   The genius of Niccolò was not precisely fitted for this class of subjects. But the composition is full of poetical feeling.   The introduction of the Madonna and Child stamps the character of the picture as devotional, not historical—it would otherwise be repulsive, and out of keeping with the subject.

There is a Martyrdom of St. Peter and St. Paul engraved after Parmigiano,[2] which I shall notice on account of its careless and erroneous treatment.   They are put to death together; an executioner prepares to decapitate St. Peter, and another drags St. Paul by the beard : the incidents are historically false, and, moreover, in a degraded and secular taste.   These are the mistakes that make us turn disgusted from the technical facility, elegance, and power of the sixteenth century, to the simplicity and reverential truth of the fourteenth.

There are various traditions concerning the relics of St. Peter and St. Paul.   According to some, the bodies of the two apostles were, in the reign of Heliogabalus, deposited by the Christian converts in the catacombs of Rome, and were laid in the same sepulchre.   After the lapse of about two hundred years, the Greek or Oriental Christians attempted to carry them off; but were opposed by the Roman Christians.   The Romans conquered; and the two bodies were transported to the church of the Vatican, where they reposed together in a magnificent shrine, beneath the church.   Among the engravings in the work of Ciampini and Bosio are two rude old pictures commemorating this event. The first represents the combat of the Orientals and the Romans

---

[1] In the Dresden Gal., No. 821.   [2] Bartsch, vii. 79.

for the bodies of the Saints; in the other, the bodies are deposited in the Vatican. In these two ancient representations, which were placed in the portico of the old basilica of St. Peter, the traditional types may be recognised—the broad full features, short curled beard, and bald head of St. Peter, and the oval face and long beard of St. Paul.

Here I must conclude this summary of the lives and characters of the two greatest apostles, as they have been exhibited in Christian Art; to do justice to the theme would have required a separate volume. One observation, however, suggests itself, and cannot be passed over. The usual type of the head of St. Peter, though often ill rendered and degraded by coarseness, can in general be recognised as characteristic; but is there among the thousand representations of the apostle Paul, *one* on which the imagination can rest completely satisfied? I know not one. No doubt the sublimest ideal of embodied eloquence that ever was expressed in Art is Raphael's St. Paul preaching at Athens. He stands there the delegated voice of the true God, the antagonist and conqueror of the whole heathen world :—' Whom ye ignorantly worship, HIM declare I unto you' —is not this what he says? Every feature, nay, every fold in his drapery, speaks; as in the other St. Paul leaning on his sword (in the famous St. Cecilia), every feature and every fold of drapery meditates. The latter is as fine in its tranquil melancholy grandeur, as the former in its authoritative energy : in the one the orator, in the other the philosopher, were never more finely rendered : but is it, in either, the Paul of Tarsus whom we know? It were certainly both unnecessary and pedantic to adhere so closely to historic fact as to make St. Paul of diminutive stature, and St. Peter weak-eyed : but has Raphael done well in wholly rejecting the traditional portrait which reflected to us the Paul of Scripture, the man of many toils and many sorrows, wasted with vigils, worn down with travel,— whose high bald forehead, thin flowing hair, and long pointed beard, spoke so plainly the fervent and indomitable, yet meditative and delicate, organisation,—and in substituting this Jupiter Ammon head, with the dark redundant hair, almost hiding the brow, and the full bushy beard? This is one of the instances in which Raphael, in yielding to the fashion of his time, has erred, as it seems to me,—

though I say it with all reverence. The St. Paul rending his garments
at Lystra, and rejecting the sacrifice of the misguided people, is
more particularly false as to the character of the man though otherwise so grandly expressive, that we are obliged to admire what our
better sense—our *conscience*—cannot wholly approve.

I shall now consider the rest of the apostles in their proper order.

St. Andrew.

Lat. S. Andreas.   *Ital.* Sant' Andrea.   *Fr.* St. André.   Patron saint of Scotland and of
Russia.   Nov. 30, A.D. 70.

St. Andrew was the brother of Simon Peter, and the first who was
called to the apostleship. Nothing farther is recorded of him in
Scripture : he is afterwards merely included by name in the general
account of the apostles.

In the traditional and legendary history of St. Andrew, we are told
that, after our Lord's ascension, when the apostles dispersed to preach
the Gospel to all nations, St. Andrew travelled into Scythia, Cappadocia, and Bithynia, everywhere converting multitudes to the faith.
The Russians believe that he was the first to preach to the Muscovites
in Sarmatia, and thence he has been honoured as titular saint of the
empire of Russia. After many sufferings, he returned to Jerusalem,
and thence travelled into Greece, and came at length to a city of
Achaia, called Patras. Here he made many converts ; among others,
Maximilla, the wife of the proconsul Ægeus, whom he persuaded to
make a public profession of Christianity. The proconsul, enraged,
commanded him to be seized and scourged, and then crucified. The
cross on which he suffered was of a peculiar form (*crux decussata*), since
called the St. Andrew's cross ; and it is expressly said that he was not
fastened to his cross with nails, but with cords,—a circumstance always
attended to in the representations of his death. It is, however, to be
remembered, that while all authorities agree that he was crucified, and
that the manner of his crucifixion was peculiar, they are not agreed as
to the form of his cross. St. Peter Chrysologos says that it was a tree :
another author affirms that it was an olive tree. The Abbé Méry

remarks, that it is a mistake to give the transverse cross to St. Andrew; that it ought not to differ from the cross of our Lord. His reasons are not absolutely conclusive:—'Il suffit pour montrer qu'ils sont là-dessus dans l'erreur, de voir *la croix véritable* de St. André, conservée dans l'Église de St. Victor de Marseille; on trouvera qu'elle est à angles droits,' &c.[1] Seeing is believing; nevertheless, the form is fixed by tradition and usage, and ought not to be departed from, though Michael Angelo has done so in the figure of St. Andrew in the Last Judgment, and there are several examples in the Italian masters.[2] The legend goes on to relate, that St. Andrew on approaching the cross prepared for his execution, saluted and adored it on his knees, as being already consecrated by the sufferings of the Redeemer, and met his death triumphantly. Certain of his relics were brought from Patras to Scotland in the fourth century, and since that time St. Andrew has been honoured as the patron saint of Scotland, and of its chief order of knighthood. He is also the patron saint of the famous Burgundian Order, the Golden Fleece; and of Russia and its chief Order, the Cross of St. Andrew.

74   St. Andrew.
(Peter Vischer.)

Since the fourteenth century, St. Andrew is generally distinguished in works of Art by the transverse cross; the devotional pictures in which he figures as one of the series of apostles, or singly as patron saint, represent him as a very old man with some kind of brotherly resemblance to St. Peter; his hair and beard silver white, long, loose, and flowing, and in general the beard is divided; he leans upon his cross, and holds the Gospel in his right hand.

The historical subjects from the life of St. Andrew, treated separately from the rest of the apostles, are very few; his crucifixion is the only

[1] Théologie des Peintres.
[2] In several ancient pictures and bas-reliefs the cross has the usual form, but he is not nailed—always bound with cords, as in the ancient bas-relief over the portal of his church at Vercelli.

one that I have found treated before the fifteenth century. On the ancient doors of San Paolo, the instrument of his martyrdom has the shape of a Y, and resembles a tree split down the middle.   The cross in some later pictures is very lofty, and resembles the rough branches of a tree laid transversely.

I know but two other subjects relating to the life of St. Andrew which have been separately treated in the later schools of Art—the Adoration of the Cross, and the Flagellation.

' St. Andrew Adoring his Cross,' by Andrea Sacchi, is remarkable for its simplicity and fine expression; it contains only three figures. St. Andrew, half undraped, and with his silver hair and beard floating dishevelled, kneels, gazing up to the cross with ecstatic devotion ; he is addressing to it his famous invocation :—' Salve, Croce preziosa ! che fosti consecrata dal corpo del mio Dio ! '—an executioner stands by, and a fierce soldier, impatient of delay, urges him on to death.[1]

' St. Andrew Taken Down from the Cross ' is a fine effective picture by Ribera.[2]

When Guido and Domenichino painted, in emulation of each other, the frescoes in the chapel of Sant' Andrea in the church of San Gregorio, at Rome, Guido chose for his subject the Adoration of the Cross.   The scene is supposed to be outside the walls of Patras in Achaia; the cross is at a distance in the background; St. Andrew, as he approaches, falls down in adoration before the instrument of his martyrdom, consecrated by the death of his Lord ; he is attended by one soldier on horseback, one on foot, and three executioners ; a group of women and alarmed children in the foreground are admirable for grace and feeling—they are, in fact, the best part of the picture. On the opposite wall of the chapel Domenichino painted the Flagellation of St. Andrew, a subject most difficult to treat effectively, and retain at the same time the dignity of the suffering apostle, while avoiding all resemblance to a similar scene in the life of Christ. Here he is bound down on a sort of table; one man lifts a rod, another seems to taunt the prostrate saint ; a lictor drives back the people.   The group of the mother and frightened children, which Domenichino so often introduces with little variation, is here very

---

[1] Gallery of the Vatican.   [2] Munich, 363.

beautiful; the judge and lictors are seen behind, with a temple and a city in the distance. When Domenichino painted the same subject in the church of Sant' Andrea-della-Valle, he chose another moment, and administered the torture after a different manner: the apostle is bound by his hands and feet to four short posts set firmly in the ground; one of the executioners in tightening a cord breaks it and falls back; three men prepare to scourge him with *thongs:* in the foreground we have the usual group of the mother and her frightened children. This is a composition full of dramatic life and movement, but unpleasing. Domenichino painted in the same church the crucifixion of the saint, and his apotheosis surmounts the whole.

All these compositions are of great celebrity in the history of Art for colour and for expression. Lanzi says, that the personages, 'if endued with speech, could not say more to the ear than they do to the eye.' But, in power and pathos, none of them equal the picture of Murillo, of which we have the original study in England.[1] St. Andrew is suspended on the high cross, formed not of planks, but of the trunks of trees laid transversely. He is bound with cords, undraped, except by a linen cloth; his silver hair and beard loosely streaming in the air; his aged countenance illuminated by a heavenly transport, as he looks up to the opening skies, whence two angels of really celestial beauty, like almost all Murillo's angels, descend with the crown and palm. In front, to the right, is a group of shrinking, sympathising women; and a boy turns away, crying with a truly boyish grief; on the left are guards and soldiers. The subject is here rendered poetical by mere force of feeling; there is a tragic reality in the whole scene, far more effective, to my taste, than the more studied compositions of the Italian painters. The Martyrdom of St. Andrew, and the Saint Preaching the Gospel, by Juan de Roelas, are also mentioned as splendid productions of the Seville school.

I think it possible that St. Andrew may owe his popularity in the Spanish and Flemish schools of Art to his being the patron saint of the far-famed Burgundian Order of the Golden Fleece. At the time that Constantinople was taken, and the relics of St. Andrew dispersed in consequence, a lively enthusiasm for this

[1] In the collection of Mr Miles at Leigh Court.

apostle was excited throughout all Christendom. He had been previously honoured chiefly as the brother of St. Peter: he obtained thenceforth a kind of personal interest and consideration. Philip of Burgundy (A.D. 1433), who had obtained at great cost a portion of the precious relics, consisting chiefly of some pieces of his cross, placed under the protection of the apostle his new order of chivalry, which, according to the preamble, was intended to revive the honour and the memory of the Argonauts. His knights wore as their badge the cross of St. Andrew.

St. James the Great.

Lat. Sanctus Jacobus Major. *Ital.* San Giacomo, or Jacopo, Maggiore. *Fr.* St. Jacques Majeur. *Spa.* San Jago, or Santiago. El Tutelar. Patron saint of Spain. July 25, A.D. 44.

St. James the Great, or the Elder, or St. James *Major*, was nearly related to Christ, and, with his brother John (the evangelist) and Peter, he seems to have been admitted to particular favour, travelled with the Lord, and was present at most of the events recorded in the Gospels. He was one of the three who were permitted to witness the glorification of Christ on Mount Tabor, and one of those who slept during the agony in the garden. After our Saviour's ascension, nothing is recorded concerning him, except the fact that Herod slew him with the sword. In the ancient traditions he is described as being of a zealous and affectionate temper, easily excited to anger: of this we have a particular instance in his imprecation against the inhospitable Samaritans, for which Christ rebuked him: 'Ye know not what manner of spirit ye are of. The Son of man is not come to destroy men's lives, but to save them.' (Luke ix. 55.)

As Scripture makes no farther mention of one so distinguished by his zeal and by his near relationship to the Saviour, the legends of the Middle Ages have supplied this deficiency; and so amply, that St. James, as St. Jago or Santiago, the military patron of Spain, became one of the most renowned saints in Christendom, and one of the most popular subjects of Western Art. Many of these subjects are so singular, that, in order to render them intelligible, I must give the legend at full length as it was followed by the artists of the fourteenth and fifteenth centuries.

According to the Spanish legend, the apostle James was the son of Zebedee, an illustrious baron of Galilee, who, being the proprietor of ships, was accustomed to fish along the shores of a certain lake called Gennesareth, but solely for his good pleasure and recreation: for who can suppose that Spain, that nation of Hidalgos and Caballeros, would ever have chosen for her patron, or accepted as the leader and captain-general of her armies, a poor ignoble fisherman? It remains, therefore, indisputable, that this glorious apostle, who was our Lord's cousin-german, was of noble lineage, and worthy of his spurs as a knight and a gentleman;—so in Dante:—

> Ecco *il Barone*
> Per cui laggiù si visita Galizia.'

But it pleased him, in his great humility, to follow, while on earth, the example of his divine Lord, and reserve his warlike prowess till called upon to slaughter, by thousands and tens of thousands, those wicked Moors, the perpetual enemies of Christ and His servants. Now, as James and his brother John were one day in their father's ship with his hired servants, and were employed in mending the nets, the Lord, who was walking on the shores of the lake, called them; and they left all and followed Him; and became thenceforward His most favoured disciples, and the witnesses of His miracles while on earth. After the ascension of Christ, James preached the Gospel in Judea; then he travelled over the whole world, and came at last to Spain, where he made very few converts, by reason of the ignorance and darkness of the people. One day, as he stood with his disciples on the banks of the Ebro, the blessed Virgin appeared to him seated on the top of a pillar of jasper, and surrounded by a choir of Angels; and the apostle having thrown himself on his face, she commanded him to build on that spot a chapel for her worship, assuring him that all this province of Saragossa, though now in the darkness of paganism, would at a future

time be distinguished by devotion to her. He did as the holy
Virgin had commanded, and this was the origin of a famous church
afterwards known as that of Our Lady of the Pillar (' *Nuestra
Señora del Pillar* '). Then St. James, having founded the Christian
faith in Spain, returned to Judea, where he preached for many years,
and performed many wonders and miracles in the sight of the people :
and it happened ,that a certain sorcerer, whose name was Hermogenes,[1] set himself against the apostle, just as Simon Magus had
wickedly and vainly opposed St. Peter, and with the like result.
Hermogenes sent his scholar Philetus to dispute with James, and
to compete with him in wondrous works ; but, as you will easily
believe, he had no chance against the apostle, and, confessing himself vanquished, he returned to his master, to whom he announced
his intention to follow henceforth James and his doctrine. Then
Hermogenes, in a rage, bound Philetus by his diabolical spells, so
that he could not move hand or foot ; saying, ' Let us now see if thy
new master can deliver thee : ' and Philetus sent his servant to St.
James, praying for aid. Then the apostle took off his cloak, and gave
it to the servant to give his master , and no sooner had Philetus
touched it, than he became free, and hastened to throw himself at
the feet of his deliverer. Hermogenes, more furious than ever, called
to the demons who served him, and commanded that they should
bring to him James and Philetus, bound in fetters ; but on their
way the demons met with a company of Angels, who seized upon
them, and punished them for their wicked intentions, till they cried
for mercy. Then St. James said to them, ' Go back to him who sent
ye, and bring him hither bound.' And they did so ; and having laid
the sorcerer down at the feet of St. James, they besought him, saying, 'Now give us power to be avenged of our enemy and thine ! '
But St. James rebuked them, saying, ' Christ hath commanded us to
do good for evil.' So he delivered Hermogenes from their hands ;
and the magician, being utterly confounded, cast his books into the
sea, and desired of St. James that he would protect him against the
demons, his former servants. Then St. James gave him his staff, as
the most effectual means of defence against the infernal spirits ; and

---

[1] Hermogenes was the name of a famous Gnostic teacher and philosopher ; thence, I
suppose, adopted into this legend.

Hermogenes became a faithful disciple and preacher of the Word from that day.

But the evil-minded Jews, being more and more incensed, took James and bound him, and brought him before the tribunal of Herod Agrippa; and one of those who dragged him along, touched by the gentleness of his demeanour, and by his miracles of mercy, was converted, and supplicated to die with him; and the apostle gave him the kiss of peace, saying, 'Pax vobis!' and the kiss and the words together have remained as a form of benediction in the Church to this day. Then they were both beheaded, and so died.

And the disciples of St. James came and took away his body; and, not daring to bury it, for fear of the Jews, they carried it to Joppa, and placed it on board of a ship: some say that the ship was of marble, but this is not authenticated; however, it is most certain that angels conducted the ship miraculously to the coast of Spain, where they arrived in seven days; and, sailing through the straits called the Pillars of Hercules, they landed at length in Galicia, at a port called Iria Flavia, now Padron.

In those days there reigned over the country a certain queen whose name was Lupa, and she and all her people were plunged in wickedness and idolatry. Now, having come to shore, they laid the body of the apostle upon a great stone, which became like wax, and, receiving the body, closed around it: this was a sign that the saint willed to remain there; but the wicked queen Lupa was displeased, and she commanded that they should harness some wild bulls to a car, and place on it the body, with the self-formed tomb, hoping that they would drag it to destruction. But in this she was mistaken; for the wild bulls, when signed by the cross, became as docile as sheep, and they drew the body of the apostle straight into the court of her palace. When Queen Lupa beheld this miracle, she was confounded, and she and all her people became Christians: she built a magnificent church to receive the sacred remains, and died in the odour of sanctity.

But then came the darkness and ruin which during the invasion of the Barbarians overshadowed all Spain; and the body of the apostle was lost, and no one knew where to find it, till, in the year 800, the place of sepulture was revealed to a certain holy friar.

Then they caused the body of the saint to be transported to Compostella; and, in consequence of the surprising miracles which graced his shrine, he was honoured not merely in Galicia, but throughout all Spain.   He became the patron saint of the Spaniards, and Compostella, as a place of pilgrimage, was renowned throughout Europe. From all countries bands of pilgrims resorted there, so that sometimes there were no less than a hundred thousand in one year.   The military Order of Saint Jago, enrolled by Don Alphonso for their protection, became one of the greatest and richest in Spain.

Now, if I should proceed to recount all the wonderful deeds enacted by Santiago in behalf of his chosen people, they would fill a volume. The Spanish historians number thirty-eight visible apparitions, in which this glorious saint descended from heaven in person, and took the command of their armies against the Moors.   The first of these, and the most famous of all, I shall now relate.

In the year of our Lord 939, King Ramirez, having vowed to deliver Castile from the shameful tribute imposed by the Moors, of one hundred virgins delivered annually, collected his troops, and defied their king Abdelraman to battle :—

> The king call'd God to witness, that, came there weal or woe,
> Thenceforth no maiden tribute from out Castile should go.—
> ' At least I will do battle on God our Saviour's foe,
> And die beneath my banner before I see it so ! '

Accordingly he charged the Moorish host on the plain of Alveida or Clavijo : after a furious conflict, the Christians were, by the permission of Heaven, defeated, and forced to retire.   Night separated the combatants, and King Ramirez, overpowered with fatigue, and sad at heart, flung himself upon his couch and slept.   In his sleep he beheld the apostle St. Jago, who promised to be with him next morning in the field, and assured him of victory.   The king, waking up from the glorious vision, sent for his prelates and officers, to whom he related it; and the next morning, at the head of his army, he recounted it to his soldiers, bidding them rely on heavenly aid.   He then ordered the trumpets to sound to battle.   The soldiers, inspired with fresh courage, rushed to the fight.   Suddenly St. Jago was seen mounted on a milk-white charger, and waving aloft a white standard; he led on the

Christians, who gained a decisive victory, leaving 60,000 Moors dead on the field. This was the famous battle of Clavijo; and ever since that day, 'SANTIAGO!' has been the war-cry of the Spanish armies.

But it was not only on such great occasions that the invincible patron of Spain was pleased to exhibit his power: he condescended oftentimes to interfere for the protection of the poor and oppressed, of which I will now give a notable instance, as it is related by Pope Calixtus II.

There was a certain German, who with his wife and son went on a pilgrimage to St. James of Compostella. Having come as far as Torlosa, they lodged at an inn there; and the host had a fair daughter, who, looking on the son of the pilgrim, a handsome and a graceful youth, became deeply enamoured; but he, being virtuous, and, moreover, on his way to a holy shrine, refused to listen to her allurements.

Then she thought how she might be avenged for this slight put upon her charms, and hid in his wallet her father's silver drinking-cup. The next morning, no sooner were they departed, than the host, discovering his loss, pursued them, accused them before the judge, and the cup being found in the young man's wallet, he was condemned to be hung, and all they possessed was confiscated to the host.

Then the afflicted parents pursued their way lamenting, and made their prayer and their complaint before the altar of the blessed Saint Jago; and thirty-six days afterwards as they returned by the spot where their son hung on the gibbet, they stood beneath it, weeping and lamenting bitterly. Then the son spoke and said, 'O my mother! O my father! do not lament for me, for I have never been in better cheer; the blessed apostle James is at my side, sustaining me and filling me with celestial comfort and joy!' The parents, being astonished, hastened to the judge, who at that moment was seated at table, and the mother called out, 'Our son lives!' The judge mocked at them: 'What sayest thou, good woman? thou art beside thyself! If thy son liveth, so do those fowls in my dish.' And lo! scarcely had he uttered the words, when the fowls (being a cock and a hen) rose up full-feathered in the dish, and the cock began to crow, to the great admiration of the judge and his attendants.[1] Then the

[1] v. Southey, 'Pilgrim of Compostella.'

judge rose up from table hastily, and called together the priests and the lawyers, and they went in procession to the gibbet, took down the young man, and restored him to his parents ; and the miraculous

75 St. James Major. (Gio. Santi.)

cock and hen were placed under the protection of the Church, where they and their posterity long flourished in testimony of this stupendous miracle.

There are many other legends of St. James; the Spanish chroniclers in prose and verse abound in such ; but, in general, they are not merely incredible, but puerile and unpoetical ; and I have here confined myself to those which I know to have been treated in Art.

Previous to the twelfth century, St. James is only distinguished among the apostles by his place, which is the fourth in the series, the second after St. Peter and St. Paul.   In some instances he is portrayed with a family resemblance to Christ, being his kinsman; the thin beard, and the hair parted and flowing down on each side.   But from the thirteenth century it became a fashion to characterise St. James as a pilgrim of Compostella : he bears the peculiar long staff, to which the wallet or gourd of water is suspended; the cloak with a long cape, the scallop-shell on his shoulder or on his flapped hat. Where the cape, hat, and scallop-shells are omitted, the staff, borne as the first of the apostles who departed to fulfil his Gospel mission, remains his constant attribute, and by this he may be recognised in the Madonna pictures, and when grouped with other saints.

The single devotional figures of St. James represent him in two distinct characters :—

1. As tutelar saint of Spain, and conqueror of the Moors.   In his

76   Santiago. (Carreño de Miranda.)

pilgrim habit, mounted on a white charger, and waving a white banner, with white hair and beard streaming like a meteor,—or sometimes armed in complete steel, spurred like a knight, his casque shadowed by white plumes,—he tramples over the prostrate Infidels; so completely was the humble, gentle-spirited apostle of Christ merged in the spirit of the religious chivalry of the time. This is a subject frequent in Spanish schools. The figure over the high altar of Santiago is described as very grand when seen in the solemn twilight.

2. St. James as patron saint in the general sense. The most beautiful example I have met with is a picture in the Florence Gallery,

77   St. James Major.   (A. del Sarto.)

painted by Andrea del Sarto for the Compagnia or Confraternita of
Sant' Jacopo, and intended to figure as a standard in their processions.   The Madonna di San Sisto of Raphael was painted for a
similar purpose : and such are still commonly used in the religious
processions in Italy ; but they have no longer Raphaels and Andrea-
del-Sartos to paint them.   In this instance the picture has a particular
form, high and narrow, adapted to its especial purpose : St. James
wears a green tunic, and a rich crimson mantle ; and as one of the
purposes of the Compagnia was to educate poor orphans, they are

represented by the two boys at his feet. This picture suffered from the sun and the weather, to which it had been a hundred times exposed in yearly processions; but it has been well restored, and is admirable for its vivid colouring as well as the benign attitude and expression.

3. St. James seated; he holds a large book bound in vellum (the Gospels) in his left hand—and with his right points to heaven: by Guercino, in the gallery of Count Harrach, at Vienna. One of the finest pictures by Guercino I have seen.

Pictures from the life of St. James singly, or as a series, are not common; but among those which remain to us there are several of great beauty and interest.

In the series of frescoes painted in a side chapel of the church of St. Antony of Padua (A.D. 1376), once called the Capella di San Giacomo, and now San Felice, the old legend of St. James has been exactly followed; and though ruined in many parts, and in others coarsely repainted, these works remain as compositions amongst the most curious monuments of the *Trecentisti*. It appears that, towards the year 1376, Messer Bonifacio de' Lupi da Parma, Cavaliere e Marchese di Serana, who boasted of his descent from the Queen Lupa of the legend, dedicated this chapel to St. James of Spain (San Jacopo di Galizia), and employed M. Jacopo Avanzi to decorate it, who no doubt bestowed his best workmanship on his patron saint. The subjects are thus arranged, beginning with the lunette on the left hand, which is divided into three compartments:

1. Hermogenes sends Philetus to dispute with St. James. 2. St. James in his pulpit converts Philetus. 3. Hermogenes sends his demons to bind St. James and Philetus. 4. Hermogenes brought bound to St. James. 5. He burns his books of magic. 6. Hermogenes and Philetus are conversing in a friendly manner with St. James. 7. St. James is martyred. 8. The arrival of his body in Spain in a marble ship steered by an angel. 9. The disciples lay the body on a rock, while Queen Lupa and her sister and another personage look on from a window in her palace. Then follow two compartments on the side where the window is broken out, much ruined; they represented apparently the imprisonment of the disciples. 12. The disciples escape and are pursued, and their pursuers with their

horses are drowned.   13. The wild bulls draw the sarcophagus into the court of Queen Lupa's palace.   14. Baptism of Lupa.   15 and 16 (lower compartments to the left) : St. Jago appears to King Ramirez, and the defeat of the Moors at Clavijo.

There is a rare and curious print by Martin Schoen, in which the apparition of St. James at Clavijo is represented not in the Spanish but the German style.   It is an animated composition of many figures.   The saint appears on horseback in the midst, wearing his pilgrim's dress, with the cockle-shell in his hat : the Infidels are trampled down, or fly before him.

78   The Miracle of the Fowls.   (Lo Spagna.)

On the road from Spoleto to Foligno, about four miles from Spoleto, there is a small chapel dedicated to St. James of Galizia. The frescoes representing the miracles of the saint were painted by Lo Spagna (A.D. 1526), the friend and fellow pupil of Raphael. In the vault of the apsis is the Coronation of the Virgin ; she kneels, attired in white drapery flowered with gold, and the whole group, though inferior in power, appeared to me in delicacy and taste far superior to the fresco of Fra Filippo Lippi at Spoleto, from which

Passavant thinks it is borrowed.[1] Immediately under the Coronation, in the centre, is a figure of St. James as patron saint, standing with his pilgrim's staff in one hand, and the Gospel in the other; his dress is a yellow tunic with a blue mantle thrown over it. In the compartment on the left, the youth is seen suspended on the gibbet, while St. James with his hands under his feet sustains him; the father and mother look up at him with astonishment. In the compartment to the right, we see the judge seated at dinner, attended by his servants, one of whom is bringing in a dish: the two pilgrims appear to have just told their story, and the cock and hen have risen up in the dish (78). These frescoes are painted with great elegance and animation, and the story is told with much naïveté. I found the same legend painted on one of the lower windows of the church of St. Ouen, and on a window of the right-hand aisle in St. Vincent's at Rouen.

Of St. John, who is the fifth in the series, I have spoken at large under the head of the Evangelists.

St. Philip.

Ital. San Filippo Apostolo. *Fr.* Saint Philippe. Patron of Brabant and Luxembourg.
May 1.

Of St. Philip there are few notices in the Gospel. He was born at Bethsaida, and he was one of the first of those whom our Lord summoned to follow Him. After the ascension, he travelled into Scythia, and remained there preaching the Gospel for twenty years; he then preached at Hieropolis in Phrygia, where he found the people addicted to the worship of a monstrous serpent or dragon, or of the god Mars under that form. Taking compassion on their blindness, the apostle commanded the serpent, in the name of the cross he held in his hand, to disappear, and immediately the reptile glided out from beneath the altar, at the same time emitting such a hideous stench, that many people died, and among them the king's son fell dead in the arms of his attendants: but the apostle, by Divine power,

[1] Passavant's Rafael, I. 508.

restored him to life. Then the priests of the dragon were incensed against him, and they took him, and crucified him, and being bound on the cross they stoned him; thus he yielded up his spirit to God, praying, like his Divine Master, for his enemies and tormentors.

According to the Scripture, St. Philip had four daughters, who were prophetesses, and made many converts to the faith of Christ (Acts xxi. 9). In the Greek calendar, St. Mariamne, his sister, and St. Hermione, his daughter, are commemorated as martyrs.

When St. Philip is represented alone, or as one of the series of apostles, he is generally a man in the prime of life, with little beard, and with a benign countenance, being described as of a remarkably cheerful and affectionate nature. He bears, as his attribute, a cross, which varies in form; sometimes it is a small cross, which he carries in his hand; sometimes a high cross in the form of a T, or a tall staff with a small Latin cross at the top of it (79). The cross of St. Philip may have a treble signification : it may allude to his martyrdom ; or to his conquest over the idols through the power of the cross; or, when placed on the top of the pilgrim's staff, it may allude to his mission among the barbarians as preacher of the cross of salvation. Single figures of St. Philip as patron are not common : there is a fine statue of him on the façade of San Michele at Florence, and a noble figure by Beccafumi, reading;[1] another, seated and reading, by Ulrich Mair.[2]

Subjects from the life of St. Philip, whether as single pictures or in a series, are also rarely met with. As he was the first called by our Saviour to leave all and follow Him, and his vocation therefore a festival in the Church, it must, I think, have been treated apart; but I have not met with it. I know but of three historical subjects taken from his life :—

79 St. Philip. (A. Durer.)

1. Bonifazio.   St. Philip stands before the Saviour : the attitude of the latter is extremely dignified, that of Philip

[1] Duomo, Siena.   [2] Belvedere, Vienna.

supplicatory; the other apostles are seen in the background: the colouring and expression of the whole like Titian. The subject of this splendid picture is expressed by the inscription underneath (John xiv. 14): 'Domine, ostende nobis Patrem, et sufficit nobis.' 'Philippe, qui videt me, videt et Patrem meum: ego et Pater unum sumus.' [1]

2. St. Philip exorcises the serpent. The scene is the interior of a temple, an altar with the statue of the god Mars: a serpent, creeping from beneath the altar, slays the attendants with his poisonous and fiery breath. The ancient fresco in his chapel at Padua, described by Lord Lindsay, is extremely animated, but far inferior to the same subject in the Santa Croce at Florence by Fra Filippo Lippi, where the dignified attitude of the apostle, and the group of the king's son dying in the arms of the attendants, are admirably effective and dramatic. St. Philip, it must be observed, was the patron saint of the painter.

3. The Crucifixion of St. Philip. According to the old Greek traditions, he was crucified with his head downwards, and he is so represented on the gates of San Paolo; also in an old picture over the tomb of Cardinal Philippe d'Alençon; where his patron, St. Philip, is attached to the cross with cords, and head downwards, like St. Peter; [2] but in the old fresco by Giusto da Padova, in the Capella di San Filippo, he is crucified in the usual manner, arrayed in a long red garment which descends to his feet.

It is necessary to avoid confounding St. Philip the apostle with St. Philip the deacon. It was Philip the deacon who baptized the chamberlain of Queen Candace, though the action has sometimes been attributed to Philip the apostle. The incident of the baptism of the Ethiopian, taking place in the road, by running water, 'on the way that goeth down from Jerusalem to Gaza,' has been introduced into several beautiful landscapes with much picturesque effect. Claude has thus treated it; Salvator Rosa; Jan Both, in a most beautiful picture in the Queen's Gallery; Rembrandt, Cuyp, and others.

[1] Venice Acad.   [2] Rome, S. Maria-in-Trastevere. A.D. 1397.

St. Bartholomew.

Lat. S. Bartholomeus.   *Ital.* San Bartolomeo.   *Fr.* St. Barthélemi.   Aug. 24.

As St. Bartholomew is nowhere mentioned in the canonical books, except by name in enumerating the apostles, there has been large scope for legendary story, but in works of Art he is not a popular saint.

80 St. Bartholomew. (Giotto.)

According to one tradition, he was the son of a husbandman; according to another, he was the son of a prince Ptolomeus. After the ascension of Christ he travelled into India, even to the confines of the habitable world, carrying with him the Gospel of St. Matthew; returning thence, he preached in Armenia and Cilicia; and coming to the city of Albanopolis, he was condemned to death as a Christian: he was first flayed and then crucified.

In single figures and devotional pictures, St. Bartholomew sometimes carries in one hand a book, the Gospel of St. Matthew; but his peculiar attribute is a large knife, the instrument of his martyrdom. The legends describe him as having a quantity of strong black hair and a bushy grizzled beard; and this portrait being followed very literally by the old German and Flemish painters, gives him, with his large knife, the look of a butcher. In the Italian pictures, though of a milder and more dignified appearance, he has frequently black hair; and sometimes dark and resolute features; yet the same legend describes him as of a cheerful countenance, wearing a purple robe and attended by angels. Sometimes St. Bartholomew has his own skin hanging over his arm, as among the saints in Michael Angelo's Last Judgment, where he is holding forth his skin in one hand, and grasping his knife in the other : and in the statue by Marco Agrati in the Milan Cathedral, famous for its anatomical precision and its boastful inscription, *Non me Praxiteles sed Marcus pinxit Agratis.* I found in the church of Nôtre Dame at Paris a picture of St. Bartholomew healing the Princess of Armenia. With this exception, I know not any historical subject where this apostle is the principal figure, except his revolting and cruel martyrdom. In the early Greek representation on the gates of San Paolo, he is affixed to a cross, or rather to a post, with a small transverse bar at top, to which his hands are fastened above his head ; an executioner, with a knife in his hand, stoops at his feet. This is very different from the representations in the modern schools. The best, that is to say, the least disgusting, representation I have met with, is a small picture by Agostino Caracci, in the Sutherland Gallery, which once belonged to King Charles I. : it is easy to see that the painter had the antique Marsyas in his mind. That dark ferocious spirit, Ribera, found in it a theme congenial with his own temperament ;[1] he has not only painted it several times with a horrible truth and power, but etched it elaborately with his own hand : a small picture, copied from the etching, is at Hampton Court.

ST. THOMAS.

Ital. San Tomaso. *Sp.* San Tomè. Dec. 21. Patron Saint of Portugal and Parma.

St. Thomas, called *Didymus* (the twin), takes, as apostle, the seventh place. He was a Galilean and a fisherman, and we find him distinguished among the apostles on two occasions recorded in the Gospel. When Jesus was going up to Bethany, being then in danger from the Jews, Thomas said, ' Let us also go, that we may die with Him ' (John xi. 16, xx. 25). After the resurrection, he showed himself unwilling to believe in the reappearance of the crucified Saviour without ocular demonstration : this incident is styled the Incredulity of Thomas. From these two incidents we may form some idea of his character : courageous and affectionate, but not inclined

[1] Stirling's ' Artists of Spain,' ii. p. 753.

to take things for granted; or, as a French writer expresses it,
'brusque et résolu, mais d'un esprit exigeant.' After the ascension,
St. Thomas travelled into the East, preaching the Gospel in far
distant countries towards the rising sun. It is a tradition received
in the Church, that he penetrated as far as India; that there meeting
with the three Wise Men of the East, he baptized them; that he
founded a church in India, and suffered martyrdom there. It is related, that the Portuguese found at Meliapore an ancient inscription,
purporting that St. Thomas had been pierced with a lance at the foot
of a cross which he had erected in that city, and that in 1523 his
body was found there and transported to Goa.

In Correggio's fresco of St. Thomas as protector of Parma he is
surrounded by angels bearing exotic fruits, as expressing his ministry
in India.

There are a number of extravagant and poetical legends relating

to St. Thomas. I shall here limit myself to those
which were adopted in ecclesiastical decoration,
and treated by the artists of the Middle Ages.

When St. Thomas figures as apostle, alone or
with others, in all the devotional representations
which are not prior to the
thirteenth century, he carries
as his attribute the builder's
rule, of this form—

Now, as he was a fisherman,
and neither a carpenter nor a mason, the origin
of this attribute must be sought in one of the
most popular legends of which he is the subject.

'When St. Thomas was at Cesarea, our Lord
appeared to him and said, "The King of the
Indies, Gondoforus, hath sent his provost Abanes
to seek for workmen well versed in the science
of architecture, who shall build for him a palace
finer than that of the Emperor of Rome. Behold,

81 St. Thomas the Apostle. now, I will send thee to him." And Thomas
went, and Gondoforus commanded him to build for him a magnificent palace, and gave him much gold and silver for the purpose.

The king went into a distant country, and was absent for two years; and St. Thomas meanwhile, instead of building a palace, distributed all the treasures entrusted to him among the poor and sick; and when the king returned, he was full of wrath, and he commanded that St. Thomas should be seized and cast into prison, and he meditated for him a horrible death. Meantime the brother of the king died; and the king resolved to erect for him a most magnificent tomb; but the dead man, after that he had been dead four days, suddenly arose and sat upright, and said to the king, " The man whom thou wouldst torture is a servant of God: behold I have been in Paradise, and the angels showed to me a wondrous palace of gold and silver and precious stones," and they said, " This is the palace that Thomas the architect hath built for thy brother King Gondoforus." And when the king heard these words, he ran to the prison, and delivered the apostle; and Thomas said to him, " Knowest thou not that those who would possess heavenly things, have little care for the things of this earth? There are in heaven rich palaces without number, which were prepared from the beginning of the world for those who purchase the possession through faith and charity. Thy riches, O King, may prepare the way for thee to such a palace, but they cannot follow thee thither." ' [1]

The builder's rule in the hand of St. Thomas characterises him as the spiritual architect of King Gondoforus, and for the same reason he has been chosen among the saints as patron of architects and builders.

There is in this legend or allegory, fanciful as it is, an obvious beauty and significance, which I need not point out. It appears to me to be one of those many legends which originally were not assumed to be facts, but were related as parables, religious fictions invented for the instruction of the people, like our Saviour's stories of the ' Good Samaritan,' the ' Prodigal Son,' &c., and were rendered more striking and impressive by the introduction of a celebrated and exalted personage—our Saviour, the Virgin, or one of the apostles— as hero of the tale. This beautiful legend of St. Thomas and King Gondoforus is painted on one of the windows of the cathedral at Bourges,—an appropriate offering from the company of builders in that ancient city. It is also the subject of one of the finest of the

[1] Legenda Aurea.

ancient French *mysteries*, which was acted with great applause at
Paris in the fourteenth century.

But, in the historical subjects from the life of St. Thomas, the
first place must be given to the one scriptural incident in which he
figures as a principal person. 'The Incredulity of St. Thomas'
occurs in all the early series of the life of Christ, as one of the events
of his mission, and one of the proofs of his resurrection. On the
ancient gates of San Paolo it is treated with great simplicity as a
sacred mystery, St. Thomas being the principal personage in the
action, as the one whose conviction was to bring conviction to the
universe. Christ stands on a pedestal surmounted by a cross; the
apostles are ranged on each side, and St. Thomas, approaching,
stretches forth his hand. The incident, as a separate subject, is of
frequent occurrence in the later schools of Italy, and in the Flemish
schools. The general treatment, when given in this dramatic style,
admits of two variations: either St. Thomas is placing his hand,
with an expression of doubt and fear, on the wounds of the Saviour;
or, his doubts being removed, he is gazing upwards in adoration and
wonder. Of the first, one of the finest examples is a well-known
picture by Rubens,[1] one of his most beautiful works, and extraordinary
for the truth of the expression in the countenance of the apostle,
whose hand is on the side of Christ; St. John and St. Peter are
behind. In Vandyck's picture at Petersburg, St. Thomas stoops to
examine the Saviour's hand. In a design ascribed to Raphael, we
have the second version: the look of astonished conviction in St.
Thomas.[2] Niccolò Poussin has painted it finely, introducing twelve
figures.[3] Guercino's picture is celebrated, but he has committed the
fault of representing the two principal figures both in profile.[4]

The legendary subject styled 'La Madonna della Cintola' belongs
properly to the legends of the Virgin, but as St. Thomas is always a
principal personage I shall mention it here. The legend relates
that when the Madonna ascended into heaven, in the sight of the
apostles, Thomas was absent; but after three days he returned, and,
doubting the truth of her glorious translation, he desired that **her**

---

[1] Gallery of Antwerp.   [2] Passavant's Rafael, II. 116.
[3] Eng. by Audran.   [4] Gal. Vatican.

The Madonna of the Girdle.

tomb should be opened; which was done, and lo! it was found empty. Then the Virgin, taking pity on his weakness and want of faith, threw down to him her girdle, that this tangible proof remaining in his hands might remove all doubts for ever from his mind: hence in many pictures of the Assumption and Coronation of the Virgin, St. Thomas is seen below holding the sacred girdle in his hand. For instance, in Raphael's beautiful ' Coronation ' in the Vatican ; and in Correggio's 'Assumption' at Parma, where St. Thomas holds the girdle, and another apostle kisses it.

The belief that the girdle is preserved in the Cathedral at Pistoia has rendered this legend a popular subject with the Florentine painters; and we find it treated, not merely as an incident in the scene of the Assumption, but in a manner purely mystic and devotional. Thus, in a charming bas-relief by Luca della Robbia,[1] the Virgin, surrounded by a choir of angels, presents her girdle to the apostle. In a beautiful picture by Granacci,[2] the Virgin is seated on the clouds; beneath is her empty sepulchre : on one side kneels St. Thomas, who receives with reverence the sacred girdle; on the other kneels the Archangel Michael. In simplicity of arrangement, beauty of expression, and tender harmony of colour, this picture has seldom been exceeded. Granacci has again treated this subject, and St. Thomas receives the girdle in the presence of St. John the Baptist, St. James Major, St. Laurence, and St. Bartholomew.[3] We have the same subject by Paolino da Pistoia ; by Sogliani ; and by Mainardi, a large and very fine fresco in the church of Santa Croce at Florence.

A poetical and truly mystical version of this subject is that wherein the Infant Saviour, seated or standing on his mother's knee, looses her girdle and presents it to St. Thomas. Of this I have seen several examples; one in the Duomo at Viterbo.[4]

In the Martyrdom of St. Thomas, several idolaters pierce him through with lances and javelins. It was so represented on the doors of San Paolo, with four figures only. Rubens, in his large picture, has followed the legend very exactly; St. Thomas embraces the cross, at the foot of which he is about to fall, transfixed by spears.

[1] Fl. Acad.　　　[2] Fl. Gal.　　　[3] Florence, Casa Ruccellai.
[4] The romantic Legend of the *sacratissima cintola,* 'the most sacred girdle of the Virgin, is given at length in the ' Legends of the Madonna,' p. 344.

A large picture in the gallery of Count Harrach at Vienna, called there the Martyrdom of St. Jude, I believe to represent the Martyrdom of St. Thomas.   Two of the idolatrous priests pierce him with lances.   Albert Dürer, in his beautiful print of St. Thomas, represents him holding the lance, the instrument of his martyrdom : but this is very unusual.

The eighth in the order of the Apostles is the Evangelist St. MATTHEW, of whom I have spoken at length.

St. James Minor.

Lat. S. Jacobus Frater Domini.   *Gr.* Adelphotheos.   *Ital.* San Jacopo or Giacomo Minore.
Fr. St. Jacques Mineur.   (May 1.)

THE ninth is St. James Minor, or the Less, called also the Just : he was a near relative of Christ, being the son of Mary, the wife of Cleophas, who was the sister of the Virgin Mary ; hence he is styled 'the Lord's brother.'   Nothing particular is related of him till after the ascension.   He is regarded as first Christian bishop of Jerusalem, and venerated for his self-denial, his piety, his wisdom, and his charity. These characteristics are conspicuous in the beautiful Epistle which bears his name.   Having excited, by the fervour of his teaching, the fury of the Scribes and Pharisees, and particularly the enmity of the high-priest Ananus, they flung him down from a terrace or parapet of the Temple, and one of the infuriated populace below beat out his brains with a *fuller's club.*

In single figures and devotional pictures, St. James is generally leaning on this club, the instrument of his martyrdom.   According to an early tradition, he so nearly resembled our Lord in person, in features and deportment, that it was difficult to distinguish them. 'The Holy Virgin herself,' says the legend, 'had she been *capable* of error, might have mistaken one for the other :' and this exact resemblance rendered necessary the kiss of the traitor Judas, in order to point out his victim to the soldiers.

This characteristic resemblance is attended to in the earliest and best representations of St. James, and by this he may usually be distinguished when he does not bear his club, which is often a thick stick or staff. With the exception of those Scripture scenes in which the apostles are present, I have met with few pictures in which St. James Minor is introduced: he does not appear to have been popular as a patron saint. The event of his martyrdom occurs very seldom, and is very literally rendered: the scene is a court of the Temple, with terraces and balconies; he is falling, or has fallen, to the ground, and one of the crowd lifts up the club to smite him.

82   St. James Minor.

Ignorant artists have in some instances confounded St. James Major and St. James Minor. The Cappella dei Belludi at Padua, already mentioned, dedicated to St. Philip and St. James, contains a series of frescoes from the life of St. James Minor, in which are some of the miraculous incidents attributed in the Legenda Aurea to St. James Major.

1. The Council of the Apostles held at Jerusalem, in which St. James was nominated chief or bishop of the infant Church. 2. Our Saviour after His resurrection appears to St. James, who had vowed not to eat till he should see Christ.[1] 3. St. James thrown down from the pulpit in the court of the Temple. 4. He is slain by the fuller. 5. A certain merchant is stript of all his goods by a tyrant,

---

[1] 'Very soon after the Lord was risen, he went to James, and showed Himself to him. For James had solemnly sworn that he would eat no bread from the time that he had drunk the cup of the Lord till he should see him risen from among them that sleep. "Bring," saith the Lord, "a table and bread." He took bread, and blessed and brake it, and then gave it to James the Just, and said to him, "My brother, eat thy bread; for the Son of man is risen from among them that sleep." '—St. Jerome, as quoted in Lardner, *Lives of the Apostles*, chap. xvi.

and cast into prison.   He implores the protection of St. James, who,
leading him to the summit of the tower, commands the tower to bow
itself to the ground, and the merchant steps from it and escapes:
or, according to the version followed in the fresco, the apostle lifts
the tower on one side from its foundation, and the prisoner escapes
from under it, like a mouse out of a trap.   6. A poor pilgrim, having
neither money nor food, fell asleep by the way-side, and, on waking,
found that St. James had placed beside him a loaf of bread, which
miraculously supplied his wants to the end of his journey.   These
two last stories are told also of St. James of Galicia, but I have
never met with any pictures of his life in which they are included.
Here they undoubtedly refer to St. James Minor, the chapel being
consecrated to his honour.

St. Simon Zelotes (or The Zealot).   St. Jude (Thaddeus, or Lebbeus).

Ital. San Simone; San Taddeo.   *Fr.* St. Simon le Zélé.   St. Thaddée.   *Ger.* Judas Thaddäus.
(Oct. 28.)

The uncertainty, contradiction, and confusion which I find in all the
ecclesiastical biographies relative to these apostles, make it impossible to give any clear account of them; and as subjects of Art they
are so unimportant, and so uninteresting, that it is the less necessary.
According to one tradition, they were the same mentioned by Matthew
as our Lord's brethren or kinsmen.   But, according to another tradition, they were not the same, but two brothers who were among the
shepherds to whom the angel and the heavenly host revealed the birth
of the Saviour.   Those painters who followed the first tradition represent Simon and Jude as young, or at least in the prime of life.   Those
who adopt the second represent them as very old, taking it for granted
that at the birth of Christ they must have been full-grown men; and
this, I think, is the legend usually followed.   It seems, however,
generally agreed, that they preached the Gospel together in Syria and
Mesopotamia, and together suffered martyrdom in Persia: in what

manner they suffered is unknown; but it is supposed that St. Simon was sawn asunder, and St. Thaddeus killed with a halberd.

In a series of apostles, St. Simon bears the saw, and St. Thaddeus a halberd. In Greek Art, Jude and Thaddeus are two different persons. Jude is represented young, Thaddeus old. St. Simon in extreme old age, with a bald head, and long white beard. In the Greek representation of his martyrdom, he is affixed to a cross exactly like that of our Saviour, so that, but for the superscription *O CIMΩN*, he might be mistaken for Christ. I do not know of any separate picture of these apostles.

There is, however, one manner of treating them, with reference to their supposed relationship to our Saviour, which is peculiarly beautiful. Assuming that the three last-named apostles, James, the son of Mary Cleophas; Simon and Jude; Joseph or Joses the Just, also named by Matthew among the brethren of Christ; together with James and John, the sons of Mary Salome,—were all nearly related to the Saviour; it was surely a charming idea to group as children around Him in His infancy those who were afterwards called to be the chosen ministers of His Word. Christianity, which has glorified womanhood and childhood, never suggested to the Christian artist a more beautiful subject, nor one which it would be more easy, by an unworthy or too picturesque treatment, to render merely pretty and commonplace. This version, however, of the *Sacra Famiglia* is rarely met with. There is an example in the Louvre, signed 'Laurentius' (Lorenzo di Pavia, A.D. 1513), which is remarkable as a religious representation; but the most beautiful instance of this treatment is a *chef-d'œuvre* of Perugino, in the Musée at Marseilles. In the centre is the Virgin, seated on a throne; she holds the infant Christ in her arms. Behind her is St. Anna, her two hands resting affectionately on the shoulders of the Virgin. In front, at the foot of the throne, are two lovely children, undraped, with glories round their heads, on which are inscribed their names, Simon and Thaddeus. To the right is Mary Salome, a beautiful young woman, holding a child in her arms—St. John, afterwards the evangelist. Near her is Joachim, the father of the Virgin. At his feet another child, James Major. To the left of the Virgin, Mary the wife of Cleophas, standing, holds by the hand

James Minor : behind her, Joseph, the husband of the Virgin, and at his feet another child, Joseph (or Joses) Justus. I have also seen this subject in illuminated MSS., and, however treated, it is surely very poetical and suggestive.[1]

St. Matthias.

Ital. San Mattia. *Fr.* St. Mathias. (Feb. 24.)

St. Matthias, who was chosen by lot to fill the place of the traitor Judas, is the last of the apostles. (Acts i.) He preached the Gospel

in Judea, and suffered martyrdom at the hands of the Jews, either by the lance or by the axe. In the Italian series of the apostles, he bears as his attribute the lance; in the German sets, more commonly the axe.[2] The ceremony of choosing St. Matthias by lot is the subject of a mediocre picture by Boschi. St. Denis says that the apostles were directed in their choice by a beam of divine splendour, for it were impious to suppose that such an election was made by chance. In this picture of Boschi, a ray of light falls from heaven on the head of St. Matthias.

There is a figure of this apostle by Cosimo Roselli, holding a sword *by the point :* what might be the intention of that capricious painter it is now impossible to guess.[3] Separate pictures of St. Matthias are very rare, and he is seldom

83   St. Matthias. (Raphael.)

included in sets of the apostles.

[1] Matt. xiii. 55; Mark xv. 40.   [2] Fl. Gal.   [3] Fl. Acad.

Judas Iscariot.

Ital. Giuda Scariota.   *Fr.* Judas Iscariote.

THE very name of Judas Iscariot has become a by-word; his person and character an eternal type of impiety, treachery, and ingratitude. We shudder at the associations called up by his memory; his crime, without a name, so distances all possible human turpitude, that he cannot even be held forth as a terror to evil-doers; we set him aside as one cut off; we never think of him but in reference to the sole and unequalled crime recorded of him. Not so our ancestors; one should have lived in the Middle Ages, to conceive the profound, the ever-present, horror with which Judas Iscariot was then regarded. The devil himself did not inspire the same passionate hatred and indignation. Being the devil, what *could* he be but devilish? His wickedness was according to his infernal nature: but the crime of Judas remains the perpetual shame and reproach of our humanity. The devil betrayed mankind, but Judas betrayed his God.

The Gospels are silent as to the life of Judas before he became an apostle, but our progenitors of the Middle Ages, who could not conceive it possible that any being, however perverse, would rush at once into such an abyss of guilt, have filled up the omissions of Scripture after their own fancy. They picture Judas as a wretch foredoomed from the beginning of the world, and prepared by a long course of vice and crime for that crowning guilt which filled the measure full. According to this legend, he was of the tribe of Reuben. Before his mother brought him forth, she dreamed that the son who lay in her womb would be accursed, that he would murder his father, commit incest with his mother, and sell his God. Terrified at her dream, she took counsel with her husband, and

they agreed to avert the threatened calamity by exposing the child.
As in the story of Œdipus, from which, indeed, this strange wild
legend seems partly borrowed, the means taken to avert the
threatened curse caused its fulfilment.   Judas, at his birth, is en-
closed in a chest, and flung into the sea ; the sea casts him up, and,
being found on the shore, he is fostered by a certain king and queen
as their own son ; they have, however, another son, whom Judas,
malignant from his birth, beats and oppresses, and at length kills
in a quarrel over a game at chess.   He then flies to Judea, where
he enters the service of Pontius Pilate as page.   In due time
he commits the other monstrous crimes to which he was predes-
tined ; and when he learns from his mother the secret of his birth,
he is filled with a sudden contrition and terror ; he hears of the
prophet who has power on earth to forgive sins ; and seeking out
Christ throws himself at His feet.   Our Saviour, not deceived, but
seeing in him the destined betrayer, and that all things may be
accomplished, accepts him as His apostle : he becomes the seneschal
or steward of Christ, bears the purse, and provides for the common
wants.   In this position, avarice, the only vice to which he was not
yet addicted, takes possession of his soul, and makes the corruption
complete.   Through avarice he grudges every penny given to the
poor, and when Mary Magdalene anoints the feet of our Lord he is
full of wrath at what he considers the waste of the precious perfume :
' Why was not this ointment sold for three hundred pence, and given
to the poor ?   This he said, not that he cared for the poor, but because he was a thief.'   Through avarice, he yields to the bribe
offered by the Jews.   Then follow the scenes of the betrayal of
Christ, and the late repentance and terrible suicide of the traitor, as
recorded in Scripture.   But in the old Mystery of the ' Passion of
Christ ' the repentance and fate of Judas are very dramatically
worked out, and with all possible circumstances of horror.   When
he beholds the mild Saviour before the judgment-seat of Herod, he
repents : Remorse, who figures as a real personage, seizes on the
fated wretch, and torments him till in his agony he invokes Despair.   Despair appears, almost in the guise of the ' accursed wight '
in Spenser, and, with like arguments, urges him to make away with
his life :—

> And brings unto him swords, rope, poison, fire,
> And all that might him to perdition draw,
> And bids him choose what death he would desire.

Or in the more homely language of the old French mystery —

> Il faut que tu passes le pas !
> Voici dagues et coutelas,
> Forcettes, poinçons, allumettes,—
> Avise, choisis les plus belles,
> Et celles de meilleure forge,
> Pour te couper à coup la gorge ;
> Ou si tu aimes mieux te pendre,
> Voici lacs et cordes à vendre.

The offer here of the bodkins and the allumettes reminds us of the speech of Falconbridge :—

> If thou would'st drown thyself,
> Put but a little water in a spoon,
> And it shall be as all the ocean,
> Enough to stifle such a villain up.

Judas chooses the rope, and hangs himself forthwith; 'and falling headlong, he burst asunder in the midst, and all his bowels gushed out:' which account is explained by an early tradition, that being found and cut down, his body was thrown over the parapet of the Temple into the ravine below, and, in the fall, was riven and dashed to pieces.

There required but one more touch of horror to complete the picture; and this is furnished by a sonnet of Giani, which I remember to have read in my youth. When Judas falls from the fatal tree, his evil genius seizes the broken rope, and drags him down to the seething abyss below: at his approach, hell sends forth a shout of rejoicing; Lucifer smooths his brow, corrugated with fire and pain, and rises from his burning throne to welcome a greater sinner than himself :—

> Poi fra le braccia incatenò quel tristo,
> E colla bocca sfavillante e nera
> Gli rese il bacio ch' avea dato a Christo !

The retribution imaged in the last two lines borders, I am afraid, on a *concetto;* but it makes one shiver, notwithstanding.

Separate representations of the figure or of the life of Judas Iscariot are not, of course, to be looked for; they would have been regarded as profane, as ominous,—worse than the evil-eye. In those Scripture scenes in which he finds a place, it was the aim of the early artists to give him a countenance as hateful, as expressive of treachery, meanness, malignity, as their skill could compass,—the Italians having depended more on expression, the German and Spanish painters on form. We have a conviction, that if the man had really worn such a look, such features, he would have been cast out from the company of the apostles; the legend already referred to says expressly that Judas was of a comely appearance, and was recommended to the service of Pontius Pilate by his beauty of person : but the painters, speaking to the people in the language of form, were right to admit of no equivocation. The same feeling which induced them to concentrate on the image of the Demon all they could conceive of hideous and repulsive, made them picture the exterior of Judas as deformed and hateful as the soul within ; and, by an exaggeration of the Jewish cast of features combined with red hair and beard, they flattered themselves that they had attained the desired object. But as if this were not enough, the ancient painters, particularly in the old illuminations, and in Byzantine Art, represent Judas as directly and literally possessed by the Devil: sometimes it is a little black demon seated on his shoulder, and whispering in his ear; sometimes entering his mouth : thus, in their simplicity, rendering the words of the Gospel, ' Then entered Satan into Judas.'

The colour proper to the dress of Judas is a dirty dingy yellow; and in Spain this colour is so intimately associated with the image of the arch-traitor, as to be held in universal dislike : both in Spain and in Italy, malefactors and galley-slaves are clothed in yellow.[1] At Venice the Jews were obliged to wear yellow hats.

[1] See Ford's ' Handbook of Spain ; ' also Goethe's ' Theory of Colours,' translated by Sir C. Eastlake. ' When a yellow colour is communicated to dull and coarse surfaces, such as common cloth, felt, or the like, on which it does not appear with full energy, the disagreeable effect alluded to is apparent. By a slight and scarcely perceptible change, the beautiful impression of fire and gold is transformed into one not undeserving the epithet foul, and the colour of honour and joy reversed to that of ignominy and aversion. To this impression, the yellow hats of bankrupts, and the yellow circles on the mantles of Jews, may have owed their origin.'—(P. 308.)

In some of the Scriptural scenes in which Judas is mentioned or supposed to be present, it is worth while to remark whether the painter has passed him over as spoiling the harmony of the sacred composition by his intrusive ugliness and wickedness, or has rendered him conspicuous by a distinct and characteristic treatment. In a picture by Niccolò Frumenti[1] of the Magdalene at the feet of our Saviour, Judas stands in the foreground, looking on with a most diabolical expression of grudging malice mingled with scorn; he seems to grind his teeth as he says, ' To what purpose is this waste?' In Perugino's beautiful picture of the washing the feet of the disciples,[2] Judas is at once distinguished, looking askance with a wicked sneer on his face, which is not otherwise ugly. In Raphael's composition of the Magdalene anointing the feet of Christ, Judas leans across the table with an angry look of expostulation.

Those subjects in which Judas Iscariot appears as a principal personage follow here.

1. Angelico da Fiesole.[3] He is bribed by the Jews. The high priest pays into the hand of Judas the thirty pieces of silver. They are standing before a doorway on some steps; Judas is seen in profile, and has the nimbus as one of the apostles : three persons are behind, one of whom expresses disapprobation and anxiety. In this subject, and in others wherein Judas is introduced, Angelico has not given him ugly and deformed features; but in the scowling eye and bent brow there is a vicious expression.

In Duccio's series of the ' Passion of our Saviour,' in the Duomo at Siena, he has, in this and in other scenes, represented Judas with regular and not ugly features; but he has a villanous, and at the same time anxious, expression ;—he has a bad conscience.

The scene between Judas and the high-priest is also given by Schalken as a candle-light effect, and in the genuine Dutch style.

2. ' Judas betrays his Master with a kiss.' This subject will be noticed at large in the Life of Christ. The early Italians, in giving this scene with much dramatic power, never forgot the Scriptural dignity required; while the early Germans, in their endeavour to render Judas as odious in physiognomy as in heart, have, in this as in many other instances, rendered the awful and the pathetic merely

[1] Fl. Gal.   [2] Manfrini P., Venice.   [3] Fl. Acad.

grotesque. We must infer from Scripture, that Judas with all his perversity, had a conscience: he would not else have hanged himself. In the physiognomy given to him by the old Germans, there is no trace of this; he is an ugly malignant brute, and nothing more.

3. Rembrandt. 'Judas throws down the thirty pieces of silver in the Temple, and departs.'[1]

4. 'The remorse of Judas.' He is seated and in the act of putting the rope about his neck; beside him is seen the purse and the money, scattered about the ground. The design is by Bloemart, and from the Latin inscription underneath, appears to be intended as a warning to all unrighteous dealers.

5. 'Judas hanging on a tree' is sometimes introduced into the background, in ancient pictures of the Deposition and the Entombment: there is one in the Frankfort Museum.

6. 'Demons toss the soul of Judas from hand to hand in the manner of a ball:' in an old French miniature.[2] This is sufficiently grotesque in representation; yet, in the idea, there is a restless, giddy horror which thrills us. At all events, it is better than placing Judas between the jaws of Satan with his legs in the air, as Dante has done, and as Orcagna in his Dantesque fresco has very literally rendered the description of the poet.[3]

[1] In the gallery of Lord Charlemont, Dublin.   [2] MS., No. 7206, Bib. du Roi.

[3] Florence, S. Maria Novella. It is clear that the extravagant legends which refer to Judas Iscariot were the inventions of the Middle Ages, and are as little countenanced by the writings of the early fathers as by the Gospels. Eusebius says, that 'Christ gave like gifts to Judas with the other apostles; that once our Saviour had good hopes of him on account of the power of the free will, for Judas was not of such a nature as rendered his salvation impossible; like the other apostles, he might have been instructed by the Son of God, and might have been a sincere and good disciple.' (Quoted in Lardner, vol. viii. p. 77.) The Mahometans believe that Christ did not die, that He ascended alive into heaven, and that Judas was crucified in His likeness.—(Curzon, p. 185.)

Lionardo da Vinci

Giotto

Raphael

H. Adlard, sc.

The Last Supper.

Ital. Il Cenacolo. La Cena. *Fr.* La Cène. *Ger.* Das Abendmal Christi.

I HAVE already mentioned the principal scenes in which the Twelve always appear together; there - is, however, one event belonging properly to the Life of Christ, so important in itself, presenting the Apostles under an aspect so peculiar, and throwing so much interest around them collectively and individually, that I must bring it under notice here.

Next to the Crucifixion, there is no subject taken from the history of our redemption so consecrated in Art as the Last Supper. The awful signification lent to it by Protestants as well as Catholics has given it a deep religious import, and caused its frequent representation in churches; it has been, more particularly, the appropriate decoration of the refectories of convents, hospitals, and other institutions having a sacred character. In our Protestant churches it is generally the subject of the altar-piece, where we have one.

Besides being one of the most important and interesting, it is one of the most difficult among the sacred subjects treated in Art. While the fixed number of personages introduced, the divine and paramount dignity of One among them, the well-known character of all, have limited the invention of the artist, they have tasked to the utmost his power of expression. The occasion, that of a repast eaten by twelve persons, is, under its material aspect, so commonplace, and, taken in the spiritual sense, so awful, that to elevate himself to the height of his theme, while keeping the ideal conscientiously bounded within its frame of circumstance, demanded in the artist aspirations of the grandest order, tempered by the utmost sobriety of reflection; and the deepest insight into the springs of character, combined with the most perfect knowledge of the indications of character as manifested through form. On the other hand, if it has been difficult to succeed, it has been equally difficult to fail signally and completely; because the spectator is not here, as in the crucifixion, in danger of being perpetually shocked, by the intrusion of anomalous incidents, and is always ready to supply the dignity and meaning of a scene so familiar in itself out of his own mind and heart.   It has followed, that mediocrity has been more prevalent and more endurable in this than in any other of the more serious subjects of Art.   But where excellence has been in some few instances attained, it has been attained in such a supreme degree, that these examples have become a perpetual source of contemplation and of emulation, and rank among the most renowned productions of human genius.

But, before I come to consider these analytically, it is necessary to premise one or two observations, which will assist us to discrimination in the general treatment.

Pictures and works of Art, which represent the Last Supper of our Lord, admit of the same classification which I have adhered to generally throughout this work.   Those which represent it as a religious mystery must be considered as *devotional;* those which represent it merely as a scene in the passion of our Saviour are *historical.*   In the first, we have the spiritual origin of the Eucharist; in the second, the highly dramatic detection of Judas.   It is evident that the predominating *motif* in each must be widely different.   In paintings which are intended for the altar, or for the chapels of the Holy Sacrament, we have the first, the mystical version;—it is the distribution of the spiritual food.   In the second form, as the Last Supper eaten by Christ with His disciples, as leading the mind to an humble and grateful sense of His sacrifice, as repressing all sinful indulgence in food, it has been the subject chosen to decorate the refectory or common dining-room of convents.

It is curious that on the Christian sarcophagi the Last Supper does not occur.   There is, in the Vatican, a rude painting taken from the catacombs representing twelve persons in a semicircle, with something like plates and dishes before them.   I could not determine whether this was our Saviour and His apostles, or merely one of those feasts or suppers instituted by the early Christians called *Agapæ* or love-feasts; but I should think the latter.

On the Dalmatica (deacon's robe) preserved in the sacristy of the Vatican, there is, if the date be exact (A.D. 795), the most ancient representation I have seen of the institution of the Sacrament.   The embroidery, which is wonderfully beautiful, is a copy from Byzantine Art. On one side, our Saviour stands by a table or altar, and presents the cup to His apostles, one of whom approaches in a reverential attitude, and with his hands folded in his robe ; on the other side, Christ presents the wafer or host: so that we have the two separate moments in separate groups.

There exists in the Duomo of Lodi the most ancient sculptural example of this subject I have met with; it is a bas-relief of the twelfth century, dated 1163, and fixed in the wall to the left of the entrance. Christ and the apostles are in a straight row, all very much alike ; six of the apostles lay their hands on their breast,— ' Lord, is it I ? ' and Christ presents the sop to Judas, who sits in front, and is as ugly as possible.

Although all the Byzantine pictures of the twelfth and thirteenth centuries which have come under my notice represent Christ breaking the bread or holding the cup, that is, the institution of the Sacrament, the Greek formula published by Didron distinguishes between this scene and that of the repast in which Judas is denounced as a traitor. The earliest representation to which I can refer in Western Art, as taking the historical form, is the Cenacolo of Giotto, the oldest and the most important that has been preserved to us ; it was painted by him in the refectory of the convent of Santa Croce at Florence. This refectory, when I visited it in 1847, was a carpet manufactory, and it was difficult to get a good view of the fresco by reason of the intervention of the carpet-looms. It has been often restored, and is now in a bad state ; still, enough remains to understand the original intention of the artist, and that arrangement which has since been the groundwork of similar compositions.

A long table extends across the picture from side to side : in the middle, and fronting the spectator, sits the Redeemer ; to the right, St. John, his head reclining on the lap of Christ : next to him, Peter; after Peter, St. James Major ; thus placing together the three favourite disciples. Next to St. James, St. Matthew, St. Bartholomew, and a young beardless apostle, probably St. Philip.

On the left hand of our Saviour is St. Andrew ; and next to him, St. James Minor (the two St. Jameses bearing the traditional re-

semblance to Christ); then St. Simon and St. Jude; and lastly, a
young apostle, probably St. Thomas. (The reader will have the
goodness to recollect that I give this explanation of the names and
position of the eleven apostles as my own, and with due deference to
the opinion of those who on a further study of the fresco may differ
from me.) Opposite to the Saviour, and on the near side of the
table, sits Judas, apart from the rest, and in the act of dipping his
hand into the dish. It is evident that the moment chosen by the
artist is, ' He that dippeth with me in the dish, the same shall betray
me.'

Although the excuse may be found in the literal adoption of the
words of the Gospel, [1] it appears to me a fault to make St. John leaning,
as one half asleep, on the lap of our Saviour, after such words have
been uttered as must have roused, or at least ought to have roused,
the young and beloved apostle from his supine attitude ; therefore, we
may suppose that Christ is about to speak the words, but has not yet
spoken them. The position of Judas is caused by the necessity of
placing him sufficiently near to Christ to dip his hand in the same
dish ; while to have placed him on the same side of the table, so as to
give him the precedence over the more favoured disciples, would have
appeared to the early artists nothing less than profane. Giotto has
paid great attention to the heads, which are individually characterised,
but there is little dramatic expression ; the attention is not yet directed to Judas, who is seen in profile, looking up, not ugly in feature,
but with a mean vicious countenance, and bent shoulders.

The arrangement of the table and figures, so peculiarly fitted for
a refectory, has been generally adopted since the time of Giotto in
pictures painted for this especial purpose. The subject is placed on
the upper wall of the chamber ; the table extending from side to side :
the tables of the monks are placed, as in the dining-rooms of our
colleges, length-ways ; thus all can behold the divine assembly, and
Christ appears to preside over and sanctify the meal.

In another Cenacolo by Giotto,[2] which forms one of the scenes in the
history of Christ, he has given us a totally different version of the

---

[1] The Greek expression, 'leaning on His bosom, or on His lap,' is not, I believe, to be
taken literally, being used to signify an intimate and affectionate intercourse.

[2] Florence Acad.

a few bones are near him—a naïve method of expressing his return
from death to life. The variety of expression in the countenances of
the assembled spectators is very fine. According to the custom of the
Florentine school at that time, many are portraits of distinguished
persons; and, considering that the fresco was painted at a period most
interesting in the Florentine history (A.D. 1440), we have much reason
to regret that these can no longer be discriminated.

4. 'The Fall of Simon Magus' is a favourite and picturesque
subject, often repeated. A most ancient and most curious version is
that on the walls of the Cathedral at Assisi, older than the time of
Giotto, and attributed to Giunta Pisano. (A.D. 1232.) On one side
is a pyramidical tower formed of wooden bars; Peter and Paul are
kneeling in front; the figure of the magician is seen floating in the
air and sustained by hideous demons;—very dreamy, poetical, and
fanciful. In Mr Ottley's collection I saw a small ancient picture of
the same subject, very curious, attributed to Benozzo Gozzoli.
Raphael's composition in the Vatican has the simplicity of a classical
bas-relief—a style which does not appear suited to this romantic
legend. The picture by L. Caracci at Naples I have not seen. Over
one of the altars of St. Peter, we now see the great mosaic, after
Vanni's picture of this subject; a clever commonplace treatment:
the scene is an amphitheatre, the emperor above in his balcony;
Peter and Paul in front, invoking the name of Christ, and Simon
Magus tumbling headlong, forsaken by his demons; in the background sit the vestals. Battoni's great picture in the S. Maria
degli Angeli at Rome is considered his best production; it is full
of well-studied academic drawing, but scenic and mannered.

The next subject in the order of events is styled the ' DOMINE, QUO
VADIS?' After the burning of Rome, Nero threw upon the Christians
the accusation of having fired the city. This was the origin of the
first persecution, in which many perished by terrible and hitherto
unheard-of deaths. The Christian converts besought Peter not to
expose his life, which was dear and necessary to the well-being of all;
and at length he consented to depart from Rome. But as he fled
along the Appian Way, about two miles from the gates, he was met
by a vision of our Saviour travelling towards the city. Struck with

Eucharist.[1] He has given us both scenes. In the first compartment,
John is leaning down with his face to the Saviour; the back of his
head only is seen, and he appears too unmindful of what is going
forward. The other apostles are well discriminated, the usual type
strictly followed in Peter, Andrew, James Major and James Minor.
To the right of Christ are Peter, Andrew, Bartholomew; to the left,
James Minor. Four turn their backs, and two young apostles
stand on each side,—I presume Thomas and Philip; they seem to be
waiting on the rest: Judas dips his hand in the dish. I suppose the
moment to be the same as in the composition of Duccio.

But in the next compartment the *motif* is different. All have risen
from table; it is no longer a repast, it is a sacred mystery; Christ
is in the act of administering the bread to St. John; all kneel; and
Judas is seen kneeling behind Christ, near an open door, and apart
from the rest, as if he were watching for the opportunity to escape.
To dispose of Judas in this holy ceremony is always a difficulty. To
represent him as receiving with the rest the sacred rite is an offence
to the pious. The expression used by St. John (xii. 30), ' After he
had received the sop he went out,' implies that Judas was not present
at the Lord's Supper, which succeeded the celebration of the paschal
supper. St. Luke and St. Mark, neither of whom were present,
leave us to suppose that Judas partook, with the other disciples, of
the mystic bread and wine; yet we can hardly believe that, after
having been pointed out as the betrayer, the conscience-stricken
Judas should remain to receive the Eucharist. Sometimes he is
omitted altogether; sometimes he is stealing out at the door. In
the composition of Luca Signorelli, which I saw at Cortona, all the
twelve apostles are kneeling; Christ is distributing the wafer; and
Judas, turning away with a malignant look, puts *his* wafer into his
satchel. In the composition of Palmezzano, in the Duomo at Forlì,
our Saviour stands, holding a plate, and is in the act of presenting
the wafer to Peter, who kneels: St. John stands by the side of Christ,
holding the cup ᐧ Judas is in the background; he kneels by the door,
and seems to be watching for the opportunity to steal away.

The fine composition, fine also in sentiment and character, of Ghir-

---

[1] In the series of compositions from the Life of Christ, now in the Academy at Florence ;
beautifully and faithfully engraved by P. Nocchi.

landajo, was painted for the small refectory in the San Marco at Florence. The arrangement is ingenious; the table is of what we call the horse-shoe form, which allows all the figures to face the spectator; and at the same time takes up less room than where the table runs across the picture from side to side. Judas sits in front, alone; Christ has just designated him. 'He it is to whom I shall give the sop when I have dipped it' (John xiii. 26). Judas holds the sop in his hand, with an alarmed conscious look. Behind sits an ill-omened cat, probably intended for the fiend. John, to the left of Christ, appears to have swooned away. The other apostles express, in various ways, amazement and horror.

It has been a question among critics, whether the purse ought to be placed in the hand of Judas when present at the Last Supper, because it is usually understood as containing the thirty pieces of silver: but this is a mistake; and it leads to the mistake of repre-senting him as hiding the purse, as if it contained the price of his treachery. Judas carries the purse openly, for he was the steward, or purse-bearer, of the party: ' he had the bag, and bare what was put therein' (John xii. 6, xiii. 29): and as the money-bag is also the attribute of St. Matthew the tax-gatherer, we must take care not to confound him with the traitor and thief. This brings me to the consideration of the subject as treated by Albert Dürer.

In the series of large woodcuts from the Passion of our Saviour (styled ' *La grande Passion*'), the Cenacolo is an event, and not a mystery. John, as a beautiful youth, is leaning against our Saviour with downcast eyes; he does not look as if he had thrown himself down half asleep, but as if Christ had put His arm around him, and drawn and pressed him fondly towards Him. On the right is Peter: the other apostles are not easily discriminated, but they have all that sort of *grandiose* ugliness which is so full of character, and so parti-cularly the characteristic of the artist: the apostle seated in front in a cowering attitude, holding the purse which he seems anxious to conceal, and looking up apprehensively, I suppose to be Judas.

In the smaller sets of woodcuts ('*La petite Passion*') I believe the apostle with the purse in the foreground to be St. Matthew; while the ugly, lank-haired personage behind Christ, who looks as if about to steal away, is probably intended for Judas: one of the apostles has laid hold of him, and seems to say, 'Thou art the man !'

There is a third Cenacolo, by Albert Dürer, which plainly represents the Eucharist. The cup only is on the table, and Judas is omitted.

In a Cenacolo by another old German, Judas is in the act of receiving the sop which Christ is putting into his mouth ; and at the same time he is *hiding* the purse :—a mistake, as I have already observed.

These examples must suffice to give some idea of the manner in which this subject was generally treated by the early German and Italian artists. But, whether presented before us as a dramatic scene expressing individual character, or as an historical event memorable in the life of Christ, or as a religious rite of awful and mysterious import—all the examples I have mentioned are in some respects deficient. We have the feeling, that, whatever may be the merit in sentiment, in intention, in detail, what has been attempted has *not* been achieved.

When Leonardo da Vinci, the greatest thinker as well as the greatest painter of his age, brought all the resources of his wonderful mind to bear on the subject, then sprang forth a creation so consummate, that since that time it has been at once the wonder and the despair of those who have followed in the same path. True, the work of his hand is perishing—will soon have perished utterly. I remember well, standing before this wreck of a glorious presence, so touched by its pale, shadowy, and yet divine significance, and by its hopelessly impending ruin, that the tears sprang involuntarily. Fortunately for us, multiplied copies have preserved at least the intention of the artist in his work. We can judge of what it *has* been, and take that for our text and for our theme.

The purpose being the decoration of a refectory in a rich convent, the chamber lofty and spacious, Leonardo has adopted the usual arrangement : the table runs across from side to side, filling up the whole extent of the wall, and the figures, being above the eye, and to be viewed from a distance, are colossal ; they would otherwise have appeared smaller than the real personages seated at the tables below. The moment selected is the utterance of the words, ' Verily, verily, I say unto you, that one of you shall betray me : ' or rather the words have just been uttered, and the picture expresses their effect on the different auditors. It is of these auditors, his apostles, that I have to speak, and not of Christ himself; for the full consideration of the subject, as it regards *Him*, must be deferred ; the intellectual elevation, the fineness of nature, the benign God-like dignity, suffused with the profoundest sorrow, in this divine head, surpassed all I could have conceived as possible in Art ; and, faded as it is, the character there, being stamped on it by the soul, not the hand, of the artist, will remain while a line or hue remains visible. It is a divine shadow, and, until it fades into nothing, and disappears utterly, will have the lineaments of divinity. Next to Christ is St. John; he has just been addressed by Peter, who beckons to him that he should ask ' of whom the Lord spake : '—his disconsolate attitude, as he has raised himself to reply, and leans his clasped hands on the table, the almost feminine sweetness of his countenance, express the character of this gentle and amiable apostle. Peter, leaning from behind, is all fire and energy ; Judas, who knows full well of whom the Saviour spake, starts back amazed, oversetting the salt; his fingers clutch the bag, of which he has the charge, with that action which Dante describes as characteristic of the avaricious :—

> Questi risurgeranno dal sepolcro
> Col pugno chiuso.

> These from the tomb with clenchèd grasp shall rise.

His face is seen in profile, and cast into shadow ; without being vulgar, or even ugly, it is hateful. St. Andrew, with his long grey beard, lifts up his hands, expressing the wonder of a simple-hearted old man. St. James Minor, resembling the Saviour in his mild features, and the form of his beard and hair, lays his hand on the shoulder of St. Peter—the expression is, ' *Can* it be possible ? Have we heard aright ? ' Bartholomew, at the extreme end of the table, has risen perturbed from his seat ; he leans forward with a look of eager attention, the lips parted ; he is impatient to hear more. (The fine copy of Uggione, in the Royal Academy, does not give this

anxious look—he is attentive only.)   On the left of our Saviour is
St. James Major, who has also a family resemblance to Christ; his
arms are outstretched, he shrinks back, he repels the thought with
horror.   The vivacity of the action and expression are wonderfully
true and characteristic.   (Morghen, the engraver, erroneously supposed this to represent St. Thomas, and placed on the border of his
robe an inscription fixing the identity; which inscription, as Bossi
asserts, never did exist in the original picture.)   St. Thomas is
behind St. James, rather young, with a short beard; he holds up
his hand, threatening—' If there be indeed such a wretch, let him
look to it.'   Philip, young and with a beautiful head, lays his hand
on his heart; he protests his love, his truth.   Matthew, also beardless, has more elegance, as one who belonged to a more educated
class than the rest; he turns to Jude and points to our Saviour, as if
about to repeat His words, ' Do you hear what He says?'   Simon and
Jude sit together (Leonardo has followed the tradition which makes
them old and brothers); Jude expresses consternation; Simon, with
his hands stretched out, a painful anxiety.

To understand the wonderful skill with which this composition has
been arranged, it ought to be studied long and minutely; and, to
appreciate its relative excellence, it ought to be compared with other
productions of the same period.   Leonardo has contrived to break
the formality of the line of heads without any apparent artifice, and
without disturbing the grand simplicity of the usual order; and he
has vanquished the difficulties in regard to the position of Judas,
without making him too prominent.   He has imparted to a solemn
scene sufficient movement and variety of action, without detracting
from its dignity and pathos; he has kept the expression of each head
true to the traditional character, without exaggeration, without effort.
To have done this, to have been the first to do this, required the far-
reaching philosophic mind, not less than the excelling hand, of this
' miracle of nature,' as Mr Hallam styles Leonardo, with reference
to his scientific as well as his artistic powers.

And now to turn to another miracle of nature, Raphael.   He has
given us three compositions for the Last Supper.   The fresco lately

discovered in the refectory of Sant' Onofrio, at Florence, is an early work painted in his twenty-third year (A.D. 1505). The authenticity of this picture has been vehemently disputed; for myself—as far as my opinion is worth anything—I never, after the first five minutes, had a doubt on the subject. As to its being the work of Neri de' Bicci, I do not believe it possible; and as for the written documents brought forward to prove this, I turn from them to ' the handwriting on the wall,' and there I see, in characters of light, RAPHAEL—and *him* only. It is, however, a youthful work, full of sentiment and grace, but deficient, it appears to me, in that depth and discrimination of character displayed in his later works. It is evident that he had studied Giotto's fresco in the neighbouring Santa Croce. The arrangement is nearly the same.

Christ is in the centre; His right hand is raised, and He is about to speak; the left hand is laid, with extreme tenderness in the attitude and expression, on the shoulder of John, who reclines upon Him. To the right of Christ is St. Peter, the head of the usual character; next to him St. Andrew, with the flowing grey hair and long divided beard; St. James Minor, the head declined resembling Christ: he holds a cup. St. Philip is seen in profile with a white beard: (this is contrary to the received tradition, which makes him young; and I doubt the correctness of this appellation). St. James Major, at the extreme end of the table, looks out of the picture; Raphael has apparently represented himself in this apostle. On the left of Christ, after St. John, is St. Bartholomew; he holds a knife, and has the black beard and dark complexion usually given to him. Then Matthew, something like Peter, but milder and more refined. Thomas, young and handsome, pours wine into a cup, last, on the right, are Simon and Jude: Raphael has followed the tradition which supposes them young, and the kinsmen of our Saviour. Judas sits on a stool on the near side of the table, opposite to Christ, and while he dips his hand into the dish he looks round to the spectators; he has the Jewish features, red hair and beard, and a bad expression. All have glories; but the glory round the head of Judas is much smaller than the others.[1]

[1] This is also observable in the Last Supper by Nicolò Petri in the San Francesco at Pisa.

In the second composition, one of the series of the Life of Christ, in the Loggie of the Vatican, Raphael has placed the apostles round a table, four on each of the three sides: our Saviour presiding in the centre. John and Peter, who are, as usual, nearest to Christ, look to Him with an animated appealing expression. Judas is in front, looking away from the rest, and as if about to rise. The other heads are not well discriminated, nor is the moment well expressed: there is, indeed, something confused and inharmonious, unlike Raphael, in the whole composition. I pass it over, therefore, without further remark, to come to the third example—a masterpiece of his later years, worthy as a composition of being compared with Leonardo's; but, never having been painted, we can only pronounce it perfect as far as it goes. The original drawing enriches the collection of the Queen of England: the admirable engraving of Marc Antonio, said to have been touched by Raphael, is before me while I write. From the disposition of the unshod feet as seen under the table, it is styled by collectors '*il pezzo dei piedi:*' from the arrangement of the table and figures it was probably designed for a refectory.

In the centre is Christ, with both hands resting on the table; in the head, a melancholy resignation. Peter is on the right, his hand on his breast. John, on the left, places both hands on his breast, with a most animated expression,—'You cannot believe it is I?' Andrew has laid his hand on the shoulder of Peter, and leans forward with a sad interrogative expression. The head of Judas has features akin to those of the antique satyr, with the look askance of a detected villain: he has heard the words, but he dares not meet the eye, of his Divine Master: he has no purse. James Minor, next to John, with his hands extended, seems to speak sadly to Philip: 'And they began to inquire among themselves, which of them should do this thing?' The whole composition is less dramatic, has less variety of action and attitude, than that of Leonardo, but is full of deep melancholy feeling.

The Cenacolo of Andrea del Sarto, in the Convent of the Salvi near Florence, takes, I believe, the third rank after those of Leonardo and Raphael. He has chosen the self-same moment, 'One of you shall betray me.' The figures are, as usual, ranged on one side of a long table.   Christ, in the centre, holds a piece of bread in His hand; on His left is St. John, and on His right St. James Major, both seen in profile.   The face of St. John expresses interrogation; that of St. James, interrogation and a start of amazement.   Next to St. James are Peter, Thomas, Andrew; then Philip, who has a small cross upon his breast.   After St. John come James Minor, Simon, Jude, Judas Iscariot, and Bartholomew.   Judas, with his hands folded together, leans forward, and looks down, with a round mean face, in which there is no power of any kind, not even of malignity.   In passing almost immediately from the Cenacolo in the St. Onofrio to that in the Salvi, we feel strongly all the difference between the mental and moral superiority of Raphael at the age of twenty, and the artistic greatness of Andrea in the maturity of his age and talent.   This fresco deserves its high celebrity.   It is impossible to look on it without admiration, considered as a work of Art.   The variety of the attitudes, the disposition of the limbs beneath the table, the ample, tasteful draperies, deserve the highest praise; but the heads are deficient in character and elevation, and the whole composition wants that solemnity of feeling proper to the subject.

The Cenacolo of Titian, painted for Philip II. for the altar of his chapel in the Escurial, is also a notable example of the want of proper reverential feeling: two servants are in attendance; Judas is in front, averting his head, which is in deep shadow; a dog is under the table, and the Holy Ghost is descending from above.

Niccolò Poussin has three times painted the Cenacolo.   In the two series of the Seven Sacraments, he has, of course, represented the institution of the Eucharist, as proper to his subject; in both instances, in that pure and classical taste proper to himself.   In the best and largest composition, the apostles are reclining on couches round the table.   Christ holds a plate full of bread, and appears as saying, 'Take, eat.'   Four are putting the morsel into their mouths.   Judas is seen behind, with an abject look, stealing out of the room.

The faults which I have observed in pictures of this subject are chiefly met with in the Venetian, Flemish, and later Bolognese schools.   When the *motif* selected is the institution of the Eucharist, it is a fault to sacrifice the solemnity and religious import of the scene in order to render it more dramatic: it ought not to be dramatic; but the pervading sentiment should be *one*, a deep and awful reverence. When Christ is distributing the bread and wine, the apostles should not be conversing with each other; nor should the figures exceed twelve in number, for it appears to me that the introduction of Judas disturbs the sacred harmony and tranquillity of the scene. When the *motif* is the celebration of the Passover, or the detection of Judas, a more dramatic and varied arrangement is necessary; but here, to make the apostles intent on eating and drinking, as in some old German pictures, is a fault. Even Albano has represented one of the apostles as peeping into an empty wine-pitcher with a disappointed look.

It appears to me, also, a gross fault to introduce dogs and cats, and other animals; although I have heard it observed, that a dog gnawing a bone is introduced with propriety, to show that the supper is over, the Paschal Lamb eaten, before the moment represented.

Vulgar heads, taken from vulgar models, or selected without any regard either to the ancient types, or the traditional character of the different apostles, are defects of frequent occurrence, especially in the older German schools; and in Titian, Paul Veronese, and Rubens, even where the heads are otherwise fine and expressive, the scriptural truth of character is in general sacrificed.

It is a fault, as I have already observed, to represent Judas anxiously concealing the purse.

Holbein, in his famous Last Supper at Basle, and in the small one in the Louvre, has adopted the usual arrangement: the heads all want elevation; but here the attention fixes at once upon Judas Iscariot—the very ideal of scoundrelism—I can use no other word to express the unmitigated ugliness, vulgarity, and brutality of the face. Lavater has referred to it as an example of the physiognomy proper to cruelty and avarice; but the dissimulation is wanting. This base, eager, hungry-looking villain stands betrayed by his own looks: he is too prominent; he is, in fact, the principal figure;—a fault in taste, feeling, and propriety.

The introduction of a great number of figures, as spectators or attendants, is a fault; excusable, perhaps, where the subject is decorative and intended for the wall of a refectory, but not otherwise. In the composition of Paul Veronese, there are twenty-three figures; in that of Zucchero, forty-five; in that of Baroccio, twenty-one. These supernumerary persons detract from the dignity and solemnity of the scene.

Tintoretto has introduced several spectators, and among them an old woman spinning in a corner, who, while she turns her spindle, looks on with an observant eye. This alludes to an early tradition, that the Last Supper was eaten in the house of Mary, the mother of Mark the evangelist. But it is nowhere said that she was present, and therefore it is an impropriety to introduce her. Magnificent architecture, as in the picture by B. Peruzzi (who, by the way, was an architect), seems objectionable: but equally unsuitable is the poor dismantled garret in this picture of Tintoretto; for the chamber in which the scene took place was 'the guest chamber,' a large upper room, ready prepared; and as it was afterwards the scene of the Pentecost, it must have held more than a hundred persons.

It is a fault, as I have already observed, to represent John as *asleep* on the breast or the shoulder of our Saviour.

Though countenanced by the highest authorities in Art, I believe it must be considered as a fault, or at least a mistake, to represent our Saviour and His apostles as seated, instead of reclining round the table. It is a fault, not merely because the use of the *triclinium* or couch at all social meals was general in the antique times,—for the custom of sitting upright was not so entirely extinct among the Jews but that it might on any other occasion have been admissible,—but, from peculiar circumstances, it became in this instance an impropriety. We know that when the Passover was first instituted the Jews were enjoined to eat it standing, as men in haste, with girded loins and sandalled feet; but afterwards it was made imperative that they should eat it in an attitude of repose, lying upon couches, and as men at ease; and the reason for this was, that all the circumstances of the meal, and particularly the attitude in which it was eaten, should indicate the condition of security and freedom which the Israelites enjoyed after their deliverance from the Egyptian bondage. In the then imperfect state of Biblical criticism, this fact seems to have been unknown to the earlier artists, or disregarded by those who employed and directed them. Among modern artists, Poussin and Le Sueur have scrupulously attended to it, even when the moment chosen is the mystical distribution of the bread and wine which succeeded the Paschal Supper. Commentators have remarked, that if Christ and His disciples *reclined* at table, then, supposing Christ to have the central place of honour, the head of John would have been near to the bosom of Christ: but under these circumstances, if Judas were sufficiently near to receive the sop from the hand of Christ, then he must have reclined next to Him on the other side, and have taken precedence of Peter. This supposed a propinquity which the early Christian artists deemed offensive and inadmissible.

In the composition by Stradano the arrangement of the table and figures is particularly well managed: all recline on couches; in the centre of the table is a dish, to which Christ extends His hand, and Judas, who is here rather handsome than otherwise, at the same time stretches forth his; the moment is evidently, ' He that dippeth with me in the dish, the same shall betray me.' Two circumstances spoil this picture, and bring it down to the level of the vulgar and the commonplace. In the background is seen a kitchen and the cooking of the supper. Under Judas crouches a hideous demon, with horns, hoof, and tail, visible only to the spectator.

When the Cenacolo represents the Eucharist, it is, perhaps, allowable to introduce angels, because it was, and I believe is, an established belief, that, visible or invisible, they are always present at the Sacrament. The Holy Ghost descending from above is unsanctioned by Scripture, but may serve to mark the mystical and peculiar solemnity of the moment chosen for representation. It may signify, ' He that receiveth me, receiveth *Him* that sent me.' But where angels attend, or where the Spiritual Comforter comes floating down from above, then the presence of Judas, or of any superfluous figures as spectators or servitors, or of dogs or other animals, becomes a manifest impropriety.

The introduction of the Devil in person as tempting Judas is rendered pardonable by the naïveté of the early painters : in the later schools of Art it is offensive and ridiculous.

The Cenacolo of Baroccio, painted by order of Clement VIII. (1594), for his family chapel in the Santa Maria-sopra-Minerva, is remarkable for an anecdote relating to it. Baroccio, who was not eminent for a correct taste, had in his first sketch reverted to the ancient fashion of placing Satan close behind Judas, whispering in his ear, and tempting him to betray his Master. The Pope expressed his dissatisfaction,—' *che non gli piaceva il demonio si dimesticasse tanto con Gesù Cristo,*'—and ordered him to remove the offensive figure. This is not the last example of the ancient manner of treatment. In the Cenacolo of Franceschini, painted nearly a century later, two angels are attending on the sacred repast, while Judas is in the act of leaving the room, conducted by Satan in person.

It is surely a fault, in a scene of such solemn and sacred import, to make the head of Judas a vehicle for public or private satire, by giving him the features of some obnoxious personage of the time.[1] This, according to tradition, has been done in some instances. Perhaps the most remarkable example that could be cited is the story of Andrea del Castagno, who, after having betrayed and assassinated his friend Domenico Veneziano, painted himself in the character of Judas : a curious instance of remorse of conscience.

Volumes might be written on the subject of the Last Supper. It extends before me, as I think and write, into endless suggestive associations, which, for the present, I dare not follow out: but I shall have occasion to return to it hereafter.[2]

---

[1] For a signal example, see Stirling's ' Artists of Spain,' p. 493.

[2] For some remarks on the subject of the Pentecost, *v.* 'Legends of the Madonna,' p. 325.

St. Barnabas.

Ital. San Barnabà.   *Fr.* Saint Barnabé.   (June 11.)

St. Barnabas is usually entitled the *Apostle* Barnabas, because he was associated with the Apostles in their high calling; 'and,' according to Lardner, 'though without that large measure of inspiration and high authority which was peculiar to the Twelve Apostles, properly so called, yet he is to be considered as *Apostolical*, and next to them in sanctity.' For this reason I place him here.

St. Barnabas was a Levite, born in the island of Cyprus and the cousin-german of Mark the evangelist. The notices of his life and character scattered through the Acts invest him with great personal interest. He it was who, after the conversion of Paul, was the first to believe in his sincerity, and took courage to present him to the other apostles, ' who were afraid of him, and would not believe that he was a disciple' (Acts xv. 39). Barnabas afterwards became the fellow-labourer of Paul, and attended him to Antioch. We are told that ' he was a good man, full of the Holy Ghost and of faith ; ' and to this the legendary traditions add, that he was a man of a most comely countenance, of a noble presence, grave and commanding in his step and deportment; and thence, when he and Paul were at Lystra together, ' they called Barnabas Jupiter, and Paul Mercurius.' Subsequently, however, Paul and Barnabas fell into a dispute concerning Mark, and separated. The tradition relates that Barnabas and Mark remained for some time together, being united by the ties of friendship, as well as by those of kindred. Barnabas preached the Gospel in Asia Minor, Greece, and Italy ; and there is an old legendary tradition that he was the first Bishop of Milan. The legend also relates that everywhere he carried with him the Gospel of St. Matthew, written by the hand of the evangelist, preaching what was written therein ; and when any were sick, or possessed, he laid the sacred writing upon their bosom, and they were healed ; (a beautiful allegory this !) and it happened that as he preached in a synagogue of Judea against the Jews, they were seized with fury and took him, and put him to a cruel death. But Mark and the other Christians buried him with many tears.

The body of St. Barnabas remained in its place of sepulture till the days of the Emperor Zeno, when, according to Nicephorus, it was revealed in a dream to Antemius, that the apostle rested in a certain spot, and would be found there, with the Gospel of St. Matthew lying on his bosom. And so it happened: the remains were found; the Gospel was carried to the emperor at Constantinople; and a church was built, dedicated to St. Barnabas.

It is, I presume, in consequence of his being the kinsman of St. Mark, that Barnabas is more popular at Venice than elsewhere, and that devotional figures of him are rarely found except in Venetian pictures. He is represented as a man of majestic presence, holding in his hand the Gospel of St. Matthew, as in a fine picture by Bonifazio: in his church at Venice he is represented over the high altar, throned as bishop, while St. Peter stands below.

He often occurs in subjects taken from the Acts and the life of St. Paul. In the scene in which he presents Paul to the other apostles, he is the principal personage; but in the scene at Paphos, where Elymas is struck blind, and at Lystra, he is always secondary to his great companion.

84   Angel. (Albert Dürer.) v. p 79.

The Doctors of the Church.

I. THE FOUR LATIN FATHERS.

THE Evangelists and the Apostles represented in Art the Spiritual Church, and took their place among the heavenly influences. The great Fathers or Doctors were the representatives of the Church Militant on earth : as teachers and pastors, as logicians and advocates, they wrote, argued, contended, suffered, and at length, after a long and fierce struggle against opposing doctrines, they fixed the articles of faith thereafter received in Christendom. For ages, and down to the present time, the prevailing creed has been that which was founded on the interpretations of these venerable personages. They have become, in consequence, frequent and important subjects of Art, particularly from the tenth century—the period when, in their personal character, they began to be regarded not merely as gifted and venerable, but as divinely inspired ; their writings appealed to as infallible, their arguments accepted as demonstration. We distinguish them as the Latin and the Greek Fathers. In Western Art, we find the Latin Fathers perpetually grouped together, or in a series : the Greek Fathers seldom occur except in their individual character, as saints rather than as teachers.

The four Latin Doctors are St. Jerome, St. Ambrose, St. Augustine, and St. Gregory. When represented together, they are generally distinguished from each other, and from the sacred personages who may be grouped in the same picture, by their conventional attributes. Thus St. Jerome is sometimes habited in the red hat and crimson robes of a cardinal, with a church in his hand ; or he is a half-naked, bald-headed, long-bearded, emaciated old man, with eager wasted features, holding a book and pen, and attended by a lion. St. Ambrose wears the episcopal robes as Bishop of Milan, with mitre and crosier, and holds his book ; sometimes, also, he carries a knotted scourge, and a bee-hive is near him. St. Augustine

The Four Latin Fathers.

is also habited as a bishop, and carries a book; he has often books at his feet, and sometimes a flaming heart transpierced by an arrow. The origin and signification of these symbols I shall explain presently.

In the most ancient churches the Four Doctors are placed after the Evangelists. In the later churches they are seen combined or grouped with the evangelists, occasionally also with the sibyls; but this seems a mistake. The appropriate place of the sibyls is neither with the evangelists nor the fathers, but among the prophets, where Michael Angelo has placed them.

Where the principal subject is the glory of Christ, or the coronation or assumption of the Virgin, the Four Fathers attend with their books as witnesses and interpreters.

1. A conspicuous instance of this treatment is the dome of San Giovanni at Parma. In the centre is the ascension of Christ, around are the Twelve Apostles gazing upwards ; below them, in the spandrils of the arches, as if bearing record, are the Four Evangelists, each with a Doctor of the Church seated by him as interpreter: St. Matthew is attended by St. Jerome; St. Mark, by St. Gregory; St. Luke, by St. Augustine; and St. John, by St. Ambrose.

2. A picture in the Louvre by Pier-Francesco Sacchi (A.D. 1640) represents the Four Doctors, attended, or rather inspired, by the mystic symbols of the Four Evangelists. They are seated at a table, under a canopy sustained by slender pillars, and appear in deep consultation : near St. Augustine is the eagle ; St. Gregory has the ox ; St. Jerome, the angel; and St. Ambrose, the lion.

3. In a well-known woodcut after Titian, ' The Triumph of Christ,' the Redeemer is seated in a car drawn by the Four Evangelists ; while the Four Latin Doctors, one at each wheel, put forth all their strength to urge it on. The patriarchs and prophets precede, the martyrs and confessors of the faith follow, in grand procession.

4. In a Coronation of the Virgin, very singularly treated, we have Christ and the Virgin on a high platform or throne, sustained by columns ; in the space underneath, between these columns, is a group of unwinged angels, holding the instruments of the Passion. (Or, as I have sometimes thought, this beautiful group may be the souls

of the Innocents, their proper place being under the throne of
Christ.)   On each side a vast company of prophets, apostles, saints,
and martyrs, ranged tier above tier.   Immediately in front, and on
the steps of the throne, are the Four Evangelists, seated each with
his symbol and book : behind them the Four Fathers, also seated.
This picture, which as a painting is singularly beautiful, the execution finished, and the heads most characteristic and expressive,
may be said to comprise a complete system of the theology of the
Middle Ages.[1]

5. We have the same idea carried out in the lower part of Raphael's
' Disputa ' in the Vatican. The Four Doctors are in the centre of what
may be called the *sublunary* part of the picture : they are the only
seated figures in the vast assembly of holy, wise, and learned men
around ; St. Gregory and St. Jerome on the right of the altar,
St. Ambrose and St. Augustine on the left. As the two latter wear
the same paraphernalia, they are distinguished by having books
scattered at their feet, on which are inscribed the titles of their
respective works.

The Madonna and Child enthroned, with the Doctors of the
Church standing on each side, is a subject which has been often, and
sometimes beautifully, treated ; and here the contrast between all we
can conceive of virginal and infantine loveliness and innocence en-
shrined in heavenly peace and glory—and these solemn, bearded,
grand-looking old Fathers, attending in humble reverence, as types
of earthly wisdom—ought to produce a magnificent effect, when
conceived in the right spirit. I can remember, however, but few
instances in which the treatment is complete and satisfactory.

1. One of these is a picture by A. Vivarini (A.D. 1446), now in
the Academy at Venice. Here, the Virgin sits upon a throne under
a rich canopy sustained by four little angels. She looks out of the
picture with a most dignified, tranquil, goddess-like expression ; she
wears, as usual, the crimson tunic and blue mantle, the latter being
of a most brilliant azure ; on her brow a magnificent jewelled crown ;
the Divine Child stands on her knee, and raises his little hand to
bless the worshipper. To the right of the Virgin, and on the plat-

[1] Acad. Venice.   Giovanni ed Antonio da Murano.   1440.

form of her throne, stands St. Jerome, robed as cardinal, and bearing his church; with St. Gregory, habited as pope. To the left stands St. Ambrose, holding his crosier and knotted scourge, and St. Augustine with his book. This is a wonderful picture, and, as a specimen of the early Venetian school, unequalled. The accuracy of imitation, the dazzling colour, the splendid dresses and accessories, the grave beauty of the Madonna, the divine benignity of the Infant Redeemer, and the sternly thoughtful heads of the old Doctors, are not only positively fine, but have a relative interest and value as being stamped with that very peculiar character which belonged to the Vivarini and their immediate followers. It was painted for the Scuola della Carità.[1]

2. A different and a singular treatment of the Four Fathers occurs in another Venetian picture.[2] Christ is represented seated on a throne, and disputing with the Jewish doctors, who are eagerly arguing or searching their books. In front of the composition stand St. Jerome, St. Ambrose, St. Augustine, and St. Gregory; who, with looks fixed on the youthful Saviour, appear to be reverentially listening to, and recording, His words. This wholly poetical and ideal treatment of a familiar passage in the life of Christ, I have never seen but in this one instance.

3. A third example is a picture by Moretto, of extraordinary beauty.[3] The Virgin sits on a lofty throne, to which there is an ascent of several steps; the Child stands on her right: she presses him to her with maternal tenderness, and his arms are round her neck. At the foot of the throne stand St. Ambrose, with his scourge, and St. Augustine; St. Gregory, wearing the papal tiara, and without a beard, is seated on a step of the throne, holding an open book; and St. Jerome, kneeling on one knee, points to a passage in it; he wears

---

[1] As I have frequent occasion to refer to pictures painted for the *Scuole* of Venice, it may be as well to observe that the word *scuola*, which we translate *school*, is not a place of education, but a confraternity for charitable purposes,—visiting the sick, providing hospitals, adopting orphans, redeeming prisoners and captives, &c. In the days of the republic these schools were richly supported and endowed, and the halls, churches, and chapels attached to them were often galleries of Art: such were the schools of St. Mark, St. Ursula, St. Roch, the Carità, and others. Unhappily, they exist no longer; the French seized on their funds, and Austria does not like confraternities of any kind. The Scuola della Carità is now the Academy of Arts.

[2] Acad. Venice. Gio. da Udine.   [3] Frankfort Museum.

the cardinal's dress complete.   This picture is worthy of Titian in
the richness of the effect, with a more sober grandeur in the colour.
The Virgin is too much like a portrait; this is the only fault.[1]

In the Chapel of San Lorenzo, in the Vatican, Angelico has painted
eight Doctors of the Church, single majestic figures standing under
Gothic canopies.   According to the names *now* to be seen inscribed
on the pedestals beneath, these figures represent St. Jerome,[2] St.
Ambrose, St. Augustine, St. Gregory, St. Athanasius, St. Leo, St.
John Chrysostom, and St. Thomas Aquinas.   St. John Chrysostom
and St. Athanasius represent the Greek doctors.   St. Leo, who
saved Rome from Attila, is with peculiar propriety placed in the
Vatican; and St. Thomas Aquinas, the angelic doctor, naturally
finds a place in a chapel painted by a Dominican for a pope who
particularly favoured the Dominicans,—Nicholas V.

The Four Fathers communing on the mystery of the Trinity, or
the Immaculate Conception, were favourite subjects in the beginning
of the seventeenth century, when church pictures, instead of being
religious and devotional, became more and more theological.   There
is an admirable picture of this subject by Dosso Dossi.[3]   Above is
seen the Messiah, as Creator, in a glory; he lays His hand on the
head of the Virgin, who kneels in deep humility before Him; St.
Gregory sits in profound thought, a pen in one hand, a tablet in the
other; St. Ambrose and St. Augustine are similarly engaged; St.
Jerome, to whom alone the celestial vision appears to be visible, is
looking up with awe and wonder.   Guido, in a celebrated picture,[4]
has represented the Doctors of the Church communing on the
Immaculate Conception of the Virgin.   The figures are admirable

---

[1] We missed the opportunity, now never more to be recalled, of obtaining this admirable picture when it was sold out of the Fesch collection.

[2] I believe the figure called St. Bonaventura to represent St. Jerome, because, in accordance with the usual scheme of ecclesiastical decoration, the greatest of the four Latin
Fathers would take the first place, and the cardinal's hat and a long flowing beard are his
proper attribute; whereas, there is no example of a St. Bonaventura with a beard, or
wearing the monastic habit, without the Franciscan cord.   The Arundel Society have
engraved this fine figure under the name of St. Bonaventura.

[3] Dresden Gal.   [4] Imp. Gal., St. Petersburg.

for thoughtful depth of character in the expression, and for the noble arrangement of the draperies ; above is seen the Virgin, floating amid clouds, in snow-white drapery, and sustained by angels; visible, however, to St. Jerome and St. Ambrose only.

Rubens has treated the Fathers several times : the colossal picture in the Grosvenor Gallery is well known, where they appear before us as moving along in a grand procession : St. Jerome comes last ; (he should be first ; but on these points Rubens was not particular) : he seems in deep contemplation, enveloped in the rich scarlet robes of a cardinal of the seventeenth century, and turning the leaves of his great book. In another picture we have the Four Fathers seated, discussing the mystery of the Eucharist; St. Jerome points to a passage in the Scriptures ; St. Gregory is turning the page; they appear to be engaged in argument ; the other two are listening earnestly. There is another picture by Rubens in which the usual attributes of the Fathers are borne aloft by angels, while they sit communing below.

These examples will suffice to give a general idea of the manner in which the four great Doctors of the Western Church are grouped in devotional pictures. We will now consider them separately, each according to his individual character and history.

St. Jerome.

Lat. Sanctus Hieronymus. *Ital.* San Geronimo or Girolamo. *Fr.* St. Jérome, Hiérome, or Géroisme. *Ger.* Der Heilige Hieronimus. Patron of scholars and students, and more particularly of students in theology. (Sept. 30, A.D. 420.)

OF the four Latin Doctors, St. Jerome, as a subject of painting, is by far the most popular. The reasons for this are not merely the exceedingly interesting and striking character of the man, and the picturesque incidents of his life, but also his great importance and dignity as founder of Monachism in the West, and as author of the universally-received translation of the Old and New Testament into the Latin language (called 'The Vulgate'). There is scarcely a collection of pictures in which we do not find a St. Jerome, either doing penance in the desert, or writing his famous translation, or meditating on the mystery of the Incarnation.

Jerome was born about A.D. 342, at Stridonium, in Dalmatia. His father, Eusebius, was rich ; and as he showed the happiest disposition for learning, he was sent to Rome to finish his studies. There, through his own passions, and the evil example of his companions, he fell into temptation, and for a time abandoned himself to worldly pleasures. But the love of virtue, as well as the love of learning, was still strong within him : he took up the profession of law, and became celebrated for his eloquence in pleading before the tribunals. When more than thirty, he travelled into Gaul, and visited the schools of learning there. It was about this time that he was baptized, and vowed himself to perpetual celibacy. In 373, he travelled into the East, to animate his piety by dwelling for a time among the scenes hallowed by the presence of the Saviour ; and, on his way thither, he visited some of the famous Oriental hermits and ascetics, of whom he has given us such a graphic account, and whose example inspired him with a passion for solitude and a monastic life. Shortly after his arrival in Syria, he retired to a desert in Chalcis, on the confines of Arabia, and there he spent four years in study and seclusion, supporting himself by the labour of his hands. He has left us a most vivid picture of his life of penance in the wilderness ; of his trials and temptations, his fastings, his sickness of soul and body : and we must dwell for a moment on his own description, in order to show with what literal and circumstantial truth the painters have rendered it. He says, in one of his epistles, ' Oh how often, in the desert, in that vast solitude which, parched by the sultry sun, affords a dwelling to the monks, did I fancy myself in the midst of the luxuries of Rome ! I sate, alone, for I was full of bitterness. My misshapen limbs were rough with sackcloth, and my skin so squalid that I might have been mistaken for an Ethiopian. Tears and groans were my occupation every day and all day long. If sleep surprised me unawares, my naked bones, which scarcely held together, rattled on the earth.' His companions, he says, ' were scorpions and wild beasts;' his home, 'a recess among rocks and precipices.' Yet, in the midst of this horrible self-torture and self-abasement, he describes himself as frequently beset by temptations to sin and sensual indulgence, and haunted by demons: at other times, as consoled by voices and visions from heaven. Besides these trials of the flesh and the spirit, he had others of the intellect. His love of learning, his admiration of the great writers of classical antiquity, —of Plato and Cicero,—made him impatient of the rude simplicity of the Christian historians. He describes himself as fasting before he opened Cicero; and, as a further penance, he forced himself to study Hebrew, which at first filled him with disgust, and this disgust appeared to him a capital sin. In one of his distempered visions, he fancied he heard the last trumpet sounded in his ear by an angel, and summoning him before the judgment-seat of God. 'Who art thou?' demanded the awful voice. 'A Christian,' replied the trembling Jerome. ''Tis false!' replied the voice, 'thou art no Christian: thou art a Ciceronian. Where the treasure is, there will the heart be also.' He persevered, and conquered the difficulties of Hebrew; and then, wearied by the religious controversies in the East, after ten years' residence there, he returned to Rome.

But neither the opposition he had met with, nor his four years of solitude and penance in the desert, had subdued the fiery enthusiasm of temperament which characterised this celebrated man. At Rome he boldly combated the luxurious self-indulgence of the clergy, and preached religious abstinence and mortification. He was particularly remarkable for the influence he obtained over the Roman women; we find them, subdued or excited by his eloquent exhortations, devoting themselves to perpetual chastity, distributing their possessions among the poor, or spending their days in attendance on the sick, and ready to follow their teacher to the Holy Land—to the desert—even to death. His most celebrated female convert was Paula, a noble Roman matron, a descendant of the Scipios and the Gracchi. Marcella, another of these Roman ladies, was the first who, in the East, collected together a number of pious women to dwell together in community: hence she is, by some authors, considered as the first nun; but others contend that Martha, the sister of Mary Magdalene, was the first who founded a religious community of women.

After three years' sojourn at Rome, St. Jerome returned to Palestine, and took up his residence in a monastery he had founded at Bethlehem. When, in extreme old age, he became sensible of the approach of death, he raised with effort his emaciated limbs, and, commanding himself to be carried into the chapel of the monastery, he received the Sacrament for the last time from the hands of the priest, and soon after expired. He died in 420, leaving, besides his famous translation of the Scriptures, numerous controversial writings, epistles, and commentaries.

We read in the legendary history of St. Jerome, that one evening, as he sat within the gates of his monastery at Bethlehem, a lion entered, limping as in pain ; and all the brethren, when they saw the lion, fled in terror : but Jerome arose, and went forward to meet him, as though he had been a guest. And the lion lifted up his paw, and St. Jerome, on examining it, found that it was wounded by a thorn, which he extracted ; and he tended the lion till he was healed. The grateful beast remained with his benefactor, and Jerome confided to him the task of guarding an ass which was employed in bringing firewood from the forest. On one occasion, the lion having gone to sleep while the ass was at pasture, some merchants passing by carried away the latter ; and the lion, after searching for him in vain, returned to the monastery with drooping head, as one ashamed. St. Jerome, believing that he had devoured his companion, commanded that the daily task of the ass should be laid upon the lion, and that the faggots should be bound on his back, to which he magnanimously submitted, until the ass was recovered ; which was in this wise. One day, the lion, having finished his task, ran hither and thither, still seeking his companion ; and he saw a caravan of merchants approaching, and a string of camels, which, according to the Arabian custom, were led by an ass ; and when the lion recognised his friend, he drove the camels into the convent, and so terrified the merchants, that they confessed the theft, and received pardon from St. Jerome.

The introduction of the lion into pictures of St. Jerome is supposed to refer to this legend : but in this instance, as in many others, the reverse was really the case. The lion was in very ancient times adopted as the symbol befitting St. Jerome, from his fervid, fiery nature, and his life in the wilderness; and in later times, the legend invented to explain the symbol was gradually expanded into the story as given above.

Representations of St. Jerome, in pictures, prints, and sculpture, are so numerous that it were in vain to attempt to give any detailed account of them, even of the most remarkable. All, however, may be included under the following classification, and, according to the descriptions given, may be easily recognised.

The devotional subjects and single figures represent St. Jerome in one of his three great characters. 1. As patron Saint and Doctor of the Church. 2. As Translator and Commentator of the Scriptures. 3. As Penitent. As Doctor of the Church, and teacher, he enters into every scheme of decoration, and finds a place in all sacred buildings. As Saint and Penitent, he is chiefly to be found in the convents and churches of the Jeronymites, who claim him as their Patriarch.

When placed before us as the patron saint and father of divinity, he is usually standing full length, either habited in the cardinal's robes, or with the cardinal's hat lying at his feet. It may be necessary to observe, that there is no historical authority for making St. Jerome a cardinal. Cardinal-priests were not ordained till three centuries later; but as the other fathers were all of high ecclesiastical rank, and as St. Jerome obstinately refused all such distinction, it has been thought necessary, for the sake of his dignity, to make him a cardinal: another reason may be, that he performed, in the court of Pope Dalmasius, those offices since discharged by the cardinal-deacon. In some of the old Venetian pictures, instead of the official robes of a cardinal, he is habited in loose ample red drapery, part of which is thrown over his head. When represented with his head uncovered, his forehead is lofty and bald, his beard is very long, flowing even to his girdle; his features fine and sharp, his nose aquiline. In his hand he holds a book or a scroll, and frequently the emblematical church, of which he was the great support and luminary: and, to make the application stronger and clearer, rays of light are seen issuing from the door of the church.

1. A signal instance of the treatment of Jerome as patron saint occurs in a fine picture by Wohlgemuth, the master of Albert Dürer.[1]

[1] Vienna Gal.

It is an altar-piece representing the glorification of the saint, and consists of three compartments. In the centre, St. Jerome *stands* on a magnificent throne, and lays his left hand on the head of a lion, raised up on his hind legs : the donors of the picture, a man and a woman, kneel in front; on each side are windows opening on a landscape, wherein various incidents of the life of St. Jerome are represented; on the right, his Penance in the Wilderness and his Landing at Cyprus ; and on the left, the merchants who had carried off the ass bring propitiatory gifts, which the saint rejects, and other men are seen felling wood and loading the lion. On the inner shutters or wings of the central picture, are represented, on the right, the three other doctors,—St. Augustine, with the flaming heart; St. Ambrose, with the beehive—both habited as bishops; and St. Gregory, wearing his tiara, and holding a large book (his famous Homilies) in his hand. On the left, three apostles with their proper attributes—St. Andrew, St. Thomas, and St. Bartholomew ; on the other side are represented, to the right, St. Henry II. holding a church (the cathedral of Bamberg), and a sword, his proper attributes ; and his wife St. Cunegunda.[1] On the left, St. Elizabeth of Hungary and St. Martin. There are besides, to close in the whole, two outer doors : on the inner side, to the right, St. Joseph and St. Kilian ; [2] on the left, St. Catherine and St. Ursula; and on the exterior of the whole the mass of St. Gregory, with various personages and objects connected with the Passion of Christ. The whole is about six feet high, dated 1511, and may bear a comparison, for elaborate and multifarious detail and exquisite painting, with the famous Van Eyck altar-piece in St. John's Church at Ghent.[3]

2. In his character of patron, St. Jerome is a frequent subject of sculpture. There is a Gothic figure of him in Henry the Seventh's Chapel, habited in the cardinal's robes, the lion fawning upon him.

When St. Jerome is represented in his second great character, as

---

[1] In the catalogue, St. Cunegunda is styled *St. Elizabeth Queen of Hungary*, and St. Elizab th of Hungary is styled *St. Elizabeth Queen of Portugal*.

[2] Irish Bishop of Würtzburg, and Patron, A.D. 689.

[3] ' In this picture we recognise the master to whom Albert Dürer was indebted for his education ; indeed, Wohlgemuth here surpasses his great scholar in the expression of gentleness and simplicity, particularly in the heads of some of the female saints.'—*Handbook of Painting : German, Flemish, and Dutch Schools*, p. 111.

the translator of the Scriptures, he is usually seated in a cave or in a cell, busied in reading or in writing; he wears a loose robe thrown over his wasted form; and either he looks down intent on his book, or he looks up as if awaiting heavenly inspiration: sometimes an angel is dictating to him.

1. In an old Italian print, which I have seen, he is seated on the ground reading, in *spectacles;* an anachronism frequent in the old painters. Sometimes he is seated under the shade of a tree; or within a cavern, writing at a rude table formed of a stump of a tree, or a board laid across two fragments of rock; as in a beautiful picture by Ghirlandajo, remarkable for its solemn and tranquil feeling.[1]

2. Very celebrated is an engraving of this subject by Albert Dürer. The scene is the interior of a cell, at Bethlehem; two windows on the left pour across the picture a stream of sunshine, which is represented with wonderful effect. St. Jerome is seen in the background, seated at a desk, most intently writing his translation of the Scriptures; in front the lion is crouching, and a fox is seen asleep. These two animals are here emblems;—the one, of the courage and vigilance, the other of the wisdom or acuteness, of the saint. The execution of this print is a miracle of Art, and it is very rare. There is an exquisite little picture by Elzheimer copied from it, and of the same size, at Hampton Court. I need hardly observe, that here the rosary and the pot of holy water are anachronisms, as well as the cardinal's hat. By Albert Dürer we have also St. Jerome writing in a cavern; and St Jerome reading in his cell; both woodcuts.

3. Even more beautiful is a print by Lucas v. Leyden, in which St. Jerome is reclining in his cell and reading intently; the lion licks his foot.

4. In a picture by Lucas Cranach, Albert of Brandenburg, elector of Mayence (1527), is represented in the character of St. Jerome, seated in the wilderness, and writing at a table formed of a plank laid across two stumps of trees: he is in the cardinal-robes; and in the foreground a lion, a hare, a beaver, a partridge, and a hind, beautifully painted, express the solitude of his life. In the background the

[1] Florence, Ogni Santi.

caravan of merchants is seen entering the gate of the monastery, conducted by the faithful lion.

5. The little picture by Domenichino, in our National Gallery, represents St. Jerome looking up from his book, and listening to the
accents of the angel. 6. In a picture by Tiarini,[1] it is St. John the
Evangelist, and not an angel, who dictates while he writes. 7. In a
picture by Titian, St. Jerome, seated, holds a book, and gazes up at a
crucifix suspended in the skies ; the lion is drinking at a fountain.
Out of twenty prints of St. Jerome after Titian, there are at least
eight which represent him at study or writing.

It is in the double character of Doctor of the Church, and translator
of the Scriptures, that we find St. Jerome so frequently introduced
into pictures of the Madonna, and grouped with other saints. Two
of the most celebrated pictures in the world suggest themselves here
as examples :—1. 'The Madonna della Pesce' of Raphael ; where
the Virgin, seated on a raised throne, holds the Infant Christ in her
arms ; on her right hand, the Archangel Raphael presents the young
Tobias, who holds the fish, the emblem of Christianity or Baptism.
On the other side kneels St. Jerome, holding an open book, his
beard sweeping to his girdle ; the lion at his feet ; the Infant Christ,
while he bends forward to greet Tobias, has one hand upon St.
Jerome's book : the whole is a beautiful and expressive allegory.[2] 2.
Correggio's picture, called 'The St. Jerome of Parma,' represents
the Infant Christ on the knees of his mother : Mary Magdalene
bends to kiss his feet : St. Jerome stands in front, presenting his
translation of the Scriptures.

The penitent St. Jerome seems to have been adopted throughout
the Christian Church as the approved symbol of Christian penitence,
self-denial, and self-abasement. No devotional subject, if we except
the 'Madonna and Child' and the 'Magdalene,' is of such perpetual
recurrence. In the treatment it has been infinitely varied. The scene
is generally a wild rocky solitude : St. Jerome, half naked, emaciated,

[1] Bologna, S. Maria Maggiore.
[2] The picture, originally at Naples, was purchased or appropriated by Philip IV. for the
Church of the Escurial, which belonged to the Jeronymites.

with matted hair and beard, is seen on his knees before a crucifix, beating his breast with a stone. The lion is almost always intro-duced, sometimes asleep, or crouching at his feet; sometimes keep-ing guard, sometimes drinking at a stream. The most magnificent example of this treatment is by Titian:[1] St. Jerome, kneeling on one knee, half supported by a craggy rock, and holding the stone, looks up with eager devotion to a cross, artlessly fixed into a cleft

85   St. Jerome doing Penance.   (Titian.)

in the rock; two books lie on a cliff behind; at his feet are a skull and hour-glass; and the lion reposes in front. The feeling of deep solitude, and a kind of sacred horror breathed over this picture, are inconceivably fine and impressive. Another by Titian, but inferior, is in the Louvre; and there are at least twelve engravings of St. Jerome doing penance, after the same painter: among them a

[1] Milan, Brera.

superb landscape, in which are seen a lion and a lioness prowling in
the wilderness, while the saint is doing penance in the foreground.
By Agostino Caracci there is a famous engraving of 'St. Jerome
doing penance in a cave,' called from its size the *great* St. Jerome.
But to particularise further would be endless: I know scarcely any
Italian painter since the fifteenth century who has not treated this
subject at least once.

The Spanish painters have rendered it with a gloomy power, and
revelled in its mystic significance.   In the Spanish gallery of the
Louvre I counted at least twenty St. Jeromes: the old German
painters and engravers also delighted in it, on account of its picturesque capabilities.

Albert Dürer represents St. Jerome kneeling before a crucifix,
which he has suspended against the trunk of a massy tree; an open
book is near it; he holds in his right hand a flint-stone, with
which he is about to strike his breast, all wounded and bleeding
from the blows already inflicted; the lion crouches behind him, and
in the distance is a stag.

The penitent St. Jerome is not a good subject for sculpture; the
undraped, meagre form, and the abasement of suffering, are disagreeable in this treatment: yet such representations are constantly
met with in churches.   The famous colossal statue by Torrigiano,
now in the Museum at Seville, represents St. Jerome kneeling on a
rock, a stone in one hand, a crucifix in the other.   At Venice, in
the Frari, there is a statue of St. Jerome, standing, with the stone
in his hand and the lion at his feet; too majestic for the Penitent.
There are several other statues of St. Jerome at Venice, from the
Liberi and Lombardi schools, all fine as statues; but the penitent
saint is idealised into the patron-saint of penitents.

When figures of St. Jerome as penitent are introduced in Màdonna
pictures, or in the Passion of Christ, then such figures are devotional,
and symbolical, in a general sense, of Christian repentance.

There is an early picture of the Crucifixion, by Raphael,[1] in which
he has placed St. Jerome at the foot of the cross, beating his breast
with a stone (86).

The pictures from the life of St. Jerome comprise a variety of

[1] Collection of Lord Ward.

subjects:—1. 'He receives the cardinal's hat from the Virgin:' sometimes it is the Infant Christ, seated in the lap of the Virgin,

86   St. Jerome, as Penitent, in a Crucifixion.   (Raphael.)

who presents it to him. 2. 'He disputes with the Jewish doctors on the truth of the Christian religion;' in a curious picture by Juan de Valdes.[1] He stands on one side of a table in an attitude of authority: the rabbis, each of whom has a demon looking over his shoulder, are searching their books for arguments against him. 3. 'St. Jerome, while studying Hebrew in the solitude of Chalcida, hears in a vision the sound of the last trumpet, calling men to judgment.' This is a common subject, and styled 'The Vision of St. Jerome.' I have met with no example earlier than the fifteenth

[1] Louvre, Sp. Gal.

century.   In general, he is lying on the ground, and an angel sounds
the trumpet from above.   In a composition by Ribera he holds a
pen in one hand and a penknife in the other: he seems to have been
arrested in the very act of mending his pen by the blast of the trumpet: the figure of the saint, wasted even to skin and bone, and his
look of petrified amazement, are very fine, notwithstanding the commonplace action.   In a picture by Subleyras, in the Louvre, St.
Jerome is gazing upwards, with an astonished look; three archangels sound their trumpets from above.   In a picture by Antonio
Pereda, at Madrid, St. Jerome not only hears in his vision the sound
of the last trump, he *sees* the dead arise from their graves around
him.   Lastly, by way of climax, I may mention a picture in the
Louvre, by a modern French painter, Sigalon: St. Jerome is in a
convulsive fit, and the three angels, blowing their trumpets in his
ears, are like furies sent to torment and madden the sinner, rather
than to rouse the saint.

While doing penance in the desert, St. Jerome was sometimes
haunted by temptations, as well as amazed by terrors.

4. Domenichino, in one of the frescoes in St. Onofrio, represents the
particular kind of temptation by which the saint was in imagination
assailed: while he is fervently praying and beating his breast, a circle
of beautiful nymphs, seen in the background, weave a graceful dance.
Vasari has had the bad taste to give us a penitent St. Jerome with
Venus and Cupids in the background: one arch little Cupid takes aim
at him;—an offensive instance of the extent to which, in the sixteenth
century, classical ideas had mingled with and depraved Christian Art.[1]

5. Guido. ' St. Jerome translating the Scriptures while an angel
dictates:' life size and very fine (except the angel, who is weak,
and reminds one of a water-nymph [2]); in his pale manner.

6. Domenichino. ' St. Jerome is flagellated by an angel for pre-
ferring Cicero to the Hebrew writings:' also in the St. Onofrio.
The Cicero, torn from his hand, lies at his feet.   Here the saint is
a young man, and the whole scene is represented as a vision.

7. But St. Jerome was comforted by visions of glory, as well as

[1] P. Pitti, Florence.   [2] Lichtenstein Gal.

haunted by terrors and temptations. In the picture by Parmigiano, in our National Gallery, St. Jerome is sleeping in the background, while St. John the Baptist points upwards to a celestial vision of the Virgin and Child, seen in the opening heavens above: the upper part of this picture is beautiful, and full of dignity; but the saint is lying stretched on the earth in an attitude so uneasy and distorted, that it would seem as if he were condemned to do penance even in his sleep; and the St. John has always appeared to me mannered and theatrical.

87   St. Jerome and the Lion. (Coll' Antonio de Fiore.)   Naples.

8. The story of the lion is often represented. St. Jerome is seated in his cell, attired in the monk's habit and cowl; the lion approaches, and lays his paw upon his knee; a cardinal's hat and

books are lying near him; and, to express the self-denial of the saint, a mouse is peeping into an empty cup (87).[1]

In another example, by Vittore Carpaccio, the lion enters the cell, and three monks, attendants on St. Jerome, flee in terror.

9. The Last Communion of St. Jerome is the subject of one of the most celebrated pictures in the world,—the St. Jerome of Domenichino, which has been thought worthy of being placed opposite to the Transfiguration of Raphael, in the Vatican. The aged saint—feeble, emaciated, dying—is borne in the arms of his disciples to the chapel of his monastery, and placed within the porch. A young priest sustains him; St. Paula, kneeling, kisses one of his thin bony hands; the saint fixes his eager eyes on the countenance of the priest, who is about to administer the sacrament, —a noble dignified figure in a rich ecclesiastical dress; a deacon holds the cup, and an attendant priest the book and taper; the lion droops his head with an expression of grief; the eyes and attention of all are on the dying saint, while four angels, hovering above, look down upon the scene.

Agostino Caracci, in a grand picture now in the Bologna Gallery, had previously treated the same subject with much feeling and dramatic power: but here the saint is not so wasted and so feeble: St. Paula is not present, and the lion is tenderly licking his feet.

Older than either, and very beautiful and solemn, is a picture by Vittore Carpaccio, in which the saint is kneeling in the porch of a church, surrounded by his disciples, and the lion is seen outside.

10. 'The Death of St. Jerome.' In the picture by Starnina he is giving his last instructions to his disciples, and the expression of solemn grief in the old heads around is very fine. In a Spanish picture he is extended on a couch, made of hurdles, and expires in the arms of his monks.

In a very fine anonymous print, dated 1614, St. Jerome is dying alone in his cell (this version of the subject is contrary to all authority and precedent): he presses to his bosom the Gospel and the crucifix; the lion looks up in his face roaring, and angels bear away his soul to heaven.

---

[1] Kugler pronounces this to be a Flemish picture (v. 'Handbook,' p. 190).

11. 'The Obsequies of St. Jerome.' In the picture by Vittore Carpaccio, the saint is extended on the ground before the high altar, and the priests around are kneeling in various attitudes of grief or devotion. The lion is seen on one side.[1]

I will mention here some other pictures in which St. Jerome figures as the principal personage.

St. Jerome introducing Charles V. into Paradise is the subject of a large fresco, by Luca Giordano, on the staircase of the Escurial.

St. Jerome conversing with two nuns, probably intended for St. Paula and St. Marcella.[2]

The sleep of St. Jerome. He is watched by two angels, one of whom, with his finger on his lip, commands silence.[3]

It is worth remarking, that in the old Venetian pictures St. Jerome does not wear the proper habit and hat of a cardinal, but an ample scarlet robe, part of which is thrown over his head as a hood (88).

The history of St. Jerome, in a series, is often found in the churches and convents of the Jeronymites, and generally consists of the following subjects, of which the fourth and sixth are often omitted :—

88   Venetian St. Jerome.

1. He is baptized. 2. He receives the cardinal's hat from the Virgin. 3. He does penance in the desert, beating his breast with a

---

[1] The three frescoes by Carpaccio are in the Church of San Giorgio de' Schiavoni at Venice.

[2] It was in the Standish Gal. in the Louvre

[3] Engraved by Loli.

stone.   4. He meets St. Augustine.   5. He is studying or writing
in a cell.   6. He builds the convent at Bethlehem.   7. He heals the
wounded lion.   8. He receives the Last Sacrament.   9. He dies
in the presence of his disciples.   10. He is buried.

Considering that St. Jerome has ever been venerated as one of the
great lights of the Church, it is singular that so few churches are
dedicated to him.   There is one at Rome, erected, according to
tradition, on the very spot where stood the house of Santa Paula,
where she entertained St. Jerome during his sojourn at Rome in 382.
For the high altar of this church, Domenichino painted his masterpiece of the Communion of St. Jerome already described.   The
embarkation of Saint Paula, to follow her spiritual teacher St. Jerome
to the Holy Land, is the subject of one of Claude's most beautiful sea
pieces, now in the collection of the Duke of Wellington; another
picture of this subject, the figures as large as life, is in the Brera,
by a clever Cremonese painter, Giuseppe Bottoni.

St. Jerome has detained us long; the other Fathers are, as subjects
of Art, much less interesting.

St. Ambrose.

Lat. **S.** Ambrosius.   *Ital.* Sant' Ambrogio.   *Fr.* St. Ambroise.   *Ger.* Der Heilige Ambrosius.
Patron Saint of Milan.   (April 4, A.D. 397.)

WE can hardly imagine a greater contrast than between the stern,
enthusiastic, dreaming, ascetic Jerome, and the statesman-like,
practical, somewhat despotic AMBROSE.   This extraordinary man, in
whose person the priestly character assumed an importance and
dignity till then unknown, was the son of a prefect of Gaul, bearing
the same name, and was born at Treves in the year 340.   It is said
that, when an infant in the cradle, a swarm of bees alighted on his
mouth, without injuring him.   The same story was told of Plato
and of Archilochus, and considered prophetic of future eloquence.
It is from this circumstance that St. Ambrose is represented with
the bee-hive near him.

Young Ambrose, after pursuing his studies at Rome with success, was appointed prefect of Æmilia and Liguria (Piedmont and Genoa), and took up his residence at Milan.   Shortly afterwards the Bishop of Milan died, and the succession was hotly disputed between the Catholics and the Arians.   Ambrose appeared in his character of prefect, to allay the tumult; he harangued the people with such persuasive eloquence that they were hushed into respectful silence; and in the midst a child's voice was heard to exclaim, 'Ambrose shall be bishop!'   The multitude took up the cry as though it had been a voice from heaven, and compelled him to assume the sacred office.   He attempted to avoid the honour thus laid upon him by flight, by entreaties,—pleading that, though a professed Christian, he had never been baptized : in vain ! the command of the emperor enforced the wishes of the people; and Ambrose, being baptized, was, within eight days afterwards, consecrated bishop of Milan. He has since been regarded as the patron saint of that city.

He began by distributing all his worldly goods to the poor; he then set himself to study the sacred writings, and to render himself in all respects worthy of his high dignity.   'The Old and the New Testament,' says Mr. Milman, 'met in the person of Ambrose : the implacable hostility to idolatry, the abhorrence of every deviation from the established formulary of belief;—the wise and courageous benevolence, the generous and unselfish devotion to the great interests of humanity.'

He was memorable for the grandeur and magnificence with which he invested the ceremonies of worship : they had never been so imposing. He particularly cultivated music, and introduced from the East the manner of chanting the service since called the Ambrosian chant.

Two things were especially remarkable in the life and character of St. Ambrose.   The first was the enthusiasm with which he advocated celibacy in both sexes : on this topic, as we are assured, he was so persuasive, that mothers shut up their daughters lest they should be *seduced* by their eloquent bishop into vows of chastity.   The other was his determination to set the ecclesiastical above the sovereign or civil power : this principle, so abused in later times, was in the days of Ambrose the assertion of the might of Christianity, of mercy, of

justice, of freedom, over heathenism, tyranny, cruelty, slavery. The
dignity with which he refused to hold any communication with the
Emperor Maximus, because he was stained with the blood of Gratian,
and his resolute opposition to the Empress Justina, who interfered
with his sacerdotal privileges, were two instances of this spirit.
But the most celebrated incident of his life is his conduct with
regard to the Emperor Theodosius, the last great emperor of Rome;—
a man of an iron will, a despot, and a warrior. That *he* should bend
in trembling submission at the feet of an unarmed priest, and shrink
before his rebuke, filled the whole world with an awful idea of the
supremacy of the Church, and prepared the way for the Hildebrands,
the Perettis, the Caraffas of later times. With regard to St.
Ambrose, this assumption of moral power, this high prerogative of
the priesthood, had hitherto been without precedent, and in this its
first application it certainly commands our respect, our admiration,
and our sympathy.

Theodosius, with all his great qualities, was subject to fits of
violent passion. A sedition, or rather a popular affray, had taken
place in Thessalonica; one of his officers was ill-treated, and some
lives lost. Theodosius, in the first moment of indignation,
ordered an indiscriminate massacre of the inhabitants, and seven
thousand human beings—men, women, and children—were sacrificed. The conduct of Ambrose on this occasion was worthy of
a Christian prelate : he retired from the presence of the emperor,
and wrote to him a letter, in which, in the name of Christ, of His
Church, and of all the bishops over whom he had any influence, he
denounced this inhuman act with the strongest expressions of
abhorrence, and refused to allow the sovereign, thus stained with
innocent blood, to participate in the sacraments of the Church;—
in fact, excommunicated him. In vain the emperor threatened, supplicated; in vain he appeared with all his imperial state before
the doors of the cathedral of Milan, and commanded and entreated
entrance. The doors were closed ; and even on Christmas-day, when
he again as a suppliant presented himself, Ambrose appeared at the
porch, and absolutely forbade his entrance, unless he should choose
to pass into the sanctuary over the dead body of the intrepid bishop.
At length, after eight months of interdict, Ambrose consented to

relent, on two conditions : the first, that the emperor should publish an edict by which no capital punishment could be executed till thirty days after conviction of a crime ; the second, that he should per- form a public penance. The emperor submitted ; and, clothed in sackcloth, grovelling on the earth, with dust and ashes on his head, lay the master of the world before the altar of Christ, because of innocent blood hastily and wrongfully shed. This was a great triumph, and one of incalculable results—some evil, some good.

Another incident in the life of St. Ambrose should be recorded to his honour. In his time, ' the first blood was judicially shed for religious opinion'—and the first man who suffered for heresy was Priscilian, a noble Spaniard : on this occasion, St. Ambrose and St. Martin of Tours raised their protest in the name of Christianity against this dreadful precedent ; but the animosity of the Spanish bishops prevailed, and Priscilian was put to death ; so early were bigotry and cruelty the characteristics of the Spanish hierarchy ! Ambrose refused to communicate with the few bishops who had countenanced this transaction : the general voice of the Church was against it.

The man who had thus raised himself above all worldly power was endued by popular enthusiasm with supernatural privileges : he per- formed cures ; he saw visions. At the time of the consecration of the new cathedral at Milan, a miraculous dream revealed to him the martyrdom of two holy men, Gervasius and Protasius, and the place where their bodies reposed. The remains were disinterred, conveyed in solemn procession to the cathedral, and deposited beneath the high altar ; and St. Gervasius and St. Protasius became, on the faith of a dream, distinguished saints in the Roman calendar. Ambrose died at Milan, in 397, in the attitude and the act of prayer.

There were many poetical legends and apologues relating to St. Ambrose current in the middle ages.

It is related that an obstinate heretic who went to hear him preach, only to confute and mock him, beheld an angel visible at his side, and prompting the words he uttered ; on seeing which, the scoffer was of course converted ; a subject represented in his church at Milan.

One day, Ambrose went to the prefect Macedonius, to entreat favour
for a poor condemned wretch ; but the doors were shut against him,
and he was refused access. Then he said, ' Thou, even thou, shalt fly
to the church for refuge, and shalt not enter ! ' and a short time afterwards, Macedonius, being pursued by his enemies, fled for sanctuary
to the church ; but, though the doors were wide open, he could not
find the entrance, but wandered around in blind perplexity till he
was slain.   Of this incident I have seen no picture.

On another occasion, St. Ambrose, coming to the house of a nobleman of Tuscany, was hospitably received ; and he inquired concerning
the state of his host; the nobleman replied, ' I have never known
adversity ; every day hath seen me increasing in fortune, in honours,
in possessions.   I have a numerous family of sons and daughters,
who have never cost me a pang of sorrow; I have a multitude of
slaves, to whom my word is law ; and I have never suffered either
sickness or pain.'   Then Ambrose rose hastily from table, and said
to his companions, ' Arise! fly from this roof, ere it fall upon us;
for the Lord is not here ! ' and scarcely had he left the house, when
an earthquake shook the ground, and swallowed up the palace with
all its inhabitants.   I have seen this story in a miniature, but cannot
at this moment refer to it.

St. Ambrose falls asleep, or into a trance, while celebrating mass,
and sees in the spirit the obsequies of St. Martin of Tours : the
sacristan strikes him on the shoulder to wake him.   This is the
subject of a very old mosaic in his church at Milan.

When St. Ambrose was on his death-bed, Christ visited him and
comforted him ; Honorat, bishop of Vercelli, was then in attendance
on him, and having gone to sleep, an angel waked him, saying, ' Arise,
for he departs in this hour ; ' and Honorat was just in time to administer the sacrament and see him expire.   Others who were present
beheld him ascend to heaven, borne in the arms of angels.

Devotional pictures of St. Ambrose alone as patron saint do not often
occur.   In general he wears the episcopal pallium with the mitre and
crosier as bishop : the bee-hive is sometimes placed at his feet ; but a
more frequent attribute is the knotted scourge with three thongs.   The
scourge is a received emblem of the castigation of sin : in the hand of

St. Ambrose it may signify the penance inflicted on the Emperor Theodosius; or, as others interpret it, the expulsion of the Arians from Italy, and the triumph of the Trinitarians. It has always this meaning, we may presume, when the scourge has three knots, or three thongs. I have seen figures of St. Ambrose holding two human bones in his hand. When this attribute occurs (as in a picture by *Vivarini, Venice Acad.*), it alludes to the discovery of the relics of Gervasius and Protasius.

Among the few representations of St. Ambrose as patron saint, the finest beyond all comparison is that which adorns his chapel in the Frari at Venice, painted conjointly by B. Vivarini and Basaiti (A.D. 1498). He is seated on a throne, raised on several steps, attired in his episcopal robes and mitre, and bearing the triple scourge in his hand. He has a short grey beard, and looks straight out of the picture with an expression of stern power;—nothing here of the benignity and humility of the Christian teacher! Around his throne stands a glorious company of saints: on the right, St. George in complete armour; St. John the Baptist; a young saint, bearing a sword and palm, with long hair, and the most beautiful expression of mild serene faith, whom I suppose to be St. Theodore; St. Sebastian; and another figure behind, part of the head only seen. On the left, St. Maurice, armed; the three Doctors, St. Gregory, St. Augustine, St. Jerome, and two other saints partly seen behind, whose personality is doubtful. All these wait round St. Ambrose, as guards and counsellors round a sovereign; two lovely little angels sit on the lower step of the throne hymning his praise. The whole picture is wonderful for colour, depth, and expression, and shows to what a pitch of excellence the Vivarini family had attained in these characteristics of the Venetian school, long before it had become a school.

Most of the single figures of St. Ambrose represent him in his most popular character, that of the stern adversary of the Arians. I remember (in the Frari at Venice) a picture in which St. Ambrose in his episcopal robes is mounted on a white charger, and flourishing on high his triple scourge. The Arians are trampled under his feet, or fly before him. I have seen an old print, in which he is represented with a short grey beard, stern countenance, and wearing the bishop's mitre; underneath is the inscription '*Antiquis ejus imaginibus Mediolani olim depictis ad vivum expressa;*' but it seems certain that no authentic portrait of him exists.

His church at Milan, the Basilica of Sant' Ambrogio Maggiore, one of the oldest and most interesting churches in Christendom, was founded by him in 387, and dedicated to all the Saints. Though rebuilt in the ninth century and restored in the seventeenth, it still retains the form of the primitive Christian churches (like some of those at Rome and Ravenna), and the doors of cypress wood are traditionally regarded as the very doors which St. Ambrose closed against the Emperor Theodosius, brought hither from the ancient cathedral. Within this venerable and solemn old church may be seen one of the most extraordinary and best-preserved specimens of Mediæval Art: it is the golden shrine or covering of the high altar, much older than the famous *pala d' oro* at Venice; and the work, or at least the design, of one man:[1] whereas the *pala* is the work of several different artists at different periods. On the front of the altar, which is all of plates of gold, enamelled and set with precious stones, are represented in relief scenes from the life of our Saviour: on the sides, which are of silver-gilt, angels, archangels, and medallions of Milanese saints. On the back, also of silver-gilt, we have the whole life of St. Ambrose, in a series of small compartments, most curious and important as a record of costume and manners, as well as an example of the state of Art at that time. I have never seen any engraving of this monument, but I examined it carefully. In the centre stand the Archangels Michael and Gabriel, in the Byzantine style; and below them, St. Ambrose blesses the donor, Bishop Angelbertus, and the goldsmith Wolvinus. Around, in twelve compartments, we have the principal incidents of the life of St. Ambrose, the figures being, as nearly as I can recollect, about six inches high.

1. Bees swarm round his head as he lies in his cradle. 2. He is appointed prefect of the Ligurian provinces. 3. He is elected Bishop of Milan in 375. 4. He is baptized. 5. He is ordained. 6. and 7. He sleeps, and beholds in a vision the obsequies of St. Martin of Tours.

---

[1] Wolvinus, A.D. 832. 'His name seems to indicate that he was of Teutonic race—a circumstance which has excited much controversy amongst the modern Italian antiquaries.' —*Murray's Handbook.*

8. He preaches in the cathedral, inspired by angels. 9. He heals the sick and lame. 10. He is visited by Christ. 11. An angel wakes the bishop of Vercelli, and sends him to St. Ambrose. 12. Ambrose dies, and angels bear away his soul to heaven.

I was surprised not to find in his church what we consider as the principal event of his life—his magnanimous resistance to the Emperor Theodosius. In fact, the grand scene between Ambrose and Theodosius has never been so popular as it deserves to be; considered merely as a subject of painting, it is full of splendid picturesque capabilities; for grouping, colour, contrast, background, all that could be desired. In the great picture by Rubens,[1] the scene is the porch of the church. On the left the emperor, surrounded by his guards, stands irresolute, and in a supplicatory attitude, on the steps; on the right and above, St. Ambrose is seen, attended by the ministering priests, and stretches out his hand to repel the intruder. There is a print, after Andrea del Sarto, representing Theodosius on his knees before the relenting prelate. In the Louvre is a small picture, by Subleyras, of the reconciliation of Ambrose and Theodosius. In our National Gallery is a small and beautiful copy, by Vandyck, of the great picture by Rubens.

As joint patrons of Milan, St. Ambrose and St. Carlo Borromeo are sometimes represented together, but only in late pictures.

There is a statue of St. Ambrose, by Falconet,[2] in the act of repelling Theodosius, which is mentioned by Diderot, with a commentary so characteristic of the French anti-religious feeling of that time,—a feeling as narrow and one-sided in its way as the most bigoted puritanism,—that I am tempted to extract it; only premising, that if, after the slaughter at Ismaël, Catherine of Russia had been placed under the ban of Christendom, the world would not have been the worse for such an exertion of the priestly power.

C'est ce fougueux évêque qui osa fermer les portes de l'église à Théodose, et à qui un certain souverain de par le monde [Frederic of Prussia] qui dans la guerre passée avoit une si bonne envie de faire un tour dans la rue des prêtres, et une certaine souveraine [Catherine of Russia] qui vient de débarrasser son clergé de toute cette richesse inutile qui l'empêchoit d'être respectable, auroient fait couper la barbe et les oreilles, en lui disant: ' Apprenez, monsieur l'abbé, que le temple de votre Dieu est sur mon domaine, et que si mon prédécesseur vous a accordé par grâce les trois arpens de terrain qu'il occupe, je puis les

[1] Belvedere Gal., Vienna.   [2] Paris, Invalides.

reprendre et vous envoyer porter vos autels et votre fanatisme ailleurs. Ce lieu-ci est la
maison du Père commun des hommes, bons ou méchans, et je veux entrer quand il me plaira.
Je ne m'accuse point à vous ; quand je daignerois vous consulter, vous n'en savez pas assez
pour me conseiller sur ma conduite, et de quel front vous immiscez-vous d'en juger ?' Mais
le plat empereur ne parla pas ainsi, et l'évêque savoit bien à qui il avoit à faire. Le
statuaire nous l'a montré dans le moment de son insolent apostrophe.

In Diderot's criticisms on Art, which are often quoted even now,
there is in general a far better taste than prevailed in his time, and
much good sense ; but a low tone of sentiment when he had to deal
with imaginative or religious Art, and an intolerable coarseness—
' most mischievous foul sin in chiding sin.'

St. Augustine.

St. Austin. *Lat.* Sanctus Augustinus. *Ital.* Sant' Agostino. *Fr.* St Augustin.
(Aug. 28, A.D. 430.)

St. Augustine, the third of the Doctors of the Church, was born at
Tagaste, in Numidia, in 354. His father was a heathen : his mother,
Monica, a Christian. Endowed with splendid talents, a vivid
imagination, and strong passions, Augustine passed his restless youth
in dissipated pleasures, in desultory studies, changing from one faith
to another, dissatisfied with himself and unsettled in mind. His
mother, Monica, wept and prayed for him, and, in the extremity of
her anguish, repaired to the bishop of Carthage. After listening to
her sorrows, he dismissed her with these words : ' Go in peace ; the
son of so many tears will not perish ! ' Augustine soon afterwards
went to Rome, where he gained fame and riches by his eloquence at
the bar ; but he was still unhappy and restless, nowhere finding peace
either in labour or in pleasure. From Rome he went to Milan ;
there, after listening for some time to the preaching of Ambrose, he
was, after many struggles converted to the faith, and was baptized
by the bishop of Milan, in presence of his mother, Monica. On this
occasion was composed the hymn called the ' Te Deum,' still in use
in our Church ; St. Ambrose and St. Augustine reciting the verses
alternately as they advanced to the altar. Augustine, after some
time spent in study, was ordained priest, and then bishop of Hippo,

a small town and territory not far from Carthage. Once installed in his bishopric, he ever afterwards refused to leave the flock intrusted to his care, or to accept of any higher dignity. His life was passed in the practice of every virtue : all that he possessed was spent in hospitality and charity, and his time was devoted to the instruction of his flock, either by preaching or writing. In 430, after he had presided over his diocese for thirty-five years, the city of Hippo was besieged by the Vandals; in the midst of the horrors that ensued, Augustine refused to leave his people, and died during the siege, being then in his seventy-sixth year. It is said that his remains were afterwards removed from Africa to Pavia, by Luitprand, king of the Lombards. His writings in defence of Christianity are numerous and celebrated; and he is regarded as the patron saint of theologians and learned men.

Of his glorious tomb, in the Cathedral of Pavia, I can only say that its beauty as a work of art astonished me. I had not been prepared for anything so rich, so elegant in taste, and so elaborate in invention. It is of the finest florid Gothic, worked in white marble, scarcely discoloured by time. Augustine lies upon a bier, and angels of exquisite grace are folding his shroud around him. The basso-relievos represent the events of his life; the statues of the evangelists, apostles, and other saints connected with the history of the Church, are full of dignity and character. It comprises in all 290 figures. This magnificent shrine is attributed by Cicognara to the Jacobelli of Venice, and by Vasari to the two brothers Agostino and Agnolo of Siena; but he does not speak with certainty, and the date 1362 seems to justify the supposition of Cicognara, the Sienese brothers being then eighty or ninety years old.

Single figures of St. Augustine are not common; and when grouped with others in devotional pictures, it is not easy to distinguish him from other bishops; for his proper attribute, the heart flaming or transpierced, to express the ardour of his piety or the poignancy of his repentance, is very seldom introduced: but when a bishop is standing with a book in his hand, or a pen, accompanied by St. Jerome and with no particular attribute, we may suppose it to be St. Augustine; and when the title of one of his famous writings is inscribed on the book, it of course fixes the identity beyond a doubt.

1. B. Vivarini.   St. Augustine seated on a throne, as patron saint, mitred and robed; alone, stern, and majestic.[1]

2. Dosso Dossi.   St. Augustine throned as patron, attended by two angels; he looks like a jovial patriarch.[2]

3. F. Filippo Lippi.   St. Augustine writing in his chamber; no emblem, no mitre; yet the *personalité* so marked, that one could not mistake him either for Ambrose or Jerome.[3]

4. Andrea del Sarto.   St. Augustine as doctor; before him stand St. Dominic and St. Peter Martyr; beside him St. Laurence, listening; in front kneel St. Sebastian and Mary Magdalen.[4]

5. V. Carpaccio.   St. Augustine standing; a fine, stern, majestic figure; he holds his book and scourge.[5]

6. Paris Bordone.   The Virgin and Child enthroned; the Virgin places on the head of St. Augustine, who kneels before her, the jewelled mitre.[6]

7. Florigerio.   St. Augustine, as bishop, and St. Monica, veiled, stand on each side of the Madonna.[7]

As a *series* of subjects, the history of St. Augustine is not commonly met with; yet certain events in his life are of very frequent occurrence.

I shall begin with the earliest.

1. Monica brings her son to school; the master receives him; the scholars are sitting in a row conning their hornbooks.   The names of Monica and Augustine are inscribed in the glories round their heads.   This is a very curious little oval picture of the early part of the fourteenth century.[8]

Benozzo Gozzoli has painted the same subject in a large fresco in the church of San Geminiano at Volterra (A.D. 1460).   Monica presents her son to the schoolmaster, who caresses him; in the background a little boy is being whipped, precisely in the same attitude in which correction is administered to this day in some of our schools.

2. St. Augustine under the fig-tree meditating, with the inscrip-

---

[1] SS. Giovan e Paolo, Venice.   [2] Brera, Milan.   [3] Fl. Gal.
[4] Pitti Pal.   This fine picture was painted for the Agostini.
[5] Brera, Milan.   [6] Berlin Gal.   [7] Acad., Venice.   [8] Vatican, Christian Museum.

tion, ' Dolores animæ salutem parturientes ; ' and the same subject
varied, with the inscription, *Tolle, lege.* He tells us in his Confessions, that while still unconverted and in deep communion with his
friend Alypius on the subject of the Scriptures, the contest within his
mind was such that he rushed from the presence of his friend and
threw himself down beneath a fig-tree, pouring forth torrents of
repentant tears ; and he heard a voice, as it were the voice of a child,
repeating several times, ' *Tolle, lege,*' ' Take and read ;' and returning
to the place where he had left his friend, and taking up the sacred
volume, he opened it at the verse of St. Paul's Epistle to the Romans,
' Not in rioting and drunkenness, not in chambering and wantonness,
not in strife and envying ; but put ye on the Lord Jesus Christ, and
make not provision for the flesh.' Considering that this was the
voice of God, he took up the religious profession, to the great joy of
his mother and his friend.

3. C. Procaccino. The Baptism of St. Augustine in the presence
of St. Monica. This is a common subject in chapels dedicated to
St. Augustine or St. Monica.[1]

4. As the supposed founder of one of the four great religious
communities, St. Augustine is sometimes represented as giving the
rules to his Order : or in the act of writing them, while his monks
stand around, as in a picture by Carletto Cagliari :[2] both are common
subjects in the houses of the Augustine friars. The habit is black.[3]

5. St. Augustine dispensing alms, generally in a black habit, and
with a bishop's mitre on his head.

6. St. Augustine, washing the feet of the pilgrims, sees Christ
descend from above to have his feet washed with the rest; a large
picture in the Bologna Academy by Desubleo, a painter whose works,
with this one exception, are unknown to me. The saint wears the
black habit of an Augustine friar, and is attended by a monk with a
napkin in his hand. I found the same subject in the Louvre, in a
Spanish picture of the seventeenth century ; above is seen a church
(like the Pantheon) in a glory, and Christ is supposed to utter the
words, ' *Tibi commendo Ecclesiam meam.*'[4]

---

[1] Cremona.   [2] Belvedere, Vienna.   [3] *v.* ' Legends of the Monastic Orders,' p. 191.
[4] I believe this picture was afterwards in the possession of Mr. Dennistoun, of Dennistoun.
Mr. Stirling mentions it as a fine specimen of Murillo's second style.

7. St. Augustine, borne aloft by angels in an ecstatic vision, beholds Christ in the opening heavens above, St. Monica kneeling below.   This fine picture, by Vandyck, is or was in the gallery of Lord Methuen at Corsham : and at Madrid there is another example, by Murillo : St. Augustine kneeling in an ecstasy sees a celestial vision ; on one hand the Saviour crucified, on the other the Virgin and angels.

This, however, is not the famous subject called, in general, 8. ' The Vision of St. Augustine,' which represents a dream or vision related

89   The Vision of St. Augustine. (Murillo.)

by himself.   He tells us that while busied in writing his Discourse
on the Trinity, he wandered along the sea-shore lost in meditation.
Suddenly he beheld a child who, having dug a hole in the sand,
appeared to be bringing water from the sea to fill it.   Augustine
inquired what was the object of his task?   He replied, that he
intended to empty into this cavity all the waters of the great deep.
' Inpossible ! ' exclaimed Augustine.   ' Not more impossible,' replied
the child, ' than for thee, O Augustine ! to explain the mystery on
which thou art now meditating.'

No subject from the history of St. Augustine has been so often
treated, yet I do not remember any very early example.   It was
adopted as a favourite theme when Art became rather theological than
religious, and more intent on illustrating the dogmas of churchmen
than the teaching of Christ.   During the 16th and 17th centuries
we find it everywhere, and treated in every variety of style ; but
the *motif* does not vary, and the same fault prevails too generally,
of giving us a material fact, rather than a spiritual vision or
revelation.   Augustine, arrayed in his black habit or his episcopal
robes, stands on the sea-shore, gazing with an astonished air on
the Infant Christ, who pauses, and looks up from his task, holding
a bowl, a cup, a ladle, or a shell in his hand.   Thus we have it
in Murillo's picture—the most beautiful example I have seen :
the child is heavenly, but not visionary, ' palpable to feeling as
to sense.'

In Garofalo's picture of this subject, now in our National Gallery,
Augustine is seated on a rock by the margin of the sea, habited in
his episcopal robes, and with his books and writing implements near
him ; and while he gazes on the mysterious child, the Virgin appears
amid a choir of angels above : behind Augustine stands St. Catherine,
the patron saint of theologians and scholars : the little red figure in
the background represents St. Stephen, whose life and actions are
eloquently set forth in the homilies of St. Augustine : the introduction of St. Catherine, St. Stephen, and the whole court of heaven,
gives the picture a visionary character.   Rubens has painted this
subject with all his powerful reality : here Augustine wears the
black habit of his Order.   Vandyck in his large grand picture has
introduced St. Monica kneeling, thus giving at once the devotional

or visionary character.[1]   Albert Dürer has designed and engraved
the same subject.   The most singular treatment is the classical
composition of Raphael, in one of the small chiaro-scuro pictures
placed significantly under the ' Dispute of the Sacrament.'   St.
Augustine is in a Roman dress, bare-headed, and on horseback ; his
horse starts and rears at the sight of the miraculous child.

There is something at once picturesque and mystical in this subject,
which has rendered it a favourite with artists and theologians ; yet
there is always, at least in every instance I can recollect, something
prosaic and literal in the treatment which spoils the poetry of the
conception.

9. ' St. Augustine and St. Stephen bury Count Orgaz'—the
masterpiece of Domenico el Greco, once in the Cathedral of Toledo,
now in the Madrid Gallery.   This Conde de Orgaz, as Mr. Ford tells
us in his Handbook, lived in 1312, and had repaired a church in his
life-time, and *therefore* St. Stephen and St. Augustine came down
from heaven to lay him in his tomb, in presence of Christ, the
Virgin, and all the court of heaven.   ' The black and gold armour of
the dead Count is equal to Titian ; the red brocades and copes of
the saints are admirable ; less good are the Virgin and celestial
groups.'   I have before mentioned the reason why St. Augustine
and St. Stephen are often represented in companionship.

St. Monica is often introduced into pictures of her son, where she
has, of course, the secondary place ; her dress is usually a black robe,
and a veil or coif, white or grey, resembling that of a nun or a widow.
I have met with but one picture where she is supreme ; it is in the
Carmine at Florence.   St. Monica is seated on a throne and attended
by twelve holy women or female saints, six on each side.   The very
dark situation of this picture prevented me from distinguishing
individually the saints around her, but Monica herself as well as the
other figures have that *grandiose* air which belongs to the painter—
Filippo Lippi.

I saw in the atelier of the painter Ary Scheffer, in 1845, an
admirable picture of St. Augustine and his mother Monica.   The
two figures, not quite full length, are seated ; she holds his hand in
both hers, looking up to heaven with an expression of enthusiastic

---

[1] Once in Lord Methuen's Gallery at Corsham.

undoubting faith ;—' the son of so many tears cannot be cast away ! '
He also is looking up with an ardent, eager, but anxious, doubtful
expression, which seems to say, ' Help thou my unbelief! '   For profound and truthful feeling and significance, I know few things in
the compass of modern Art that can be compared to this picture.[1]

St. Gregory.

Lat. Sanctus Gregorius Magnus.   *Ital.* San Gregorio Magno or Papa.   *Fr.* St. Grégoire.
Ger. Der Heilige Gregor.   (March 12, A.D. 604.)

THE fourth Doctor of the Latin Church, St. Gregory, styled, and
not without reason, Gregory the Great, was one of those extraordinary men whose influence is not only felt in their own time, but
through long succeeding ages.   The events of his troubled and
splendid pontificate belong to history; and I shall merely throw
together here such particulars of his life and character as may
serve to render the multiplied representations of him both intelligible and interesting.   He was born at Rome in the year 540.   His
father, Gordian, was of senatorial rank : his mother, Sylvia, who, in
the history of St. Gregory, is almost as important as St. Monica in
the story of St. Augustine, was a woman of rare endowments, and,
during his childish years, the watchful instructress of her son.   It is
recorded that when he was still an infant she was favoured by a
vision of St. Antony, in which he promised to her son the supreme
dignity of the tiara.   Gregory, however, commenced his career in
life as a lawyer, and exercised during twelve years the office of
prætor or chief magistrate of his native city ; yet, while apparently
engrossed by secular affairs, he became deeply imbued with the
religious enthusiasm which was characteristic of his time and here-
ditary in his family.   Immediately on the death of his father he
devoted all the wealth he had inherited to pious and charitable purposes, converted his paternal home on the Celian Hill into a monastery and hospital for the poor, which he dedicated to St. Andrew ;
then, retiring to a little cell within it, he took the habit of the Bene-

---

[1] It was in possession of Her Majesty the Ex-Queen of the French, who paid for it
25,000f.

dictine Order, and gave up all his time to study and preparation for
the duties to which he had devoted himself.   On the occasion of a
terrific plague which almost depopulated Rome, he fearlessly undertook the care of the poor and sick.   Pope Pelagius having died at
this time, the people with one voice called upon Gregory to succeed
him ; but he shrank from the high office, and wrote to the Emperor
Maurice, entreating him not to ratify the choice of the people. The Emperor sent an edict confirming his election, and thereupon Gregory
fled from Rome, and hid himself in a cave.   Those who went in search
of him were directed to the place of his concealment by a celestial
light, and the fugitive was discovered and brought back to Rome.

No sooner had he assumed the tiara, thus forced upon him against
his will, than he showed himself in all respects worthy of his elevation.   While he asserted the dignity of his station, he was distinguished by his personal humility : he was the first pope who took
the title of ' Servant of the Servants of God ; ' he abolished slavery
throughout Christendom on religious grounds ; though enthusiastic
in making converts, he set himself against persecution ; and when
the Jews of Sardinia appealed to him, he commanded that the syna-
gogues which had been taken from them, and converted into churches,
should be restored.   He was the first who sent missionaries to
preach the Gospel in England, roused to pity by the sight of some
British captives exposed for sale in the market at Rome.   Shocked
at the idea of an eternity of vengeance and torment, if he did not
orginate the belief in purgatory, he was at least the first who
preached it publicly, and made it an article of faith.   In his hatred
of war, of persecution, of slavery, he stepped not only in advance of
his own time, but of ours.   He instituted the celibacy of the clergy,
one of the boldest strokes of ecclesiastical power ; he reformed the
services of the Church ; defined the model of the Roman liturgy,
such as it has ever since remained—the offices of the priests, the
variety and change of the sacerdotal garments ; he arranged the
music of the chants, and he himself trained the choristers.   ' Experi-
ence,' says Gibbon, 'had shown him the efficacy of these solemn and
pompous rites to soothe the distress, to confirm the faith, to mitigate
the fierceness, and to dispel the dark enthusiasm of the vulgar and
he readily forgave their tendency to promote the reign of priesthood

and superstition.' If, at a period when credulity and ignorance were universal, he showed himself in some instances credulous and ignorant, it seems hardly a reproach to one in other respects so good and so great.

His charity was boundless, and his vigilance indefatigable: he considered himself responsible for every sheep of the flock intrusted to him; and when a beggar died of hunger in the streets of Rome, he laid himself under a sentence of penance and excommunication, and interdicted himself for several days from the exercise of his sacerdotal functions.

Such was St. Gregory the Great, the last pope who was canonised: celestial honours and worldly titles have often been worse—seldom so well—bestowed.

During the last two years of his life, his health, early impaired by fasts and vigils, failed entirely, and he was unable to rise from his couch. He died in 604, in the fourteenth year of his pontificate. They still preserve, in the church of the Lateran at Rome, his bed, and the little scourge with which he was wont to keep the choristers in order.

The monastery of St. Andrew, which he founded on the Celian Hill, is now the church of San Gregorio. To stand on the summit of the majestic flight of steps which leads to the portal, and look across to the ruined palace of the Cæsars, makes the mind giddy with the rush of thoughts. *There,* before us, the Palatine Hill—pagan Rome in dust: *here,* the little cell, a few feet square, where slept in sackcloth the man who gave the last blow to the power of the Cæsars, and first set his foot as sovereign on the cradle and capital of their greatness.

St. Gregory was in person tall and corpulent, and of a dark complexion, with black hair, and very little beard. He speaks in one of his epistles of his large size, contrasted with his weakness and painful infirmities. He presented to the monastery of St. Andrew his own portrait, and those of his father, and his mother St. Sylvia: they were still in existence 300 years after his death, and the portrait of Gregory probably furnished that particular type of physiognomy which we trace in all the best representations of him, in which he appears of a tall, large, and dignified person, with a broad full face, black hair and eyebrows, and little or no beard.

As he was, next to St. Jerome, the most popular of the Four Doctors, single figures of him abound. They are variously treated : in general, he bears the tiara as pope, and the crosier with the double cross, in common with other papal saints; but his peculiar attribute is the dove, which in the old pictures is always close to his ear. He is often seated on a throne in the pontifical robes, wearing the tiara : one hand raised in benediction ; in the other a book, which represents his homilies, and other famous works attributed to him : the dove either rests on his shoulder, or is hovering over his head. He is thus represented in the fine statue, designed, as it is said, by M. Angelo, and executed by Cordieri, in the chapel of St. Barbara, in San Gregorio, Rome ; and in the picture over the altar-piece of his chapel, to the right of the high altar. In the Salviati Chapel, on the left, is the ' St. Gregory in prayer,' by Annibal Caracci. He is seen in front bareheaded, but arrayed in the pontifical habit, kneeling on a cushion, his hands outspread and uplifted ; the dove descends from on high ; the tiara is at his feet, and eight angels hover around :—a grand, finely-coloured, but, in sentiment, rather cold and mannered picture.[1]

By Guercino, St. Gregory seated on a throne, looking upwards, his hand on an open book, in act to turn the leaves ; the dove hovers at his shoulder : to the left stands St. Francis Xavier; on the right, and more in front, St. Ignatius Loyola. Behind St. Gregory is an angel playing on the viol, in allusion to his love and patronage of sacred music; in front an infant angel holds the tiara. The type usually adopted in figures of St. Gregory is here exaggerated into coarseness, and the picture altogether appears to me more remarkable for Guercino's faults than for his beauties.[2]

Several of the legends connected with the history of St. Gregory are of singular interest and beauty, and have afforded a number of picturesque themes for Art : they appear to have arisen out of his exceeding popularity. They are all expressive of the veneration in which he was held by the people ; of the deep impression left on their minds by his eloquence, his sanctity, his charity; and of the

---

[1] There is a duplicate in the Bridgewater Gallery.   [2] Sutherland Gal.

authority imputed to his numerous writings, which were commonly said to have been dictated by the Holy Spirit.

1. John the deacon, his secretary, who has left a full account of his life, declares that he beheld the Holy Ghost in the form of a dove perched upon his shoulder while he was writing or dictating his famous homilies. This vision, or rather figure of speech, has been interpreted as a fact by the early painters. Thus, in a quaint old picture in the Bologna Gallery, we have St. Gregory seated on a throne writing, the celestial dove at his ear. A little behind is seen John the deacon, drawing aside a curtain, and looking into the room at his patron with an expression of the most naïve astonishment.

2. The Archangel Michael, on the cessation of the pestilence, sheathes his sword on the summit of the Mole of Hadrian. I have never seen even a tolerable picture of this magnificent subject. There is a picture in the Vatican, in which Gregory and a procession of priests are singing litanies, and in the distance a little *Mola di Adriano*, with a little angel on the summit;—curious, but without merit of any kind.

3. The Supper of St. Gregory. It is related that when Gregory was only a monk, in the Monastery of St. Andrew, a beggar presented himself at the gate, and requested alms: being relieved, he came again and again, and at length nothing was left for the charitable saint to bestow, but the silver porringer in which his mother, Sylvia, had sent him a *potage;* and he commanded that this should be given to the mendicant. It was his custom, when he became pope, to entertain every evening at his own table twelve poor men, in remembrance of the number of our Lord's apostles. One night, as he sat at supper with his guests, he saw, to his surprise, not twelve, but thirteen seated at his table. And he called to his steward, and said to him, ' Did I not command thee to invite twelve? and behold, there are thirteen !' And the steward told them over, and replied, ' Holy Father, there are surely twelve only!' and Gregory held his peace; and after the meal, he called forth the unbidden guest, and asked him, ' Who art thou?' And he replied, ' I am the poor man whom thou didst formerly relieve; but my name is the Wonderful, and through me thou shalt obtain whatever thou shalt ask of God. Then

Gregory knew that he had entertained an angel (or, according to another version of the story, our Lord Himself). This legend has been a frequent subject in painting, under the title of ' The Supper of St. Gregory.' In the fresco in his church at Rome, it is a winged angel who appears at the supper-table. In the fresco of Paul Veronese, one of his famous banquet-scenes, the stranger seated at the table is the Saviour habited as a pilgrim.[1] In the picture painted by Vasari, his masterpiece, now in the Bologna Gallery, he has introduced a great number of figures and portraits of distinguished personages of his own time, St. Gregory being represented under the likeness of Clement VII. The unbidden guest, or angel, bears the features of the Saviour.

This is one of many beautiful mythic legends, founded on the words of St. Paul in which he so strongly recommends hospitality as one of the virtues: ' Be not forgetful to entertain strangers: for thereby some have entertained angels unawares.' (Heb. xiii. 2.) Or, as Massinger has rendered the apostolic precept,—

> Learn all,
> By this example, to look on the poor
> With gentle eyes, for in such habits often
> Angels desire an alms.

4. The Mass of St. Gregory. On a certain occasion, when St. Gregory was officiating at the mass, one who was near him doubted the real presence; thereupon, at the prayer of the saint, a vision is suddenly revealed of the crucified Saviour Himself, who descends upon the altar, surrounded by the instruments of his passion. This legend has been a popular subject of painting from the beginning of the fifteenth century, and is called ' The Mass of St. Gregory.' I have met with it in every variety of treatment and grouping; but, however treated, it is not a pleasing subject. St. Gregory is seen officiating at the altar, surrounded by his attendant clergy. Sometimes several saints are introduced in a poetical manner, as witnesses of the miracle: as in an old picture I saw in the gallery of Lord Northwick; —the crucified Saviour descends from the cross, and stands on the altar, or is upborne in the air by angels; while all the incidental circumstances and instruments of the Passion,—not merely the crown

[1] Vicenza. S. Maria del Monte.

of thorns, the spear, the nails, but the kiss of Judas, the soldiers' dice, the cock that crew to Peter,—are seen floating in the air. As a specimen of the utmost naïveté in this representation may be mentioned Albert Dürer's woodcut.

The least offensive and most elegant in treatment is the marble bas-relief in front of the altar in the Chapel of St. Gregory at Rome.

5. The miracle of the Brandeum. The Empress Constantia sent to St. Gregory requesting some of the relics of St. Peter and St. Paul. He excused himself, saying that he dared not disturb their sacred remains for such a purpose, but he sent her part of a consecrated cloth (*Brandeum*) which had enfolded the body of St. John the Evangelist. The Empress rejected this gift with contempt: whereupon Gregory, to show that such things are hallowed not so much in themselves as by the faith of believers, laid the Brandeum on the altar, and after praying he took up a knife and pierced it, and blood flowed as from a living body. This incident, called the 'miracle *dei Brandei*,' has also been painted. Andrea Sacchi has represented it in a grand picture now in the Vatican; the mosaic copy is over the altar of St. Gregory in St. Peter's. Gregory holds up to view the bleeding cloth, and the expression of astonishment and conviction in the countenances of the assistants is very fine.

6. St. Gregory releases the soul of the emperor Trajan. In a little picture in the Bologna Academy, he is seen praying before a tomb, on which is inscribed TRAJANO IMPERADOR; beneath are two angels raising the soul of Trajan out of the flames. Such is the usual treatment of this curious and poetical legend, which is thus related in the Legenda Aurea:—'It happened on a time, as Trajan was hastening to battle at the head of his legions, that a poor widow flung herself in his path, and cried aloud for justice, and the emperor stayed to listen to her; and she demanded vengeance for the innocent blood of her son, killed by the son of the emperor. Trajan promised to do her justice when he returned from his expedition. "But, Sire," answered the widow, "should you be killed in battle, who then will do me justice?" "My successor," replied Trajan. And she said, "What will it signify to you, great emperor, that any other than yourself should do me justice? Is it not better that you

should do this good action yourself than leave another to do it?"
And Trajan alighted, and having examined into the affair, he gave
up his own son to her in place of him she had lost, and bestowed on
her likewise a rich dowry.   Now it came to pass that as Gregory
was one day meditating in his daily walk, this action of the Emperor
Trajan came into his mind, and he wept bitterly to think that a man
so just should be condemned as a heathen to eternal punishment.
And entering into a church he prayed most fervently that the soul of
the good emperor might be released from torment.   And a voice said
to him, " I have granted thy prayer, and I have spared the soul of
Trajan for thy sake ; but because thou hast supplicated for one whom
the justice of God had already condemned, thou shalt choose one of
two things : either thou shalt endure for two days the fires of
purgatory, or thou shalt be sick and infirm for the remainder of thy
life."   Gregory chose the latter, which sufficiently accounts for the
grievous pains and infirmities to which this great and good man was
subjected, even to the day of his death.'

This story of Trajan was extremely popular in the middle ages : it
is illustrative of the character of Gregory, and the feeling which gave
rise to his doctrine of purgatory.   Dante twice alludes to it ; he describes it as one of the subjects sculptured on the walls of Purgatory,
and takes occasion to relate the whole story :—

> . . . There was storied on the rock
> Th' exalted glory of the Roman prince,
> Whose mighty worth moved Gregory to earn
> His mighty conquest—Trajan the Emperor.
> A widow at his bridle stood attired
> In tears and mourning.   Round about them trooped
> Full throng of knights : and overhead in gold
> The eagles floated, struggling with the wind.
> The wretch appeared amid all these to say :
> ' Grant vengeance, Sire ! for, woe beshrew this heart,
> My son is murdered !'   He, replying, seemed :
> ' Wait now till I return.'   And she, as one
> Made hasty by her grief : ' O Sire, if thou
> Dost not return ?'—' Where I am, who then is,
> May right thee.'—' What to thee is other's good,
> If thou neglect thy own ?'—' Now comfort thee,'
> At length he answers.   ' It beseemeth well
> My duty be performed, ere I move hence.
> So justice wills ; and pity bids me stay.'   Cary's DANTE, *Purg.* x.

It was through the efficacy of St. Gregory's intercession that Dante afterwards finds Trajan in Paradise, seated between King David and King Hezekiah. (*Par.* xx.)

As a subject of painting, the story of Trajan was sometimes selected as an appropriate ornament for a hall of justice. We find it sculptured on one of the capitals of the pillars of the Ducal Palace at Venice: there is the figure of the widow kneeling, somewhat stiff, but very simple and expressive, and over it in rude ancient letters—'*Trajano Imperador, che die justizia a la Vedova.*' In the Town Hall of Ceneda, near Belluna, are the three Judgments (*i tre Giudizi,*) painted by Pompeo Amalteo : the Judgment of Solomon, the Judgment of Daniel, and the Judgment of Trajan. It is painted in the Town Hall of Brescia by Giulio Campi, one of a series of eight righteous judgments.

I found the same subject in the Church of St. Thomas of Canterbury at Verona. 'The son of the Emperor Trajan trampling over the son of the widow' is a most curious composition by Hans Schaufelein.[1]

7. There was a monk, who, in defiance of his vow of poverty, secreted in his cell three pieces of gold. Gregory, on learning this, excommunicated him, and shortly afterwards the monk died. When Gregory heard that the monk had perished in his sin, without receiving absolution, he was filled with grief and horror ; and he wrote upon a parchment a prayer and a form of absolution, and gave it to one of his deacons, desiring him to go to the grave of the deceased and read it there : on the following night the monk appeared in a vision, and revealed to him his release from torment.

This story is represented in the beautiful bas-relief in white marble in front of the altar of his chapel ; it is the last compartment on the right. The obvious intention of this wild legend is to give effect to the doctrine of purgatory, and the efficacy of prayers for the dead.

St. Gregory's merciful doctrine of purgatory also suggested those pictures so often found in chapels dedicated to the service of the dead, in which he is represented in the attitude of supplication, while

[1] Bartsch, *Le Peintre Graveur*, vii. 234.

on one side, or in the background, angels are raising the tormented souls out of the flames.

In ecclesiastical decoration I have seen the two popes, St. Gelasius, who reformed the calendar in 494, and St. Celestinus, who arranged the discipline of the Monastic Orders, added to the series of beatified Doctors of the Church.

II. THE FOUR GREEK FATHERS.

THE Four Greek Fathers are St. John Chrysostom, St. Basil the Great, St. Athanasius, and St. Gregory Nazianzen. To these, in Greek pictures, a fifth is generally added, St. Cyril of Alexandria.

From the time of the schism between the Eastern and Western Churches, these venerable personages, who once exercised such an influence over all Christendom, who preceded the Latin Fathers, and were in fact their teachers, have been almost banished from the religious representations of the west of Europe. When they are introduced collectively as a part of the decoration of an ecclesiastical edifice, we may conclude in general, that the work is Byzantine and executed under the influence of Greek artists.

A signal example is the central dome of the baptistery of St. Mark's at Venice, executed by Greek artists, of the 12th and 13th centuries. In the four spandrils of the vault are the Greek Fathers seated, writing (if I well remember), and in the purest Byzantine style of Art. They occupy the same places here that we find usually occupied by the Latin Doctors in church decoration : each has his name inscribed in Greek characters. We have exactly the same representation in the Cathedral of Monreale at Palermo. The Greek Fathers have no attributes to distinguish them, and the general custom in Byzantine Art of inscribing the names over each figure renders this unnecessary : in general, each holds a book, or, in some instances, a scroll, which represents his writings; while the right hand is raised in benediction, in the Greek manner, the first and second finger extended, and the thumb and third finger forming a cross. According to the formula published by M. Didron, each of

The five Greek Fathers.

the Greek Fathers bears on a scroll the first words of some remark-able passage from his works : thus, St. John Chrysostom has ' God, our God, who hath given us for food the bread of life,' &c. : St. Basil, ' None of those who are in the bondage of fleshly desires are worthy,' &c. : St. Athanasius, ' Often, and anew, do we flee to thee, O God,' &c. : St. Gregory Nazianzen, ' God, the holy among the holies, the thrice holy,' &c. : and St. Cyril, ' Above all, a Virgin without sin or blemish,' &c.

The Greek bishops do not wear mitres; consequently, when in the Italian or German pictures St. Basil or any of his companions wear the mitre, it is a mistake arising from the ignorance of the artist.

The Fathers of the Greek Church have been represented by Dome-nichino at Grotta Ferrata, placed over the cornice and under the evangelists, their proper place : they are majestic figures, with fine heads, and correctly draped according to the Greek ecclesiastical costume. They are placed here with peculiar propriety, because the convent originally belonged to the Greek order of St. Basil, and the founder, St. Nilus, was a Greek.[1]

The etched outline, from a beautiful ancient Greek miniature, will give an accurate idea of the characteristic figures and habits of the Greek Fathers.

As separate devotional and historical representations of these Fathers do sometimes, though rarely, occur, I shall say a few words of them individually.

St. John Chrysostom.

Lat. Sanctus Johannes Chrysostom. *Ital.* San Giovanni Crisostomo, San Giovanni Bocca d' Oro. *Fr.* St. Jean Chrysostome. Died Sept. 14, A.D. 407. His festival is celebrated by the Greeks on the 13th of November, and by the Latin Church on the 27th of January.

St. John, called Chrysostom, or of the Golden Mouth, because of his extraordinary eloquence, was born at Antioch in 344. His parents were illustrious, and the career opened to him was of arts and arms :

[1] For an account of St. Nilus, and the foundation of Grotta Ferrata, see the ' Legends of the Monastic Orders.'

but from his infancy the bent of his mind was peculiar.   He lost his
father when young; his mother Arthusia, still in the prime of her
life, remained a widow for his sake, and superintended his education
with care and intelligence.   The remark of Sir James Mackintosh
that 'all distinguished men have had able mothers,' appears especially
true of the great churchmen and poets.   The mother of St. John
Chrysostom ranks with the Monicas and Sylvias, already described.

John, at the age of twenty, was already a renowned pleader at the
bar.   At the age of twenty-six, the disposition to self-abnegation
and the passion for solitude, which had distinguished him from boyhood, became so strong, that he wished to retire altogether from the
world; his legal studies, his legal honours, had become hateful to
him: he would turn hermit.   For a time his mother's tears and
prayers restrained him.   He has himself recorded the pathetic remonstrance in which she reminded him of all she had done and suffered in her state of widowhood for his sake, and besought him not
to leave her.   For the present he yielded: but two years later he fled
from society, and passed five or six years in the wilderness near
Antioch, devoting himself solely to the study of the Scriptures, to
penance and prayer; feeding on the wild vegetables, and leading a
life of such rigorous abstinence that his health sank under it, and
he was obliged to return to Antioch.

All this time he was not even an ordained priest; but shortly
after he had emerged from the desert, Flavian, bishop of Antioch,
ordained him, and appointed him preacher.   At the moment of his
consecration, according to the tradition, a white dove descended on
his head, which was regarded as the sign of immediate inspiration.
He then entered on his true vocation as a Christian orator, the
greatest next to Paul.   On one occasion, when the people of Antioch
had offended the Emperor Theodosius, and were threatened with a
punishment like that which had fallen on Thessalonica, the eloquence
of St. John Chrysostom saved them: he was so adored by the people,
that when he was appointed patriarch of Constantinople, it was
necessary to kidnap him, and carry him off from Antioch by a force
of armed soldiers, before the citizens had time to interfere.

From the moment he entered on his high office at Constantinople,
he became the model of a Christian bishop.   Humble, self-denying,

sleeping on a bare plank, content with a little bread and pulse, he entertained with hospitality the poor and strangers: indefatigable as a preacher, he used his great gift of eloquence to convert his hearers to what he believed to be the truth: he united the enthusiasm and the imagination of the poet, the elegant taste of the scholar, the logic of the pleader, with the inspired earnestness of one who had authority from above. He was, like St. Jerome, remarkable for his influence over women; and his correspondence with one of his female converts and friends, Olympias, is considered one of the finest of his works remaining to us; but, inexorable in his denunciations of vice, without regard to sex or station, he thundered against the irregularities of the monks, the luxury and profligacy of the Empress Eudosia, and the servility of her flatterers, and brought down upon himself the vengeance of that haughty woman, with whom the rest of his life was one long contest. He was banished: the voice of the people obliged the emperor to recall him. Persisting in the resolute defence of his church privileges, and his animadversions on the court and the clergy, he was again banished; and, on his way to his distant place of exile, sank under fatigue and the cruel treatment of his guards, who exposed him, bare-headed and bare-footed, to the burning sun of noon : and thus he perished, in the tenth year of his bishopric, and the sixty-third of his age. Gibbon adds, that, ' at the pious solicitation of the clergy and people of Constantinople, his relics, thirty years after his death, were transported from their obscure sepulchre to the royal city. The Emperor Theodosius advanced to receive them as far as Chalcedon, and, falling prostrate on the coffin, implored, in the name of his guilty parents, Arcadius and Eudosia, the forgiveness of the injured saint.'

It is owing, I suppose, to the intercourse of Venice with the East, that one of her beautiful churches is dedicated to San Gian Grisostomo, as they call him there, in accents as soft and sonorous as his own Greek. Over the high altar is the grandest devotional picture in which I have seen this saint figure as a chief personage. It is the masterpiece of Sebastian del Piombo,[1] and represents St. John

---

[1] According to Sansovino, begun by Giorgione, and finished by Sebastian.

Chrysostom throned and in the act of writing in a great book ; behind
him, St. Paul.   In front to the right, stands St. John the Baptist,
and behind him St. George as patron of Venice ; to the left Mary
Magdalene, with a beautiful Venetian face ; behind her, St. Catherine, patroness of Venice ; close to St. J. Chrysostom stands St. Lucia
holding her lamp ; she is here the type of celestial light or wisdom.[1]
This picture was for a long time attributed to Giorgione.   There was
also a very fine majestic figure of this saint by Rubens, in the collection of M. Schamp ; he is in the habit of a Greek bishop ; in one
hand he holds the sacramental cup, and the left hand rests on the
Gospel : the celestial dove hovers near him, and two angels are in
attendance.

I cannot quit the history of St. John Chrysostom without alluding
to a subject well known to collectors and amateurs, and popularly
called ' *La Pénitence de St. Jean Chrysostome.*'   It represents a
woman undraped, seated in a cave, or wilderness, with an infant in
her arms ; or lying on the ground with a new-born infant beside her;
in the distance is seen a man with a glory round his head, meagre,
naked, bearded, crawling on his hands and knees in the most abject
attitude : beneath, or at the top, is inscribed S. JOHANNES CRISOSTOMUS.

For a long time this subject perplexed me exceedingly, as I was
quite unable to trace it in any of the biographies of Chrysostom,
ancient or modern : the kindness of a friend, learned in all the
byways as well as the *highways* of Italian literature, at length assisted
me to an explanation.

The bitter enmity excited against St. John Chrysostom in his life-
time, and the furious vituperations of his adversary, Theophilus of
Alexandria, who denounced him as one stained by every vice, '*hostem
humanitatis, sacrilegorum principem, immundum dæmonem,*' as a
wretch who had absolutely delivered up his soul to Satan, were apparently disseminated by the monks.   Jerome translated the abusive
attack of Theophilus into Latin ; and long after the slanders against
Chrysostom had been silenced in the East, they survived in the West.
To this may be added the slaughter of the Egyptian monks by the

_____

[1] Dante, *Inf.* c. xi.

90   The Penance of St. Chrysostom. (Albert Dürer.)

friends of Chrysostom in the streets of Constantinople; which, I
suppose, was also retained in the traditions, and mixed up with the
monkish fictions.   It seems to have been forgotten who John Chrysostom really was; his name only survived in the popular ballads and
legends as an epitome of every horrible crime; and to account for
his being, notwithstanding all this, a *saint*, was a difficulty which
in the old legend is surmounted after a very original, and I must
needs adds, a very audacious fashion.   ' I have,' writes my friend,
' three editions of this legend in Italian, with the title *La Historia*
di San Giovanni Boccadoro.   It is in *ottava rima*, thirty-six stanzas
in all, occupying two leaves of letter-press.   It was originally composed in the fifteenth century, and reprinted again and again, like

the ballads and tales hawked by itinerant balladmongers, from that day to this, and as well known to the lower orders as " Jack the Giant-killer " here.   I will give you the story as succinctly and as properly as I can.   A gentleman of the high roads, named Schitano, confesses his robberies and murders to a certain Frate, who absolves him, upon a solemn promise not to do three things—

> Che tu non facci falso sacramento,
> Nè homicidio, nè adulterare.

Schitano thereupon takes possession of a cave, and turns *Romito* (Hermit) in the wilderness.   A neighbouring king takes his daughter out hunting with him ; a white deer starts across their path ; the king dashes away in pursuit ten miles or more, forgetting his daughter ; night comes on ; the princess, left alone in the forest, wanders till she sees a light, and knocks for admittance at the cave of Schitano.   He fancies at first that it must be the " Demonio," but at length he admits her after long hesitation, and turns her horse out to graze.   Her beauty tempts him to break one of his vows ; the fear of discovery induces him to violate another by murdering her, and throwing her body into a cistern.   The horse, however, is seen by one of the cavaliers of the court, who knocks and inquires if he has seen a certain " donzella " that way ?   The hermit swears that he has not beheld a Christian face for three years, thus breaking his third vow ; but, reflecting on this three-fold sin with horror, he imposes on himself a most severe penance (" un' aspra penitenza,") to wit—

> Di stare sette anni nell' aspro diserto,
> Pane non mangerò nè berò vino,
> Nè mai risguarderò il ciel scoperto,
> Non parlerò Hebraico nè Latino,
> Per fin che quel ch' io dico non è certo,
> Che un fantin di sei dì porga favella,
> " Perdonato t' ha Dio ; va alla tua cella."

That is, he swears that for seven years he will neither eat bread nor drink wine, nor look up in the face of heaven, nor speak either Hebrew or Latin, until it shall come to pass that an infant of seven days old shall open its mouth and say, " Heaven hath pardoned thee

—go in peace." So, stripping off his clothes, he crawls on hands and knees like the beasts of the field, eating grass and drinking water.

'Nor did his resolution fail him—he persists in this "aspra penitenza" for seven years—

> Sette anni e sette giorni nel diserto ;
> Come le bestie andava lui carpone,
> E mai non risguardò il ciel scoperto,
> Peloso egli era a modo d' un montone ;
> Spine e fango il suo letto era per certo,
> Del suo peccato havea contrizione ;
> E ogni cosa facea con gran fervore,
> Per purgar il suo fallo e grand' errore.

In the meantime it came into the king's head to draw the covers where the hermit was leading this life. The dogs of course *found*, but neither they nor the king could make anything of this new species of animal, "*che pareva un orso.*" So they took him home in a chain and deposited him in their zoological collection, where he refused meat and bread, and persisted in grazing. On new year's day the queen gives birth to a son, who, on the seventh day after he is born, says distinctly to the hermit,—

> Torna alla tua cella,
> Che Dio t' ha perdonato il tuo peccato,
> Levati su, Romito ! ora favella!

But the hermit does not *speak* as commanded; he makes signs, that he will write. The king orders the inkstand to be brought, but there is no ink in it: so Schitano at once earns his surname of Boccadoro (Chrysostom) by a simple expedient: he puts the pen to his mouth, wets it with his saliva, and writes in letters of gold—

> Onde la penna in bocca si metteva,
> E a scrivere cominciò senza dimoro,
> Col sputo, lettere che parevan d' oro !

'After seven years and seven days, he opens his golden mouth in speech, and confesses his foul crimes to the king; cavaliers are despatched in search of the body of the princess; as they approach the cavern they hear celestial music and in the end they bring the

donzella out of the cistern alive and well, and very sorry to leave the
blessed Virgin and the angels, with whom she had been passing her
time most agreeably: she is restored to her parents with universal
festa e allegrezza, and she announces to the hermit that he is pardoned and may return to his cell, which he does forthwith, and ends
in leading the life of a saint, and being beatified. The " *discreti
auditori* " are invited to take example—

> Da questo Santo pien di leggiadria
> Che Iddio sempre perdona a' peccatori,

and are finally informed that they may purchase this edifying history
on easy terms, to wit, a halfpenny—

> Due quattrini dia senza far più parole.

The price, however, rose; for in the next century the line is altered
thus :—

> Pero ciascun che comperarne vuole,
> Tre quattrini mi dia senza più parole.'

The woodcuts prefixed to the ballad represent this saintly Nebu-
chadnezzar on all fours, surprised by the king with his hunstmen
and dogs; but no female figure, as in the German prints, in which
the German version of the legend has evidently been in the mind of
the artists. It differs in some respects from the Italian ballad. I
shall therefore give as much of it here as will explain the artistic
treatment of the story.

' When John Chrysostom was baptized, the Pope [1] stood godfather.
At seven years old he went to school, but he was so dull and back-
ward, that he became the laughing-stock of his schoolfellows. Unable to endure their mockery, he took refuge in a neighbouring
church, and prayed to the Virgin ; and a voice whispered, " Kiss me
on the mouth, and thou shalt be endowed with all learning." He
did so, and, returning to the school, he surpassed all his companions,

[1] The Greek word *Papa,* here translated *der Papst* (the Pope), betrays the Eastern
origin of the story. It is the general title of the Greek priesthood, and means simply a
priest, elevated in the German legend into ' the Pope.'

so that they remained in astonishment: as they looked, they saw a
golden ring or streak round his mouth, and asked him how it came
there? and when he told them they wondered yet more. Thence he
obtained the name of Chrysostom. John was much beloved by his
godfather the Pope, who ordained him priest at a very early age; but
the first time he offered the sacrifice of the mass, he was struck to
the heart by his unworthiness, and resolved to seek his salvation in
solitude; therefore, throwing off his priestly garments, he fled from
the city, and made his dwelling in a cavern of the rock, and lived
there a long while in prayer and meditation.

'Now not far from the wilderness in which Chrysostom dwelt, was
the capital of a great king; and it happened that one day, as the
princess his daughter, who was young and very fair, was walking
with her companions, there came a sudden and violent gust of wind,
which lifted her up and carried her away, and set her down in the
forest, far off; and she wandered about till she came to the cave of
Chrysostom, and knocked at the door. He, fearing some temptation
of the devil, would not let her in; but she entreated, and said, "I
am no demon, but a Christian woman; and if thou leavest me here,
the wild beasts will devour me!" So he yielded perforce, and arose
and let her in. And he drew a line down the middle of his cell, and
said, "That is your part, this is mine; and neither shall pass this
line." But this precaution was in vain, for passion and temptation
overpowered his virtue; he overstepped the line, and sinned.
Both repented sorely; and Chrysostom, thinking that if the damsel
remained longer in his cave it would only occasion further sin,
carried her to a neighbouring precipice, and flung her down. When
he had done this deed, he was seized with horror and remorse; and
he departed and went to Rome to his godfather the Pope, and
confessed all, and entreated absolution. But his godfather knew
him not; and, being seized with horror, he drove him forth, and
refused to absolve him. So the unhappy sinner fled to the wilderness, and made a solemn vow that he would never rise from the
earth nor look up, but crawl on his hands and knees, until he had
expiated his great sin and was absolved by Heaven.

'When he had thus crawled on the earth for fifteen years, the queen
brought forth a son; and when the Pope came to baptize the child,

the infant opened its mouth and said, " I will not be baptized by thee, but by St. John ; " and he repeated this three times : and none could understand this miracle ; but the Pope was afraid to proceed.   In the meantime, the king's huntsmen had gone to the forest to bring home game for the christening feast : there as they rode, they beheld a strange beast creeping on the ground ; and not knowing what it might be, they threw a mantle over it and bound it in a chain and brought it to the palace.   Many came to look on this strange beast, and with them came the nurse with the king's son in her arms ; and immediately the child opened its mouth and spake, " John, come thou and baptize me ! "   He answered, " If it be God's will, speak again ! "   And the child spoke the same words a second and a third time.   Then John stood up ; and the hair and the moss fell from his body, and they brought him garments ; and he took the child, and baptized him with great devotion.

' When the king heard his confession, he thought, " Perhaps this was my daughter, who was lost and never found ; " and he sent messengers into the forest to seek for the remains of his daughter, that her bones at least might rest in consecrated ground.   When they came to the foot of the precipice, there they found a beautiful woman seated, naked, and holding a child in her arms ; and John said to her, " Why sittest thou here alone in the wilderness ? "   And she said, " Dost thou not know me ?   I am the woman who came to thy cave by night, and whom thou didst hurl down this rock ! "   Then they brought her home with great joy to her parents.' [1]

This extravagant legend becomes interesting for two reasons : it shows the existence of the popular feeling and belief with regard to Chrysostom, long subsequent to those events which roused the hatred of the early monks ; and it has been, from its popular notoriety, embodied in some rare and valuable works of art, which all go under the name of ' the Penance or Penitence of Johannes Chrysostom or Crisostomos.'

1. A rare print by Lucas Cranach, composed and engraved by himself.   In the centre is an undraped woman reclining on the

[1] Koburgher, ' Legendensammlung,' 1488, p. 325.   Heller's ' Leben und Werke Albrecht Dürer's,' p. 440.

ground against a rock, and contemplating her sleeping infant, which is lying on her lap ; a stag, a hind crouching, a pheasant feeding near her, express the solitude of her life ; in the background is ' the savage man ' on all fours, and browsing : here, he has no glory round his head. The whole composition is exceedingly picturesque.

2. A rare and beautiful print by B. Beham, and repeated by Hans Sibald Beham, represents a woman lying on the ground with her back turned to the spectator ; a child is near her ; Chrysostom is seen crawling in the background, with the glory round his head.

3. A small print by Albert Dürer, also exquisitely engraved (from which I give a sketch). Here the woman is sitting at the entrance of a rocky cave, feeding her child from her bosom : in the background the ' savage man' crawling on all fours, and a glory round his head. This subject has been called St. Geneviève of Brabant ; but it is evidently the same as in the two last-named compositions.

All these prints, being nearly contemporaneous, show that the legend must have been particularly popular about this time (1509— 1520). There is also an old French version of the story which I have not seen.

ST. BASIL THE GREAT.

Lat. St. Basilius Magnus. *Ital.* San Basilio Magno. *Fr.* St. Basile. (June 14, A.D. 380.)

ST. BASIL, called the Great, was born at Cesarea in Cappadocia, in the year 328. He was one of a family of saints. His father St. Basil, his mother St. Emmelie, his two brothers St. Gregory of Nyssa and St. Peter of Sebaste, and his sister St. Macrina, were all distinguished for their sanctity, and renowned in the Greek calendar. The St. Basil who takes rank as the second luminary of the Eastern Church, and whose dogmatical and theological works influenced the faith of his own age, and consequently of ours, was the greatest of all. But, notwithstanding his importance in the Greek Church, he figures so seldom in the productions of Western Art, that I shall content myself with relating just so much of his life and actions as may render the few representations of him interesting and intelligible.

He owed his first education to his grandmother St. Macrina, the elder, a woman of singular capacity and attainments, to whom he has in various parts of his works acknowledged his obligations. For several years he pursued his studies in profane learning, philosophy, law, and eloquence, at Constantinople, and afterwards at Athens, where he had two companions and fellow-students of very opposite character: Gregory of Nazianzen, afterwards the *Saint;* and Julian, afterwards the *Apostate.*

The success of the youthful Basil in all his studies, and the reputation he had obtained as an eloquent pleader, for a time swelled his heart with vanity, and would have endangered his salvation but for the influence of his sister, St. Macrina, who in this emergency preserved him from himself, and elevated his mind to far higher aims than those of mere worldly science and worldly distinction. From that period, and he was then not more than twenty-eight, Basil turned his thoughts solely to the edification of the Christian Church; but first he spent some years in retreat among the hermits of the desert, as was the fashion of that day, living, as they did, in abstinence, poverty, and abstracted study; acknowledging neither country, family, home, nor friends, nor fortune, nor worldly interests of any kind, but with his thoughts fixed solely on eternal life in another world. In these austerities he, as was also usual, consumed and ruined his bodily health; and remained to the end of his life a feeble wretched invalid,—a circumstance which was supposed to contribute greatly to his sanctity. He was ordained priest in 362, and bishop of Cesarea in 370; his ordination on the 14th of June being kept as one of the great feasts of the Eastern Church.

On the episcopal throne he led the same life of abstinence and humility as in a cavern of the desert; and contended for the doctrine of the Trinity against the Arians, but with less of vehemence, and more of charity, than the other Doctors engaged in the same controversy. The principal event of his life was his opposition to the Emperor Valens, who professed Arianism, and required that, in the Church of Cesarea, Basil should perform the rites according to the custom of the Arians. The bishop refused: he was threatened with exile, confiscation, death: he persisted. The emperor, fearing a tumult, resolved to appear in the church on the day of the Epiphany, but not to communicate. He came, hoping to overawe the impracticable bishop, surrounded by all his state, his courtiers, his guards. He found Basil so intent on his sacred office as to take not the slightest notice of him; those of the clergy around him continued to chant the service, keeping their eyes fixed in the profoundest awe and respect on the countenance of their bishop. Valens, in a situation new to him, became agitated: he had brought his oblation; he advanced with it; but the ministers at the altar, not knowing whether Basil would accept it, dared not take it from his hands. Valens stood there for a moment in sight of all the people, rejected before the altar,—he lost his presence of mind, trembled, swooned, and would have fallen to the earth, if one of the attendants had not received him in his arms. A conference afterwards took place between Basil and the emperor; but the latter remained unconverted, and some concessions to the Catholics was all that the bishop obtained.

St. Basil died in 379, worn out by disease, and leaving behind him many theological writings. His epistles, above all, are celebrated, not only as models of orthodoxy, but of style.

Of St. Basil, as of St. Gregory and St John Chrysostom, we have the story of the Holy Ghost, in visible form as a dove of wonderful whiteness, perched on his shoulder, and inspiring his words when he preached. St. Basil is also celebrated as the founder of Monachism in the East. He was the first who enjoined the vows of poverty, chastity, and obedience; and his Rule became the model of all other monastic Orders. There is, in fact, no other Order in the Greek Church, and when either monks or nuns appear in a Greek or a Russian picture they must be Basilicans, and no other: the habit is a plain black tunic with a cowl, the tunic fastened round the waist with a girdle of cord or leather. Such is the dress of the Greek caloyer, and it never varies.

The devotional figures of St. Basil represent him, or ought to represent him, in the Greek pontificals, bareheaded, and with a thin worn countenance, as he appears in the etching of the Greek Fathers.

' The Emperor Valens in the church at Cesarea,' an admirably picturesque subject, has received as little justice as the scene between

Ambrose and Theodosius. When the French painter Subleyras was
at Rome in 1745, he raised himself to name and fame by his portrait
of Benedict XIV.,[1] and received, through the interest of his friend
Cardinal Valenti, the commission to paint a picture for one of the
mosaics in St. Peter's. The subject selected was the Emperor
Valens fainting in presence of St. Basil. We have all the pomp of
the scene:—the altar, the incense, the richly attired priests on one
side; on the other, the imperial court. It is not easy to find fault,
for the picture is well drawn, well composed, in the mannered taste
of that time; well coloured, rather tenderly than forcibly; and
Lanzi is enthusiastic in his praise of the draperies; yet, as a whole,
it leaves the mind unimpressed. As usual, the original sketch for
this picture far excels the large composition.[2]

The prayers of St. Basil were supposed by the Armenian Christians, partly from his sanctity, and partly from his intellectual
endowments, to have a peculiar, almost resistless, power; so that
he not only redeemed souls from purgatory, but even lost angels from
the abyss of hell. 'On the sixth day of the creation, when the
rebellious angels fell from heaven through that opening in the
firmament which the Armenians call Arocea, and we the Galaxy,
one unlucky angel, who had no participation in their sin, but seems
to have been entangled in the crowd, fell with them.' (A moral, I
presume, on the consequences of keeping bad company.) 'And this
unfortunate angel was not restored till he had obtained, it is not
said how, the prayers of St. Basil. His condition meantime, from
the sixth day of the creation to the fourth century of the Christian
era, must have been even more uncomfortable than that of Klop-
stock's repentant demon in "The Messiah."'

There are many other beautiful legendary stories of St. Basil, but,
as I have never met with them in any form of Art, I pass them over
here. One of the most striking has been versified by Southey in his
ballad-poem, 'All for Love.' It would afford a great variety of
picturesque subjects.

---

[1] Sutherland Gal.
[2] '*La Messe de saint Basile.*' Louvre, École française, No. 508.

St. Athanasius.

Lat. S. Athanasius, Pater Orthodoxiæ. *Ital.* Sant' Atanasio. *Fr.* St. Athanase.
(May 2, A.D. 373.)

St. Athanasius, whose famous Creed remains a stumbling-block in Christendom, was born at Alexandria, about the year 298; he was consequently the eldest of the Greek Fathers, though he does not in that Church take the first rank. He, like the others, began his career by the study of profane literature, science, and eloquence ; but, seized by the religious spirit of the age, he, too, fled to the desert, and became, for a time, the pupil of St. Anthony. He returned to Alexandria, and was ordained deacon. His first appearance as a public character was at the celebrated council of Nice (A.D. 325), where he opposed Arius and his partisans with so much zeal and eloquence, that he was thenceforth regarded as the great pillar of orthodoxy. He became Bishop of Alexandria the following year; and the rest of his life was a perpetual contest with the Arians. The great schism of the early Church blazed at this time in the East and in the West, and Athanasius, by his invincible perseverance and intrepidity, procured the victory for the Catholic party. He died in 372, after having been Bishop of Alexandria forty-six years, of which twenty years had been spent in exile and tribulation.

It is curious that, notwithstanding his fame and his importance in the Church, St. Athanasius should be, as a patron and a subject of Art, of all saints the most unpopular. He figures, of course, as one of the series of Greek Doctors ; but I have never met with any separate representation of him, and I know not any church dedicated to him, nor any picture representing the vicissitudes of his unquiet life, fraught as it was with strange reverses and picturesque incidents. Such *may* exist, but in Western Art, at least, they have never been prominent. According to the Greek formula, he ought to be represented old, bald-headed, and with a long white beard, as in the etching.

St. Gregory Nazianzen.

Gr. St. Gregory Theologos. *Lat.* S. Gregorius Nazianzenus. *Ital.* San Gregorio Nazianzeno
Fr. St. Grégoire de Naziance. *Ger.* St. Gregor von Nazianz. (May 9, A.D. 390.)

This Doctor, like St. Basil, was one of a family of saints ; his father, St. Gregory, having been bishop of Nazianzus before him ; his mother, St. Nonna, famous for her piety ; and two of his sisters, St. Gorgonia and St. Cesarea, also canonized. Gregory was born about the year 328 ; and his mother, who fondly believed that he had been granted to her prayers, watched over his early education, and guided his first steps in piety and literature. When a boy, he had a singular dream, which he has related himself. He beheld in his sleep two virgins of celestial beauty ; they were clothed in white garments, and their faces shone upon him like two stars out of heaven :. they took him in their arms and kissed him as if he had been their child. He, charmed by their virgin beauty and their caresses, asked who they were, and whence they came ? One of them replied, ' I am called Chastity, and my sister here is Temperance ; we come to thee from Paradise, where we stand continually before the throne of Christ, and taste ineffable delights : come to us, my son, and dwell with us for ever ; ' and having spoken thus, they left him and flew upwards to heaven. He followed them with longing eyes till they disappeared, and as he stretched his arms towards them he awoke.

This dream—how natural in a boy educated between a tender mother, who had shielded him, as only mothers can, against all sinful temptations, and a lovely and saintly sister !—he regarded as a direct revelation from heaven : it decided his future life, and he made a vow of perpetual continence and temperance. Like the other Greek doctors, he began by the study of profane literature and rhetoric. He went to Athens, where he formed an enduring friendship with St. Basil, and pursued his studies with Julian, afterwards Cæsar and Apostate. After leaving Athens, in his thirtieth year, he was baptized ; and, devoting himself solemnly to the service of God and the study of the Scriptures, like his friend Basil, he destroyed his health by his austerities and mortifications :

he confesses that they were wholly repugnant to his nature—a nature sensitive, imaginative, poetical; but this of course only added to their merit and efficacy. His aged father withdrew him from his solitude, and ordained him as his coadjutor: in 362 he succeeded to the bishopric of Nazianzus: but great part of his time was still spent at Constantinople, whither he was invited to preach against the Arians. It was a strange spectacle to see, in the capital of the world, a man, from a distant province and an obscure town, of small shrunken stature, bald-headed, wrinkled, haggard with vigils and fasting, poor, ill-clothed, and in his address unpolished and abrupt, stand up to oppose himself to a luxurious court and prevalent sect. The people began by stoning him; but at length his earnestness and eloquence overcame all opposition.

Religious disputes were the fashion at that time in Constantinople, not merely among the priesthood, but among the laity, the lawyers, and above all the women, who were heard, in assemblies and at feasts, at home and abroad, declaiming and arguing on the most abstruse mysteries of the evangelical doctrine, till they lost temper and modesty:—so true it is, that there is nothing new under the sun. This was in 378, and St. Gregory found more difficulty in silencing their squabbles than in healing the schisms of the Church. He was ordained Bishop of Constantinople by the favour of Theodosius; but, unable to endure the odious cabals and uncharitable contests which at that time distracted and disgraced Christianity, he resigned his sacred office, and retired to a small paternal estate, where he lived, with his usual self-denial and austerity, till his death. He composed in his retreat a number of beautiful poems in his native Greek: he was, in fact, the earliest Christian poet on record. These poems are not hymns only, but lyrics, in which he poured forth his soul, his aspirations, his temptations, his joys, his sufferings, his plaintive supplications to Christ, to aid him in his perpetual combats against a too vivid imagination, and feelings and passions which not even age and penance had subdued.

St. Gregory Nazianzen ought to be represented as an old man wasted by fasting and vigils, with a bald head, a long beard of a reddish colour, and eyebrows the same. He is always the last in a series of the Four Greek Fathers, and, though often occurring in Greek Art, the popularity of St. Gregory the GREAT has completely banished St. Gregory the POET from Western Art.

There remains, however, a very valuable and singular monument to the honour of St. Gregory Nazianzen, in the Greek MS. of his sermons preserved in the Imperial Library at Paris, and adorned with Byzantine miniatures, which must once have been beautiful and brilliant: ruined as they are, they present some of the most ancient examples which remain to us of the treatment of many sacred subjects from the Old and the New Testament, and give a high idea of the classic taste and the skill of the Byzantine limners of the ninth century. Besides the sacred subjects, we have numerous scenes interspersed from the life of Gregory himself, his friend St. Basil, and the Emperor Theodosius. As these are subjects which are exceptional, I need not describe them. Of the style of the miniatures I have already spoken, and given one example (*v.* p. 75).

St. Cyril.

Lat. S. Cyrillus. *Ital.* San Cirillo. *Fr.* S⁺. Cyrille. (Jan. 28, A.D. 444.)

ST. CYRIL, Patriarch of Alexandria from the year 412 to 444, was famous in his time as deeply engaged in all the contests which disturbed the early Christian Church. He has left a great number of theological writings, which are regarded as authority in matters of faith. He appears to have been violent against the so-called heresies of that day, and opposed Nestorius with the same determined zeal and inexorable firmness with which Athanasius had opposed Arius. The ascendency of Cyril was disgraced by the death of the famous female mathematician and philosopher Hypatia, murdered with horrible cruelty, and within the walls of a church, by the fanatic followers of the Patriarch, if he did not himself connive at it. He is much more venerated in the Greek than in the Latin Church. In the Greek representations he is the only bishop who has his head covered; he wears a veil or hood, coming over his head, falling down on his shoulders, and the front embroidered with a cross, as in the illustration.

With the Greek Fathers I conclude the list of those saints who are generally represented in their collective character, grouped, or in a series.

St. Mary Magdalene, St. Martha, St. Lazarus, St. Marimin, St. Marcella, St. Mary of Egypt, and the Beatified Penitents.

St. Mary Magdalene.

Lat. Sancta Maria Magdalena. *Ital.* Santa Maria Maddalena. *Fr.* La Madeleine. La Sainte Demoiselle pécheresse. (July 22, A.D. 68.) Patroness of Provence, of Marseilles, and of frail and penitent women.

OF all the personages who figure in history, in poetry, in art, Mary Magdalene is at once the most unreal and the most real :—the most *unreal,* if we attempt to fix her identity, which has been a subject of dispute for ages; the most *real,* if we consider her as having been, for ages, recognised and accepted in every Christian heart as the impersonation of the penitent sinner absolved through faith and love. In this, her mythic character, she has been surrounded by associations which have become fixed in the imagination, and which no reasoning, no array of facts, can dispel. This is not the place to enter into disputed points of biblical criticism; they are quite beside our present purpose. Whether Mary Magdalene, ' out of whom Jesus cast seven devils,' Mary of Bethany, and the ' woman who was a sinner,' be, as some authorities assert, three distinct persons, or, as others affirm, one and the same individual under different designations, remains a question open to dispute, nothing having been demonstrated on either side, from Scripture or from tradition; and I cannot presume even to give an opinion where doctors—and doctors of the Church, too—disagree; Origen and St. Chrysostom taking one side of the question, St. Clement and St Gregory the other. Fleury, after citing the opinions of both sides, thus beautifully sums up the whole question :—' Il importe de ne pas croire témérairement ce que l'Évangile ne dit point, et de ne pas mettre la religion à suivre aveuglement toutes les opinions populaires : *la foi est trop précieuse pour la prodiguer ainsi;* mais la charité l'est encore plus; et ce qui est le plus important, c'est d'éviter les disputes qui peuvent l'altérer tant soit peu.' And this is most true ;—in his time the fast hold which the Magdalene had taken of the affections of the people was not to be shaken by theological researches and doubts. Here critical accuracy was nothing less than profanation and scepticism, and to have attacked the sanctity of the Blessed Mary Magdalene would have embittered and alienated many kindly and many believing spirits. It is difficult to treat of Mary Magdalene; and this difficulty would be increased infinitely if it were absolutely necessary to enter on the much-vexed question of her scriptural character and identity; one thing only appears certain,—that such a person, whatever might have been her veritable appellation, did exist. The woman who, under the name of Mary Magdalene,—whether that name be rightfully or wrongfully bestowed,—stands before us sanctified in the imagination and in the faith of the people in her combined character of Sinner and of Saint, as the first-fruits of Christian penitence,—is a reality, and not a fiction. Even if we would, we cannot do away with the associations inseparably connected with her name and her image. Of all those to whom much has been forgiven, she was the first; of all the tears since ruefully shed at the foot of the cross of suffering, hers were the first; of all the hopes which the Resurrection has since diffused through nations and generations of men, hers were the first. To her sorrowful image how many have looked up through tears, and blessed the pardoning grace of which she was the symbol—or rather the impersonation! Of the female saints, some were the chosen patrons of certain virtues—others of certain vocations; but the accepted and glorified penitent threw her mantle over all, and more especially over those of her own sex who, having gone astray, were recalled from error and from shame, and laid down their wrongs, their sorrows, and their sins in trembling humility at the feet of the Redeemer.

Nor is it only the popularity of Mary Magdalene as the representative and the patroness of repentant sinners which has multiplied her image through all Christendom. As a subject for painting,

Whether the fair one sinner it or saint it,

it is rich in picturesque capabilities. It combines all that can inspire with all that can chasten the fancy; yet, when we review what has been done, how inadequate the result! In no class of subjects have the mistakes of the painters, even the most distinguished, been so conspicuous as in the representation of the penitent Magdalene; and it must be allowed that, with all its advantages and attractions, it is a subject full of perils and difficulties. Where the penitent prevails, the saint appears degraded; where the wasted, unclad form is seen attenuated by vigils and exposed in haggard unseemliness, it is a violation of that first great rule of Art which forbids the repulsive and the painful. And herein lies the fault of the earlier schools, and particularly of the old Greek and German painters;—their matter-of-fact ugliness would be intolerable, if not redeemed by the intention and sentiment. On the other hand, where sensual beauty has obviously been the paramount idea in the artist's work, defeating its holiest purpose and perverting its high significance, the violation of the moral sentiment is yet more revolting. This is especially the fault of the later painters, more particularly of the schools of Venice and Bologna: while the French painters are yet worse, adding affectation to licentiousness of sentiment; the Abbé Mèry exclaims with reasonable and pious indignation against that '*air de galanterie*' which in his time was regarded as characteristic of Mary Magdalene. The 'larmoyantes' penitents of Greuze—Magdalenes *à la Pompadour* —are more objectionable to my taste than those of Rubens.

I shall give the legend of the Magdalene here as it was accepted by the people and embodied by the arts of the middle ages, setting aside those Eastern traditions which represent the Mary of Bethany and the Magdalene as distinct personages, and place the death and burial-place of Mary Magdalene at Ephesus. Our business is with the Western legend, which has been the authority for Western Art. This legend, besides attributing to one individual, and blending into one narrative, the very few scattered notices in the Gospels, has added some other incidents, inconceivably wild and incredible, leaving her, however, the invariable attributes of the frail loving woman, the sorrowing penitent, and the devout enthusiastic saint.

Mary Magdalene was of the district of Magdala, on the shores of

the Sea of Galilee, where stood her castle, called Magdalon; she was
the sister of Lazarus and of Martha, and they were the children of
parents reputed noble, or, as some say, of royal race.   On the death
of their father, Syrus, they inherited vast riches and possessions in
land, which were equally divided between them.   Lazarus betook
himself to the military life; Martha ruled her possessions with great
discretion, and was a model of virtue and propriety,—perhaps a little
too much addicted to worldly cares; Mary, on the contrary, abandoned
herself to luxurious pleasures, and became at length so notorious for
her dissolute life, that she was known through all the country round
only as 'THE SINNER.' Her discreet sister, Martha, frequently rebuked her for these disorders, and at length persuaded her to listen
to the exhortations of Jesus, through which her heart was touched
and converted.   The seven demons which possessed her, and which
were expelled by the power of the Lord, were the seven deadly sins
to which she was given over before her conversion.   On one occasion
Martha entertained the Saviour in her house, and, being anxious to
feast him worthily, she was 'cumbered with much serving.'   Mary,
meanwhile, sat at the feet of Jesus, and heard his words, which completed the good work of her conversion; and when, some time afterwards, he supped in the house of Simon the Pharisee, she followed
him thither, 'and she brought an alabaster box of ointment, and
began to wash his feet with tears, and did wipe them with the hair
of her head, and kissed his feet, and anointed them with ointment;
and He said unto her, Thy sins are forgiven.'   She became afterwards
one of the most devoted of his followers; 'ministered to him of her
substance;' attended him to Calvary, and stood weeping at the foot
of the cross.   She, with the other Mary, watched by his tomb, and
was the first to whom he appeared after the resurrection; her un-
faltering faith, mingled as it was with the intensest grief and love,
obtained for her this peculiar mark of favour.   It is assumed by
several commentators that our Saviour appeared first to Mary
Magdalene, because she, of all those whom he had left on earth, had
most need of consolation :—' *The disciples went away to their own
home ; but Mary stood without the sepulchre, weeping.*'

Thus far the notices in the Gospel and the suggestions of commentators : the old Provençal legend then continues the story.   After the ascension, Lazarus with his two sisters, Martha and Mary; with Maximin, one of the seventy-two disciples, from whom they had received baptism; Cedon, the blind man whom our Saviour had restored to sight ; and Marcella, the handmaiden who attended on the two sisters, were by the heathens set adrift in a vessel without sails, oars, or rudder ; but, guided by Providence, they were safely borne over the sea till they landed in a certain harbour which proved to be Marseilles, in the country now called France.   The people of the land were pagans, and refused to give the holy pilgrims food or shelter ; so they were fain to take refuge under the porch of a temple ; and Mary Magdalene preached to the people, reproaching them for their senseless worship of dumb idols ; and though at first they would not listen, yet being after a time convinced by her eloquence, and by the miracles performed by her and by her sister, they were converted and baptized.   And Lazarus became, after the death of the good Maximin, the first bishop of Marseilles.

These things being accomplished, Mary Magdalene retired to a desert not far from the city.   It was a frightful barren wilderness, in the midst of horrid rocks and caves ; and here for thirty years she devoted herself to solitary penance for the sins of her past life, which she had never ceased to bewail bitterly.   During this long seclusion, she was never seen or heard of, and it was supposed that she was dead.   She fasted so rigorously, that but for the occasional visits of the angels, and the comfort bestowed by celestial visions, she must have perished.   Every day during the last years of her penance, the angels came down from heaven and carried her up in their arms into regions where she was ravished by the sounds of unearthly harmony, and beheld the glory and the joy prepared for the sinner that repenteth.   One day a certain hermit, who dwelt in a cell on one of those wild mountains, having wandered farther than usual from his home, beheld this wondrous vision—the Magdalene in the arms of ascending angels, who were singing songs of triumph as they bore her upwards ; and the hermit, when he had a little recovered from his amazement, returned to the city of Marseilles, and reported what he had seen.   According to some of the legends, Mary Magdalene died within the walls of the Christian church, after receiving the sacrament from the hand of St. Maximin; but the more popular accounts represent her as dying in her solitude, while angels watched over and ministered to her.

The middle of the thirteenth century was an era of religious excitement all over the south of Europe. A sudden fit of penitence—'una subita compunzione,' as an Italian anthor calls it—seized all hearts; relics, and pilgrimages, and penances, and monastic ordinances filled all minds. About this period, certain remains, supposed to be those of Mary Magdalene and Lazarus, were discovered at a place since called St. Maximin, about twenty miles north of Toulon. The discovery strongly excited the devotion and enthusiasm of the people; and a church was founded on the spot by Charles, Count of Provence (the brother of St. Louis), as early as 1279. A few years afterwards, this prince was vanquished and taken prisoner by the king of Aragon, and when at length set free after a long captivity, he ascribed his deliverance particularly to the intercession of his chosen patroness, Mary Magdalene. This incident greatly extended her fame as a saint of power; and from this time we may date her popularity, and those sculptural and pictorial representations of her, under various aspects, which, from the fourteenth century to the present time, have so multiplied, that scarcely any Catholic place of worship is to be found without her image. In fact, it is difficult for us, in these days, to conceive, far more difficult to sympathise with, the passionate admiration and devotion with which she was regarded by her votaries in the middle ages. The imputed sinfulness of her life only brought her nearer to them. Those who did not dare to lift up their eyes to the more saintly models of purity and holiness,—to the martyrs who had suffered in the cause of chastity,—took courage to invoke her intercession. The extravagant titles bestowed upon her in the middle ages—' 'l'amante de Jésus-Christ,' 'la bien-aimée du Sauveur,' 'la très-saincte demoiselle pécheresse,'—and others which I should hardly dare to transcribe, show the spirit in which she was worshipped, particularly in the south of France, and the kind of chivalrous sentiment which mingled with the devotion of her adorers. I found in an old French sermon a eulogium of Mary Magdalene, which for its eloquence and ingenuity seems to me without a parallel

The preacher, while acknowledging the excesses which brought her a penitent to the feet of Christ, is perfectly scandalised that she should be put on a par with common sinners of the same class, and that on the faith of a passage in St. Luke, ' on a osé flétrir une des plus belles âmes qui soient jamais sorties des mains du Créateur!' He rather glorifies her as a kind of Aspasia, to whom, indeed, he in a manner compares her.[1]

[1] 'Pour vous ramener à des idées plus favorables à la Madeleine, vous transportant au temps et aux circonstances où vécut cette célèbre Israélite, je pourrais vous dire, MESSIEURS, que l'antiquité, ne jugeant pas équitable d'exiger plus de vertu du sexe réputé pour le plus faible, ne croyait pas les femmes déshonorées de ce qui ne déshonorait pas les hommes à ses yeux ; qu'elle a d'ailleurs toujours été bien moins sévère à des sentiments qui, naissant avec nous, lui paraissaient une partie de nous-mêmes, et qu'elle n'attacha jamais aucune idée flétrissante aux suites d'une passion qu'elle trouvait presque aussi pardonnable que naturelle. Les grâces de la beauté étaient alors regardées comme les autres talents ; et l'art de plaire, aussi autorisé que les autres arts, loin d'inspirer de l'éloignement,' &c.

After describing, in glowing terms, her splendid position in the world, her illustrious rank, her understanding, '*droit, solide, et délicat*,' her '*grâce*,' her '*esprit*,' her wondrous beauty, particularly her superb hair, '*cultivé avec tant de soin, arrangé avec tant d'art ;*'— and lamenting that a creature thus nobly gifted should have been cast away upon the same rock which had shipwrecked the greatest, the most illustrious, of her *compatriotes, le fort Samson, le preux David, le sage Salomon ;*' he goes on to describe, with real eloquence, and in a less offensive strain of panegyric, her devotion at the foot of the cross, her pious visit to the tomb by break of day, braving the fury of the guards, the cruelty of the Jews, and taking the place of the apostles, who were dispersed or fled. And thus he winds up with a moral, most extraordinary when we recollect that it was preached from a pulpit by a grave doctor in theology :—

'Jeunes personnes qui vivez encore dans l'innocence ! apprenez donc de la Madeleine combien grands sont les périls de la jeunesse, de la beauté, de tous les dons purement naturels ; souvenez-vous que le désir excessif de plaire est toujours dangereux, rarement innocent, et qu'il est bien difficile de donner beaucoup de sentiments, sans en prendre soi-même. A la vue des faiblesses de la jeune Israélite, comprenez de quelle importance est, pour vous, la garde de votre cœur ; et à quels désorders il vous expose, si vous ne vous accoutumez à le contrarier sans cesse, en tous ses penchants.

'Femmes mondaines, et peut-être voluptueuses ! apprenez de la Madeleine à revenir de vos écarts ; ils ont été, dans vous, le fruit de la faiblesse humaine ; que votre retour soit le fruit de votre correspondance à la grâce. Et pourriez-vous ou vous proposer un modèle plus digne d'être suivi que celui que vous présente Madeleine, ou trouver ailleurs un motif plus puissant de le suivre ?

'Et vous qui, fières d'une réserve que vous ne devez peut-être qu'à votre insensibilité, vous en faites un rempart, à l'abri duquel vous croyez pouvoir mépriser toute la terre, et dont la mondanité de Madeleine elle-même a peut-être scandalisé la précieuse vertu ! femmes plus vaines que sages ! apprenez de notre Sainte, qu'il n'y a que la grâce de Dieu

The traditional scene of the penance of the Magdalene, a wild spot between Toulon and Marseilles, is the site of a famous convent called La Sainte Beaume (which in the Provençal tongue signifies *Holy Cave*), formerly a much frequented place of pilgrimage. It is built on the verge of a formidable precipice ; near it is the grotto in which the saint resided ; and to Mount Pilon, a rocky point about six hundred feet above the grotto, the angels bore her seven times a day to pray. This convent was destroyed and pillaged at the commencement of the French Revolution. It was filled with relics and works of art, referring to the life and the worship of the Magdalene.

But the most sumptuous fane ever erected to her special honour is that which, of late years, has arisen in the city of Paris. The church, or rather the temple, of La Madeleine stands an excelling monument, if not of modern piety, at least of modern Art. It is built on the model of the temple of Jupiter at Athens :—

> That noble type is realised again
> In perfect form ; and dedicate—to whom ?
> To a poor Syrian girl of lowliest name—
> A hapless creature, pitiful and frail,
> As ever wore her life in sin and shame !
>   R. M. MILNES.

The saint, whether she were ' the lowly Syrian girl,' or the ' Princess of Magdala,' would be equally astonished to behold herself thus honoured with a sort of pagan magnificence in the midst of a luxurious capital, and by a people more remarkable for scoffing than for praying. Even in the successive vicissitudes of this splendid edifice there is something strange. That which is now the temple of the lowly penitent, was a few years ago *Le Temple de la Gloire.*

Let us now turn to those characteristic representations with which painting and sculpture have made us familiar, and for which both

et une attention continuelle sur nous-mêmes qui puissent nous aider constamment contre la pente qui nous précipite vers le mal, et craignez qu'on ne puisse vous dire, à son sujet, ce que Saint Augustin disait à une dévote de votre caractère, pleine d'elle-même et médisante : " Plût à Dieu que vous eussiez donné dans les mêmes excès dont vous croyez si volontiers les autres capables ! vous seriez moins éloignée du royaume de Dieu ; du moins vous auriez de l'humanité ! " '

Le Brun's Magdalene is just the Magdalene described by this preacher : both one and the other are as like the Magdalene of Scripture as Leo X. was like St. Peter.

Scripture and legendary tradition have furnished the authority and the groundwork. These are so numerous and so infinitely varied, that I find it necessary here, as in the case of St. Jerome, to arrange them under several heads.

The devotional representations may be divided into two classes. 1. Those which represent the Magdalene as patron saint. 2. Those which represent her penitence in the desert.

The historical subjects may also be divided into two classes. 1. Those scenes from Gospel story in which Mary Magdalene figures as a chief or conspicuous personage. 2. The scenes taken from her legendary life.

In all these subjects the accompanying attribute is the alabaster box of ointment, which has a double significance : it may be the perfume which she poured over the feet of the Saviour, or the balm and spices which she had prepared to anoint his body. Sometimes she carries it in her hand, sometimes it stands at her feet, or near her ; frequently, in later pictures, it is borne by an attendant angel. The shape varies with the fancy of the artist; it is a small vase, a casket, a box, a cup with a cover ; more or less ornamented, more or less graceful in form ; but always there—the symbol at once of her conversion and her love, and so peculiar that it can leave no doubt of her identity.

Her drapery in the ancient pictures is usually red, to express the fervour of her love ; in modern representations, and where she figures as penitent, it is either blue or violet ; violet, the colour of mourning and penitence—blue, the colour of constancy. To express both the love and the sorrow, she sometimes wears a violet-coloured tunic and a red mantle. The luxuriant hair ought to be fair or golden. Dark-haired Magdalenes, as far as I can remember, belong exclusively to the Spanish school.

1. When exhibited to us as the patron saint of repentant sinners, Mary Magdalene is sometimes a thin wasted figure, with long dishevelled hair of a pale golden hue, falling over her shoulders almost to the ground ; sometimes a skin or a piece of linen is tied round her loins, but not seldom her sole drapery is her long redundant hair. The most ancient single figure of this character to which I can refer is an old picture in the Byzantine manner, as old perhaps

as the thirteenth century, and now in the Academy at Florence. She is standing as patroness, covered only by her long hair, which falls in dark brown masses to her feet; the colour, I imagine, was originally much lighter. She is a meagre, haggard, grim-looking figure, and holds in her hand a scroll, on which is inscribed in ancient Gothic letters—

𝔑𝔢 𝔡𝔢𝔰𝔭𝔢𝔠𝔱𝔢𝔱𝔢𝔰
𝔙𝔬𝔰 𝔮𝔲𝔦 𝔭𝔢𝔠𝔠𝔞𝔯𝔢 𝔰𝔬𝔩𝔢𝔱𝔦𝔰
𝔈𝔵𝔢𝔪𝔭𝔩𝔬 𝔪𝔢𝔬
𝔙𝔬𝔰 𝔯𝔢𝔭𝔞𝔯𝔞𝔱𝔢 𝔇𝔢𝔬.[1]

Rude and unattractive as is this specimen of ancient Art, I could not look at it without thinking how often it must have spoken hope and peace to the soul of the trembling sinner, in days when it hung, not in a picture-gallery to be criticised, but in a shrine to be worshipped. Around this figure, in the manner of the old altar-pieces, are six small square compartments containing scenes from her life.

The famous statue carved in wood by Donatello, in point of character, may be referred to this class of subjects : she stands over her altar in the Baptistery at Florence, with clasped hands, the head raised in prayer; the form is very expressive of wasting grief and penance, but too meagre for beauty. *'Egli la volle specchio alle penitenti, non incitamento alla cupidizia degli sguardi, come avenne ad altri artisti,'* says Cicognara ; and, allowing that beauty has been sacrificed to expression, he adds, ' but if Donatello had done all, what would have

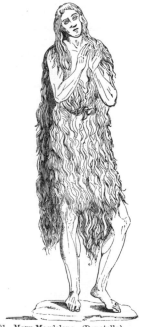

91   Mary Magdalene   (Donatello).

The original Latin distich runs thus :—
Ne desperetis vos qui peccare soletis,
Exemploque meo vos reparate Deo.

remained for Canova?' That which remained for Canova to do, he has done; he has made her as lovely as possible, and he has dramatised the sentiment: she is more the penitent than the patron saint. The display of the beautiful limbs is chastened by the humility of the attitude—half kneeling, half prostrate; by the expression of the drooping head—'all sorrow's softness charmed from its despair.' Her eyes are fixed on the cross which lies extended on her knees; and she weeps—not so much her own past sins, as the sacrifice it has cost to redeem them. This is the prevailing sentiment, or, as the Germans would call it, the *motive* of the representation, to which I should feel inclined to object as deficient in dignity and severity, and bordering too much on the *genre* and dramatic style: but the execution is almost faultless. Very beautiful is another modern statue of the penitent Magdalene, executed in marble for the Count d'Espagnac, by M. Henri de Triqueti. She is half seated, half reclining on a fragment of rock, and pressing to her bosom a crown of thorns, at once the mourner and the penitent: the sorrow is not for herself alone.

But, in her character of patron saint, Mary Magdalene was not always represented with the squalid or pathetic attributes of humiliation and penance. She became idealised as a noble dignified creature bearing no traces of sin or of sorrow on her beautiful face; her luxuriant hair bound in tresses round her head; her drapery rich and ample; the vase of ointment in her hand or at her feet, or borne by an angel near her. Not unfrequently she is attired with the utmost magnificence, either in reference to her former state of worldly prosperity, or rather, perhaps, that with the older painters, particularly those of the German school, it was a common custom to clothe all the ideal figures of female saints in rich habits. In the fourteenth and fifteenth centuries such representations of the Magdalene are usual both in Italian and German Art. A beautiful instance may be seen in a picture by Signorelli, in the Cathedral of Orvieto, where she is standing in a landscape, her head uncovered, and the rich golden hair partly braided, partly flowing over her shoulders; she wears a magnificent tunic embroidered with gold, over it a flowing mantle descending to her feet; she holds the vase with her left hand, and points to it with her right. If it were not for the saintly aureole encircling her head, this figure, and others similar to it, might be mistaken for Pandora.   See, for example, the

Mary Magdalene   (Lucas v. Leyden)

famous print by Lucas v. Leyden, where she stands on clouds with an embroidered coif and flowing mantle, holding the vase in her left hand, and lifting the cover with her right (in the sketch it is reversed): and in the half-length by Leonardo, or one of his school.

The want of a religious sentiment gives such figures a very heathen and *Pandora* look, so that the aureole alone fixes the identity. This is not the case with a noble Magdalene by Dennis Calvert, in the Manfrini Palace at Venice. She is standing in a fine bold landscape; one hand sustains her ample crimson drapery, the other holds her vase; her fair hair falls in masses over her shoulders, and she looks down on her worshippers with a serious dignified compassion. This is one of the finest pictures of the later Bologna school, finer and truer in sentiment than any of the Caracci and Guido Magdalenes.

In this her wholly divine and ideal character of saint and intercessor, Mary Magdalene is often most beautifully introduced as standing near the throne of the Virgin, or as grouped with other saints. In two of the most famous pictures in the world she is thus represented. In the St. Cecilia of Raphael, she stands on the left, St. Paul being on the right of the principal figure; they are here significant of the conversion of the man through *power*, of the woman through *love*, from a state of reprobation to a state of reconcilement and grace. St. Paul leans in deep meditation on his sword. Mary Magdalene is habited in ample drapery of blue and violet, which she sustains with one hand, and bears the vase in the other. She looks out of the picture with a benign countenance and a particularly graceful turn of the head. Raphael's original design for this picture (engraved by Marc Antonio) is, however, preferable in the sentiment given to the Magdalene: she does not look *out* of the picture, but she looks *up* : *she* also hears the divine music which has ravished St. Cecilia. In the picture she is either unconscious or inattentive.

In the not less celebrated St. Jerome of Correggio she is on the left of the Madonna, bending down with an expression of the deepest adoration to kiss the feet of the infant Christ, while an angel behind holds up the vase of ointment: thus recalling to our minds, and shadowing forth in the most poetical manner, that memorable act of love and homage rendered at the feet of the Saviour. Parmigiano has represented her, in a Madonna picture, as standing on one side, and the prophet Isaiah on the other. Lord Ashburton has a fine picture by Correggio, in which we have the same ideal representation: she is here grouped with St. Peter, St. Margaret, and St. Leonardo.

There are two classes of subjects in which Mary Magdalene is richly habited, and which must be carefully distinguished; those above described, in which she figures as patron saint, and those which represent her *before* her conversion, as the votary of luxury and pleasure. In the same manner we must be careful to distinguish those figures of the penitent Magdalene which are wholly devotional in character and intention, and which have been described in the first class, from those which represent her in the act of doing penance, and which are rather dramatic and sentimental than devotional.

2. The penance of the Magdalene is a subject which has become, like the penance of St. Jerome, a symbol of Christian penitence, but still more endeared to the popular imagination by more affecting and attractive associations, and even more eminently picturesque,—so tempting to the artists, that by their own predilection for it they have assisted in making it universal. In the display of luxuriant female forms, shadowed (not hidden) by redundant fair hair, and flung in all the *abandon* of solitude, amid the depth of leafy recesses, or relieved by the dark umbrageous rocks; in the association of love and beauty with the symbols of death and sorrow and utter humiliation; the painters had ample scope, ample material, for the exercise of their imagination, and the display of their skill: and what has been the result? They have abused these capabilities even to licence; they have exhausted the resources of Art in the attempt to vary the delineation; and yet how seldom has the ideal of this most exquisite subject been—I will not say realised—but even approached? We have Magdalenes who look as if they never could have sinned, and others who look as if they never could have repented; we have Venetian Magdalenes with the air of courtesans, and Florentine Magdalenes with the air of Ariadnes; and Bolognese Magdalenes like sentimental Niobes; and French Magdalenes, *moitié galantes, moitié dévotes;* and Dutch Magdalenes, who wring their hands like repentant washerwomen. The Magdalenes of Rubens remind us of nothing so much as of the ' unfortunate Miss Bailey;' and the Magdalenes of Van Dyck are fine ladies who have turned Methodists. But Mary Magdalene, such as we have conceived her, mournful yet hopeful,—tender yet dignified,—worn with grief and fasting, yet

radiant with the glow of love and faith, and clothed with the beauty of holiness,—is an ideal which painting has not yet realised. Is it beyond the reach of Art? We might have answered this question, had Raphael attempted it;—but he has not. His Magdalene at the feet of Christ is yet unforgiven—the forlorn castaway, not the devout penitent.

The Magdalene doing penance in her rocky desert first became a popular subject in the sixteenth century; in the seventeenth it was at the height of favour. There are two distinct versions of the subject, infinitely varied as to detail and sentiment: either she is represented as bewailing her sins, or as reconciled to Heaven.

In the former treatment she lies prostrate on the earth, or she is standing or kneeling at the entrance of the cave (in some of the old illuminated missals the upper part of her body is seen emerging from a cave or rather a hole in the ground,) the hands clasped, or extended towards heaven; the eyes streaming with tears; the long yellow hair floating over her shoulders. The crucifix, the skull, and sometimes the scourge, are introduced as emblems of faith, mortality, and penance; weeping angels present a crown of thorns.

In the latter treatment she is reading or meditating; the expression is serene or hopeful; a book lies beside the skull; angels present the palm, or scatter flowers; a vision of glory is seen in the skies.

The alabaster box is in all cases the indispensable attribute. The eyes are usually raised, if not in grief, in supplication or in aspiration. The ' uplifted eye ' as well as the ' loose hair ' became a characteristic; but there are some exceptions. The conception of character and situation, which was at first simple, became more and more picturesque, and at length theatrical—a mere vehicle for sentiment and attitude.

1. The earliest example I can remember of the Penitent Magdalene, *dramatically* treated, remains as yet unsurpassed;—the reading Magdalene of Correggio, in the Dresden Gallery. This lovely creation has only one fault—the virginal beauty is that of a Psyche or a Seraph. In Oelenschläger's drama of ' Correggio,' there is a beautiful description of this far-famed picture; he calls it ' Die Gottinn des Waldes Frömmigkeit,'—the goddess of the religious solitude. And in truth, if we could imagine Diana reading instead

of hunting, she might have looked thus. Oelenschläger has made poetical use of the tradition that Correggio painted this Magdalene for a poor monk who was his confessor or physician ; and thus he makes Silvestro comment on the work :—

> What a fair picture !—
> This dark o'erhanging shade, the long fair hair,
> The delicate white skin, the azure robe,
> The full luxuriant life, the grim death's head,
> The tender womanhood, and the great book :—
> These various contrasts have you cunningly
> Brought into sweetest harmony.

But truer, at least nobler in sentiment, is the Magdalene by the same painter (in the Manfrini Palace, Venice,) of the same size and similarly draped in dark blue ; but here *standing* at the entrance of her cave. She leans her elbow on the book which lies on the rock, and appears to be meditating on its contents. The head, seen in front, is grand and earnest, with a mass of fair hair, a large wide brow, and deep, deep eyes full of mystery. The expression of power in this head pleases me especially, because true to the character, as I conceive it.

> Doch ist es schön von einem Weibe, mein' ich,
> Einmal gefallen wieder sich zu heben ;
> Es gibt sehr wen'ge Männer, die das können !

> Yes ! it is good to see a hapless woman,
> That once has fallen, redeem herself ! In truth,
> There be few men, methinks, could do as much.

> *Correggio,* Act i. Scene 1.

I do not know why this lovely Manfrini picture should be so much less celebrated than the Dresden Magdalene : while the latter has been multiplied by copies and engravings, I do not remember a single print after the Manfrini Magdalene. There is a bad feeble copy in the Louvre ; [1] I know no other.

2. There is a celebrated picture by Timoteo della Vite, in the Bologna Gallery. She is standing before the entrance of her cavern, arrayed in a crimson mantle ; her long hair is seen beneath descending to her feet ; the hands joined in prayer, the head declined on

---

[1] It was in the Standish Gallery belonging to Louis-Philippe, and now dispersed.

93   Mary Magdalene (Timoteo della Vite)

one side, and the whole expression that of girlish innocence and
simplicity, with a touch of the pathetic.   A mendicant, not a Magdalene, is the idea suggested ; and, for myself, I confess that at the
first glance I was reminded of the little Red-Riding-Hood, and could
think of no sin that could have been attributed to such a face and
figure, beyond the breaking of a pot of butter : yet the picture is
very beautiful.

3. The Magdalene of Titian was so celebrated in his own time,
that he painted at least five or six repetitions, of it, and copies and

engravings have since been multiplied. The eyes, swimming, in tears, are raised to heaven ; the long dishevelled hair floats over her shoulders; one hand is pressed on her bosom, the other rests on the skull ; the forms are full and round, the colouring rich ; a book and a box of ointment lie before her on a fragment of rock. She is sufficiently woeful, but seems rather to regret her past life than to repent of it, nor is there anything in the expression which can secure us against a relapse. Titian painted the original for Charles V. His idea of the *pose* was borrowed, as we are told, from an antique statue, and his model was a young girl, who being fatigued with long standing, the tears ran down her face, 'and Titian attained the desired expression.'(!) His idea therefore of St. Mary Magdalene was the fusion of an antique statue and a girl taken out of the streets; and with all its beauties as a work of Art—and very beautiful it is—this *chef-d'œuvre* of Titian is, to my taste, most unsatisfactory.

4. Cigoli's Magdalene is seated on a rock, veiled *only* by her long hair, which falls over the whole figure ; the eyes, still wet with tears, are raised to heaven ; one arm is round a skull, the right hand rests on a book which is on her knees.

5. The Magdalene of Carlo Cignani, veiled in her dishevelled hair, and wringing her hands, is also most affecting for the fervent expression of sorrow; both these are in the Florence Gallery.[1]

6. Guido, regarded as the painter of Magdalenes *par excellence*, has carried this mistake yet farther ; he had ever the classical Niobe in his mind, and his saintly penitents, with all their exceeding loveliness, appear to me utterly devoid of that beauty which has been called 'the beauty of holiness; ' the reproachful grandeur of the Niobe is diluted into voluptuous feebleness ; the tearful face, with the loose golden hair and uplifted eyes, of which he has given us at least ten repetitions, however charming as Art—as painting, are unsatisfactory as religious representations. I cannot except even the beautiful study in our National Gallery, nor the admired full-

---

[1] There is a beautiful half-length female figure, attributed to Correggio, and engraved under the title of ' Gismunda ' weeping over the heart of her lover, in the collection of the Duke of Newcastle. The duplicate in the Belvedere Gallery at Vienna is there styled a Magdalene, and attributed correctly to Francesco Furini.

length in the Sciarra Palace, at Rome; the latter, when I saw it last, appeared to me poor and mannered, and the pale colouring not merely delicate, but vapid. A head of Mary Magdalene reading,

94   Mary Magdalene (Murillo).

apparently a study from life, is, however in a grand style.[1]

7. Murillo's Magdalene, in the Louvre, kneeling, with hands crossed on her bosom, eyes upraised, and parted lips, has eager devout hope as well as sorrow in the countenance. 8. But turn to the Magdalene of Alonzo Cano, which hangs near : drooping, negligent of self; the very hands are nerveless, languid, dead.[2] Nothing but woe, guilt, and misery are in the face and attitude , *she* has not yet looked into the face of Christ, nor sat at his feet, nor heard from his lips, ' Woman, thy

[1] Lichtenstein Gal.
[2] These two pictures were sold out of the Louvre with King Louis-Philippe's pictures.

sins be forgiven thee,' nor dared to hope; it is the penitent only; the
whole head is faint, and the whole heart sick.   9. But the beautiful
Magdalene of Annibal Caracci has heard the words of mercy, *she* has

95   Mary Magdalene (Annibal Caracci).

memories which are not of sin only; angelic visions have already come
to her in that wild solitude; she is seated at the foot of a tree; she
leans her cheek on her left hand, the other rests on a skull; she is in
deep contemplation; but her thoughts are not of death: the upward
ardent look is full of hope, and faith, and love.   The fault of this beautiful little picture lies in the sacrifice of the truth of the situation to the
artistic feeling of beauty—the common fault of the school; the forms
are large, round, full, untouched by grief and penance.

10. Vandyck's Magdalenes have the same fault as his Madonnas;
they are not feeble nor voluptuous, but they are too elegant and lady-
like.   I remember, for example, a Deposition by Vandyck, and one of

his finest pictures, in which Mary Magdalene kisses the hand of the
Saviour quite with the air of a princess.   The most beautiful of his
penitent Magdalenes is the half-length figure with the face in profile,
bending with clasped hands over the crucifix; the skull and knotted
scourge lie on a shelf of rock behind ; underneath is the inscription,
' *Fallit gratia, et vana est pulchritudo ; mulier timens Dominum ipsa
laudabitur.*' (Prov. xxxi. 30.) 11. Rubens has given us thirteen
Magdalenes, more or less coarse ; in one picture [1] she is tearing her
hair like a disappointed virago ; in another, the expression of grief is
overpowering, but it is that of a woman in the house of correction.
From this sweeping condemnation I must make one exception ; it is
the picture known as ' The Four Penitents.' [2] In front the Magdalene
bows down her head on her clasped hands with such an expression of
profound humility as Rubens only, when painting out of nature and
his own heart, could give.   Christ, with an air of tender yet sublime
compassion, looks down upon her :—' Thy sins be forgiven thee ! '
Behind Christ and the Magdalene stand Peter, David, and Didymus,
the penitent thief ; the faces of these three, thrown into shadow to
relieve the two principal figures, have a self-abased, mournful expression.   I have never seen anything from the hand of Rubens at once
so pure and pathetic in sentiment as this picture, while the force and
truth of the painting are, as usual, wonderful.   No one should judge
Rubens who has not studied him in the Munich Gallery.

The HISTORICAL SUBJECTS from the life of Mary Magdalene are
either scriptural or legendary ; and the character of the Magdalene, as
conceived by the greatest painters, is more distinctly expressed in
those scriptural scenes in which she is an important figure, than in
the single and ideal representations.   The illuminated Gospels of
the ninth century furnish the oldest type of Mary, the penitent
and the sister of Lazarus, but it differs from the modern conception
of the Magdalene.   She is in such subjects a secondary scriptural
personage, one of the accessories in the history of Christ, and nothing more ; no attempt was made to give her importance, either by

---

[1] Turin Gallery.
[2] Munich Gallery, No. 266. There is an inferior repetition in the Royal Gallery at Turin.

beauty or dignity, or prominence of place, till the end of the thirteenth century.

The sacred subjects in which she is introduced are the following :—

1. Jesus at supper with Simon the Pharisee.—' And she began
to wash his feet with tears, and did wipe them with the hair of her
head, and kissed his feet, and anointed them with ointment.' (Luke
vii. 30.)

2. Christ is in the house of Martha and Mary.—' And she sat at
Jesus' feet, and heard his words; but Martha was cumbered with
much serving.' (Luke x. 39, 40.)

3. The raising of Lazarus.—' Lord, if thou hadst been here, my
brother had not died.' (John xi. 32.)

4. The Crucifixion.—' Now there stood by the cross Mary Magdalene.' (John xix. 25 ; Matt. xxvii. 56.)

5. The Deposition from the Cross.—' And Mary Magdalene, and the
mother of Jesus, beheld where he was laid.' (Mark xv. 47.)

6. The Maries at the Sepulchre.—' And there was Mary Magdalene
and the other Mary, sitting over against the sepulchre.' (Matt. xxvii.
61.)

7. Christ appears to Mary Magdalene in the Garden, called the
Noli me tangere.—' Touch me not, for I am not yet ascended to my
Father.' (John xx. 17.)

In the first, second, and last of these subjects, the Magdalene is
one of the two principal figures, and necessary to the action ; in the
others she is generally introduced, but in some instances omitted ; and
as all belong properly to the life of Christ, I shall confine myself
now to a few remarks on the characteristic treatment of the Magdalene
in each.

1. The supper with Simon has been represented in every variety
of style. The earliest and simplest I can call to mind is the fresco
of Taddeo Gaddi in the Rinuccini Chapel at Florence. The Magdalene bends down prostrate on the feet of the Saviour; she is in a red
dress, and her long yellow hair flows down her back ; the seven devils
by which she was possessed are seen above, flying out of the roof of the
house in the shape of little black monsters. Raphael, when treating
the same subject, thought only of the religious significance of the action,
and how to express it with the utmost force and the utmost simplicity.

There are few figures—our Saviour, the Pharisee, four apostles, and two attendants: Mary Magdalene in front bends over the feet of Christ while her long hair half conceals her face and almost sweeps the ground; nothing can exceed the tenderness and humility of the attitude and the benign dignity of Christ. As an example of the most opposite treatment let us turn to the gorgeous composition of Paul Veronese; we have a stately banquet-room, rich architecture, a crowd of about thirty figures; and the Magdalene is merely a beautiful female with loose robes, dishevelled tresses, and the bosom displayed; this gross fault of sentiment is more conspicuous in the large picture in the Durazzo Palace at Genoa than in the beautiful finished sketch in the collection of Mr. Rogers.[1] A fine sketch by the same painter, but quite different, is at Alton Towers. The composition of Rubens, of which a very fine sketch is in the Windsor collection, is exceedingly dramatic; the dignity of Christ and the veneration and humility of the Magdalene are admirably expressed; but the disdainful surprise of some of the assistants, and the open mockery of others—the old man in spectacles peering over to convince himself of the truth—disturb the solemnity of the feeling: and this fault is even more apparent in the composition of Philippe de Champagne, where a young man puts up his finger with no equivocal expression. In these two examples the moment chosen is not ' *Thy sins are forgiven thee,*' but the scepticism of the Pharisee becomes the leading idea; ' *This man, if he were a prophet, would have known who and what manner of woman this is.*'

2. Christ in the house of Martha and Mary. Of this beautiful subject I have never seen a satisfactory version; in the fresco by Taddeo Gaddi in the Rinuccini Chapel the subject becomes legendary rather than scriptural. Mary Magdalene is seated at the feet of Christ in an attitude of attention; Martha seems to expostulate; three of the disciples are behind; a little out of the principal group, St. Marcella, also with a glory round her head, is seen cooking. At Hampton Court there is a curious picture of this subject by Hans Vries, which is an elaborate study of architecture :- the rich decora-

---

[1] The great picture formerly in the Durazzo Palace is now in the Royal Gallery at Turin. It is wonderful for life and colour, and dramatic feeling—a masterpiece of the painter in his characteristic style

tion of the interior has been criticised; but, according to the legend,
Martha and Mary lived in great splendour; and there is no impropriety in representing their dwelling as a palace, but a very great
impropriety in rendering the decorations of the palace more important than the personages of the scene.   In a picture by Old Bassano,
Christ is seen entering the house; Mary Magdalene goes forward to
meet him; Martha points to the table where Lazarus sits composedly
cutting a slice of sausage, and in the corner St. Marcella is cooking
at a fire.   In a picture by Rubens, the treatment is similar.   The
holy sisters are like two Flemish farm servants, and Christ—but I
dare not proceed:—in both these instances, the colouring, the
expression, the painting of the accessories—the vegetables and fruit,
the materials and implements for cooking a feast—are as animated
and true to nature as the conception of the whole scene is trivial,
vulgar, and, to a just taste, intolerably profane.

One of the most modern compositions of this scene which has
attracted attention is that of Overbeck, very simple and poetical, but
deficient in individual expression.

3. The raising of Lazarus was selected by the early Christians as
an emblem both of the general resurrection and the resurrection of
our Saviour, at a time that the resurrection of the Saviour in person
was considered a subject much too solemn and mysterious to be
dealt with by the imitative arts.   In its primitive signification, as
the received emblem of the resurrection of the dead, we find this
subject abounding in the catacombs, and on the sarcophagi of the
third and fourth centuries.   The usual manner of representation shows
the dead man swathed like a mummy, under the porch of a temple
resembling a tomb, to which there is an ascent by a flight of steps.
Christ stands before him, and touches him with a wand.   Sometimes
there are two figures only, but in general Mary Magdalene is kneeling by.   There is one instance only in which Christ stands surrounded by the apostles, and the two sisters are kneeling at his feet:
—'Lord, hadst thou been here, my brother had not died.'[1]

In more modern Art this subject loses its mystic signification,
and becomes simply a scriptural incident.   It is treated like a scene
in a drama, and the painters have done their utmost to vary the

[1] Bottari, Tab. xxx.

treatment. But, however varied as regards the style of conception and the number of personages, Martha and Mary are always present, and, in general, Mary is at the feet of our Saviour. The incident is of course one of the most important in the life of Christ, and is never omitted in the series, nor yet in the miracles of our Saviour. But, from the beginning of the fourteenth century, it forms one of the scenes of the story of Mary Magdalene. The fresco of Giovanni da Milano at Assisi contains thirteen figures, and the two sisters kneeling at the feet of Christ have a grand and solemn simplicity; but Mary is not here in any respect distinguished from Martha, and both are attired in red.

In the picture in our National Gallery, the kneeling figure of Mary looking up in the face of Jesus, with her grand severe beauty and earnest expression, is magnificent : but here, again, Mary of Bethany is not Mary Magdalene, nor the woman ' who was a sinner ;' and I doubt whether Michael Angelo intended to represent her as such. On the other hand, the Caracci, Rubens and the later painters are careful to point out the supposed identity, by the long fair hair, exposed and dishevelled, the superior beauty and the superior prominence and importance of the figure, while Martha stands by, veiled, and as a secondary personage.

4. In the crucifixion, where more than the three figures (the Redeemer, the Virgin, and St. John) are introduced, the Magdalene is almost always at the foot of the cross, and it is said that Giotto gave the first example. Sometimes she is embracing the cross, and looking up with all the abandonment of despairing grief, which is more picturesque than true in sentiment; finer in feeling is the expression of serene hope tempering the grief. In Rubens' famous ' Crucifixion' at Antwerp, she has her arms round the cross, and is gazing at the executioner with a look of horror : this is very dramatic and striking, but the attention of the penitent ought to be fixed on the dying Saviour, to the exclusion of every other thought or object. In Vandyck's ' Crucifixion,' the face of the Magdalene seen in front is exquisite for its pathetic beauty. Sometimes the Virgin is fainting in her arms. The box of ointment is frequently placed near, to distinguish her from the other Maries present.

5. In the Descent or Deposition from the Cross, and in the Entombment, Mary Magdalene is generally conspicuous. She is often
supporting the feet or one of the hands of the Saviour; or she stands
by weeping; or she sustains the Virgin; or (which is very usual in
the earlier pictures) she is seen lamenting aloud, with her long
tresses disordered, and her arms outspread in an ecstasy of grief and
passion; or she bends down to embrace the feet of the Saviour, or to
kiss his hand; or contemplates with a mournful look one of the nails,
or the crown of thorns, which she holds in her hand.

In the Pietà of Fra Bartolomeo, in the Pitti Palace, the prostrate
abandonment in the figure of the Magdalene, pressing the feet of
Christ to her bosom, is full of pathetic expression; in the same gallery
is the Pietà by Andrea del Sarto, where the Magdalene, kneeling,
wrings her hands in mute sorrow. But in this, as in other instances,
Raphael has shown himself supreme; there is a wonderful little
drawing by him, in which Nicodemus and others sustain the body of
the Saviour, while Mary Magdalene lies prostrate bending her head
over his feet, which she embraces; the face is wholly concealed by
the flowing hair, but never was the expression of overwhelming love
and sorrow conveyed with such artless truth.

6. The Maries at the Sepulchre. The women who carry the spices
and perfumes to the tomb of Jesus are called, in Greek Art, the
Myrrhophores, or myrrh-bearers : with us there are usually three—
Mary Magdalene, Mary the mother of James and John, and Mary
Salome. In Matthew, two women are mentioned; in Mark, three;
in Luke, the number is indefinite; and in John, only one is mentioned, Mary Magdalene. There is scarcely a more beautiful subject
in the whole circle of scripture story than this of the three desolate
affectionate women standing before the tomb in the grey dawn, while
the majestic angels are seen guarding the hallowed spot. I give, as
one of the earliest examples, a sketch from the composition of Duccio;
the rules of perspective were then unknown—but what a beautiful
simplicity in the group of women ! how fine the seated angel !—' The
angel of the Lord descended from heaven, and came and rolled back
the stone from the door and sat upon it.' I have seen one instance,
and only one, in which the angel is in the act of descending; in
general, the version according to St. John is followed, and the ' two

men in shining garments' are seated within the tomb. There is a famous engraving, after a design by Michael Angelo, called 'The Three Maries going to the Sepulchre;' it represents three old women veiled, and with their backs turned—very awful; but they might as well be called the three Fates, or the three Witches, as the three Maries. The subject has never been more happily treated than by Philip Veit, a modern German artist, in a print which has become popular; he has followed the version of Matthew: 'As it began to dawn, came Mary Magdalene and the other Mary to see the sepulchre.' The attitude of motionless sorrow; the anxious expectant looks, fixed on the tomb; the deep shadowy stillness; the morning light just breaking in the distance, are very truly and feelingly expressed.

7. The 'Noli me tangere' is the subject of many pictures; they do not vary in the simplicity of the *motif*, which is fixed by tradition, and admits but of two persons. The composition of Duccio, as one of the series of the Passion of Christ, is extremely grand; and the figure of Mary, leaning forward as she kneels, with outstretched hands full of expression. The old fresco of Taddeo Gaddi, in the Rinuccini Chapel,[1] is also exquisite. Two of the finest in conception and treatment are, notwithstanding, in striking contrast to each other. One is the Titian in the collection of Mr Rogers:[2] the Magdalene, kneeling, bends forward with eager expression, and one hand extended to touch him: the Saviour, drawing his linen garment round him, shrinks back from her touch—yet with the softest expression of pity. Besides the beauty and truth of the expression, this picture is transcendent as a piece of colour and effect; while the rich landscape and the approach of morning over the blue distance are conceived with a sublime simplicity. Not less a miracle of Art, not less poetical, but in a far different style, is the Rembrandt in the Queen's Gallery: at the entrance of the sepulchre the Saviour is seen in the habiliments of a gardener, and Mary Magdalene at his feet, adoring. This picture exhibits, in a striking degree, all the wild originality and peculiar feeling of Rembrandt: the forms and characters are common; but the deep shadow of the cavern tomb, the dimly-seen

---

[1] Santa Croce, Florence.

[2] This beautiful and valuable picture has been bequeathed by the poet to the National Gallery.

supernatural beings within it, the breaking of the dawn over the distant city, are awfully sublime, and worthy of the mysterious scene. Barroccio's great altar-piece, which came to England with the Duke of Lucca's pictures, once so famous, and well known from the fine engraving of Raphael Morghen, is poor compared with any of these: Christ is effeminate and commonplace—Mary Magdalene all in a flutter.

I now leave these scriptural incidents, to be more fully considered hereafter, and proceed to the fourth class of subjects pertaining to the life of the Magdalene—those which are taken from the wild Provencal legends of the thirteenth and fourteenth centuries.

1. 'La Danse de la Madeleine' is the title given to a very rare and beautiful print by Lucas v. Leyden. It represent Mary Magdalene abandoned to the pleasures of the world. The scene is a smiling and varied landscape; in the centre Mary Magdalene, with the anticipative glory round her head, is seen dancing along to the sound of a flute and tabor, while a man in a rich dress leads her by the hand: several groups of men and women are diverting themselves in the foreground; in the background Mary Magdalene, with a number of gay companions, is chasing the stag; she is mounted on horseback, and has again the glory round her head: far in the distance she is seen borne upwards by the angels. This singular and suggestive composition is dated 1519. There is a fine impression in the British Museum.

2. 'Mary Magdalene rebuked by her sister Martha for her vanity and luxury.' I believe I am the first to suggest that the famous picture in the Sciarra Palace, by Leonardo da Vinci, known as 'Modesty and Vanity,' is a version of this subject. When I saw it, this idea was suggested, and no other filled my mind. The subject is one often treated, and here treated in Leonardo's peculiar manner. The attitude of the veiled figure is distinctly that of remonstrance and rebuke; the other, decked and smiling, looks out of the picture holding flowers in her hand, as yet unconvinced, unconverted: the vase of ointment stands near her. In other pictures there is no doubt as to the significance of the subject; it has been gracefully treated in a picture by Giovanni Lopicino, now in the gallery of the Belvedere at Vienna. She is seated at her toilette; her maid is binding her luxuriant hair;

Martha, standing by, appears to be remonstrating with great fervour. There is a pretty picture by Elisabetta Sirani of the same scene, similarly treated.

3. 'Mary Magdalene conducted by her sister Martha to the feet of Jesus.' Of this most beautiful subject, I know but one composition of distinguished merit. It is by Raphael, and exists only in the drawing, and the rare engraving by Marc Antonio. Christ sits within the porch of the Temple, teaching four of his disciples who stand near him. Martha and Mary are seen ascending the steps which lead to the portico: Martha, who is veiled, seems to encourage her sister, who looks down. I observe that Passavant and others are uncertain as to the subject of this charming design: it has been styled 'The Virgin Mary presenting the Magdalene to Christ;' but with any one who has carefully considered the legend there can be no doubt as to the intention of the artist. 'Mary Magdalene listening to the preaching of our Saviour, with Martha seated by her side,' is one of the subjects in the series by Gaudenzio Ferrari at Vercelli: it is partly destroyed. We have the same subject by F. Zucchero; Mary, in a rich dress, is kneeling at the feet of the Saviour, who is seated under a portico; Martha, veiled, stands near her, and there are numerous spectators and accessories.

4. 'The Magdalene renouncing the Vanities of the World' is also a very attractive subject. In a picture by Guido she has partly divested herself of her rich ornaments, and is taking some pearls from her hair, while she looks up to heaven with tearful eyes. In a sketch by Rubens, in the Dulwich Gallery, she is seated in a forest solitude, still arrayed in her worldly finery, blue satin, pearls, &c., and wringing her hands with an expression of the bitterest grief. The treatment, as usual with him, is coarse, but effective. In his large picture at Vienna, with the figures life-size, Mary is spurning with her feet a casket of jewels, and throwing herself back with her hands clasped in an agony of penitence; while Martha sits behind, gazing on her with an expression so demurely triumphant as to be almost comic. There is an exquisite little picture by Gerard Douw in the Berlin Gallery, in which the Magdalene, in a magnificent robe of crimson and sables, is looking up to heaven with an expression of sorrow and penitence; the table before her is covered with gold and

jewels. 'Mary Magdalene renouncing the World,' by Le Brun, is a famous picture, now in the Louvre. She looks up to heaven with tearful eyes, and is in the act of tearing off a rich mantle; a casket of jewels lies overturned at her feet. This picture is said to be the portrait of Madame de la Vallière, by whose order it was painted for the church of the Carmelites at Paris, where she had taken refuge from the court and from the world. It has that sort of theatrical grace and grandeur, that mannered mediocrity, characteristic of the painter and the time.[1] There is a Magdalene in the Gallery at Munich by Le Brun, which is to me far preferable; and this, and not the Paris one, I presume to be the portrait of the Duchesse de la Vallière. In a picture by Franceschini she has flung off her worldly ornaments, which lie scattered on the ground, and holds a scourge in her hand, with which she appears to have castigated herself: she sinks in the arms of one of her attendant maidens, while Martha, standing by, seems to speak of peace, and points towards heaven: the figures are life-size.[2] None of these pictures, with the exception of the precious Leonardo in the Sciarra Palace, have any remarkable merit as pictures. The scenes between Mary and Martha are capable of the most dramatic and effective illustration, but have never yet been worthily treated.

5. 'The embarkation of the Magdalene in Palestine, with Martha, Lazarus, and the others, cast forth by their enemies in a vessel without sails or rudder, but miraculously conducted by an angel,' is another subject of which I have seen no adequate representation. There is a mediocre picture by Curradi in the Florence Gallery. Among the beautiful frescoes of Gaudenzio Ferrari in the Church of St. Cristoforo at Vercelli, is the voyage of the Magdalene and her companions, and their disembarkation at Marseilles.[3]

6. 'Mary Magdalene preaching to the inhabitants of Marseilles' has been several times represented in the sculpture and stained glass of the old cathedrals in the south of France. In the Hôtel de Cluny there is a curious old picture in distemper attributed to King René of Provence, the father of our Margaret of Anjou, and famous for his skill as a limner. Mary Magdalene is standing on some steps,

---

[1] The print by Edelinck is considered as the masterpiece of that celebrated engraver.
[2] Dresden Gal.   [3] See p. 379, *note*.

96   The Assumption of the Magdalene   (Albert Dürer).

arrayed in loose white drapery, and a veil over her head. She is
addressing earnestly a crowd of listeners, and among them we see
King René and his wife Jeanne de Laval on thrones with crown and
sceptre :—a trifling anachronism of about 1400 years, but it may be
taken in a poetical and allegorical sense. The port of Marseilles is

seen in the background.   The same subject has been classically
treated in a series of bas-reliefs in the porch of the Certosa at Pavia:
there is a mistake, however, in exhibiting her as half naked, clothed
only in a skin, and her long hair flowing down over her person : for
she was at this time the missionary saint, and not yet the penitent
of the desert.

7. ' Mary Magdalene borne by angels above the summit of Mount
Pilon,' called also ' The Assumption of the Magdalene,' is a charming subject when treated in the right spirit.   Unfortunately, we are
oftener reminded of a Pandora, sustained by a group of cupids, or
a Venus rising out of the sea, than of the ecstatic trance of the
reconciled penitent.   It was very early a popular theme.   In the
treatment we find little variety.   She is seen carried upwards very
slightly draped, and often with no other veil than her redundant
hair, flowing over her whole person.   She is in the arms of four,
five, or six angels.   Sometimes one of the angels bears the alabaster
box of ointment; far below is a wild mountainous landscape, with
a hermit looking up at the vision, as it is related in the legend.   The
illustration is from a fine woodcut of Albert Dürer (96).

In a hymn to the Magdalene, by an old Provençal poet (Balthazar
de la Burle), there is a passage describing her ascent in the arms of
angels, which, from its vivid graphic naïveté, is worthy of being
placed under this print of Albert Dürer :—

> Ravengat lou jour los anges la portavan
> Ben plus hault que lou roc.
> Jamais per mauvais temps que fessa ne freddura,
> Autre abit non avia que la sien cabellura,
> Que como un mantel d'or tant eram bels e blonds
> La couvria de la testa fin al bas des talons.

The fresco by Giulio Romano, in which she is reclining amid
clouds, and sustained by six angels, while her head is raised and her
arms extended with the most ecstatic expression, was cut from the
walls of a chapel in the Trinità di Monte, at Rome, and is now in
our National Gallery.

One of the finest pictures ever painted by Ribera is the Assumption
of the Magdalene in the Louvre, both for beauty of expression and
colour.   She is here draped, and her drapery well managed.   The

Spanish painters never fell into the mistake of the Italians ; they give us no Magdalenes which recall the idea of a Venus Meretrix. The rules of the Inquisition were here absolute, and held the painters in wholesome check, rendering such irreligious innovations inadmissible and unknown. In the Turin Gallery there is an Assumption of the Magdalene by Dennis Calvert, admirably painted, in which she is carried up by four Apollo-like angels, who, with their outstretched arms, form a sort of throne on which she is seated : she is herself most lovely, draped in the thin undress of a Venus ; and the whole composition, at first view, brought to my fancy the idea of a Venus rising from the sea, throned in her shell and sustained by nymphs and cupids.

In general, the early painters, Albert Dürer, Vivarini, Lorenzo di Credi, Benedetto Montagna, represent her in an upright position, with hands folded in prayer, or crossed over her bosom, and thus soaring upwards, without effort of will or apparent consciousness ; while the painters of the seventeenth century (with whom this was a favourite subject) strained their imagination to render the form and attitude voluptuously graceful, and to vary the action of the attendant angels, until, in one or two instances, the representation became at once absurdly prosaic and offensively theatrical. F. Zucchero, Cambiasi, Lanfranco, Carlo Maratti, have all given us versions of this subject in a florid, mannered style.

Over the high altar of the Madeleine, at Paris, is the same subject in a marble group, by Marochetti, rather above life-size. Two angels bear her up, while on each side an archangel kneels in adoration.

8. The Last Communion of the Magdalene is represented in two different ways, according to the two different versions of the story : in the first, she expires in her cave, and angels administer the last sacrament ; one holds a taper, another presents the cup, a third the wafer. This has been painted by Domenichino. In the other version, she receives the sacrament from the hand of St. Maximin, who wears the episcopal robes, and the Magdalene kneels before him, half-naked, emaciated, and sustained by angels : the scene is the porch of a church.

9. The Magdalene dying in the Wilderness, extended on the bare

earth, and pressing the crucifix to her bosom, is a frequent subject
in the seventeenth century.   One of the finest examples is the
picture of Rustichino in the Florence Gallery.   The well-known
' Dying Magdalene ' of Canova has the same merits and defects as
his Penitent Magdalene.

I saw a picture at Bologna by Tiarini, of which the conception
appeared to me very striking and poetical.   The Virgin, ' La Madre
Addolorata,' is seated, and holds in her hand the crown of thorns,
which she contemplates with a mournful expression; at a little
distance kneels Mary Magdalene with long dishevelled hair, in all
the abandonment of grief.   St. John stands behind, with his hands
clasped, and his eyes raised to heaven.

When the Magdalene is introduced into pictures of the ' Incredulity
of Thomas,' it is in allusion to a famous parallel in one of the
Fathers, in which it is insisted ' that the faith of Mary Magdalene
and the doubts of Thomas were equally serviceable to the cause of
Christ.'

Among the many miracles imputed to the Magdalene, one only
has become popular as a subject of Art.   Besides being extremely
naïve and poetical, it is extremely curious as illustrating the manners
of the time.   It was probably fabricated in the fourteenth century,
and intended as a kind of parable, to show that those who trusted in
Mary Magdalene, and invoked her aid, might in all cases reckon
upon her powerful intercession.   It is thus related :—

' Soon after Mary Magdalene landed in Provence, a certain prince
of that country arrived in the city of Marseilles with his wife, for the
purpose of sacrificing to the gods ; but they were dissuaded from doing
so by the preaching of Mary Magdalene : and the prince one day said
to the saint, " We greatly desire to have a son.   Canst thou obtain
for us that grace from the God whom thou preachest ?"   And the
Magdalene replied, " If thy prayer be granted, wilt thou then
believe ?"   And he answered, " Yes, I will believe." But shortly
afterwards, as he still doubted, he resolved to sail to Jerusalem to
visit St. Peter, and to find out whether his preaching agreed with that
of Mary Magdalene.   His wife resolved to accompany him : but the
husband said, " How shall that be possible, seeing that thou art with

child, and the dangers of the sea are very great?" But she insisted, and, throwing herself at his feet, she obtained her desire. Then, having laden a vessel with all that was necessary, they set sail, and when a day and a night were come and gone, there arose a terrible storm. The poor woman was seized prematurely with the pains of childbirth; in the midst of the tempest she brought forth her first-born son, and then died. The miserable father, seeing his wife dead, and his child deprived of its natural solace, and crying for food, wrung his hands in despair, and knew not what to do. And the sailors said, "Let us throw this dead body into the sea, for as long as it remains on board the tempest will not abate." But the prince, by his entreaties, and by giving them money, restrained them for a while. Just then, for so it pleased God, they arrived at a rocky island, and the prince laid the body of his wife on the shore, and, taking the infant in his arms, he wept greatly, and said, "O, Mary Magdalene! to my grief and sorrow didst thou come to Marseilles. Why didst thou ask thy God to give me a son only that I might lose both son and wife together? O, Mary Magdalene! have pity on my grief, and if thy prayers may avail, save at least the life of my child!" Then he laid down the infant on the bosom of the mother, and covered them both with his cloak, and went on his way, weeping. And when the prince and his attendants had arrived at Jerusalem, St. Peter showed him all the places where our Saviour had performed his miracles and the hill on which he had been crucified, and the spot from whence he had ascended into heaven. Having been instructed in the faith by St. Peter, at the end of two years the prince embarked to return to his own country, and passing near to the island in which he had left his wife, he landed in order to weep upon her grave.

'Now, wonderful to relate!—his infant child had been preserved alive by the prayers of the blessed Mary Magdalene: and he was accustomed to run about on the sands of the sea-shore, to gather up pebbles and shells; and when the child, who had never beheld a man, perceived the strangers, he was afraid, and ran and hid himself under the cloak which covered his dead mother; and the father, and all who were with him, were filled with astonishment; but their surprise was still greater when the woman opened her eyes, and stretched out her arms to her husband. Then they offered up thanks, and all

returned together to Marseilles, where they fell at the feet of Mary
Magdalene, and received baptism. From that time forth, all the
people of Marseilles and the surrounding country became Christians.'

The picturesque capabilities of this extravagant but beautiful
legend will immediately suggest themselves to the fancy—the wild
sea-shore—the lovely naked infant wandering on the beach—the
mother, slumbering the sleep of death, covered with the mysterious
drapery—the arrival of the mariners—what opportunity for scenery
and grouping, colour and expression! It was popular in the Giotto
school, which arose and flourished just about the period when the
enthusiasm for Mary Magdalene was at its height; but later painters
have avoided it, or, rather, it was not sufficiently accredited for a
Church legend; and I have met with no example later than the end
of the fourteenth century.

The old fresco of Taddeo Gaddi in the S. Croce at Florence will give
some idea of the manner in which the subject was usually treated.
In the foreground is a space representing an island; water flowing
round it, the water being indicated by many strange fishes. On the
island a woman lies extended with her hands crossed upon her
bosom; an infant lifts up the mantle, and seems to show her to a
man bending over her; the father on his knees, with hands joined,
looks devoutly up to heaven; four others stand behind expressing
astonishment or fixed attention. In the distance is a ship, in which
sits a man with a long white beard, in red drapery; beside him
another in dark drapery; beyond is a view of a port with a light-
house, intended, I presume, for Marseilles. The story is here told
in a sort of Chinese manner as regards the drawing, composition,
and perspective; but the figures and heads are expressive and
significant.

In the Chapel of the Magdalene at Assisi, the same subject is given
with some variation. The bark containing the pilgrims is guided by
an angel, and the infant is seated by the head of the mother, as if
watching her.

The life of Mary Magdalene in a series of subjects, mingling the
scriptural and legendary incidents, may often be found in the old

French and Italian churches, more especially in the chapels dedicated to her: and I should think that among the remains of ancient painting now in course of discovery in our own sacred edifices they cannot fail to occur.[1]   In the mural frescoes, in the altar-pieces, the stained glass, and the sculpture of the fourteenth and fifteenth centuries, such a series perpetually presents itself; and, well or ill executed, will in general be found to comprise the following scenes:—

1. Her conversion at the feet of the Saviour.   2. Christ entertained in the house of Martha: Mary sits at his feet to hear his words.   3. The raising of Lazarus.   4. Mary Magdalene and her companions embark in a vessel without sails, oars, or rudder.   5. Steered by an angel, they land at Marseilles.   6. Mary Magdalene preaches to the people.   7. The miracle of the mother and child.   8. The penance of the Magdalene in a desert cave.   9. She is carried up in the arms of angels.   10. She receives the Sacraments from the hands of an angel or from St. Maximin.   11. She dies, and angels bear her spirit to heaven.[2]

The subjects vary of course in number and in treatment, but, with some attention to the foregoing legend, they will easily be understood and discriminated.   Such a series was painted by Giotto in the Chapel of the Bargello at Florence (where the portrait of Dante was lately discovered), but they are nearly obliterated; the miracle of the mother and child is, however, to be distinguished on the left

---

[1] There are about 150 churches in England dedicated in honour of Mary Magdalene.

[2] There is a fine series of frescoes from the life of Mary Magdalene by Gaudenzio Ferrari, in the Church of St. Cristoforo at Vercelli. 1. Mary and Martha are seated, with a crowd of others, listening to Christ, who is preaching in a pulpit.   Martha is veiled and thoughtful: Mary, richly dressed, looks up eagerly.—Half destroyed. 2. Mary anoints the feet of the Saviour : she lays her head down on his foot with a tender humiliation: in the background the Maries at the sepulchre and the *Noli me tangere.*—This also in great part ruined. 3. The legend of the Prince of Provence and his wife, who are kneeling before Lazarus and Mary.   Martha is to the left, and Marcella behind.   In the background are the various scenes of the legend—the embarkation ; the scene on the island ; the arrival at Jerusalem ; the return to Marseilles with the child.—This is one of the best preserved, and the heads are remarkably fine. 4. Mary Magdalene sustained by angels, her feet resting between the wings of one of them, is borne upwards. All the upper part of the figure is destroyed.. In the background are the last communion and burial of the Magdalene. I saw these frescoes in October 1855.   They suffered greatly from the siege in 1638, when several bombs shattered this part of the wall, and will soon cease to exist.   They are engraved in their present state in Pianazzi's ' Opere di Gaudenzio Ferrari,' No. 19.

near the entrance. The treatment of the whole has been imitated
by Taddeo Gaddi in the Rinuccini Chapel at Florence, and by
Giovanni da Milano and Giottino in the Chapel of the Magdalene
at Assisi; on the windows of the Cathedrals of Chartres and Bourges;
and in a series of bas-reliefs round the porch of the Certosa of Pavia,
executed in the classical style of the sixteenth century.

On reviewing generally the infinite variety which has been given
to these favourite subjects, the life and penance of the Magdalene, I
must end where I began—in how few instances has the result been
satisfactory to mind or heart, or soul or sense! Many have well
represented the particular situation, the appropriate sentiment, the
sorrow, the hope, the devotion : but who has given us the *character?*
A noble creature, with strong sympathies and a strong will, with
powerful faculties of every kind, working for good or evil—such a
woman Mary Magdalene must have been, even in her humiliation;
and the feeble, girlish, commonplace, and even vulgar women who
appear to have been usually selected as models by the artists, turned
into Magdalenes by throwing up their eyes and letting down their
hair, ill represent the enthusiastic convert or the majestic patroness.

I must not quit the subject of the Magdalene without some allusion
to those wild legends which suppose a tender attachment (but of
course wholly pure and Platonic) to have existed between her and
St. John the Evangelist.[1] In the enthusiasm which Mary Magdalene
excited in the thirteenth century, no supposition that tended to exalt
her was deemed too extravagant: some of her panegyrists go so far
as to insist that the marriage at Cana, which our Saviour and his
mother honoured by their presence, was the marriage of St. John
with the Magdalene; and that Christ repaired to the wedding-feast
on purpose to prevent the accomplishment of the marriage, having
destined both to a state of greater perfection. This fable was never
accepted by the Church; and among the works of Art consecrated to

---

[1] Bayle, Dict. Hist. ; Molanus, lib. iv., de Hist. Sacrar. S. Mag., cap. xx. p. 428 ;
Thomasium, prefat. 78. The authority usually cited is Abdius, a writer who pretended to
have lived in the first century, and whom Bayle styles 'the most impudent of legendary
impostors.'

Martha presents her sister Mary to our Lord.

religious purposes I have never met with any which placed St. John
and the Magdalene in particular relation to each other, except when
they are seen together at the foot of the cross, or lamenting with the
Virgin over the body of the Saviour : but such was the popularity of
these extraordinary legends towards the end of the thirteenth and in
the beginning of the fourteenth century, that I think it possible such
may exist, and, for want of this key, may appear hopelessly enig-
matical.

In a series of eight subjects which exhibit the life of St. John prefixed to a copy of the Revelation,[1] there is one which I think admits
of this interpretation. The scene is the interior of a splendid building sustained by pillars. St. John is baptizing a beautiful woman,
who is sitting in a tub ; she has long golden hair. On the outside of
the building seven men are endeavouring to see what is going
forward : one peeps through the key-hole ; one has thrown himself
flat on the ground, and has his eye to an aperture ; a third, mounted
on the shoulders of another, is trying to look in at a window ; a fifth,
who cannot get near enough, tears his hair in an agony of impa-
tience ; and another is bawling into the ear of a deaf and blind
comrade a description of what he has seen. The execution is
French, of the fourteenth century ; the taste, it will be said, is also
French; the figures are drawn with a pen and slightly tinted: the design is incorrect ; but the vivacity of gesture and expression, though
verging on caricature, is so true, and so comically dramatic, and the
whole composition so absurd, that it is impossible to look at it without a smile.

St. Martha.

Ital. Santa Marta, Vergine, Albergatrice di Cristo. *Fr.* Sainte Marthe, la Travailleuse.
Patroness of cooks and housewives. (June 29, A.D. 84.)

MARTHA has shared in the veneration paid to her sister. The important part assigned to her in the history of Mary has already been
adverted to ; she is always represented as the instrument through
whom Mary was converted, the one who led her first to the feet of
the Saviour. 'Which thing,' says the story, 'should not be

Paris, Bibliothèque du Roi, MS. 7013, fourteenth century.

accounted as the least of her merits, seeing that Martha was a
chaste and prudent virgin, and the other publicly contemned for her
evil life; notwithstanding which, Martha did not despise her, nor
reject her as a sister, but wept for her shame and admonished her
gently and with persuasive words; and reminded her of her noble
birth, to which she was a disgrace, and that Lazarus, their brother,
being a soldier, would certainly get into trouble on her account.
So she prevailed, and conducted her sister to the presence of
Christ, and afterwards, as it is well known, she lodged and entertained the Saviour in her own house.'[1]

According to the Provençal legend, while Mary Magdalene converted the people of Marseilles, Martha preached to the people of
Aix and its vicinity. In those days the country was ravaged by a
fearful dragon, called the *Tarasque*, which during the day lay concealed in the river Rhône. Martha overcame this monster by
sprinkling him with holy water, and having bound him with her girdle
(or, as others say, her garter), the people speedily put an end to
him. The scene of this legend is now the city of *Tarascon*, where
there is, or was, a magnificent church, dedicated to St. Martha, and
richly endowed by Louis XI.

The same legends assure us that St. Martha was the first who
founded a monastery for women; the first, after the blessed Mother
of Christ, who vowed her virginity to God; and that when she had
passed many years in prayer and good works, feeling that her end
was near, she desired to be carried to a spot where she could see the
glorious sun in heaven, and that they should read to her the history
of the passion of Christ; and when they came to the words, ' Father,
into thy hands I commend my spirit,' she died.

As Mary Magdalene is the patroness of repentant frailty, so
Martha is the especial patroness of female discretion and good house-
keeping. In this character, she is often represented with a
skimmer or ladle in her hand, or a large bunch of keys is attached
to her girdle. For example, in a beautiful old German altar-piece
attributed to Albert Dürer,[2] she is standing in a magnificent dress,
a jewelled turban, and holding a well-known implement of cookery
in her hand. In a missal of Henry VIII.[3] she is represented with

[1] Il Perfetto Legendario.   [2] Queen's Gal.   [3] Bodleian MSS., Oxford.

the same utensil, and her name is inscribed beneath. In general, however, her dress is not rich but homely, and her usual attributes as patron saint are the pot of holy water, the asperge in her hand, and a dragon bound at her feet. In the chapels dedicated to the Magdalene, she finds her appropriate place as pendant to her sister, generally distinguished by her close coif and by being draped in blue or dark brown or grey; while the Magdalene is usually habited in red. When attended by her dragon, St. Martha is some-times confounded with St. Margaret, who is also accompanied by a dragon : but it must be remembered that St. Margaret bears a cruci-fix or palm, and St. Martha the pot of holy water ; and in general the early painters have been careful to distinguish these attributes.

St. Martha, besides being a model of female discretion, sobriety, and chastity, and the patroness of good housewives, was, according to the old legends, the same woman who was healed by Christ, and who in gratitude erected to his honour a bronze statue, which statue is said to have existed in the time of Eusebius, and to have been thrown down by Julian the Apostate.[1]

When Martha and Mary stand together as patronesses, one repre-sents the *active*, the other the *contemplative*, Christian life.

Martha is generally introduced among the holy women who attend the crucifixion and entombment of our Lord. In a most beautiful Entombment by Ambrogio Lorenzetti, Martha kisses the hand of the Saviour, while Mary Magdalene is seen behind with outspread arms : Lazarus and Maximin stand at the head of the Saviour.

LAZARUS, the brother of Martha and Mary, is revered as the first bishop and patron saint of Marseilles, and is generally represented with the mitre and stole. There are at least fifty saints who wear the same attire ; but when a figure in episcopal robes is introduced into the same picture, or the same series, with Martha and Mary, it

----

[1] It is perhaps in reference to this tradition that St. Martha has become the patroness of an order of charitable women, who serve in the hospitals, particularly the military hos-pitals, in France and elsewhere—her brother Lazarus having been a soldier.

may be presumed, if not otherwise distinguished, to be St. Lazarus : sometimes, but rarely, the introduction of a bier, or his resurrection, in the background, serves to fix the identity. Grouped with these three saints, we occasionally find St. Marcella (or Martilla), who accompanied them from the East, but who is not distinguished by any attribute ; nor is anything particular related of her, except that she wrote the life of Martha, and preached the Gospel in Sclavonia.

There are beautiful full-length figures of Mary, Martha, Lazarus, and Marcella in the Brera at Milan—painted by one of the Luini school, and treated in a very classical and noble style—draped, and standing in niches to represent statues. At Munich are the separate figures of Mary, Martha, and Lazarus, by Grünewald ; Lazarus is seen standing by his bier ; Mary, in the rich costume of a German lady of rank, presents her vase ; and Martha is habited like a German *hausfrau*, with her dragon at her feet. They are much larger than life, admirably painted, and full of character, though somewhat grotesque in treatment.

Over the altar of the church ' La Major,' at Marseilles, stands Lazarus as bishop ; Mary on the right, and Martha on the left ; underneath these three statues runs a series of bas-reliefs containing the history of Lazarus. 1. He is recalled to life. 2. Seated on the edge of his tomb, he addresses the spectators. 3. He entertains Christ. 4. The arrival at Marseilles. 5. He preaches to the people. 6. He is consecrated bishop. 7. He suffers martyrdom.

In a tabernacle or triptica by Nicolò Frumenti (A.D. 1461),[1] the central compartment represents the raising of Lazarus, who has the truest and most horrid expression of death and dawning life I ever beheld. On the volet to the right is the supper in the house of Levi, and the Magdalene anointing the feet of the Saviour ; on the left volet, Martha meets him on his arrival at Bethany : ' Lord, if thou hadst been here, my brother had not died.'

In the chapel of Mary Magdalene at Assisi, we find, besides the history of her life, full-length figures of Mary, Martha, Lazarus, and Maximin. Mary, a beautiful dignified figure, as usual in rich red

[1] Fl. Gal.

drapery, stands to the right of the altar, holding out her hand to a kneeling Franciscan : on the left Martha stands in grey drapery with a close hood : Lazarus and Maximin as bishops.

This will give an idea of the manner in which these personages are either grouped together or placed in connection with each other.

St. Mary of Egypt.

Ital. Santa Maria Egiziaca Penitente.   *Fr.* Sainte Marie l'Égyptienne, La Gipesienne, La Jussienne.   (April 2, A.D. 433.)

I PLACE the story of St. Mary of Egypt here, for though she had no real connection with the Magdalene, in works of art they are perpetually associated as *les bienheureuses pécheresses*, and in their personal and pictorial attributes not unfrequently confounded.   The legend of Mary *Egyptiaca* is long anterior to that of Mary Magdalene.   It was current in a written form so early as the sixth century, being then received as a true history ; but it appears to have been originally one of those instructive parables or religious romances which, in the early ages of the Church, were composed and circulated for the edification of the pious.   In considering the manners of that time, we may easily believe that it may have had some foundation in fact.   That a female anchoret of the name of Mary lived and died in a desert of Palestine near the river Jordan—that she there bewailed her sins in solitude for a long course of years, and was accidentally discovered— is a very ancient tradition, supported by contemporary evidence.   The picturesque, miraculous, and romantic incidents with which the story has been adorned, appear to have been added to enhance the interest ; and, in its present form, the legend is attributed to St. Jerome.

' Towards the year of our Lord 365, there dwelt in Alexandria a woman whose name was Mary, and who in the infamy of her life far exceeded Mary Magdalene.   After passing seventeen years in every species of vice, it happened that one day, while roving along the sea-

shore, she beheld a ship ready to sail, and a large company preparing
to embark. She inquired whither they were going? They replied
that they were going up to Jerusalem, to celebrate the feast of the
true cross. She was seized with a sudden desire to accompany them;
but having no money, she paid the price of her passage by selling
herself to the sailors and pilgrims, whom she allured to sin by every
means in her power. On their arrival at Jerusalem, she joined the
crowds of worshippers who had assembled to enter the church; but
all her attempts to pass the threshold were in vain; whenever she
thought to enter the porch, a supernatural power drove her back in
shame, in terror, in despair. Struck by the remembrance of her sins,
and filled with repentance, she humbled herself and prayed for help;
the interdiction was removed, and she entered the church of God,
crawling on her knees. Thenceforward she renounced her wicked
and shameful life, and, buying at a baker's three small loaves, she
wandered forth into solitude, and never stopped or reposed till she
had penetrated into the deserts beyond the Jordan, where she remained in severest penance, living on roots and fruits, and drinking
water only; her garments dropped away in rags piecemeal, leaving
her unclothed; and she prayed fervently not to be left thus exposed:
suddenly her hair grew so long as to form a covering for her whole
person (or, according to another version, an angel brought her a garment from heaven). Thus she dwelt in the wilderness in prayer and
penance, supported only by her three small loaves, which, like the
widow's meal failed her not, until, after the lapse of forty-seven
years, she was discovered by a priest named Zosimus. Of him she
requested silence, and that he would return at the end of a year, and
bring with him the elements of the holy sacrament, that she might
confess and communicate before she was released from earth. And
Zosimus obeyed her, and returned after a year; but not being able to
pass the Jordan, the penitent, supernaturally assisted, passed over the
water to him; and having received the sacrament with tears, she
desired the priest to leave her once more to her solitude, and to return in a year from that time. And when he returned he found her
dead, her hands crossed on her bosom. And he wept greatly; and,
looking around, he saw written in the sand these words :—" O Father
Zosimus, bury the body of the poor sinner, Mary of Egypt! Give

earth to earth, and dust to dust, for Christ's sake!" He endeavoured to obey this last command, but being full of years, and troubled and weak, his strength failed him, and a lion came out of the wood and aided him, digging with his paws till the grave was sufficiently large to receive the body of the saint, which being committed to the earth, the lion retired gently, and the old man returned home praising God, who had shown mercy to the penitent.'

In single figures and devotional pictures, Mary of Egypt is portrayed as a meagre, wasted, aged woman, with long hair, and holding in her hand three small loaves. Sometimes she is united with Mary Magdalene, as joint emblems of female penitence; and not in painting only, but in poetry,—

> Like redeemèd Magdalene,
> Or that Egyptian penitent, whose tears
> Fretted the rock, and moisten'd round her cave
> The thirsty desert.

Thus they stand together in a little rare print by Marc' Antonio, the one distinguished by her vase, the other by her three loaves. Sometimes, when they stand together, Mary Magdalene is young, beautiful, richly dressed; and Mary of Egypt, a squalid, meagre, old woman, covered with rags: as in a rare and curious print by Israel von Mecken.[1]

Pictures from her life are not common. The earliest I have met with is the series painted on the walls of the Chapel of the Bargello, at Florence, above the life of Mary Magdalene: they had been whitewashed over. In seeking for the portrait of Dante, this whitewash has been in part removed; and it is only just possible for those acquainted with the legend to trace in several compartments the history of Mary of Egypt.

1. Detached subjects are sometimes met with. In the church of San Pietro-in-Pò, at Cremona, they preserve relics said to be those of Mary of Egypt: and over the altar there is a large picture by

[1] B. Museum.

Malosso, representing the saint at the door of the Temple at Jerusalem, and repulsed by a miraculous power.   She is richly dressed, with a broad brimmed hat, and stands on the step, as one endeavouring to enter, while several persons look on,—some amazed, others mocking.

2. Mary of Egypt doing penance in the desert is easily confounded with the penitent Magdalene.   Where there is no skull, no vase of ointment, no crucifix near her, where the penitent is aged, or at least not young and beautiful, with little or no drapery, and black or grey hair, the picture may be presumed to represent Mary of Egypt, and not the Magdalene, however like in situation and sentiment.   There is a large fine picture of this subject at Alton Towers.

3. The first meeting of Mary and the hermit Zosimus has been painted by Ribera : in this picture her hair is grey and short, her skin dark and sunburnt, and she is clothed in rags.

4. In another picture by the same painter she is passing over the Jordan by the help of angels ; she is seen floating in the air with her hands clasped, and Zosimus is kneeling by.   This subject might easily be confounded with the Assumption of the Magdalene, but the sentiment ought to distinguish them ; for, instead of the ecstatic trance of the Magdalene, we have merely a miraculous incident : the figure is but little raised above the waters, and the hermit is kneeling on the shore.[1]

5. St. Mary receives the last communion from the hands of Zosimus. I have known this subject to be confounded with the last communion of the Magdalene.   The circumstances of the scene, as well as the character, should be attended to.   Mary of Egypt receives the sacrament in the desert ; a river is generally in the background : Zosimus is an aged monk.   Where the Magdalene receives the sacrament from the hands of Maximin, the scene is a portico or chapel with rich architecture, and Maximin wears the habit of a bishop.

6. The death of Mary of Egypt.   Zosimus is kneeling beside her, and the lion is licking her feet or digging her grave.   The presence of the lion distinguishes this subject from the death of Mary Magdalene.

[1] It was in the Sp. Gal. in the Louvre, now dispersed.

97   The Death of Mary of Egypt.

St. Mary of Egypt was early a popular saint in France, and particularly venerated by the Parisians, till eclipsed by the increasing
celebrity of the Magdalene.   She was styled, familiarly, La Gipesienne
(the Gipsy), softened by time into La Jussienne.   The street in which
stood a convent of reformed women, dedicated to her, is still *La Rue
Jussienne.*

We find her whole story in one of the richly painted windows of
the cathedral of Chartres; and again in the 'Vitraux de Bourges,'
where the inscription underneath is written 'Segiptiaca.'

Among the best modern frescoes which I saw at Paris, was the decoration of a chapel in the church **of St. Merry,** dedicated to Ste.
Marie l'Égyptienne: the religious sentiment and manner of middle-
age Art are as usual imitated, but with a certain unexpected originality

in the conception of some of the subjects which pleased me. 1. On the wall, to the right, she stands leaning on the pedestal of the statue of the Madonna in a meditative attitude, and having the dress and the dark complexion of an Egyptian dancing-girl ; a crowd of people are seen behind entering the gates of the Temple, at which she alone has been repulsed. 2. She receives the communion from the hand of Zosimus, and is buried by a lion.

On the left-hand wall. 3. Her apotheosis. She is borne aloft by many angels, two of whom swing censers, and below is seen the empty grave watched by a lion. 4. Underneath is a group of hermits, to whom the aged Zosimus is relating the story of the penitence and death of St. Mary of Egypt.

I do not in general accept modern representations as authorities, nor quote them as examples ; but this resuscitation of Mary of Egypt in a city where she was so long a favourite saint, appears to me a curious fact. Her real existence is doubted even by the writers of that Church which, for fourteen centuries, has celebrated her conversion and glorified her name. Yet the poetical, the moral significance of her story remains ; and, as I have reason to know, can still impress the fancy, and, through the fancy, waken the conscience and touch the heart.

There were several other legends current in the early ages of Christianity, promulgated, it should seem, with the distinct purpose of calling the frail and sinning woman to repentance. If these were not pure inventions, if the names of these beatified penitents retained in the offices of the Church must be taken as evidence that they *did* exist, it is not less certain that the prototype in all these cases was the reclaimed woman of the Scriptures, and that it was the pitying charity of Christ which first taught men and angels to rejoice over the sinner that repenteth.

The legend of MARY, the niece of the hermit Abraham,[1] must not be confounded with that of Mary of Egypt. The scene of this story

[1] Santa Maria Penitente.

is placed in the deserts of Syria. The anchoret Abraham had a
brother, who lived in the world and possessed great riches, and when
he died, leaving an only daughter, she was brought to her uncle
Abraham, apparently because of his great reputation for holiness,
to be brought up as he should think fit. The ideas of this holy man,
with regard to education, seem to have been those entertained by
many wise and religious people since his time; but there was this
difference, that he did not show her the steep and thorny way to
heaven, and choose for himself ' the primrose path of dalliance.'
Instead of applying to his charge a code of morality as distinct as
possible from his own, he, more just, only brought up his niece in
the same ascetic principles which he deemed necessary for the salvation of all men.

Mary, therefore, being brought to her uncle when she was only
seven years old, he built a cell close to his own, in which he shut
her up; and, through a little window, which opened between their
cells, he taught her to say her prayers, to recite the Psalter, to sing
hymns, and dedicated her to a life of holiness and solitude, praying
continually that she might be delivered from the snares of the arch-
enemy, and keeping her far, as he thought, from all possibility of
temptation ; while he daily instructed her to despise and hate all the
pleasures and vanities of the world.

Thus Mary grew up in her cell till she was twenty years old; then
it happened that a certain youth, who had turned hermit and dwelt
in that desert, came to visit Abraham to receive his instructions;
and he beheld through the window the face of the maiden as she
prayed in her cell, and heard her voice as she sang the morning and
the evening hymn ; and he was inflamed with desire of her beauty,
till his whole heart became as a furnace for the love of her; and forgetting his religious vocation, and moved thereto by the devil, he
tempted Mary, and she fell. When she came to herself, her heart
was troubled ; she beat her breast and wept bitterly, thinking of what
she had been, what she had now become; and she despaired, and
said in her heart, ' For me there is no hope, no return; shame is
my portion evermore ! ' So she fled, not daring to meet the face of
her uncle, and went to a distant place, and lived a life of sin and
shame for two years.

Now, on the same night that she fled from her cell, Abraham had a dream; and he saw in his dream a monstrous dragon, who came to his cell, and finding there a beautiful white dove, devoured it, and returned to his den. When the hermit awoke from his dream he was perplexed, and knew not what it might portend; but again he dreamt, and he saw the same dragon, and he put his foot on its head, and crushed it, and took from its maw the beautiful dove, and put it in his bosom, and it came to life again, and spread its wings and flew towards heaven.

Then the old man knew that this must relate to his niece Mary; so he took up his staff, and went forth through the world seeking her everywhere. At length he found her, and seeing her overpowered with shame and despair, he exhorted her to take courage, and comforted her, and promised to take her sin and her penance on himself. She wept and embraced his knees, and said, 'O my father! if thou thinkest there is hope for me, I will follow thee whithersoever thou goest, and kiss thy footsteps which lead me out of this gulf of sin and death!' So he prayed with her, and reminded her that God did not desire the death of a sinner, but rather that he should turn from his wickedness and live; and she was comforted. And the next morning Abraham rose up and took his niece by the hand, leaving behind them her gay attire and jewels and ill-gotten wealth.

And they returned together to the cell in the wilderness.

From this time did Mary lead a life of penitence and of great humility, ministering to her aged uncle, who died glorifying God: after his death, she lived on many years, praising God, and doing good in humbleness and singleness of heart, and having favour with the people; so that from all the country round they brought the sick, and those who were possessed, and she healed them,—such virtue was in her prayers, although she had been a sinner! Nay, it is written, that even the touch of her garment restored health to the afflicted.

At length she died, and the angels carried her spirit out of the shadow and the cloud of sin into the glory and the joy of heaven.

Although the legend of Mary the Penitent is accepted by the Church, which celebrates her conversion on the 29th of October, effigies of her must be rare; I have never met with any devotional representation of her.   A print attributed to Albert Dürer represents the hermit Abraham bringing back his penitent niece to his cell.[1]

In the Louvre are two large landscapes by Philippe de Champagne, which in poetry and grandeur of conception come near to those of Niccolò Poussin; both represent scenes from the life of Mary the Penitent.   In the first, amid a wild and rocky landscape, is the cell of Abraham, and Mary, sitting within it, is visited by the young hermit who tempted her to sin; in the second, we have the same wilderness, under another aspect; Mary, in a rude secluded hut, embowered in trees, is visited by pilgrims and votaries, who bring to her on their shoulders and on litters, the sick and the afflicted, to be healed by her prayers.   The daughter of Champagne, whom he tenderly loved, was a nun at Port-Royal, and I think it probable that these pictures (like others of his works) were painted for that celebrated convent.

St. Thais, a renowned Greek saint, is another of these '*bienheureuses pécheresses*,' not the same who sat at Alexander's feast, and fired Persepolis, but a firebrand in her own way.   St. Pelagia, called *Pelagia Meretrix* and *Pelagia Mima* (for she was also an actress), is another.   These I pass over without further notice, because I have never seen nor read of any representation of them in Western Art.

St. Afra, who sealed her conversion with her blood, will be found among the Martyrs.

Poets have sung, and moralists and sages have taught, that for the frail woman there was nothing left but to die; or if more remained for her to suffer, there was at least nothing left for her to be or do: no choice between sackcloth and ashes and the livery of sin.

The beatified penitents of the early Christian Church spoke another lesson; spoke divinely of hope for the fallen, hope without self-abasement or defiance.   We, in these days, acknowledge no such saints; we have even done our best to dethrone Mary Magdalene; but we have martyrs,—'by the pang without the palm,'—and *one*

---

[1] 'Leben und Werke von Albrecht Dürer,' No. 2067.

at least among these who has not died without lifting up a voice of
eloquent and solemn warning; who has borne her palm on earth, and
whose starry crown may be seen on high even now, amid the constel-
lations of Genius.